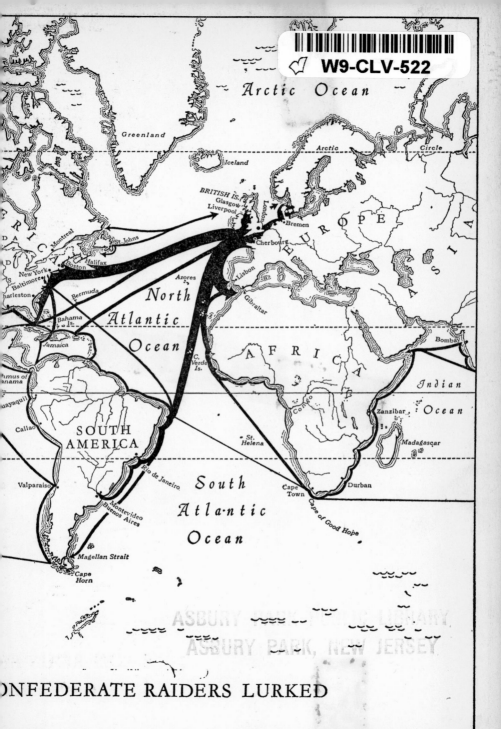

CONFEDERATE RAIDERS LURKED

Garnet W. Jex

★ THE CIVIL WAR AT SEA

Books by the same author

RANGER MOSBY
THE HATFIELDS AND THE MCCOYS
GRAY GHOSTS AND REBEL RAIDERS
EIGHT HOURS BEFORE RICHMOND
THE CIVIL WAR AT SEA, *Volumes I and II*

 *Volume II*

THE CIVIL WAR AT SEA

MARCH 1862 ★ JULY 1863

# ★ THE RIVER WAR

by Virgil Carrington Jones

FOREWORD BY ADMIRAL E. M. ELLER
DIRECTOR OF NAVAL HISTORY

illustrated with maps and photographs

HOLT ★ RINEHART ★ WINSTON
New York

★ Foreword

Like a ship plunging toward the eye of a great storm, this second volume of Virgil Carrington Jones' account of the Civil War at sea takes on even more drama than the first. The narration increases in vividness of portrayal of accumulating doom for the South—like the giant waves that mount higher and higher as the typhoon approaches its climax.

The effect of power at sea intelligently integrated with power ashore has seldom shown more clearly than in the Civil War, including the fall of New Orleans, "the night the war was lost." This disaster to the South was only one of the many that followed the policy decisions which early in the war set the course for the wise employment of the North's great advantage at sea. It was, however, perhaps the most stunning and is told here with powerful impact.

The North was fortunate to have this advantage at sea and fortunate in employing it effectively—which is not always true of man's use of an advantage. That it did so may be credited to a number of key people. In the Navy these included Secretary Welles and Gustavus Fox of the Navy Department, Farragut, Dahlgren, Du Pont, Foote, Porter, Rodgers and many others afloat. Of perhaps greatest importance, Lincoln, close friend of Dahlgren and frequent visitor to confer with him at the Washington Navy Yard, knew the far-reaching possibilities of sea-based power; and so did many able generals, including especially Scott and Grant.

The vision of many men thus developed and carried out policies that employed the crushing forces of sea power to destroy the South. Some of these that surge through this dramatic volume are:

a. *Blockade.* By control of the sea the North reduced overseas aid for the industrially deficient South, while the already far superior industrial North continued to import freely from all the world. It is interesting that one of the ships that participated in the blockade, the fine old frigate *Constellation,* still floats in Baltimore.

b. *Capture of Southern ports and harassing the coast.* These operations facilitated the blockade, captured or destroyed resources, and forced the South to disperse substantial strength from the main armies to counterattack from the sea.

c. *Splitting the South along the Mississippi* and using the river highways to speed her destruction.

d. *Combined operations* with the Army, providing massive concentrations of big-gun fire, flexible change of plans, swiftness of movement, ease of shifting base, transport of supplies, and support of the Army in most of its other problems wherever water reached.

e. *Deferring and ultimately preventing foreign intervention* that could have turned this into a world war with the South receiving powerful allies and major reinforcements from overseas.

In this volume one can see, as in the first, where the South's earlier awareness of crucial dangers from the sea and more energetic exertions to meet them could have had far-reaching effects upon the war. In a crisis one cannot depend on normal slow speed ahead. One must move with vigor and intensity, with determination to overcome all obstacles and to brook no delay. "Let courage rise with danger, and strength to strength oppose," cannot wait until the last fateful moment. Slowness in throwing every effort into overcoming the North's sea advantages had fatal results for the South.

This was especially true on the Western rivers from Nashville to Memphis to New Orleans, where means to overcome them

were more nearly in the South's grasp. Too little and too late
show clearly from the fall of Fort Henry to that of New Orleans
and Vicksburg.

Perhaps nothing the South could have done would have overcome the superiority the North enjoyed and so well exploited.
Perhaps dynamic action to meet the superiority would have succeeded, thus resulting in a divided nation. That it did not seems
surely an act of Providence in the strange and stirring history
of the great American dream that today even more than then
seems "the last, best hope of earth."

—*E. M. Eller*
Rear Admiral, USN (Ret.)
Director of Naval History

★ *Preface*

The number of volumes an author writes on a subject, I find, in no way lessens his indebtedness to the people who have assisted him. A parallel is found in ordinary life: the longer a person lives, the more obligated he is to his friends and to others around him.

So with the second volume of this trilogy on the sea, gratitude extends to even more individuals than in the case of the first. For, in most instances, those who helped me with Volume One have helped me with Volume Two and, in addition, new sources and new faces have been drawn into the circle. I recognize this to be a continuing factor, an endless chain that will be broken only when the end-product is completed or abandoned.

Experienced researchers in the field of historical narrative know that their work is never finished in the sense that an undertaking has a definite, fixed goal, specifically identifiable before it is begun. Always, out of musty records, remote attics, and memories, new material crops up, to be mulled over longingly and regretfully by the person who has spent hours and days and perhaps years looking for it. "Why couldn't I have found this in time for inclusion in my book?" The answer is supplied by the commonplace that luck is unpredictable and by the history-supported fact that the author who waits to finish his research never completes a book.

This has been my experience with Volume Two. It has been pursued with the same painstaking care as Volume One, but with the advantage of the additional material that has been turned up since its predecessor went to press. Its subject matter is broader, owing to the more advanced stage of the war, and I believe it offers the most complete account of the river campaigns now available.

My assistance has come mainly from the three principal standard sources—the Library of Congress, the National Archives, and the Navy Department. But I also have traveled in new areas, done many additional interviews, and tapped the files of regional libraries in heretofore unvisited parts of the nation.

I again owe much to my friend, Rear Admiral E. M. Eller, Director of Naval History, who has guided and encouraged me, and who has lent a hand in scouring the manuscript for technical errors. His introductions to the two first volumes are an invaluable blessing. Somewhat similar assistance has been given me by Rear Admiral John D. Hayes, USN (Ret.), of Annapolis, Maryland. When I asked him, an expert on the history of the U.S. Navy and at present engaged in editing the letters of Admiral Samuel F. du Pont, if he would "take" the time to read my manuscript, he replied that he not only would "take" it, but, if necessary, would "make" it. Such generous and magnanimous co-operation on the part of both of these busy gentlemen can contribute only toward a better book.

Unexpected help has come from my friend, Hulen Stuart of the U.S. Department of Commerce, a man who best represents in my estimation a walking encyclopedia of the Civil War. I also am indebted especially to Elwood L. Bear, Jr., of the U.S. Coast and Geodetic Survey, who went out of his way to supply me with maps and other information helpful in fitting that agency into the war picture and in demonstrating the faith placed in it by both the Army and Navy.

As all publishers know and few laymen realize, much praise is due the editor who frets and worries to make sure the text of a book is accurate and readable. In this volume, as with the first, the "angel" has been Mrs. Beulah Harris of Holt, Rinehart and

Winston, Inc. When I think of the gloss she adds to my copy, I am surprised that she has time to be pleasant toward me, too.

Another unsung "angel" is my secretary, Mrs. June Marshall, of the Curtis Publishing Company's Washington office. Her role has been in a category that extends from plain, ordinary patience to the actual contribution of historical data.

To turn my thoughts homeward, I am immeasurably indebted to my wife, Peyton, who should share equally in the glory and satisfaction of turning out a book. She still would rather play bridge than scan musty pages, and yet she has devoted many hours and many days to copying records I needed and could not find time to copy myself.

Lastly, I speak about the author. He daily has read and written of naval activities, of fleets steaming into battle with great noise and furor, and of heroes in epaulettes standing dauntlessly at the helm while their ships are torn to pieces by shot and shell. The interest is there, but the experience and the salty background are lacking. While he has labored, he has looked off at wooded acreage and dreamed of the day when he might be able to put out from shore in even so small a craft as an open boat without the usual attack of seasickness.

—*V. C. J.*

Centreville, Virginia

CONTENTS

Dramatis Personae

ALDEN, JAMES—Commander of U.S.S. *Richmond.*

ARMSTRONG, JAMES F.—Commander of the U.S.S. *State of Georgia.*

ARMSTRONG, RICHARD F.—Crewman on board C.S.S. *Alabama* (alias *290*).

BAILEY, THEODORUS—Union naval officer commanding division in Battle of New Orleans.

BAKER, MARION A.—Secretary to mayor of New Orleans.

BANKHEAD, JOHN PINE—Commander of U.S.S. *Monitor.*

BARNEY, JOSEPH NICHOLSON—Confederate naval officer.

BEAUREGARD, PIERRE G. T.—Confederate general.

BELL, HENRY HAYWOOD—Union naval officer commanding division in Battle of New Orleans.

BISSELL, JOSIAH W.—Union engineer assigned task of opening canal at Island No. 10.

BOGGS, CHARLES S.—Commander of U.S.S. *Varuna.*

BROWN, ISAAC NEWTON—Confederate naval officer assigned task of completing C.S.S. *Arkansas.*

BUCHANAN, FRANKLIN—First commander of the C.S.S. *Virginia* (alias *Merrimack*).

BUCHANAN, THOMAS MCKEAN—Union ship commander killed at Bayou Teche.

BULLOCH, I. D.—Brother of James D. Bulloch.

BULLOCH, JAMES DUNWODY—Confederate purchasing agent in Europe.

BURNSIDE, AMBROSE EVERETT—Union general.

BURRELL, ISAAC S.—Commander of Federal troops at Galveston, Texas.

xv

BUTCHER, MATTHEW J.—Superintendent constructing Confederate ship *290*.

BUTLER, BENJAMIN FRANKLIN—Union general.

CABLE, GEORGE W.—Author who, as a boy, witnessed the Battle of New Orleans.

CALDWELL, CHARLES H. B.—Commander of the U.S.S. *Itasca*.

CARRELL, THOMAS R.—Pilot on Farragut's flagship.

CHURCHILL, THOMAS J.—Confederate general commanding at Arkansas Post.

CITY, GEORGE—Confederate naval officer on board *Arkansas*.

CONOVER, FRANCIS S.—Commander of U.S.S. *Isaac Smith*.

CRAVEN, T. AUGUSTUS—Union naval officer.

CRAVEN, THOMAS T.—Commander of U.S.S. *Brooklyn*.

CROSBY, PEIRCE—Commander of U.S.S. *Pinola*.

CUMMINGS, A. BOYD—Executive officer of U.S.S. *Richmond*.

CURTIS, SAMUEL R.—Union general commanding White River expedition.

DAHLGREN, JOHN A.—Union naval officer and armament expert.

DAVIS, CHARLES HENRY—Union naval officer who succeeded Andrew H. Foote as fleet commander.

DAVIS, JEFFERSON—President of the Confederate States of America.

DE CAMP, JOHN—Commander of U.S.S. *Iroquois*.

DEWEY, GEORGE—First lieutenant on U.S.S. *Mississippi*.

DONALDSON, EDWARD—Commander of U.S.S. *Sciota*.

DUNCAN, JOHNSTON K.—Confederate general commanding defenses of New Orleans.

DU PONT, SAMUEL FRANCIS—Union commander of South Atlantic Blockading Squadron (SABS).

ELLET, ALFRED W.—Brother of Charles Ellet and commander of Union Marine Brigade.

ELLET, CHARLES—Naval engineer who constructed Union ram fleet.

ELLET, CHARLES RIVERS—Son of Charles Ellet and active Union officer in Mississippi campaign.

FARRAGUT, DAVID GLASGOW—Union naval officer in command of fleet pushing up the Mississippi River.

FARRAGUT, LOYALL—Son of Admiral David G. Farragut.

FARRAND, EBENEZER—Confederate officer at battle of Drewry's Bluff.

FOOTE, ANDREW HULL—Union naval officer in command of fleet pushing down the Mississippi River.

FOX, GUSTAVUS VASA—Union Assistant Secretary of the Navy.

FULLER, EDWARD W.—Confederate naval officer.

GABAUDAN, EDWARD C.—Admiral Farragut's secretary.

GANSEVOORT, GUERT—Union naval officer.

GETTY, ROBERT—Commander of U.S.S. *Marmora*.

GIFT, GEORGE W.—Confederate naval officer on board *Arkansas*.

GOLDSBOROUGH, LOUIS MALESHERBES—Union commander of North Atlantic Blockading Squadron (NABS).

GRANT, ULYSSES S.—Union general commanding troops in the Mississippi River campaign.

GREENE, SAMUEL DANA—Lieutenant on board U.S.S. *Monitor*.

GRIMES, JAMES WILSON—United States Senator.

GWIN, WILLIAM—Union naval officer and ship commander.

HALLECK, HENRY WAGER—Union general in chief.

HIGGINS, EDWARD—Confederate lieutenant colonel commanding Forts Jackson and St. Philip.

HITCHCOCK, ROBERT BRADLEY—Union naval officer.

HOLLINS, GEORGE NICHOLS—Confederate naval officer and fleet commander.

HOLMES, THEOPHILUS H.—Confederate general.

HUGER, BENJAMIN—Confederate general.

HUGER, THOMAS BEE—Confederate naval officer killed in New Orleans campaign.

HUNLEY, HORACE L.—Inventor of Confederate submarine.

INGRAHAM, DUNCAN NATHANIEL—Confederate naval officer on duty at Charleston, South Carolina.

JEFFERS, WILLIAM NICHOLSON—Union naval officer who succeeded Worden in command of U.S.S. *Monitor*.

JENKINS, THORNTON A.—Commander of U.S.S. *Oneida*.

JOHNSTON, JOSEPH EGGLESTON—Confederate general.

JONES, CATESBY ap R.—Confederate naval officer who succeeded Buchanan in command of C.S.S. *Virginia* (alias *Merrimack*).

KELL, JOHN MCINTOSH—Officer on board C.S.S. *Alabama* (alias *290*).

KENNON, BEVERLY—Confederate naval officer.

KIMBALL, JAMES B.—Union naval officer.

KING, E. T.—Confederate lieutenant temporarily in command of C.S.S. *J. A. Cotton.*

LEE, ROBERT E.—Military advisor to Jefferson Davis and later commander of the Army of Northern Virginia.

LEE, SAMUEL PHILLIPS—Union naval officer and successor to Goldsborough as commander of North Atlantic Blockading Squadron.

LEE, SIDNEY SMITH—Confederate naval officer and brother of Robert E. Lee.

LINCOLN, ABRAHAM—Union President during the Civil War.

LOCKWOOD, THOMAS J.—Blockade runner and ship commander.

LOVELL, MANSFIELD—Confederate general in command of troops at New Orleans.

LOW, JOHN—One-time commander of C.S.S. *Oreto* (later the *Florida*).

LOWE, JOHN—Officer on board C.S.S. *Alabama* (alias *290*).

McCLELLAN, GEORGE B.—Union general in command of Peninsula campaign.

McCLERNAND, JOHN A.—Union Army general assigned to the Mississippi.

McINTOSH, CHARLES F.—Confederate naval officer.

MAFFITT, EUGENE A.—Son of John Newland Maffitt.

MAFFITT, JOHN NEWLAND—Commander of C.S.S. *Florida* (alias *Oreto*).

MAGRUDER, JOHN BANKHEAD—Confederate general.

MALLORY, STEPHEN R.—Confederate Secretary of the Navy.

MAURY, MATTHEW FONTAINE—Noted hydrographer and developer of mines for Confederacy.

MEIGS, MONTGOMERY C.—Union Army engineer and quartermaster general.

MEREDITH, WILLIAM T.—Secretary to Admiral Farragut.

MITCHELL, JOHN K.—Commander of Confederate forts at New Orleans.

MONROE, JOHN T.—Mayor of New Orleans.

MONTGOMERY, JAMES E.—Confederate naval officer.

MOORE, THOMAS O.—Governor of Louisiana.

MORRIS, HENRY W.—Commander of U.S.S. *Pensacola.*

MURRAY, EDWARD C.—Shipbuilder for the Confederacy.

NICHOLS, EDWARD T.—Union naval officer.

PALMER, EDWARD A.—Clerk to Admiral Farragut.

PARRISH, WILLIAM—Pilot on C.S.S. *Virginia* (alias *Merrimack*).

POLK, LEONIDAS—Confederate general commanding along the Mississippi.

POPE, JOHN—Union general leading attack on New Madrid.

PORTER, DAVID DIXON—Union naval officer and fleet commander assigned to the Mississippi campaign. Brother of William D.

PORTER, JOHN L.—Confederate marine architect and engineer.

PORTER, WILLIAM D.—Union naval officer.

PREBLE, GEORGE HENRY—Union naval officer.

RAMSAY, H. ASHTON—Chief engineer of C.S.S. *Virginia* (alias *Merrimack*).

RANSOM, GEORGE M.—Union naval officer.

READ, CHARLES WILLIAM—Confederate naval officer and commander of the *Clarence*.

RENSHAW, WILLIAM B.—Union naval officer.

RODGERS, JOHN—Union naval officer.

ROE, FRANCIS A.—Commander of U.S.S. *Katahdin*.

SCALES, DABNEY—Officer on board C.S.S. *Arkansas*.

SELFRIDGE, THOMAS O.—Union naval officer.

SEMMES, RAPHAEL—Commander of Confederate cruisers *Sumter* and *Alabama* (alias *290*).

SEWARD, WILLIAM H.—Union Secretary of State.

SHERMAN, W. T.—Union general.

SHIRLEY, JOHN T.—Ship constructor awarded contract to build C.S.S. *Arkansas*.

SINCLAIR, ARTHUR, JR.—Confederate naval engineer.

SMITH, ANDREW JACKSON (Whiskey)—Union general.

SMITH, MARTIN LUTHER—Confederate army engineer commanding defenses of New Orleans and Vicksburg.

SOULÉ, PIERRE—Local civil leader in New Orleans.

STANTON, EDWIN McMASTERS—Union Secretary of War.

STELLWAGEN, HENRY S.—Union naval officer.

STEVENS, HENRY K.—Officer on board C.S.S. *Arkansas*.

STRIBLING, JOHN M.—Officer on board C.S.S. *Sumter* and later on C.S.S. *Florida* (alias *Oreto*).

TATTNALL, JOSIAH—Confederate fleet commander and last captain of C.S.S. *Merrimack*.

TEMPLE, WILLIAM G.—Union naval officer.

TESSIER, E. L.—Blockade runner.

THOMPSON, M. JEFFERSON—Confederate general.

TIFT, ASA F.—Builder, with his brother, of C.S.S. *Mississippi.*

TIFT, NELSON—Co-builder of C.S.S. *Mississippi* and brother of Asa
Tift.

TRENCHARD, STEPHEN DECATUR—Union naval officer.

TUCKER, JOHN RANDOLPH—Confederate naval officer.

VANDERBILT, CORNELIUS—Union philanthropist.

VAN DORN, EARL—Confederate general assigned to the Lower Mississippi.

VILLEPIQUE, JOHN B.—Confederate army officer commanding at
Fort Pillow.

WADDELL, JAMES IREDELL—Confederate naval officer.

WAINWRIGHT, JONATHAN M.—Union naval officer killed in the battle
of Galveston.

WAINWRIGHT, RICHARD—Union naval officer.

WALKE, HENRY—Union naval officer.

WELLES, GIDEON—Union Secretary of the Navy.

WILKES, CHARLES—Union naval officer.

WILKINSON, JOHN—Confederate naval officer.

WILLIAMS, THOMAS—Union general aiding in attack on Vicksburg.

WOOD, JOHN TAYLOR—Grandson of President Zachary Taylor and
former U.S. Naval Academy instructor fighting for the Confederacy.

WOOL, JOHN E.—Union general.

WORDEN, JOHN L.—First commander of U.S.S. *Monitor.*

WRIGHT, DAVID—Pilot on C.S.S. *Virginia* (alias *Merrimack*).

WYNNE, THOMAS H.—Chief engineer in charge of defenses at Richmond, Virginia.

YONGE, C. R.—Officer on board C.S.S. *Alabama* (alias *290*).

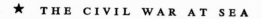 THE CIVIL WAR AT SEA

1

An ironclad for Davy Jones

MARCH 1862

Had the public been able to view the panic in the White House the morning of March 9, 1862, bedlam might have been general throughout the Union capital. But the alarm of the Government's top administrators over what had taken place the day before down in Hampton Roads on the Virginia coast was well concealed. Along Pennsylvania Avenue and out across the meadow spreading from the presidential mansion to the unfinished Washington Monument, only the routine of a country at war could be observed.

Uniformed men hustled about their chores, regimented and alert. Others, off duty for the moment, loitered in groups or strolled along the sidewalks, some with girls on their arms. Through the streets, muddy from recent spring rains, horses trotted with a monotonous clop-clop that spelled industry and activity, some of it social. Over at Ford's Theater on Tenth Street, billboards announced that Mr. and Mrs. Barney Williams were playing their second week in a fascinating comedy, *Ireland As It Was,* and intellectually minded patrons of the

1

Smithsonian Institution were looking forward to a lecture on *Popular Taste in Art and Literature* by the Reverend A. Cleveland Coxe, D.D. The green of the trees along the capital's streets was pleasingly reflected in the carpet of grass at their feet.

At an early hour that morning, Union Navy Secretary Gideon Welles, all whiskers and dignity, came bustling up to the White House, his brisk stride denoting crisis. The reason for the visit was twofold: first had come a message that the naval chief's presence was desired in the council chamber of the President, and then a messenger brought a telegram that would have sent him there anyway. It announced that the ironclad ship the Confederates at Norfolk had made out of the frigate *Merrimack* had appeared the previous afternoon and had sunk the *Cumberland* and the *Congress*, two of the North's mightiest warships.

Upstairs at the White House, Welles found closeted with Abraham Lincoln a department head who caused him great irritation. This individual was War Secretary Edwin McMasters Stanton.

From the atmosphere of the room the naval official could tell that the news he brought was already known, for the attitudes of both men reflected desperation. They were walking about in little circles, occasionally stopping at a window to stare down the Potomac River, and Welles assumed they were watching for the appearance of the Confederate ironclad. (He did not know that the ship was even then on its way into Hampton Roads to take part in the most unusual battle in history.)

Shortly after the Navy Secretary arrived, other Cabinet members put in their appearance—Salmon Chase of the Treasury and William Seward from the Department of State. In solemn conclave they gathered, but before their thoughts could be pooled, the President ordered his carriage and rushed off to the Navy Yard, there to seek professional advice from Admiral John A. Dahlgren and others.[1]

But Lincoln's trip was futile. Dahlgren, although attentive and courtly, could offer no advice. His only knowledge was of matters that came under his jurisdiction around the Navy Yard.

Any action the Navy Department had taken to stop this monster that only the day before had steamed ominously and awkwardly out of a dock at Norfolk, he told Lincoln, would have to be revealed by Secretary Welles.

Back to the White House hurried the President, and to Welles it seemed that the Chief Executive's panic had increased.[2] Encouraged by Seward, a summons went out for Quartermaster General Montgomery C. Meigs, engineer officer in whom the Secretary of State placed great reliance for military advice. But this man, too, could offer no help.

As the morning advanced, the atmosphere of the President's council chamber became more strained. Officials, among them Dahlgren, came in as the excitement spread. "The most frightened man on that gloomy day," noted Welles, "was the Secretary of War. He was at times almost frantic, and as he walked the room with his eyes fixed on me, I saw well the estimation in which he held me with my unmoved and unexcited manner and conversation." [3]

The men gathered around Lincoln that day could feel the fire that flashed between Stanton and Welles. The two Cabinet members were never in stronger contrast than at that moment. Welles, ex-newspaperman and cotton-mill executive, appeared calm. But Stanton, lawyer and statesman, paced the floor like a caged lion, occasionally halting to toss bitter comments at the naval chief. The *Merrimack,* he said, would destroy every vessel in the service, place every city on the coast under levy, and take Fort Monroe. What would that mean? It would mean that the aspiring young General George B. McClellan would have to abandon his proposed advance up the Peninsula toward Richmond, the Confederate capital; and Ambrose Burnside, so successful in capturing Roanoke Island down on the coast of North Carolina—with the aid of the North Atlantic Blockading Squadron and Flag Officer Louis Malesherbes Goldsborough —would inevitably be captured. What was more, the next move of the ironclad likely would be to come up the Potomac, disperse Congress, and destroy the Capitol and other public buildings; or she might go to New York and Boston and either destroy those cities or levy on them contributions sufficient to carry on the war.

"What vessel or means do you have to resist or prevent her from doing whatever she pleases?" he threw at Welles.

The Navy Secretary, running patient fingers through a drapery of beard, answered solemnly, and with aggravating smugness. What Stanton had in mind was possible, he admitted. And maybe the vessels at his disposal were not as powerful or as numerous as he would like. But he dismissed the idea that the *Merrimack* could attack Washington or New York.

"I wish she would come up the Potomac," he declared, "for if so we could take efficient measures to dispose of her. As for Burnside, he is safe from her because her draft of water is such that she cannot reach him. Moreover, our ironclad, the *Monitor,* is in Hampton Roads, and I have confidence in her power to resist and, I hope, overcome the *Merrimack*. She should have been there sooner, but the contractors disappointed us." [4]

Seward brightened with Welles' remarks. Mention of the *Merrimack*'s draft, he said, gave him the first moment's relief he had experienced since hearing of the ironclad.

"What about this new vessel, the *Monitor?*" asked Stanton. "I know little or nothing about her." [5]

Welles described the *Monitor,* adding that it was the intention, had she been completed within contract time, to send her to engage the batteries on the Potomac and break the blockade of Washington.

"What about her armament?" asked Stanton.

With Welles' answer the War Secretary seemed at the breaking point. "His mingled look of incredulity and contempt cannot be described," the Navy Secretary wrote, "and the tone of his voice, as he asked if my reliance was on that craft with her two guns, is equally indescribable."

Stanton's critical anxiety spread to the others, as he continued bitter, censorious, malevolent. Throughout it all Welles remained calm, carrying the burden alone. His assistant, Gustavus V. Fox, was down at Hampton Roads watching developments, and Dahlgren and Meigs, as the Secretary saw them, were "by nature and training cautious, not to say timid."

This day and its incidents would go down for Welles as the most unpleasant and uncomfortable of his life.

"In all that painful time," he wrote in his diary, "my composure was not disturbed, so that I did not perhaps as fully realize and comprehend the whole impending calamity as others, and yet to me there was throughout the whole day something inexpressibly ludicrous in the wild, frantic talk, action, and rage of Stanton as he ran from room to room, sat down and jumped up after writing a few words, swung his arms, scolded, and raved."

The President found himself torn between the two Secretaries. He wanted to give Welles his sympathy, and yet Stanton's wailing and woeful predictions were so disturbing that the Chief Executive could not keep away from the window where he stood staring down the Potomac.

"What would we do if the *Merrimack* were now in sight?" asked someone.

Welles directed his answer to the President. With her heavy armor, he said, she could not possibly cross Kettle Bottom Shoals, a considerable distance downstream. Someone turned to Dahlgren for confirmation. This officer nodded. He doubted, he said, that she could reach Washington, even if she entered the river.

Stanton asked what protection could be given New York and other coastal cities. In answer, Welles cited the numerous reports that had come in from Union spies assigned to watch the *Merrimack*. According to their information, he stated, she was to be used only in Hampton Roads and Chesapeake Bay and would not venture outside.

Welles' calm assurance failed to convince Stanton. Still pacing the floor, he gave orders for messages to be sent to military commanders at Northern ports, cautioning them to watch out for the *Merrimack* and to "do your best to stop her should she endeavor to run by." [6]

As with residents of the Hampton Roads area, sleep that night was slow in coming to top officials in Washington. Late in the evening, Welles received by wire from his assistant, Gustavus Fox, news of the terrific battle that had been waged during the middle of the day between the *Merrimack* and the *Monitor*.

"The damage to the *Merrimac* [7] cannot be ascertained," Fox telegraphed. "Nearly all here are of the opinion that she is disabled. I was the nearest person to her, outside of the *Monitor,* and I am of opinion she is not seriously injured. She retreated under steam without assistance. The *Monitor* is all ready for her tomorrow, but I think the *Merrimac* may be obliged to lay up for a few days. She is an ugly customer and it is too good luck to believe we are yet clear of her. Our hopes are upon the *Monitor* and this day's work shows that the *Merrimac* must attend to her alone."

Another telegram reached Welles that evening. It was from Dahlgren, announcing that he had rounded up a large number of boats to be sunk in the channel of the Potomac. At the moment, he reported, he had a full force loading them with stone and gravel. Was this in conformance with the Secretary's wishes? Welles replied that he had given no such orders.

An explanation of Dahlgren's action awaited the Navy Secretary at the White House next morning. Stanton was there, and with a voice trembling with anger he inquired whether Welles had given orders to prevent the loading of the boats. Welles answered that he had ordered no boats loaded and had no intention of doing so. The War Secretary then revealed that he had instructed Meigs and Dahlgren to take the step to protect Washington and had done so with the approval of the President. Lincoln, standing by, remarked that Stanton had thought it imperative that something be done, that he himself thought no harm would come of it, even if it did no good.

"I'm sorry to hear it," Welles said, straightening with dignified disapproval. "For five or six months we have labored with General McClellan and the War Department to keep this important avenue open to unrestricted navigation, and now we are about to shut ourselves off with these obstructions."

Stanton announced that sixty canal boats had been rounded up and that the War Department would bear both the expense and the responsibility. Again Lincoln was torn between his two department heads. But several hours later he forbade the sinking of the boats until it was known that the *Merrimack* was actually approaching. So they were moored on the Maryland side of the river, near Kettle Bottom Shoals, to await developments, and thus it was that they were seen by Lincoln while making a trip down the river and referred to by him as "Stanton's navy." [8]

Later in the day the informal Cabinet meeting of the 10th was interrupted as suddenly as had been that of the 9th, again by the departure of the President. This time he hurried away in answer to an announcement that Lieutenant John Worden, commander of the *Monitor,* wounded in the fight with the *Merrimack,* had arrived by ship and been taken to the home of a friend, Lieutenant Henry A. Wise, assistant chief of the Bureau of Ordnance.

"Excuse me, gentlemen," Lincoln said, reaching for his hat, "I must see this fellow."

Eyewitnesses recorded the scene when Lincoln walked into Worden's presence. The wounded officer lay on a sofa, his eyes and face bandaged to cover the wounds made by the peppering of bits of concrete and steel from a shell that had struck inches away while he peered from the tiny pilothouse of the ironclad.

"Mr. President," said Worden, "you do me great honor by this visit."

Lincoln was silent for a moment. Then he said: "Sir, I am the one who is honored."

The President spent some time with Worden, listening to his account of the battle of the ironclads and asking questions about the individual performances of the ships. One particular comment from the wounded skipper added to his concern. This was to the effect that the *Monitor* was not invincible, that she might be captured by boarding parties. All they would have to do, Worden explained, would be to wedge her turret and flood her machinery by pouring water upon it.

The Chief Executive returned to the White House with a firm conviction: the *Monitor* must be carefully guarded, even to the point of avoiding battle. This was important strategy, as he saw it. For if the Union ironclad were put out of the way, the *Merrimack* would have nothing to stop her from steaming out of Hampton Roads and laying waste to coastal cities in the North. In compliance with this decision, Welles sent off an urgent telegram to Fox: "It is directed by the President that the *Monitor* be not too much exposed; that in no event shall any attempt be made to proceed with her unattended to Norfolk." [9]

Lincoln's fears regarding the *Monitor* were supported by a telegram from Major General John E. Wool, commanding Union troops at Fort Monroe. Addressed to General McClellan, his message opened with the calm statement that "nothing of importance has occurred today." This was followed by the announcement that the *Merrimack* had not reappeared. "If I can get the number of men and batteries asked for," he added, "I think I will be able to keep Newport News, that is, if no accident happens to the *Monitor*." [10]

Abraham Lincoln was determined that "no accident" should happen.

Newspapers that morning carried full and fairly complete accounts of the battle of the ironclads. THE *Merrimack* CATCHES TARTAR IN THE *Monitor,* read a headline in the Washington *Star*. Included in the accompanying article was the statement that the Union ironclad was furnished with four hundred wrought-iron shot, each costing forty-seven dollars and made by forging square blocks of iron and turning them at the lathe. News of the sea battle shared prominence with the announcement that the Confederates had abandoned their lines near Manassas and fallen back toward Richmond.

By the 11th, newspapers were trying to fix the blame for the destruction wrought by the *Merrimack* on the 8th. Wrote one editor: "Had Congress promptly responded to the President's and Secretary's recommendations in this connection, instead of wasting their time over the inevitable Negro, and in intrigues to wholly overturn the Constitution of the United States, under the pleas of there being a military necessity for so doing, which no military man sees, we would not have lost the *Cumberland* and *Congress,* all must now know." [11]

As the days passed, attention in the North remained on the question of when the *Merrimack* would reappear and what could be done to stop her. Quartermaster General Meigs offered his suggestions in a message dated from the White House. The best defense, he thought, would be an attack on the ironclad by a number of swift steamers filled with men who would board her in a sudden rush, fire through her hatches or grated deck, and throw cartridges, grenades, or shells down her smokestack. A delegation from Northern cities, headed by the mayor of New York, called on Welles to urge that the Confederate ironclad be bottled up in Norfolk by sinking vessels across the mouth of the Elizabeth River. This idea was passed on to Flag Officer Goldsborough, who promptly termed it infeasible and proposed instead that the enemy vessel be run down with large and fast steamers. He ordered the chartered vessels *Illinois* and *Arago* to stand by for this purpose, and then ran into trouble with the crews, who refused to work the ships in such an operation. They were immediately replaced with naval personnel.

War Secretary Stanton, again usurping Welles' prerogative, wired the shipping magnate, Cornelius Vanderbilt, America's first multimillionaire, to inquire what sum he would ask to destroy the *Merrimack.*[12] Vanderbilt replied by coming to Washington to confer with the President.

"Can you stop this ironclad?" Lincoln asked.

"Yes," Vanderbilt replied. "At least, there are nine chances out of ten I can. I will take my ship, the *Vanderbilt,* cover her machinery with five hundred bales of cotton, raise the steam, and rush her with overwhelming force on the ironclad, and sink her before she can escape or cripple us."

"How much money will you demand for such a service?"

"I will accept no money. I will give the vessel free of charge to the Government." [13]

Three days after the battle of the ironclads, the ambitious General McClellan, moving in a whirlwind of plans for his advance on Richmond by way of the coast, wired Fox: "Can I rely on the *Monitor* to keep the *Merrimack* in check, so that I can make Fort Monroe a base of operations?" Fox answered cautiously: "The *Monitor* is more than a match for the *Merrimack,* but she might be disabled in the next encounter. I cannot advise so great dependence upon her." [14] At the same time he wrote Senator James Wilson Grimes in Washington, urging him to provide Dahlgren with money to produce larger guns, at least twenty-inchers, adding: "I have not thought the *Merrimack* was much injured, but we are now better prepared for her, by the harbor being cleared of non-combatants. Everybody here feels the *Monitor* can sink the *Merrimack,* but it will be a terrible struggle." [15]

Fox's optimism was not shared by Goldsborough, who wrote him a day or two later: ". . . On a careful scrutiny of the *Monitor,* it will not do, in my judgment, to count too largely on her prowess. She is scarcely enough for the *Merrimack.* It should be remembered that the latter was injured when the *Monitor* engaged her—had been injured the day before in her exploits both in her beak and others. The *Merrimack*'s mere weight, with a velocity of say even five knots, would, I fear, be too much for the *Monitor* to withstand in case she should be able to deliver such a blow." [16]

The opinion prevailed among other Union military leaders that the *Monitor* should not be risked against the *Merrimack.* General Wool, answering a query from McClellan regarding the possibility of blocking the channel between Sewell's Point and Craney Island, wrote that it could not be done without the *Monitor* to aid in resisting the fire from batteries on shore, and added: ". . . It would not do to use the *Monitor* for that service, lest she should become crippled. She is our only hope against the *Merrimack*." [17]

Fear of risking the *Monitor* posed the serious problem of how to dispose of the *Merrimack*. The proposal to block the channel to Norfolk and prevent her exit received serious consideration, although it was advised against by such old heads as Goldsborough, who longed for half a dozen large and fast steamers, "such as those running on the Hudson and East Rivers," so he could capture the *Merrimack* by running her down any time she made her appearance.[18] McClellan passed along a proposal that the *Monitor* take a long hemp cable in tow and, by running around the *Merrimack,* endeavor to foul her propeller.[19]

The idea of paralyzing the Confederate ironclad's means of propulsion caused men to lie awake at night and scheme. Welles was taken in by it and wired Lieutenant R. H. Wyman, commanding the Potomac Flotilla: "Nets and hawsers stretched across the narrow part of the channel will foul the *Merrimack*'s propeller, and you are authorized to prepare such for obstructing her progress." [20]

The Confederates meanwhile, with their ironclad in dock undergoing repairs, were expecting a Federal advance on the James River. General John B. Magruder, commanding the Southern troops thrown out along the Peninsula to stop McClellan, recommended that not a moment be lost in bringing out the *Merrimack*. His spies reported that Union officers were saying the Rebel ironclad was badly damaged and that they had no apprehensions regarding her for the present. This led him to believe the advance would be made before the *Merrimack* could be brought into action again.[21]

Tension increased as March advanced. Telegrams, passing along intelligence on developments or asking information, went back and forth daily. Those of Federal origin invariably referred to the Rebel ironclad as the *Merrimack,* while those of the Confederates identified her under her new name, the *Virginia.*

The South at this time suddenly awoke to an alarming situation, one somewhat in the nature of the individual who finds himself holding a lion by the tail. What was to be done with this monster it had created? Major General Benjamin Huger, commanding the Confederate Headquarters Department at Norfolk, posed the problem in a message to the Adjutant General's office at Richmond: "The only means of stopping them is by vessels of the same kind. The *Virginia,* being the most powerful, can stop the *Monitor;* but a more powerful one would run her down or ashore. As the enemy can build such boats faster than we, they could, when so prepared, overcome any place accessible by water. How these powerful machines are to be stopped is a problem I cannot solve. At present, in the *Virginia,* we have the advantage; but we cannot tell how long this may last." [22]

While each side debated this problem, the Union went ahead with its plans for an advance on Richmond. McClellan at Washington began moving his army down the Potomac toward Fort Monroe, actually getting the first transports off a day ahead of the date given in a general order from the White House.[23] By the 20th, signal officers and pickets on both sides of the river approaching Hampton Roads were reporting activity and sighting evidence of an impending campaign: "Twenty-six sails of different kinds, all loaded with hay and horses" . . . "Nineteen steamers bearing troops" . . . "Several gunboats moving south." The great push was on, encouraged by a rumor that the *Merrimack* would not be in condition for service for eight or ten days, during which period the Federal transports might attempt to get past and make their way up the James River, into water too shallow for the ironclad to follow.

Plans for ramming the *Merrimack* should she appear continued to progress. The U.S.S. *Illinois* and the U.S.S. *Arago* dropped anchor at Fort Monroe, and then four days later appeared the *Vanderbilt.* Immediately, Union headaches increased. To begin with, the crews of the first two, on learning of their assignment, balked: their lives were too dear to be risked on vessels used as rams. With the *Vanderbilt,* the troubles stemmed more from a question of diplomacy. Stanton, who had taken it upon himself to negotiate with her wealthy owner, smugly gave him full authority to direct the activities of his ship under special orders of the War Department. But at Fort Monroe things didn't work that way. War vessels in those waters were under the experienced direction of Louis Goldsborough of the Navy, and it was days later, and after several angry protests, that Stanton was forced to bow to protocol.

The Confederates in the meantime were feeling the approach of doom. They were determined that the *Merrimack* would not be shut in and were taking steps to prevent it, even to leaving a gap in a line of hulks scuttled in the Elizabeth River. But their army was a different problem. Magruder and his principal officers held a council of war on March 25. The outcome was not optimistic. To check the invasion, they decided, ten thousand additional troops were needed immediately and ten thousand more must be supplied as soon as possible. Where these were to come from no one knew. It was obvious that Yorktown was the best line of defense east of Richmond, for they realized that if the Peninsula were lost, Norfolk and the *Merrimack* would be lost. But there seemed no way to prevent such a calamity. Preparing for it, Stephen Mallory, Confederate Secretary of the Navy, wired on March 26: "You will begin at once, without attracting special notice to the subject, to carefully pack and get ready for transportation all the fine machinery and tools not required for your workshops." This message went to Captain Sidney Smith Lee, brother of the rising Southern general, Robert E. Lee.

As March drew to a close, both sides were talking of the day on which the *Merrimack* would reappear. Deserters from Norfolk told Union officers that she was ready to come out, even better prepared to encounter the *Monitor,* and that her guns had been replaced by ones of larger caliber. Her name was on every tongue. It was said that she had had six feet of water in her hold when she limped into the Navy Yard after her conflict with the Federal ship, that her pumps then could not keep her free. But no matter how badly crippled she had been, rumor now left no doubt that her repairs were nearing completion. Spies able to get within hearing distance brought back unanimous confirmation. When a northeaster raged over the area on March 30, driving all vessels into safe harbor, they reported that they could still hear hammering and other evidence of industry from the dock where she nestled. Much of this labor, they were able to learn, was confined to the strengthening of her armor. More than four hundred additional plates were to cover her sides.[24]

The Confederates were also engaged in the spy business. By April they had enough information concerning the *Monitor* to work out a definite plan of attack. Some of this came from a friend of Mallory's at Baltimore; part of it was out of a recent number of *Scientific American.*[25] Among other things, the article stated that little preparation had been made to resist boarders, and that a wet sail thrown over the little pilothouse which protruded above her deck would effectively shut off the view of the steersman. Mallory became so aroused over this intelligence that he forwarded the advice in a message that read: "Her grated turret, her smokestack, ventilators, and air holes invite attack with inflammables or combustibles, and it would seem that twenty men, thus provided, once upon her deck, as her turret is but nine feet high, might drive every man out of her."

Mallory gave clearance for the *Merrimack* to come out at any time. "Please telegraph me," he wired her captain, "when you will probably leave, and to avoid the leaky telegraph you can say that Captain Smith will leave here at blank o'clock."

On April 2, McClellan appeared at Old Point Comfort and

revealed his plan of march. It was to begin on the 4th, a multi-pronged thrust aimed at cutting off both Yorktown and Norfolk. As for any danger of opposition from the Confederate ironclad, he wired Stanton: "Have seen Goldsborough, and feel sure that he will crush the *Merrimack* if she appears."

Union divisions began moving on schedule. As they marched, plans were under way to release the *Merrimack* from dry dock.[26] Standing nearby watching her was a new commander, the veteran Josiah Tattnall, brought up from South Carolina to shoulder the responsibility which had fallen upon the younger but capable Catesby Jones after the wounding of Franklin Buchanan in the fight against the Union fleet on March 8. Tattnall was one of the most experienced seamen on the Southern side, a fiery man with a sense of humor that could be wrecked in a moment by a temper that flashed like a stroke of lightning. He viewed the ironclad with a critical eye. Some features of her reconstruction pleased him, but he was concerned over the fact that several of her iron port covers were missing. Buchanan had advised him not to engage the *Monitor* without them.[27] Also bothering him was the report of her chief engineer, H. Ashton Ramsay, an able technician who had been attached to her while in the U. S. Navy prior to the war. He advised from experience that little reliance could be placed in her engines.

These factors caused the veteran to act with caution. He knew the Union troops were pushing forward for a siege at Yorktown, but he also knew that many men had died on the *Merrimack* and her guns had been damaged because she had no port covers. Work on her continued night and day, Sunday included, and weather was never a consideration. Each plate had to be heated and cut in two, then shaped by means of molds, and finally transferred to the machine shop to be drilled. Next came the tedious task of putting the plates in place, difficult because of their weight and because only a few men at a time could get to them. But determination brought its reward: the *Merrimack* slid down the ways April 7.

What she would do next was still undetermined. From Richmond, General Lee, newly mantled with the responsibility of advising President Davis on military affairs, suggested that she pass Fort Monroe at night and destroy enemy gunboats and transports standing by in the York River. On the other hand, Mallory, convinced that the Union Army was held to the Peninsula by fear of the ironclad, urged that she be kept in the Elizabeth River as a safeguard against the capture of Norfolk.[28]

With these and many other things to consider, Tattnall debated, while thick weather held him to his anchors. The ship was still without port covers, her engines still faulty. For these reasons, he hesitated to pass the forts thrown up by the invaders, although he consented to make the attempt if authorities at Richmond so ordered. His suggestion was to attack above the forts, not venturing too far away from Norfolk. "The *Monitor* is off Hampton Creek, and will doubtless engage this ship," he informed Mallory. "I shall not notice her until she closes with me, but direct my fire on the transports. There must be, however, a combat with the *Monitor*." [29]

Tattnall looked upon the *Monitor*'s weak points as her smokestack, ventilators, pilothouse, and joint, or opening between the revolving turret and the deck. She would have to be boarded. Then, by covering the smokestack with wet blankets or sailcloth, he would shut in the smoke and gas and thus drive the crew into the open. A sail or cloth over the pilothouse would render the helm useless, and wedges driven between the turret and the deck would keep the turret from revolving. He spread the word: captains of the ships in the tiny Confederate fleet surrounding him were to assign crews to each duty.

It was April 11 before the *Merrimack* appeared in the neighborhood of the Federal fleet. Lookouts in the *Minnesota*'s mizzen crosstrees had been cautioned to remain alert, for three days earlier spyglasses had shown the Rebel ironclad to be under steam at Craney Island.

This day of her appearance a gentle breeze stirred from the southwest, and the tide ran at a moderate ebb. Charles C.

Fulton, correspondent of the Baltimore *American* was on hand and excitedly wired his newspaper:

> I said two days since that we were looking for the *Merrimack* and sunshine together; both are here this morning. Day opened bright and clear, with the broad expanse of Hampton Roads almost unruffled by wave. About seven o'clock a signal gun from the *Minnesota* turned all eyes toward Sewell's Point, and, coming out from under the land, almost obscured by a dim haze, the *Merrimack* was seen, followed by the *Yorktown, Jamestown,* and four small vessels, altogether seven in number. There was instantaneous activity among the transports and vessels in the upper roads to get out of the way of the steamboats, several of which were crowded with troops, and moved down out of danger. Steam tugs ran whistling and screaming about, towing strings of vessels behind them, whilst sloops, schooners, and brigs, taking advantage of what air there was, got up sail and moved out of harm's way. In the course of an hour the appearance of crowded roads was greatly altered. Forests of masts between Fort Monroe and Sewell's Point disappeared, and the broad, open expanse of water bore on its surface only the Rebel fleet and two French and one English men-of-war, which, with steam up, still maintained position.

Spectators who soon crowded along the beaches saw the *Merrimack* stand directly across the mouth of the Elizabeth River as if bound for Newport News. But she was headed for the foreign ships, the *Rinaldo, Catinat,* and *Gassendi*. Drawing near, she apparently communicated with them, and then fell back toward her consorts. Immediately, the visiting vessels hauled anchor and changed position, obviously warned to get out of range.

For the next hour the Confederate ships maneuvered about halfway between Sewell's and Newport News points, without maintaining any specific direction. Charles Fulton was convinced they were trying to draw the Union fleet up toward Sewell's Point.

But if this was a challenge, it was not accepted. The *Monitor,* with steam up and in fighting trim, lay quietly near her usual anchorage, commanded now by William Nicholson Jeffers, a pudgy, bewhiskered native of New Jersey in his thirty-seventh year, twenty-two of them spent in the Navy. He had fought in the Mexican War, received a sword from the Queen of Spain for rescuing a Spanish steamer, and, at the start of this war, been detailed to ordnance duty at Norfolk. But soon he was transferred to the command of a ship, and in the recent operations in the sounds of North Carolina had brought such acclaim upon himself that he was looked upon as the logical choice to succeed the wounded Worden as captain of the *Monitor*.

As the Union ironclad waited at anchor, the *Naugatuck,* a small ship covered with iron, lay alongside, an addition contributing more to morale than to offense.[30] Signals were exchanged among the vessels and Fort Monroe and the Rip Raps, but no movements resulted.

In the face of this refusal of action, the Southerners became audacious. The *Yorktown* rapidly moved up, advanced well toward Newport News, and then steamed toward Hampton, to Bates' Dock, where it captured and took in tow three vessels of the Union Quartermaster Department.[31] These were the brigs *Marcus* and *Saboah* and the schooner *Catherine T. Dix,* one of the brigs loaded with hay, the other ships in ballast. They were towed away in plain view of the Federal fleet, the flag of each hoisted with Union down.[32]

But not even this insult stirred the Federal ships to action. Wrote the Baltimore *American* reporter: "The bold impudence of maneuvering continued; the apparent apathy of our fleet excited surprise and indignation." The New York *Herald* quickly followed with a blistering editorial on April 15, scoring the Union ships for their refusal to fight. Gideon Welles was the victim of this caustic blast. "It was red tape which tied the hands of our sailors and restrained them from victory," the newspaper charged. "The wretched imbecility of the management of the Navy Department has paralyzed the best sailors and the best navy of the world. . . . If the Rebels will only send a gunboat or two up the Potomac and throw a large shell into the sleeping apartment of the venerable head of the Navy

Department, we will forgive them all the other damage they may do us in a year."

From then until late afternoon the Confederate fleet continued its maneuvering out in deep water, where the *Merrimack* was free to move about. Occasionally she ran within range of the guns of the Federal ships, as well as those at Fort Monroe and on the Rip Raps, but not once did they fire at her.[33] It was obviously a game of waiting, and it was so frustrating to the *American* correspondent that he dashed off another report:

> Our inaction seems unaccountable except upon the supposition that the desire is to get the Rebels farther down. Still it is painful to see these vessels carried off without an attempt at resistance.
>
> . . . The *Merrimack* is black with men who cluster on the edge of her iron roof. The other vessels are also thronged with men.
>
> The *Jamestown* is armed with an iron prow, which can be seen protruding about six feet beyond the water line of her bow. The position is simply one of defiance on both sides. The Rebels are challenging us to come to their field of battle, and we are daring them to come down.
>
> The events of this morning are much commented on and have caused much feeling of irritation and some humiliation. Beyond the capture of three transports the demonstration of the Rebel fleet has been little less than a reconnaissance. It cannot but be concluded, however, that the Rebels have had the best of the affair. The capture of the three prizes was a bold affair, and we can well imagine the hurrah with which their arrival at Norfolk was greeted.

At four o'clock the *Merrimack,* as if in frustration, fired three shots at the *Monitor,* all falling short. Ten minutes later they were answered by several shots from the *Naugatuck,* a gesture equally as ineffective.

But there was no other response to the challenge from the Confederates. At five o'clock the *Merrimack* turned slowly and steamed away, followed by her consorts. A short while later she disappeared behind Sewell's Point.

The land troops and the civilian spectators were stunned. They could not understand the strategy of the Union high command, but they were still hopeful of action, of some demonstration of offensive power, of an answer to this obvious and insulting challenge of the South. "What the night may bring forth I am unable to say," General Wool wrote War Secretary Stanton.[34]

But the night brought nothing. Shouts of defiance and ridicule sounded in the streets of Norfolk and Newport News, but Louis Goldsborough turned deaf ears. "Had the *Merrimack* engaged the *Monitor,* which she might have done, I was quite prepared, with several vessels, to avail myself of a favorable moment and run her down. This experiment, however, must not be made too rashly, or until the right opportunity presents itself, as to fail in it would be to enable the *Merrimack* to place herself before Yorktown." These words constituted his only explanation as to why the *Monitor* had not come out of shallow water so she could be reached by the shells of the *Merrimack.*

At Richmond, Judith White McGuire, a lady who made daily recordings in a diary, noted: "The *Virginia* went out again today. The Federal *Monitor* would not meet her, but ran to Fortress Monroe, either for protection, or to tempt her under the heavy guns of the fortress." [35]

Next day was quiet. Goldsborough, watching closely, could see the Confederate vessel and her consorts hovering inside Sewell's Point, and for some reason he concluded that she was preparing to attack that night. A warning went out to every Navy vessel in the Roads. This caution was taken despite a conviction, arrived at as early as four o'clock in the afternoon, that the Rebel ship was aground. The tide was low and she could be seen with a cluster of tugboats around her. The only noticeable movement during the day was by a sassy little tug that ran around the point and scurried about in circles for a time, apparently on reconnaissance.

The 13th and 14th went by without change. On the 15th Goldsborough notified Welles that the *Merrimack* and consorts still remained at anchor. "Their next move," he added, "is to shell Newport News. The place is no longer of any material consequence to us, and it is not my intention to be drawn up there by the enemy. Our troops stationed there, as both Generals McClellan and Wool assure me, can easily fall back out of the way of all harm."

This message brought approval from Welles. "The measures adopted by the Government and yourself in relation to the armored steamer *Merrimack* will, I think under your direction and execution, be effective in overpowering her, provided she gives you the opportunity," he wrote. ". . . Should she venture out, the *Minnesota,* or some one or more of the large steamers, will be able, I doubt not, under full speed, to run her down. . . . I commend your determination not to be drawn into a conflict where the enemy can take you at disadvantage. . . ."

Welles was writing with harassment at his elbow. Zealots, remembering the brazen appearance of the *Merrimack* on the 11th and the refusal of the *Monitor* to fight, were hounding him with propositions to dispose of the Rebel craft—for certain remuneration. One proposition promised to destroy the vessel in twenty days with four "submarine armors," provided the Navy Department would supply fifteen hundred pounds of gunpowder and other material necessary to manufacture torpedoes. If successful, Congress would be expected to appropriate one hundred thousand dollars as compensation.[36]

The *Merrimack* meanwhile remained quiet, although official Confederate channels indicated she had activity in mind. General Lee notified General Joseph E. Johnston, who, as commander of the Army of Northern Virginia had moved to the Peninsula from the Manassas area, that she was at the Navy Yard having her port shutters put in place. "She is ready for active service at any moment," he added.[37] Tattnall indicated to Mallory she was preparing for action. "When the ship is fully prepared with the covers for her ports," he wrote, "I shall have great hopes of passing the forts successfully, but the attempt should not be made but for a sufficient object." [38]

The spy system of the Federals, aided by contrabands and deserters, kept them fully informed on developments concerning the *Merrimack*. On April 23, Wool notified Stanton that she would be out in a day or two. At this time, also, the Navy Department was cautioned that the Confederates planned to capture the *Monitor* by boarding her, after which she would be towed up the Elizabeth River. "Suppose half a dozen men were to spring on the *Monitor*'s decks with grapnels and chains," wrote an officer stationed on the U.S.S. *Anacostia* in the Rappahannock River, "and make them fast, just after her two guns had been fired; undoubtedly she could be towed off and they could not help themselves. . . . In such an event it strikes me that the 'liquid fire,' with which you witnessed an experiment four or five months ago at the navy yard, Washington, would be a good thing to drive them off with. The pipe of a hose thrown out of the small holes in the 'dome,' or out of the pilothouse, would, I think, clear the decks sooner than the heaviest discharge of musketry that could possibly be brought to bear."

This idea took hold. Lieutenant H. A. Wise, assistant inspector of ordnance for the Union Navy, acknowledged that the moment he jumped on board the *Monitor* after her fight on the 9th he realized that a steam tug with twenty men could have taken the upper part of her in as many seconds—and perhaps the inside, too, by dropping two or three twelve-pounder shrapnel down her steampipe, or by blocking the turret or dancing around with it as it moved. But he reminded Union officers that the *Monitor* was not intended to be fought by itself alone and that her consorts would keep her deck clear. "With respect to that 'liquid fire' stuff, which is petroleum, naphtha, and benzine," he added, "it might do very well in an emergency, in all save the risk of the fire running down the gratings of the *Monitor* or the crevices about the turret and setting her going below. Moreover, we have sent to all the big guns in the Roads shells filled with Birney's preparation, nearly the same elements as the 'liquid fire,' which will puzzle the devil himself, even in his own dominions, to put out, should one crack over or into hell." [39]

Goldsborough added the alarm that chloroform was to be

used in abundance by the *Merrimack* to produce insensibility on board the *Monitor*.[40]

April closed with thick weather and rain pouring in torrents. Tattnall was still pondering the suggestion that the *Merrimack* run past the forts and Union fleet and make its way into York River. The more he thought of it, the more he was convinced such a plan would be useless.

At the Norfolk Navy Yard at this period more construction was in progress than ever before. The South was trying desperately to complete another ironclad, the *Richmond,* said to be free of some of the major faults found in the *Merrimack.* Labor crews to hurry her along were brought in from Fredericksburg, from North Carolina and elsewhere, and Mallory gave orders for operations to go on through the night, even if girls had to be employed to hold lanterns so the workmen could see.

As May moved into its first week, the Confederates recognized the handwriting on the wall. General Lee wrote General Johnston: "If it is possible for the *Virginia,* which upon the fall of Norfolk must be destroyed, to run into Yorktown at the last moment and destroy the enemy's gunboats and transports, it would greatly cripple his present and future movements, relieve your army from pursuit, and prevent its meeting the same army in Northern Virginia." [41]

As early as the 3rd, there was sound of heavy cannonading in the direction of Yorktown, and plans for the evacuation of that center were speeded. Mallory directed that all public property be removed to North Carolina, assembling it at Raleigh or elsewhere. Apparently fearing the results of the campaign against Richmond, he cautioned that nothing should be sent to the Confederate capital.

The cannonading was still in progress next morning, and at nine o'clock Goldsborough signaled from his flagship: "Yorktown is ours." During divine service on board ship, Dr. Joseph Beale, chief surgeon, stepped forth and uttered an impressive prayer of thanksgiving. Men bowed their heads, but almost all irreverently looked up now and then to peer toward Sewell's Point. There the *Merrimack* could be seen anchored beside a small tug, the nearest she had been to the Union fleet since April 11. Swung around by the action of the tide, she presented a broadside to the face of the channel. They could see that her armor was covered with a thick coat of grease and black lead, which, as the sun reflected on it, gave it a brilliant, glassy appearance. Her ports resembled the eyes of cadavers, and those who stared at her sensed her conviction of strength, of unequaled superiority. But this advantage was wasted, for her challenge was ignored, and in the late afternoon she steamed back to Craney Island, lying to with steam up.

The evening of the 6th, Abraham Lincoln arrived at Fort Monroe. His visit was prompted by public impatience over the stalemate at Hampton Roads. Plans for the advance on Richmond were stepped up immediately. The President informed Goldsborough that, if he had "tolerable confidence" he could contend with the *Merrimack* without the help of the *Galena,* a new gunboat, and two other similar vessels, they should be sent up the James River immediately.

Lincoln's directive set off a chase. At two o'clock the morning of the 8th the Confederate ships *Patrick Henry* and *Jamestown* stood off Newport News. They were returning from a trip up the James, where they had towed some of the ships partially completed at Norfolk, including the ironclad *Richmond.* Suddenly signal lights flashed on shore and were answered by Federal vessels moored out in the roadstead. This was all the evidence the Confederates needed to determine that they had been discovered, so they slowly returned up the James. At 9:30 A.M. they saw three steamers standing up the river toward them, and lookouts reported they were the *Galena,* the *Aroostook,* and the *Port Royal,* the latter two, gunboats. Steadily the Federals pushed along, but at Day's Point they swung about and opened fire on a battery until it was silenced. While the bombardment was in progress, the *Jamestown* hurried off to report at Richmond what was happening below.

John R. Tucker of the *Patrick Henry,* remaining behind, watched for a time while the enemy vessels shelled another battery at Hardens Bluff, and then he, too, scurried on up the river, determined if necessary to scuttle his ship and create a blockade for the defense of the Confederate capital.

In Hampton Roads later that morning of the 8th, six Union ships, including the *Monitor,* steamed out and began shelling the batteries on Sewell's Point. This attack could be blamed on a disgruntled Southerner. His name was Byers, and he was master of a tugboat, the *J. B. White,* that for nearly a year had been employed on a canal construction project. He deserted, taking his vessel with him, and soon he was in front of Lincoln, telling all he knew. The Confederates, he said, were preparing to evacuate Norfolk and Portsmouth.[42]

When the Federal ships appeared, the *Merrimack* could not be seen anywhere. Byers had told Lincoln she was at Norfolk.

But soon smoke was seen rising beyond the far side of the woods on Sewell's Point, and a little later the *Merrimack* appeared and steamed toward the Union fleet. Goldsborough had verbal orders to the effect that, if the Confederate ironclad appeared, the *Monitor* was to fall back into fair channel way, "and only to engage her seriously in such a position" that the *Minnesota,* together with other vessels standing by for that purpose, could run her down.[43]

There are different versions of what went on that day. Goldsborough reported:

"The *Merrimack* came out, but was even more cautious than ever. The *Monitor* was kept well in advance and so that the *Merrimack* could have engaged her without difficulty had she been so disposed, but she declined to do it, and soon returned and anchored under Sewell's Point." [44]

The log of the *Minnesota* recorded: "Battery on Sewell's Point opened fire. At one-thirty the *Monitor* went close to the battery. At two-fifteen the fleet began to draw off, and the *Merrimack* appeared coming out. The *Merrimack,* coming round Sewell's Point, fired a gun and made signal to ship to keep underway; slipped chain. At four-thirty the *Merrimack* retired." [45]

In the log of the U.S.S. *Susquehanna* it was reported that the flag of the Confederate battery on Sewell's Point was shot away about 2:00 P.M. and that its fire soon ceased. "Made signal to the fleet 'Enemy's fort appears abandoned,'" it was added. "At three P.M. made signal to 'Follow our motions,' and stood toward Fortress Monroe, the Rebel steamer *Merrimack* steaming down from Craney Island toward us. Flagship made signal 'Resume your moorings.' At four-thirty *Merrimack* turned and stood toward Craney Island again." [46]

From the commander of the *Naugatuck* came this report: "I selected a position off the battery of the enemy within a distance varying from three-quarters of a mile to a mile and a quarter (a distance less than that of one-quarter of the actual range of our heavy gun), from which I threw shell into the enemy's battery with good effect until the *Merrimack* made her appearance, coming out of Elizabeth River, when, with the rest of the squadron, led by the flagship, we slowly retired toward Hampton Bar." [47]

The commander of the British ship *Rinaldo,* supposedly an unbiased observer, also described what happened. "With the exception of a few shots fired from the Rip Raps at the *Virginia,* the Federals made no attempt to molest her, but, on the contrary, as she approached them they steamed away from her. They left off firing at Sewell's Point immediately on sighting her coming from Norfolk. She would most likely have made her appearance before had the water been sufficiently high. The *Virginia,* having driven the Federal fleet away, returned and anchored under Sewell's Point, where she now remains." [48]

The Confederates had planned to hold a conference that morning on the final disposition of the *Merrimack.* Before the officers could assemble, however, the shelling of Sewell's Point began, and Tattnall set out with the ironclad. "We passed the battery and stood directly for the enemy, for the purpose of engaging him," he reported, "and I thought an action certain,

particularly as the *Minnesota* and *Vanderbilt,* which were anchored below Fortress Monroe, got underway and stood up to
that point, apparently with the intention of joining their squadron in the roads. Before, however, we got within gunshot the
enemy ceased firing and retired with all speed under the protection of the guns of the fortress, followed by the *Virginia*
until the shells from the Rip Raps passed over her." [49]

Tattnall steamed about in disgust until the tide began to ebb,
a development he recognized as his warning to be careful
where he moved with the *Merrimack.* But before leaving the
scene, he ordered a gun fired to windward, a sailor's gesture of
supreme contempt.

The Confederates were able to hold their conference on the
9th. They agreed unanimously that the *Merrimack* should continue to protect Norfolk, affording time for the public property
there to be removed. The day went by peaceably. That night
was beautiful. Union soldiers at Fort Monroe sat outdoors and
wrote letters home by moonlight. Off in the distance they could
see a bright light, and, judging by their sense of direction, they
were sure it was on the *Merrimack.*[50]

But on the 10th, with Lincoln as an eyewitness, Union troops
were landed at Willoughby Point, and soon they were pouring
across land toward Norfolk. Smoke could be seen rising at
different points, one cloud in the direction of the Navy Yard.

Tattnall got evidence of impending collapse at 10:00 A.M.,
when from the *Merrimack* he noticed that the flag on Sewell's
Point was no longer flying. Hastily Lieutenant J. P. Jones was
sent to Craney Island, where the Confederate colors were still
visible, and there he learned that the enemy was marching on
Norfolk. This same officer then was directed to go to Norfolk.
He returned with a report that the Navy Yard was in flames,
the Confederate forces had fled, the enemy was within half a
mile of the city, and the mayor was treating for its surrender.[51]

By the time the officer returned it was seven o'clock in the
evening. Tattnall debated his next move. His chief pilot, William Parrish, and his chief assistant, David Wright, had assured

him that the *Merrimack,* if lightened to a draft of eighteen feet, could proceed to within forty miles of Richmond.[52] With this assurance, the flag officer called all hands on deck. He spoke in sharp tones, explaining the emergency and expressing hope that the ironclad could be taken up the James and could capture enemy vessels there before its design was known. The crew replied with cheers and immediately went to work.

Tattnall had been ill all day and, after speaking to the men, was forced to return to bed. Between one and two o'clock his first lieutenant, Catesby Jones, aroused him to report that the ship had been lightened by nearly two feet, but that the pilots now were saying eighteen feet would not carry her above the Jamestown Flats, the shores on each side of which were occupied by the enemy.

Tattnall sent for Parrish and demanded an explanation. The pilot replied that the ship with an eighteen-foot draft could be taken upstream with prevailing easterly winds, but that for the last two days they had been westerly.

"I had no time to lose," Tattnall reported. "The ship was not in a condition for battle even with an enemy of equal force, and their force was overwhelming. I therefore determined, with the concurrence of the first and flag lieutenants, to save the crew for future service by landing them at Craney Island, the only road for retreat open to us, and to destroy the ship to prevent her falling into the hands of the enemy. I may add that, although not formally consulted, the course was approved by every commissioned officer in the ship." [53]

The *Merrimack* swung around toward Craney Island. Her iron sheathing still extended three feet under water.[54] At her destination, she was driven hard up on the mainland. Sadly her crew abandoned her, starting a march in the dark toward Suffolk. Behind they left Catesby Jones, entrusted with the unpleasant duty of firing her.[55]

It was around three o'clock that morning when a match was applied, after which Jones hurried ashore and set out on the trail of his companions. He must have felt certain satisfaction over what he had just done. Confederate officials had not considered him capable of commanding the *Merrimack,* and yet it was his lot to destroy her.

At two minutes to five o'clock, as dawn was creeping in, she blew up. "It is said to have been a grand sight," Union War Secretary Stanton reported.[56] Goldsborough heard the "awful explosion" from the direction of Craney Island and inferred immediately that either the *Merrimack* or the Confederate works at that point had been blown up. A few minutes later an officer from the U.S.S. *Dacotah* arrived on board to tell him it was the *Merrimack*.

Union officers at a signal station agreed it was the grandest sight imaginable. For nearly an hour before the explosion, they told a New York *Herald* reporter, the roof was red from the heat, and at short intervals the guns would discharge, awesomely breaking in upon the stillness of the night. Just at the first grayness of daylight the whole red and black mass heaved skyward. Then came the report, so terrific as to shake houses eight miles away. The flash, an unearthly hissing sound, ended and "the *Merrimack* ceased to exist in the form in which she had been such a terror to us for two long, weary, watchful months."

And then there was an epitaph. "It was a beautiful Sunday morning that the *Congress* exploded. How strange that the destroyer should be blasted out of her existence on a Sunday morning, too." [57]

Thus came the end of the ironclad in which the Southerners had placed so much faith.[58] It was left to Josiah Tattnall to add the benediction: "The *Virginia* no longer exists, but three hundred brave and skillful officers and seamen are saved to the Confederacy." [59]

Drewry's Bluff

APRIL-MAY 1862

The night of May 14 was not one the refugee crew from the C.S.S. *Merrimack* cared to remember. They had been facing emergencies for what seemed an interminable period, beginning with the hour of flight over the side of the doomed ironclad. Their course since then had led from Suffolk to Richmond, and then down the muddy, swollen course of the James, eight miles to Drewry's Bluff, the first high ground below the city.[1] Everywhere they were met by confusion and excitement and alarm. How to stop the Union gunboats from storming up the river and shelling the Confederate capital, now that the mighty *Merrimack* was gone, was the dominant problem.

It was well known the enemy's vessels were coming, even without the assurance embraced in a message McClellan sent War Secretary Stanton the morning the Rebels blew up their ironclad: "I congratulate you from the bottom of my heart upon the destruction of the *Merrimack*. I would now most earnestly urge that our gunboats and the ironclad boats be sent as far as possible up the James River without delay. This

will enable me to make our movements much more decisive." [2]
Elation over the blowing up of the Confederate ship was not
confined alone to the commander of Union troops. Gustavus
Fox, the Navy executive, wrote Flag Officer Du Pont in the
tone of a man waking from a bad dream: "I have not written
you lately, the confounded *Merrimack* has set like a nightmare
upon our Department." [3]

At Drewry's Bluff the *Merrimack's* crewmen were received
with joyous welcome by men toiling frantically in mud and
dampness. For two months, ever since the *Monitor* had made
its timely appearance in Hampton Roads, the race to build a
fort that would stop the Union monster had been in progress,
and still it was not completed. Spring freshets and the difficulty
of hauling in materials, including stone to go in the cribs under
construction as a barrier out in the channel, had delayed matters alarmingly.[4] Deficiencies included men, timber, ropes, and
stone. As late as April 29, Thomas H. Wynne, chief engineer
assigned to the defenses of Richmond, had estimated the river
would not be fully obstructed for two months. Most discouraging were the freshets, the sudden surges of water brought
on by the frequent spring rains, one of which during the last
week had carried off some of the stone, making it necessary
for certain work to be redone. Part of the supply of stone was
concentrated on the wharf at Richmond, dumped there after
being hauled from sites of buildings razed in the city, and it
was a problem to get it moved the eight miles downstream to
the Bluff. Only two boats—the *John Farrar* and the *E. J. Duval*
—had been called into use, while two others, as well as several
canal boats, lay idle in the basin, much to Engineer Wynne's
disgust.

But there was hope that what had been accomplished would
do the job. Five guns—three thirty-two's and two sixty-
four's, some Army, some Navy—were in position behind strong
earthworks, with wooden platforms beneath to keep the artillerists' feet out of the soft, sticky mud.[5] This stronghold already had been given the name of Fort Darling. It sat on top of

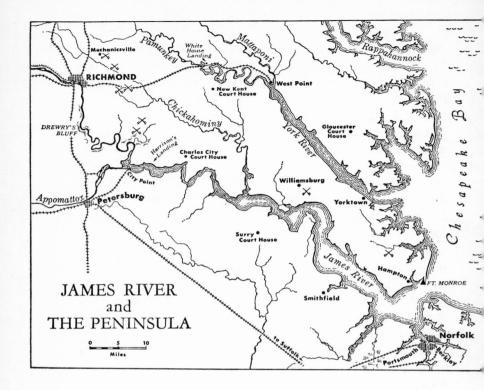

JAMES RIVER
and
THE PENINSULA

the bluff, two hundred feet above the surface of the river, and the mouths of its pieces, all powerful and capable of hurling eight- and ten-inch shot, pointed downstream, almost due east, along a straight stretch looking toward a curve around which the enemy would have to come and on the other side of which the river again turned toward the southeast. Across the stream, directly in front of the fort, stretched a line of piles and scuttled hulks. Some of the latter had been there for weeks, chained to shore to keep them from washing away in the flood waters which during the spring rose and fell in a matter of hours. They were so arranged that a one-hundred-foot gap was left for navigation, with the understanding that this, too, could be closed on fifteen to twenty minutes' notice.

Nightfall of the 14th came too quickly for the Confederates. Rain had been falling in a drizzle all day, and the mire underfoot was deeper and stickier than ever. But the men worked on unceasingly, desperation prodding them. Just before dark the *Jamestown* was scuttled, and she settled down in the water to block the gap left in the line of hulks. Work continued even after the sun disappeared and night closed in. Torches burned in the damp air until a late hour, spreading their flickering glow over men who slogged about, wet and muddy and tired, some in uniform, some in civilian dress, and all as bent on attaining a goal as a family of beavers scuttling about the slippery foundation of a new dam.

Downstream on both sides campfires burned sullenly in the night, adding a feeling of security to the scene, for each marked a spot where riflemen—an entire brigade brought in by forced march—hovered on the banks, waiting for the enemy to approach so they could let loose their hail of well-aimed bullets at every animate object in sight. This support lent great comfort to the forces drawn into the frantic struggle to save the Confederate capital, and so did the presence of a company of sappers and miners hurried down from their temporary camp at the Fair Grounds in Richmond. For more than a week these fellows had been busy rigging water mines out in the river as a further obstruction against the invaders.

For the last two days the *Merrimack's* crew had been subjected to this merciless struggle, exposed to constant rain, in bottomless mud, without shelter, and living on scant rations. Aiding them were men who could be spared from the vessels that had managed to make their way through the gap before it was closed. The *Patrick Henry* was among them. She lay upstream now, waiting.

Rain still fell as the men from the *Merrimack* finally extinguished their last torch and stumbled, tired and hungry, to beds in a hastily constructed casemate. But the restful sleep their aching muscles cried for was not to be their lot that night. During the early hours of morning a heavy rain and wind storm swept through, knocking the roof from their shelter. With no other haven, they huddled together in their misery, awaiting the dawn. Slowly it came, baring a sodden landscape. On all sides water dripped from trees and gun carriages, from man and his accouterments, and down on the river mists hung over the banks, enveloping the land and blending with a day that promised more rain and mud.

Up on the bluff, soldiers and their civilian helpers grumbled freely in the grayish dawn. Then suddenly, at six o'clock, the grumbling stopped and eyes were turned due east toward the curve where the guns pointed. Somewhere down there in the misty screen of bushes a signal musket had cracked, sounding an alarm that told the enemy had been sighted.

Higher upstream, riding out on horseback in the early dawn, was President Jefferson Davis' military adviser, Robert E. Lee. Behind in the Confederate capital he had left government officials in a state bordering on panic. Only the day before, when news had arrived in the late afternoon that the Federal ships were making their way past City Point in an atmosphere of white flags and burning tobacco, boxes of government archives, all addressed to Columbia, South Carolina, had been taken away in the very canal boats Engineer Wynne had wanted to use for hauling stone. The Confederate Treasury's reserve of gold was packed and ready to be placed aboard a special train standing by under steam. As another evidence of evacuation intent, planks for the passage of artillery lay across bridges over the James. But Lee had no notion of surrendering Richmond, although the possibility that he might have to threatened annoyingly. At a Cabinet meeting called by Davis he had reacted to the suggestion emotionally, declaring with tears in his eyes: "Richmond must not be given up; it shall not be given up!" [6]

Calming the public's fears had been one of Davis' major chores for days. Committees from the City of Richmond and the State Legislature had called on him in alarm. During one interview, held at a time when the gap still existed in the line of hulks at Drewry's Bluff, the President gave assurance that everything was being done that could be done and blamed the slow progress on the spring freshets. In the midst of the session, General Lee arrived with Navy Secretary Mallory and conferred with Davis in an anteroom. When the Chief Executive returned to the conference with the committee, he was pressed for more specific information.

"I should have given you a very different answer to your question a few moments ago from which I shall be compelled to give you now," he said. "Those traitors at Norfolk, I fear, have defeated our plans."

"What traitors?" asked the committee.

Davis answered with details concerning the tugboat Captain Byers had deserted to give Abraham Lincoln information that led to the attack on Sewell's Point, May 8.

"Can nothing be done to counteract this?" asked a committee member.

"Everything will be done, I assure you, which can be done," Davis replied.

"But, Mr. President, what will be done?" pursued the committeeman.

Davis declined to answer, saying there were some things it was not proper to communicate.

The member was determined. "This is a confidential meeting," he told Davis, "and of course nothing transpiring here will reach the public."

Cornered, Davis smiled and said: "Gentlemen, I think there was much wisdom in the remark of old John Brown at Harpers Ferry: 'A man who is not capable of keeping his own secrets is not fit to be trusted with the business of other people.'" The committee went away unsatisfied, but with no unpleasant feeling.[7]

It is unlikely that the signal gun fired below Drewry's Bluff was heard by Lee, but the bombardment that started little more than an hour and a half later certainly came clearly and dishearteningly to his ears. For three hours and twenty minutes, by actual count, it rattled the windows of the Confederate capital.

The muddy men huddling up on Drewry's Bluff watched while the Federal ships steamed slowly into sight, one after another. The commander of the post, Ebenezer Farrand, a patriot of the Confederate cause from the very beginning and one of the officers most responsible for keeping Florida's Pensacola Navy Yard in the hands of Southerners, stood looking through a pair of glasses. In front was the ironclad *Galena,* commanded by John Rodgers, a veteran officer with a long career as a coast surveyor and conductor of scientific expeditions, carrying on a name made famous by a Revolutionary patriot grandfather and a naval hero father who had had the distinction of firing the first shot of the War of 1812. Behind the *Galena* moved the *Monitor, Port Royal, Naugatuck,* and *Aroostook.* From the moment of raising anchor near Kingsland Creek a few miles below, they had passed through a gantlet of small-gun fire. Sharpshooters blazed away from both banks, from rifle pits, and from treetops, giving the crews of the vessels ample warning they were in enemy territory. A few shots from twenty-four-pounders silenced these snipers momentarily, and then they opened again, more furiously than ever, peppering portholes and pilothouses.

Rodgers' orders directed him to go up the James, reducing the works of the Confederates as he moved, spiking their guns, blowing up their magazines, and at Richmond to "shell the city to a surrender." Already he had grave doubts that the last of these missions would be accomplished, and sight of the fort up on the bluff strengthened his misgivings. His experience in coming up the river had convinced him that the ironclad he commanded was not as formidable as she was rumored to be.[8]

Without hesitating he ran the *Galena* up to within six hundred yards of the enemy battery, to a point where the width of the stream was no more than double the ship's length. There he let go her starboard anchor, ran out the chains, put her head inshore, backed astern, let go her stream anchor from the starboard quarter, hove ahead, and made ready for action before firing a gun. Wrote one of the Confederate officers staring down from Fort Darling: "Nothing could have been more beautiful than the neatness and precision of movement with which Rodgers placed the *Galena,* as if in target practice, directly under the enemy's fire." [9] The *Monitor* lay near, the others farther back.

At 7:45 A.M. the *Galena* opened fire from one of her six guns. For the next hour and a quarter the bombardment continued. Rodgers' ship was as vulnerable as a sitting duck, the plunging shot from the fort tearing through her deck and sides, and the riflemen along the banks sniping at her crewmen whenever they showed themselves. Recognizing the *Galena's* dilemma, the *Monitor,* at nine o'clock, passed above and attempted to shell the enemy battery, but her guns could not be elevated enough to reach the top of the bluff. She then dropped below, to take advantage of distance, and continued to fire.

All the while the Confederates blasted away mercilessly from the bluff, observing a pattern of action designed to reduce their own mortality rate. When the ships were firing rapidly, there was rarely an answering shot from the battery above, but the moment the Federals slackened the rate of their bombardment the Rebel guns were remanned furiously. One problem for the Southerners was caused by the angle at which their guns had to be depressed in order to aim at the ships below. So slanting were the barrels that grommets of rope had to be placed around cannon balls to keep them from rolling out before the firing could take place.[10]

The men up there and out along the banks where rifles cracked were some of the best fighters siding with the South. Among them, seeing action for the Confederacy for the first times as a corps, were the Confederate Marines, most of them officers and privates who had resigned from the United States service. For months they had been cooped up in Richmond, idle and impatient, but now they were free to give battle as they had been trained. Only one of their units was untroubled by former lethargy: it had seen service on the *Merrimack* up to the time of her destruction. Although their allegiance had changed, they might have looked on at least with a mite of pride at one of their former buddies, Corporal John L. Mackie. So gallantly was he fighting on board the *Galena* that his service would bring as an award the first Congressional Medal of Honor ever presented to a member of his corps.[11]

Up there on the bluff was an officer newly arrived from the battlefront around New Orleans. He was James I. Waddell, better than six feet tall, well-proportioned, limping slightly from a duel he had fought with a messmate during his years in the old navy. After a battle with yellow fever, he had sailed on duty to the Orient, and there he was when the war began. It was January '62 before he returned, but his resignation had been dated weeks earlier. Disguised as an oysterman, he made his way south to join the Confederacy, twirling a neat mustache not usually found on men of the occupation he had temporarily assumed.[12]

Down among the Confederate riflemen along the bank was one officer who was conducting himself in such a manner that he would be cited in an official report. He was John Taylor Wood, grandson of President Zachary Taylor and a former faculty member at the U. S. Naval Academy. He lay at the front of a band of sharpshooters, all busy firing and reloading.

Out on the *Galena* a port cover jammed. Quickly through the gap a sailor's arm appeared in a panicky attempt to shake it loose. A barrage of rifle shots sounded from the bushes along the bank, and the arm dropped into the water.[13]

Rodgers soon had sufficient evidence that the *Galena* was not shotproof. A ball penetrated just above the water line and exploded in the steerage. Others followed, breaking the iron and penetrating the wood backing. Knees, timbers, and planks were started. In three places on the deck, holes appeared, one a yard long and eight inches wide, made by a glancing shot that broke through and killed several men with fragments of the deck plating. This was a major problem: to stave off fatalities from the ship's own iron.

Downstream the *Naugatuck* lay in silence. At the first fire from her one-hundred-pounder, the rifle itself exploded, half of the part abaft the trunnions going overboard. That no one was killed seemed a miracle. Peter Dixon, seaman, was the worst hurt, receiving a severe contusion of the left shoulder. Another seaman was shot in the arm by a sharpshooter.

The *Port Royal* remained in the background, but the Confederates found her. A shell struck on the port bow below the water line, and water poured in so freely it was necessary to draw off and repair the damage. When it returned to action, another shot hit forward the wheel and also below the water line. Again the vessel withdrew, and on her return found her greatest trouble in the riflemen lurking in the woods. One of their balls struck the captain of the ship, George U. Morris, commander of the *Cumberland* at the time she was sunk by the *Merrimack* on March 8. It caused a severe flesh wound in the right leg.

Slow to get into action, the *Aroostook* opened with an eleven-inch gun and did very well for more than an hour. Then a shell struck at the water line under the after part of the starboard forechains, cutting off the planking and laying the timbers bare. Shortly afterward an eight-inch solid shot passed through the starboard bow a foot above the sheet hawsehole and lodged in the harness cask. Reported her captain: "Seeing that the enemy had my range perfectly, I changed my position about one hundred yards farther down and again opened fire." [14]

Emboldened by the resistance from the top of Drewry's Bluff, the little *Patrick Henry* drifted down, almost unnoticed, to a point a short distance above the barricade and opened fire. Her target was the *Galena,* and her gunners were capable. At eleven o'clock one of her eight-inch solid shots passed into the bow of the enemy ship and immediately smoke began to pour out of the portholes. Five minutes later John Rodgers had had enough. He signaled to discontinue the action and withdraw.

As the *Galena* slipped her cables and moved down the river, men on board the *Patrick Henry* cheered loudly, a reaction echoed by the gunners on the bluff. A Rebel picket concealed on the bank of the stream heard Rodgers call to one of the other vessels in passing: "She's in a sinking condition." [15]

Rodgers' ship limped away, followed by the others. Her sides, her deck, her smokestacks were riddled. Forty-four shot, by actual count, had found their mark in her.[16] She had been tested and found wanting. Because of the failure, her armor would be removed and she would serve out the war as a wooden gunboat, a great letdown from the high hopes held for her at the time of her launching the preceding February at Mystic, Connecticut.

So this armada, the first against the Confederate capital, ended in complete failure. Ships were damaged, men were killed and wounded. The wounded outnumbered the dead, as usually was the case. Thirteen corpses lay in a row on the *Galena*. The bodies, taken downriver, soon began to smell, and the odor became so bad they were interred in graves hurriedly dug along the bank, where the Southerners could walk and count the results of the terrific resistance they had managed to organize at Drewry's Bluff. Seven of their number had been killed and eight wounded.[17]

Rodgers withdrew downstream with a conclusive report on the *Galena* and a firm conviction that Fort Darling atop Drewry's Bluff would fall only in the face of a joint operation.

Island No. 10

MARCH-MAY 1862

Only a man steeped in the ways of God and the Church could have withstood without strong oath the pain Commodore Andrew Foote suffered after the battle of Fort Donelson. The shrapnel wound he had received in the attack failed to heal, and a doctor, examining it later, found the anterior portion of the instep of the left foot considerably swollen, although without discoloration of the skin. It was his conclusion that "very little, if any, improvement has taken place in consequence of neglect of the main requirements of a cure, viz., absolute rest and horizontal position of the whole extremity."

Foote, directing the Union's drive from the north to close the Mississippi and cut the Confederacy in two, unaware that the wound would spell his end in a matter of months, would take no time for rest. Even the death of a favorite son failed to divert him from his duties. He wrote his wife: "I have pain in my foot; but you will see from the certificate that there is no danger to be apprehended, unless it is to the government from my not being able to give personal attention to my varied duties. Still every moment of my time from seven A.M. till eleven P.M. is occupied with office duties. I am on crutches." [1]

Through it all his eyes remained steadily focused on a goal. But no longer did he stand on deck and preach, a form of indulgence that was the obvious outlet for a self-nurtured belief that he was a great orator, something his friends said he was not.[2] Broad of forehead, square-built and neatly dressed, at times wearing green goggles, he stumped about ship on crutches with the belligerence of a bulldog, yet with a heart and soul that would cause him to be referred to as the Stonewall Jackson of the Navy.

Foote's campaign was moving well despite his wound. After the capture of Forts Henry and Donelson, the Confederate stronghold at Columbus, Kentucky, fell in the final breakup of the first line of the Confederate defense in the West. Everyone recognized it was a blow to the South, for this point was considered the Confederacy's "Gibraltar." On duty there, under General Leonidas Polk, were twenty thousand Confederates, stationed behind guns well situated on high bluffs overlooking the river. But the fall of Forts Henry and Donelson isolated the garrison and forced its evacuation.

After the fall of Columbus, the Rebels moved forty miles downstream and fortified another place from which they thought they could not be blasted. It was Island No. 10, so numbered in the order of the succession of islands below the mouth of the Ohio.[3] It lay toward the east bank, near the Kentucky-Tennessee line, in a great turn of the river known as Madrid Bend. Over a period of months it had been strengthened with every device of military skill, in a frantic drive carried on under the direction of General Pierre G. T. Beauregard, a new commander of the Department of Mississippi, an officer who had resigned as an engineer for the Federal Government to lead the Southerners at Charleston, South Carolina, and later at Manassas, Virginia, in the first major battle of the war.

This island stood high out of the water and, owing to its

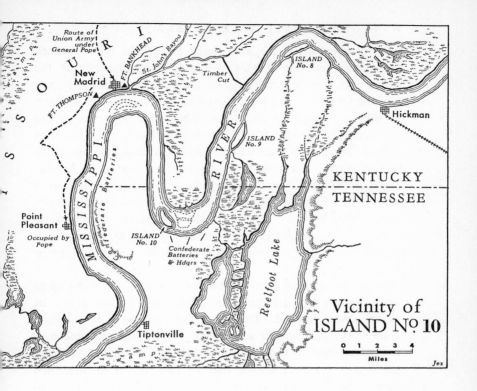

Route of
Union Army
under
General Pope

New
Madrid

FT. BANKHEAD

St. John's Bayou

Timber
Cut

ISLAND
No. 8

FT. THOMPSON

MISSISSIPPI

Confederate Batteries

RIVER

ISLAND
No. 9

Hickman

KENTUCKY
TENNESSEE

Point
Pleasant

Occupied by
Pope

ISLAND
No. 10

Confederate
Batteries
& Hdqrs

Reelfoot Lake

Vicinity of
ISLAND Nº 10

Tiptonville

0   1   2   3   4
Miles

Jex

location in Madrid Bend, commanded the river for some distance
in both directions. It was fifty-five miles below the Union naval
base at Cairo, Illinois, and between the Tennessee and Missouri shores. Because of a wide surrounding area of swamps
and bayous, teeming with black and miasmatic water, rank
vegetation, rotting trees, and poisonous snakes, land forces
could not reach it, so Beauregard centered his attention on
defense against gunboats. For two miles along the banks approaching it he had constructed earthworks commanding the
swift current by which enemy vessels must come. Fifty-two
guns were ready to be fired by the Confederates. At the island
the river made a sharp bend and ran northwest several miles
to another bend, where it once more turned southward, and
there on the Missouri side, at New Madrid, the Southerners built
strong fortifications and stationed a large number of troops,

most of them from the abandoned stronghold at Columbus. Since the preceding August they had been constructing the earthworks, handicapped most of the time by sickness. Nearly half the force of better than thirty-five hundred men were down with bowel complaint and fever. They were under command of a forty-six-year-old West Pointer, Brigadier General William Whann Mackall, a pleasant sort of individual who somehow lacked what it takes to make an inspired leader. In his defense, of course, it could be held later, was the might thrown against him by the North in its drive to split the Confederacy. But behind him was a record that, except for a wound received in the Seminole War, would tag him as an armchair officer. After the impending campaign, he would disappear from history.

As Union commanders viewed the situation, the first step to invest Island No. 10 would be to cut it off from below by taking New Madrid. This task was assigned to General John Pope, an engineer officer and West Point graduate who had taken part in the fighting in Missouri from the very beginning of the war. Before that he had put in distinguished service—exploring, surveying, fighting in the Mexican War, and even escorting Abraham Lincoln to Washington for his inauguration. Simultaneously with Pope's advance by land, Andrew Foote would bring his boats downstream from Cairo and they would meet at Island No. 10.

Fighting by Pope's army began at New Madrid March 1, and continued through several days of skirmishing and picket fire. Foote still had not moved from Cairo, and Major General Henry W. Halleck, commanding the Western Department from St. Louis, became impatient. He wanted Pope's forces for a movement up the Tennessee River.

By the 6th, Halleck would wait no longer. He sent word that he wanted an attack on Monday, the 10th. Foote said he could not be ready before Wednesday, the 12th.[4]

Halleck fretted. So did Pope. But Foote was adamant. On board his flagship, the U.S.S. *Benton,* James Eads' masterpiece and the most powerful fighting vessel on the Mississippi, he painfully struggled about on crutches, black eyes flashing fire, his brown hair, surprisingly free of gray, waving in the breeze. Still clear in his memory was the roar of the cannon at Fort Donelson, the steady pace with which the Confederates had kept up their fire, and the damage they had done to him and to his gunboats. His foremost concern now was the cautious use of his vessels and the welfare of the men serving under him. He repeated that his fleet was not ready, that he hoped General Pope and the land forces could maintain position until it was. If ordered to move before the 12th, he said he would do it, "but under a remonstrance that I shall deem it an act involving, in all probability, the most disastrous consequences to the flotilla and to the service for which it was designed to perform." His delay, he explained, was caused by the fact that the pilothouses, the target the Southerners had learned to shoot at first, were unsafe, and the vessels were not in a condition to enable them to make a stand "against such a resistance as the Rebels have made in every instance." [5]

As promised, Foote had his forces in shape by the 12th. "I am ready to move with seven gunboats and ten mortar boats upon Island No. 10 and New Madrid," he wired, "but the troops and transports are not here and I consider it unsafe to move without troops to occupy No. 10 if we capture it, as we can not take prisoners with gunboats." He had visions of the Confederates returning on the Tennessee side, manning their batteries, and closing the river in his rear.

At seven o'clock on the 14th, with transports at hand, he got his flotilla under way and started downstream. His movement was not unnoticed. While passing through banks of fog, the Confederate *Grampus,* described as "the sauciest little vessel on the river," ran up, whirled about, and dashed off before Union gunners could fire a shot. On ahead she scurried, yawing and flirting and blowing her whistle, all to warn the Rebel artillerists stationed above Island No. 10 that the enemy was coming.[6]

While Foote was moving downstream, Pope was sending off messages of victory. He had pushed in with heavy guns and twenty thousand men at New Madrid, and the Confederates, awed by what was before them, gave virtually no resistance. Their fleet, under veteran Flag Officer George N. Hollins—the *McRae, Livingston, Maurepas, General Polk, Ivy,* and *Pontchartrain,* only two armored sufficiently to protect them from small arms and light artillery—moved out of action, dropping downriver to Tiptonville, a point thirty miles from Island No. 10 by river, but only four miles by land. The land troops quickly followed them.

The Confederates made their departure during a violent thunderstorm.

They went away very badly scared and in an awful hurry [Charles W. Willis, one of the pursuing Federals reported] for there were tables with wine on, and cards and beds that had been used last night, and they left all their heavy artillery. They must have had all of their light artillery with the horses hitched to it and harnessed, and a lot of horses saddled and tied, for the halters were cut with the ties left on the posts, showing that they were in too much of a hurry to untie. They also left all their tents, some five hundred, standing, most of them as good as the best of ours, and barracks for several regiments, quarters in all for probably ten thousand men, the generals say, but I don't think they will hold so many. I think we got forty guns, twenty-fours and larger, besides some field pieces. We also got a big lot of ammunition, lots of mules and wagons, and the boys are now fishing out of the river whole boxes of quartermaster's goods—clothing, blankets, etc., that the secesh rolled in as they ran.[7]

Pope was delighted that he had cut off the little fleet protecting Island No. 10—one gunboat and ten large steamers, as well as a floating battery with nine guns. These vessels must either be destroyed or surrendered, he telegraphed.[8]

Foote, moving down a badly flooded Mississippi, arrived within two miles of Island No. 10 at nine o'clock the morning of the 15th. Fog lay in a dense cloud along the river, and a heavy rain was falling. Because of weather conditions, only two mortar boats could be maneuvered into position, and they just for the purpose of ascertaining the range. They fired only four shots. The *Benton* also used up a few shells, testing the Rebels, but nothing brought a reply.

That night the Confederates took a final defense step: they sank a large steamboat in the slough on the Missouri side of Island No. 10.

The morning of the 16th dawned clear. As soon as it was light, Captain Edmund W. Rucker, commanding Confederate Battery No. 1, lying on the Kentucky shore two miles above Island No. 10, looked out to find four Union mortar boats in position. About nine o'clock a small tugboat dropped down from the Federal flotilla, bearing a flag of truce, and her captain yelled a query as to whether the Southerners wanted to communicate with the fleet.

"No!" shouted Rucker.

"Then why the white flag?" asked the Union officer, pointing.

Rucker turned and stared at the flag he was using to signal headquarters. It was indeed white, something he had not noticed before.[9]

At intervals throughout the day Foote's mortars dropped shells on the island. The wind had blown in diagonally across the river from the northeast, carrying all smoke and fog away and giving the Federals a clear view of the Rebel works. A sweep with glasses showed them a threatening picture: batteries above and below high bluffs, guns visible over breastworks, troops drawn up in large bodies, and a sea of white tents and log huts, denoting strength. Tall smokestacks of half a dozen steamers were visible on the Tennessee side, and others could be seen against the head of the island; also plainly visible was the boat sunk in the channel during the night. Long rows of tents gleamed in the sunlight. Occasionally the white flag at the upper battery stirred, giving signals, and Foote ordered the gunners to concentrate on it.[10]   But only an annoying silence came from the Confederates.

The 17th was a big day. Soon after sunrise the flagship *Benton* was lashed between the steamers *Cincinnati* and *St. Louis* and, with the other ironclad steamers in the flotilla, drifted down to make an attack on the Rebel batteries. Within two thousand yards of No. 1 they stopped, fearing the rapid current would carry them under the enemy's guns. At noon the firing reached maximum pace—one gun a minute from the Federals—and continued through the afternoon. This time the Confederates replied. The last shot was touched off from Battery No. 1 by Captain Rucker at 7:00 P.M.[11]

As the hours passed, Foote's respect for his enemy increased. With his glasses he examined the layout of fortifications, each commanding the one next above it on the river. Forty-nine guns he counted, and he concluded Island No. 10 was better adapted for defense than Columbus. His flagship bore evidence of the strength involved. Four shots had struck it, one of them bouncing along the upper deck, striking the lower deck, breaking several beams en route, and finally winding up in a drawer of the flag officer's desk, "depositing itself in the drawer as quietly as possible." [12] The *Cincinnati's* engines were so damaged she would have to return to Cairo for repairs. And on board the *St. Louis* a rifled gun had burst, killing and wounding fifteen officers and men.

Other worries for Foote were created during the day by John Pope. He had taken New Madrid, but by this time he realized he could not reach Island No. 10 without moving his troops across the river. This would call for transports, tugboats, and possibly gunboats. He sent off a message to the Chief of Staff: "If Commodore Foote can run past the batteries of Island No. 10 with two or three gunboats and reach here, I can cross my whole force and capture every man of the enemy at Island No. 10 and on the mainland." [13] The same proposal was made by letter to Foote, but got an immediate turndown on the grounds of impracticability.

Pope had been so certain that Foote would comply with his suggestion that he had sent his chief engineer, Colonel

Josiah W. Bissell, by dugout across the overflow of the river to escort the gunboats down. Bissell reached the flagship in the late afternoon to find Foote firmly opposed to the suggestion of running past the forts. Other procedures were discussed, and there was some talk of cutting a channel across the neck of the swampy peninsula formed by the bend in the river, but the idea at the time was without detail and seemed somewhat fantastic.[14] A day or so later, while standing on the levee near Island No. 8, the engineer spied an opening through the trees that activated his interest in a channel crossing.

Soon dugouts with guides were carrying Bissell along what had been an old wagon road, now several feet under water. The engineer thought only in terms of success. Before the war he had had a mixed career of banking and engineering, both successful, and he was accustomed to having things work out to his satisfaction and benefit. So it was with him in this venture. Thirty-six hours later he and his companions appeared before Pope. They had moved from Island No. 8 up bayous five miles to a locality known as "The Sag," an indentation left by an earthquake in 1811, and had passed through it several miles to Chepousa Creek, thence down that stream to emerge into the Mississippi half a mile above New Madrid.

Bissell was beaming. He told Pope the plan could not fail; he was sure the way could be opened for vessels of light draft, though possibly not gunboats. Easily convinced, Pope gave orders for him to use his entire regiment on the project and to call on other regiments for whatever else he needed in the way of manpower and material. Thousands of trees would have to be cut and dragged away from the banks in order for the vessels to pass through. To Cairo went a call for four steamers, and soon they were on their way down—the *W. B. Terry, John Trio, Gilmore,* and *Emma,* all stern-wheelers drawing only thirty to thirty-six inches of water. With them came six large coal barges. Bissell worked madly to assemble needed supplies—flatboats, saws, lines, tools, tackle, siege guns, ammunition, and two million feet of lumber.

While Bissell was getting ready, Foote continued to shell the Confederates with his mortars. He wrote his wife: "We are throwing mortar shells into the forts at night, which, showing the burning fuses, makes a beautiful sight, like a shooting star in a parabola." [15] On the 18th, the Rebel fleet bottled up at Island No. 10 tried to escape, firing for some time at Pope's batteries at New Madrid, but was driven back.

Although he continued to shell the island, Foote knew this bombardment alone would not bring victory.

This place is admirably chosen for defense by the Rebels, as its rear can only be approached in this stage of water from the river side opposite New Madrid, its being surrounded by bayous and sloughs, while its long line of six forts commanding one another from the river front renders it almost impregnable to an attacking force [he reported to Welles]. General Pope having no transports, and without our reaching him by running the blockade, is unable to cross over to the Tennessee side from New Madrid, where he now is in force, and it is impossible for him, from the inundated state of the country, to send or march his troops to this point. . . . When the object of running the blockade becomes adequate to the risk, I shall not hesitate to do it. The place may be occupied by us in a short time without an assault, as the Rebels must be cut off from their necessary supplies; still, if this does not soon take place, it may become necessary to force the blockade or adopt some other measures which have not yet suggested themselves.[16]

On the 20th, Bissell and his regiment—twelve full companies of trained workmen, mostly mechanics—disappeared up Dry Bayou. During the next fifteen days they would accomplish one of the most amazing engineering feats of the war.

On this date Foote sent off a report to Navy Secretary Welles:

Today, for the first time since I have been in command of the flotilla, I called a council of war, with the view of ascertaining the opinion of the officers with reference to sending, or attempting to send, aid requested to General Pope. The officers, with one exception, were decidedly opposed to running the blockade, believing that it would result in the almost certain destruction of the boats which should attempt to pass the six forts with fifty guns bearing upon the vessels.

I have been seriously disposed to run the blockade myself in the *Benton*, which is better protected than the other boats, although she is slow and works sluggishly, but upon reconsideration, as her loss would be so great if we failed, and my personal services here considered so important with the fleet and transports, I have for the present abandoned the idea.[17]

Foote's decision drew favorable comment from Halleck.

I am very glad [he wrote the flag officer] that you have not necessarily exposed your gunboats.[18] If they had been disabled, it would have been a most serious loss to us in the future operations of the campaign, whereas the reduction of these batteries this week or next is a matter of very little importance indeed. I think it will turn out in the end that it is much better for us that they are not reduced till we can fully cut off the retreat of their troops. . . . The reduction of these works is only a question of time and we are in no hurry on that point.

The ultimate fate of the Confederates at Island No. 10 was generally recognized. They were running short of ammunition and, isolated as they were by a combination of the enemy and the surrounding swampy country, had no prospect of getting a new supply. A resident of Memphis, in a letter to Beauregard, correctly interpreted what the Federals had in mind: "I fear from all the rumors current that they design throwing a large force on the Tennessee shore from New Madrid, landing as far above Tiptonville as they can so as to elude our gunboats, and then moving in our rear while their gunboats attack us in front. If our gunboats get out of ammunition, as they must in a few more fights or harmless bombardments, this crossing the river on rafts or launches can easily be effected, and our men and guns all lost." [19]

Foote's reluctance to run past Island No. 10 stirred the disdain of John Pope. Apparently influenced by the perennial jealousy between services, the Army leader wired Halleck: "Will take Island 10 within a week. Trust me. As Commodore Foote is unable to reduce and unwilling to run his boats past it, I would ask, as they belong to the United States, that he be directed to remove his crews from two of them and turn over the boats to me. I will bring them here. I can get along without them, but will have several days' delay." [20]

While Pope fumed, the bombardment of Island No. 10 continued. Every half hour a mortar shell was fired. Much attention was given the floating battery, for the Federal gunners had found a landmark that aided them in finding the range. Just above the point where the floating battery was anchored, a thriving peach orchard was in full bloom and appeared against the landscape a mass of color.[21] Meanwhile Mother Nature was giving aid to the Confederates. For days the Mississippi had been at flood stage, the waters rushing past bringing trees, buildings, and other debris, and at the same time submerging banks that were ordinarily dry. The *Carondelet,* tied up near the bank in support of the mortar boats, got a direct demonstration of what this soaking of dry soil meant. Within a few minutes of each other, two huge cottonwood trees, their roots loosened, fell across her deck, killing John McBride, ship's cook, and dangerously wounding Seaman Hugh Maguire. Carpenters were kept busy for more than a week making repairs.

Pope continued to needle Foote in the hope of getting him to run a gunboat past Island No. 10, telling him it would be essential to a successful crossing of troops from New Madrid. On the 28th the flag officer held another council with his officers. Henry Walke, commanding the *Carondelet,* favored making the attempt to run past Island No. 10 and volunteered to do it. Walke was nearly as old as Foote, a Mexican War veteran prominent in opposing the Southerners even before the start of hostilities. He had a rare gift, the ability to sketch a scene with pen and ink, and even in the midst of a campaign he spent some of his idle time drawing pictures, many of which would appear later in national publications.

This time, when Walke made his offer to attempt the dash down the river, Foote accepted it. Soon he was issuing written orders: "On this delicate and somewhat hazardous service I assign you. I must enjoin upon you the importance of keeping your lights secreted in the hold, or put out; keeping your officers and men from speaking at all when passing the forts above a whisper, and then only on duty; and of using every other precaution to prevent the Rebels suspecting that you are dropping below their batteries. Should you meet with disaster, you will, as a last resort, destroy the steam machinery, and, if possible to escape, set fire to your gunboat or sink her, and prevent her from falling into the hands of the Rebels." [22]

In the next few days Walke made the *Carondelet* look like a farmer's wagon prepared for market. All loose material at hand was collected and stacked on deck to deflect plunging shot. Hawsers and chain cables were strung around the pilot-house, and cordwood was stacked around the boilers. A coal barge laden with hay and coal was lashed to the port side on which there was no iron plating. Pipes directed the escape steam into the wheelhouse to avoid the puffing sound it made when blown through the smokestacks. Hose was attached to the boilers so hot water could be thrown on boarders. Pistols, cutlasses, boarding pikes, and hand grenades were placed at various points about the decks. As these preparations were made, Walke watched the weather: his orders directed him to make the dash the first foggy or rainy night.

By the 29th, the Confederates knew what Bissell's engineers were doing up Dry Bayou.[23] Here was engineering genius at its best. Over a route of twelve miles they were cutting a chan-nel fifty feet wide, half of this distance through a heavily wooded area.

First, men stood on platforms on small rafts and sawed off the trees eight feet above water. As these giants of the forest fell, a line was fastened about them and run back through a snatch block to a steam capstan on a steamboat, and thus they were hauled out of the way. Other capstans on other vessels were worked by hand. It took four sets of lines to keep pace with twelve saws. In order to cut the trees off below water, a raft was attached to the stump and saws set to work in a frame fastened by a pivot, thus enabling them to work back and forth like a clock pendulum. This was the most difficult part of the undertaking. In one short stretch seventy-five trees, not one of them less than two feet in diameter, were cut in this manner. Frequently the saw ran crooked and pinched. If it ran upward, the top was notched and the frame set farther in; if downward, powerful tackle was rigged to pull the stump over and thus ease the pinch. "When the saw runs right," wrote one of the participants, "we have cut off a stump two feet in diameter in fourteen minutes. Often it pinched and ran crooked; then a gang would be two or three hours on one of the same size. If there happened to be any brush under water it added much to the labor; it all had to be fished up and got out of the way." [24]

Because of the emergency, work was pushed in relays, from dawn to dark. Through swamps, forests, cornfields, and bayous —Wilson's, East, St. John's—the engineers labored. Occasionally there were frustrating delays. It sometimes took a crew of men an entire day to get out a tree half-sunken across a bayou, during which time the advance was at a standstill and the other workers stood by idling. But Bissell was determined, and he could see his goal.

While the men worked, they could hear the mortar boats a few miles away hammering at Island No. 10, firing their shells at regular intervals. They lay so close to the bank a derrick on shore could drop the huge balls, each twelve inches in diameter and weighing two hundred and fifteen pounds, into the mouths of the guns. Twenty-four pounds of powder went behind each charge. A newspaper reporter described the shell as being as large as a soup plate. "So your readers may imagine, when they sit down to dinner," he wrote, "the emotions they would happen to experience if they happened to see a ball of iron of those dimensions coming toward them at the rate of a thousand miles a minute. The men go ashore when the mortar is fired. A pull of the string does the work, and the whole vicinity is shaken with the concussion. The most enthusiastic person gets enough of it with two or three discharges." [25]

But one bit of excitement the engineers could not hear. On the night of March 31, five boats carrying one hundred and six men, including officers, stole toward Captain Edmund W. Rucker's Battery No. 1 on the Tennessee shore. This was a redan, the first of the earthworks along the shore to be built. But at the moment it was useless: for days floodwater from the swollen river had kept it from being manned. Keeping close under the shadow of the shore, the Federals approached with muffled oars in such silence they got within ten yards of the sentinels on duty before they were discovered. The guards shouted, fired twice, and ran. After spiking the six guns in the battery, the Federals returned to their boats and rowed away without a single injury.

On April 2, Foote wrote his wife: "The Rebels are firing briskly upon us this morning, which we are returning. I suppose they are indignant and demoralized somewhat at the spiking of their guns . . . We all feel a little more encouraged from putting to rest Fort No. 1. The men are singing psalm tunes near the cabin, but, I am sorry to say, I hear more oaths than praises among them." 26

On this same date Pope, impatient and more disgusted than ever, got off a letter to Halleck: "I have no hope of Commodore Foote. He has postponed trying to run any of his gunboats past Island No. 10 until some foggy or rainy night. The moon is beginning to make the nights light, and there is no prospect of fogs during this sort of weather. We must do without him." 27

Pope was writing without full information. Up the river near Island No. 8, Walke had the *Carondelet* ready for the run and was watching for favorable weather conditions. These came the night of the 4th. At sundown the atmosphere was hazy, and the wind gradually changed to the northwest. Toward ten o'clock the roar of an approaching thunderstorm could be heard. Soon a dark cloud spread out over the heavens, blotting out the moon, and bright flashes of lightning zigzagged across the darkened sky. Walke ordered the first master to cast off.

This officer, William R. Hoel, was on special assignment, brought on board that day from the *Cincinnati* because for twenty-one years he had seen service on the Mississippi and was, at the moment, boasting that he was on his 194th trip toward New Orleans. Going along this time were reporters from the St. Louis *Democrat* and New York *Times*. Also on hand was Company H of the 42nd Illinois, a unit of sharpshooters called into duty to repel boarders.

The *Carondelet* swung out into the channel. She ran in the dark, with lights out, but the repeated flashes of lightning bared her hulk as though it were broad daylight. These came frequently, in one of the worst cloudbursts in the area's history, a great storm of wind and rain that blew down trees, one falling in a camp and killing some of Pope's soldiers.[28]

Down past Rucker's Battery No. 1 she ran, and then a short distance farther to Battery No. 2. It was there Walke got his first serious scare. Suddenly the soot in the smokestack, now dry since removal of the steam-escape pipes, flared up into the night, vying with the storm in brightness, and the Federals knew such an abnormal torch could not escape the attention of the enemy. Crewmen frantically ran to tell the engineer to open the flue caps and, when this was done, the flames gradually subsided.

But it was not until she moved toward Battery No. 3 that the Confederates began firing at her. Gunfire opened in a roar of defiance, and shells with their fuses burning arched out into the blackness and struck the water on the far side of the *Carondelet*. She chugged on, giving no answer in return, most of her men on deck staring at the wild scene from behind bales of hay. All at once her smokestack again caught fire, and another call went to the engineer. Past Battery No. 4 she ran, and on to the point of Island No. 10, barely grazing it, with Confederate guns roaring and shells passing harmlessly overhead. A formidable object still lay ahead of her—the floating battery tied up just to the side of the island. Guns on its deck now joined in the bombardment. "No reply from the *Caron-*

delet," wrote the *Democrat's* reporter. "Slowly she steamed ahead, the sky all ablaze about her, the shore vomiting fierce flames; the thunder of the storm and the roar of the Rebel artillery commingling, as if heaven and earth had joined to crush the audacious intruder." The *Carondelet* veered toward the Missouri shore and forged on, one moment clearly in view, the next shut out by darkness. Later the men on her deck would find that two of the shots from the battery found a mark, one in the coal barge tied to the side of the steamer and one in a bale of hay.

It was midnight when Walke arrived at New Madrid. There he drew in to report to Pope and to participate in double rejoicing. Just before dark Bissell and his engineers had stormed into town, the last stretch of the canal completed.

Pope was elated, more over the canal, his report would indicate, than over the appearance of Walke. "For nineteen days," he wrote, "the work was prosecuted with untiring energy and determination, under exposures and privations very unusual even in the history of warfare. It will long remain a monument of enterprise and skill." [29]

On the night of the 6th another thunderstorm shook the area, and another vessel, this time the *Pittsburg,* one of the Union's original ironclads, well girded with hay, ran the blockade and drew alongside the *Carondelet.* During the hours of darkness four shallow-draft steamers improved Pope's hand by making their way through Bissell's canal.

Earlier this day, over on the Tennessee River at Pittsburg Landing, or Shiloh, the Navy gave the Army another demonstration of its value in combined operations. Confederate forces under General Albert Sidney Johnston began an attack at dawn on Federal troops under General U. S. Grant. Throughout the morning it raged, and in the afternoon the Southerners began driving toward the river, pushing the Federals back against the stream. But there they encountered an enemy with which they were unable to cope. Standing by at the landing were the little wooden gunboats *Lexington* and *Tyler,* both already rich in war service, and they opened with their guns and turned the tide. Reporting this engagement that went into the records as the battle of Shiloh, Grant casually mentioned that "in this repulse much is due to the presence of the gunboats." [30] It was the second time the Navy had saved him from defeat. Only five months had passed since these same two gunboats, the *Tyler* commanded by Walke, rescued his panicked troops in the hot little fight at Belmont, Missouri.[31]

The morning of the 7th was dark, and rain fell heavily. At daylight the *Carondelet* and *Pittsburg* steamed down toward Tiptonville and shelled and captured several Confederate batteries. About the same time, at New Madrid, Pope loaded his troops on transports brought through Bissell's canal and sent them across to the Tennessee side. "The passage of this wide, furious river by our large force was one of the most significant spectacles I ever witnessed," the general wrote animatedly in his report. "By twelve o'clock that night all the forces designed to cross the river were over, without delay or accident." [32]

This day saw the fall of Island No. 10. As the Federals landed, the Confederates retreated. Throughout the afternoon and on into the night the pursuit continued. Occasionally the Southerners tried to make a stand, but the effort was futile. At four o'clock in the morning, driven back into the swamps, they surrendered. Into the bag went three generals, seven colonels, seven regiments, several battalions of infantry, five companies of artillery, more than one hundred heavy siege guns, twenty-four pieces of field artillery, an immense quantity of ammunition and supplies, several thousand stand of small arms, and a large number of tents, horses, and wagons.

Back at the island the Confederate fleet bottled up by Pope waited, some at the bottom of the Mississippi. Included among the sunken vessels were the *De Soto, Yazoo,* and *Red Rover,* all side-wheelers, all first-class steamboats; the *Ohio Belle,* second-class steamboat; the saucy little *Grampus,* the *John Simonds, Admiral, Prince, Champion, Mars, Mohawk, L. B. Winchester,* and *Kanawha Valley.* The floating battery was scuttled and turned adrift, but it refused to sink and was anchored ashore by the Federals below New Madrid.

When the Federals reached the island, the precipitate flight of the Confederates was obvious. "The haste of the evacuation is plainly seen by the cooked and uncooked meals, the quantity of private baggage and other personal effects, the undamaged stores—ordnance, commissary and quartermaster's —left in the encampment for our forces to capture," reported a New York *Herald* correspondent. "The whole encampment was left as if the forces intended returning immediately in time for supper. As one deserter described it, 'they went like a flock of sheep.' The only thought they seemed to have for the future occupants of the works was to spike their guns." [33]

An officer of Foote's squadron, pushing across the island, stopped in surprise at one point along his route. In a grove on a hill, amid colorful wild flowers and all the charm of a rural retreat, stood several tents. But what caught his eye were the traces of femininity—hoop skirts and pantaloons hanging from trees, and on the inside dimity, calico, silk, and feathers. Around campfires, cooking breakfast, sat fifteen or more young women, "more or less fair to look upon." He saw stray locks of hair and here and there an unlaced bodice "granting chary glimpses of vast luxuriance of bust," a garter with drooping tendencies, and a stocking down at the heel.

"I will not say much for their fame," he wrote in shocked astonishment, "or for the good fame of the Confederate officers, whose baggage was mingled in admirable confusion with the rumpled dimity and calico, whose boots and spurs hung among the hoop skirts and unmentionables, and whose old hats ornamented the tent poles or decked the heads of the fair adventuresses. It was a new feature in war." [34]

★ *4*

New Orleans: passing the forts

MARCH-APRIL 1862

Louisiana's "Crescent City" of New Orleans, largest metropolis in the South and sixth in size in the nation, was a community born of a medley of tongues, a municipality that lay in the sun of deep Dixieland. It had in its atmosphere happiness and hospitality and the usual assortment of sins. Nature seemed to have intended it for a land of relaxed vacation and rollicking pleasure, but in '62 unrest and desperate activity, so alien to its fun-loving people, drove all thought of the usual delights from their minds. Faced with the reality that their city was the doorway to the vitals of the Confederacy and, as an important commercial center one hundred miles inland from the Gulf of Mexico, would be a prize and perhaps even a battleground, they were disturbed by tensions they had never before known. Beyond the outskirts stretched the delta of the Mississippi, described as "a long, watery arm, gauntleted in swamps and mud, spread out into a grasping hand," the thumb and fingers represented by the five passes into which the river divided.[1] Because of the swamps the natives knew that Union armies would never come marching overland, but must gain their access by vessel.

Records show that the North and South simultaneously realized the importance of the Mississippi River. The experienced, West Point-trained engineer, Pierre G. T. Beauregard, himself a Louisianian who had devoted years to laying out the river's defenses, called attention early in the struggle to the advantages this long, winding stream gave the side that controlled it; and about the same time, Abraham Lincoln's Cabinet began to discuss the best procedure for regaining mastery of it from the South. The way Federal officers looked upon a drive against New Orleans was summed up by Brigadier General J. G. Barnard: "Its failure would be a terrible blow; its success would bring us almost to the close of the war." [2]

Over the months the Union advanced its plans; the Confederacy vacillated. Because of the *Monitor* threat, the Southerners centered their attention chiefly on the defense of their capital in Virginia. In this concentration of effort history has shown they made a mistake. Better than to defend the seat of government, a movable factor, would it have been to preserve control over the Mississippi, the vital artery to the South's bread basket. [3]

By the spring of '62 the Union had organized its plans through frequent conference and deliberate foresight. What would be the best way to take New Orleans? The answer had been fairly well worked out by November of '61, the gist of it apparently coming from one of the Navy's top officers, David Dixon Porter. [4]

All the summer of '61 Porter had lain off the mouth of the Mississippi. During this period he did considerable spying, through interviews with fishermen supplying New Orleans, and even through night trips up the river—thirty-odd, he remembered—in a mail steamer. The more he learned and the more he saw, the more convinced he was New Orleans could be taken.

On November 9, he brought his ship into New York, and three days later waited by order outside the office of Secretary

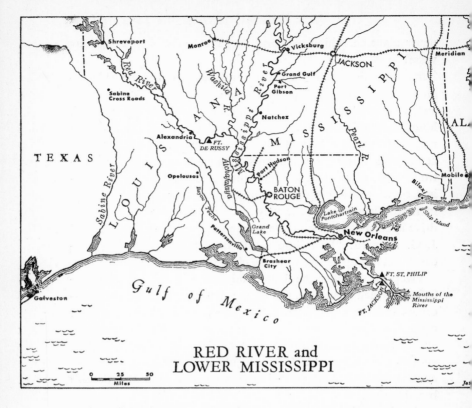

RED RIVER and
LOWER MISSISSIPPI

Welles in Washington. He had been there most of the morning when two United States Senators who recognized him, James Wilson Grimes of Iowa and John Parker Hale of New Hampshire, entered and engaged him in conversation regarding his experiences in the Gulf. While they talked, Porter mentioned his plan for the capture of New Orleans. The legislators were impressed, and in a few minutes, backed by their influence as responsible men on Capitol Hill, they put in motion the wheels of official Washington. Conferences with Welles and Lincoln and General McClellan, the Union's new hope for military victories on land, followed in quick succession, and it was left to McClellan and Porter to work out the details.

Porter already had the problem and the solution pretty well in mind. The attack should be made by a fleet of war vessels, supported by a flotilla of mortar ships, none drawing more than eighteen feet. No fewer than two hundred and fifty heavy guns should be included, and so also should a body of troops to occupy the city when captured.

One question the Navy Department would have to answer concerned the leader who would be chosen to head this expedition. What officer in Union naval ranks could attempt such an enterprise without losing many of his men and possibly his entire fleet? This cloak of responsibility settled eventually on a Southern-born veteran then in his sixtieth year and at the moment cooling his heels behind a desk in the Navy Retirement Board offices in New York—David Glasgow Farragut.

Farragut's past record had been commendable, but not of a nature that would cause him to be remembered by future generations. For half a century—since 1810 when he became a midshipman at age nine—he had served the Navy, rising in rank to a captaincy in 1851, and there he had remained, a veteran who, from all appearances, would soon lay aside his uniform and take to the rocking chair, slippers, and clay pipe. But destiny suddenly ruled otherwise, and destiny's tap needs only a certain amount of ability, mixed with a degree of luck, to provide immortality.

The Navy Department's search for a leader of the expedition included a group, among them Farragut, singled out as officers who had the experience and capabilities needed.[5] But what features were there about this man to lend support to his selection? In fifty years of service he had been faithful to duty, but he had done nothing particularly outstanding. True he had fought in the War of 1812, while still a boy not yet in his teens, and later in the Mexican War. But his career since then had been more or less routine and never spectacular. He had shown always a stubborn, plodding efficiency, and he had performed what was required of him well, yet never were his actions such as to single him out as an especially great leader.

These things were all taken into consideration in the departmental routine of selecting a commander. On his service record Farragut stacked up over many others. But above all considerations was the important question whether this officer, born in the little Tennessee hamlet known as Campbell's Station, not far from Knoxville, could be trusted to lead a fleet against his own people. A strong affirmative came from Porter, the one individual in the service who had family ties with Farragut and knew most about him.

Farragut had the background of a patriot, the strong influence of a frontier family, Porter cited. His father was George Farragut, a Spaniard born on the Island of Minorca in the Mediterranean; his mother Elizabeth Shine of North Carolina, daughter of the good Scotch lass, Ellenor McIven. Coming to America in 1776, George had fought in the Revolution for his adopted country with honorable record, meeting among the men of the naval service one David Porter, grandfather of the man who now was recommending Farragut for one of the most responsible roles of the war.

The tie went further. Years after the Revolution, when George Farragut was living in New Orleans, he happened one day upon his old friend David Porter, stricken with yellow fever while trying to get back from a fishing trip to the home of a son of the same name with whom he was living. George had Porter taken to his own residence, and there he died. On the day of his burial, Elizabeth Shine Farragut also was buried, victim of the disease she had contracted while nursing her husband's friend.

The son with whom Porter had lived, commander of the naval station at New Orleans, was attracted to young David Farragut, an alert, spirited lad. One day while on a visit at the Farragut home, he made an offer: he, a naval officer with what promised to be a bright future, would adopt the boy and assume responsibility for his training and education. George Farragut asked for time to consider, but eventually accepted.

Thus fate prescribed a new life for David Farragut. From New Orleans he was taken to Chester, Pennsylvania, where, under the watchful eye of his foster parent, he received appointment as a midshipman and where, in 1813 when he was twelve, his foster brother was born, a third David Porter—David Dixon Porter—who through the years would become convinced that David Farragut was one of the best officers in the entire Union Navy.

As for Farragut's allegiance to the Union, ample evidence could be provided. Residents of Norfolk, Virginia, remembered well the David Farragut who used to come to the neighborhood store at night to sit among the loiterers and to argue against secession, even though it made of him an enigma. Two wives he had taken from the community, Susan Marchant first and, after her death, Virginia Loyall. But the day the state seceded he departed, with wife and son, bound for a new home on the Hudson River in New York, where he hoped to escape the people he charged with trying to break up the nation. As he left he shot a warning to his friends at the store: "Mind what I tell you: you fellows will catch the devil before you get through with this business." [6]

Farragut spoke with conviction. During the nullification troubles of 1833 he had been sent as a shipmaster to South Carolina to support the Presidential mandate that "the Union must and shall be preserved." [7]

So, largely on the strength of his foster brother's endorsement, Farragut was called into conference. To the gathering he came, bearing the air and the confidence of a man who had spent a lifetime on deck with the brine of the world's seas beating in his face. Of medium height, leather-skinned, eyes small and sparkling above a nose that curved like the beak of a hawk, he took his seat to listen. His attitude was friendly, but his demeanor solemn. And yet officers present knew he was not always like this, that at times he was an animated and interesting talker, almost boyish in his enthusiasm. They knew, too, that he had a tender heart and a fine sense of humor, that his habits were clean and his speech picturesque, and that the fire that danced in his eyes denoted a will that would not stand denial. [8] What was more, the gray of his hair was misleading. Each birthday he celebrated by turning a handspring. And frequently, in moments of relaxation, he clasped the toe of his left foot and jumped back and forth over his leg.

Farragut came away from the Navy Department conference and wrote a note, possibly intended for his wife, that was found later in his papers. Dated December 21, 1861, it ended with these sentences: "I am to have a flag in the Gulf, and the rest depends upon myself. Keep calm and silent. I shall sail in three weeks." [9]

During the next month this Tennesseean whom fate had tapped was kept busy with organization details. Working at his side was his foster brother, David Porter, given the assignment of rounding up vessels suitable for the mortar fleet— twenty of them, each mounting one heavy thirteen-inch mortar and at least two thirty-two-pounders. These two leaders were not in complete agreement. Farragut had no use for mortars, feeling that shells lobbed over onto a target in an arc were much less effective than horizontal fire. He also looked askance at ironclads, under the argument that shot passed clean through a wooden vessel and did less damage than that which penetrated a mailed ship.[10] "When a shell makes its way into one of those damn teakettles," he would say, "it can't get out again. It sputters around inside doing all kinds of mischief." [11]

Gustavus Fox was in the picture, too, handling the chore of assembling in New York the warships to be used on the expedition. One of these was the *Hartford,* on which Farragut would hoist his flag.

By January 20 everything was ready. The men-of-war— six sloops and sixteen gunboats—were standing by alongside the mortar vessels. Thousands of shells cast at Pittsburgh were stored on board. Seven hundred picked men waited to be divided into crews and assigned to the mortars.

On this day Farragut was given his orders. He was to proceed to the Gulf of Mexico and take command of the West Gulf Blockading Squadron, leaving the East Gulf Squadron to

Flag Officer W. W. McKean. There, after rounding up all available vessels, he was to push up the Mississippi, having in mind as his great object "the certain capture of the city of New Orleans." [12] If by that time Foote's flotilla, battling its way down from Cairo, had not appeared, he was to forge ahead and take the Confederate defenses in the rear.

Under this strategy two separate fleets would be pressing toward each other, their goal the complete monopoly of a river. While their purposes were identical, the vessels were not: Foote's gunboats were ironclad; those coming upstream, wooden. Farragut would have it no other way.

During the middle of February, the fleet under Farragut was brought together at Ship Island, the Gulf base the Union had established months earlier not far from the mouth of the Mississippi. Vessels on duty there were found in poor condition, due largely to "young and inexperienced engineers." But this did not dampen Farragut's spirits. He wrote Fox that he would keep all in as good condition "as my means will allow until I have made my debut." [13] Sailors serving on his ships were mostly greenhorns. Only two officers on board the *Cayuga*, for instance, had ever been to sea before. One of these, George Hamilton Perkins, just back from Africa, looked over the ninety-five neophytes serving under him and wrote home: "So my berth as first lieutenant is as onerous as honorary." [14]

Now, week after week, Farragut was busy with final plans for the dash up the Mississippi. The men watching him these days said he had a bee buzzing in his bonnet. From before dawn until well after usual bedtime he rushed about, appearing first on one vessel and then another. His principal place for filing papers was his coat pocket. Orders he wrote himself, usually on his knee braced against a ship's rail. This was Farragut: no fondness had he for written detail. The Navy Department noted he did one thing at a time, but that he did "strong and well." Secretary Welles said of him that he would "more willingly take great risks in order to obtain great results than any officer in high position in either Navy or Army and, unlike most of them, prefers that others should tell the story of his well-doing rather than relate it himself." [15]

As Farragut worked, he also earned the respect of observers around him. The New York *Herald* correspondent described him in a dispatch: "He is a man of the age, and one, though being honored by years, who is in appearance a young man— a man destined to rank with the brightest of our naval officers. Not rash, but a go-ahead man, he combines valor with discretion, and will not rush into anything he cannot see his way out of. Every one respects him, and our men will fight to the death for him." [16]

But his behavior in some instances was puzzling. One day two men visited him on the deck of the *Hartford*. They found him dressed in a common flannel sack coat, white pants with tight legs, an old straw hat, and a pair of patent leather pumps badly run down at the heel. "He is a great talker, very opinionated, very stubborn, has no discretion or fear, nor much judgment," one of them recorded. "No military knowledge, a great contempt for all recent innovations in the shape of rams and ironclads, swears that no such damn thing which was ever made, or may hereafter be made, can stand five minutes before his ships. He despises that kind of cowardly fighting, and is full of all such trumpery as you would suppose a man to be who had been in the service fifty years. Still he is very brave, and is not contented unless getting ready for or engaged in some desperate enterprise." [17]

Soon after reaching Ship Island, Farragut startled Fox by sending a request to Washington for vessels of not more than five-foot draft that would carry two or three twenty-pounder rifles. The Assistant Secretary hurried off a message to David Porter: "This is not the time for such requests. . . . If he does the work laid out for him there will be no use for these frail boats. . . . I trust we have made no mistake in our man but his despatches are very discouraging. It is not too late to rectify our mistake." Porter himself was puzzled at first, and then eventually came an explanation that put things in order again: Farragut wanted the boats of light draft to combat blockade runners, not to further the expedition.[18]

The flag officer found the runners a new and strange problem. "I am told," he reported to Welles, "that they come out through little places that would not be supposed anything larger than a rowboat could pass." [19] At first he was much concerned, and then, reconsidering, was not sure that too much effort should be made to eliminate this evasion of the blockade. "To stop it altogether may be impracticable," he observed. "These vessels are necessarily so small that it takes a great many of them to make one decent cargo."

In the exchange of correspondence between Washington and Ship Island, Welles assigned Farragut another responsibility. There were rumors of ironclads under construction at Mobile and New Orleans, all of which involved a disturbing threat. The Secretary said they should be captured, that the danger they represented was implied by the fact that "no unclad ship can contend, except at great odds, with even a moderately armored vessel." [20] Farragut, having no use for ironclads, replied unexcitedly that he had no definite knowledge of any that were building and that he would endeavor to deal with them to the best advantage.[21]

As Farragut worked he had time to think occasionally of himself. "I have now attained what I have been looking for all my life—a flag—and, having attained it, all that is necessary to complete the same is a victory," he wrote home to his wife. "If I die in the attempt it will only be what every officer has to expect. He who dies in doing his duty to his country, and at peace with his God, has played out the drama of life to the best advantage. The great men in our country must not only plan but execute. Success is the only thing listened to in this war, and I know that I must sink or swim by that rule." And again: "Men are not easily elated or depressed by victory, but as for being prepared for defeat I certainly am not. Any man who is prepared for defeat would be half defeated before he commenced. I hope for success; shall do all in my power to secure it, and trust to God for the rest." [22]

Farragut was well aware of his responsibility. One of his first problems concerned the matter of getting the ships over the bar at the mouth of the Mississippi. The depth there, Welles wrote him, was nineteen feet. If so, vessels like the *Mississippi* and the *Richmond* would have no trouble. But the *Colorado,* a giant that drew twenty-three feet, would have to be lightened to the maximum, and the Navy Secretary helpfully advised that every twenty-four tons of weight taken from her would raise her one inch. "The Department relies upon your skill to give direction to the powerful force placed at your disposal," he encouraged, "and upon your personal character to infuse a hearty cooperation amongst your officers, free from unworthy jealousies. If successful, you open the way to the sea for the great West, never again to be closed. The rebellion will be riven in the center, and the flag to which you have been so faithful will recover its supremacy in every state." [23]

Such a message from Washington did little to help Farragut in this hour of mounting cares. His chief worry was what lay ahead of him, and about this deserters gave a confused picture. By their accounts it sounded rather formidable, although they were able to learn that the Rebels were sending all the men they could to the armies fighting in Virginia.[24]

While his intelligence may have failed to reveal it, there actually was much less to worry about than appeared on the surface. History would show that the Confederates were relying too much on gentlemanly relations and not enough on military methods to get results. Organization was lacking, and day by day they were becoming more and more the victims of bad management. Nowhere was there unison of effort. Authority was divided between the Louisiana and the Confederate governments, as well as between the Army and Navy and the self-governing river-steamboat captains. General Mansfield Lovell, ordered down the preceding October to direct defense preparations at New Orleans, and General J. K. Duncan, directing work on the exterior lines, often were unable to agree. Moreover, there was the naval station. Captain W. C. Whittle, the commander, was never given a clear pattern of jurisdiction and virtually no authority. When urged to hurry the construction of ships, he could comply only with messenger service, for he had no power by which to force action. And funds were a constant source of worry. In February Louisiana's Governor Thomas O. Moore had wired Richmond: "The Navy Department here owes nearly a million. Its credit is stopped." [25]

One part of the picture of the situation at New Orleans, Farragut knew, must be left to conjecture. Whatever the Confederates were placing in his way, he could be confident it would have variety. Newspapers reported they were lining the river with explosives, each charge capable of blowing up the largest steamer. Just how effective these weapons would be was demonstrated by a flatboat that broke loose and was blown to smithereens. "Fire balls, chain shot and stink balls," they added, "are reported to be ready to be thrown into gunboats and mortar batteries. The composition for the stink balls is said to be made of rashed hoofs, asafoetida, tar, brimstone, pot grease and turpentine, with the tincture of polecat so mixed that it would suffocate the denizens of pandemonium." [26]

Farragut knew his first step in the approach upon New Orleans would be the passing of Forts Jackson and St. Philip.[27] These stood on opposite sides of the river twenty-two and a half miles above the Head of the Passes, where the river made its last great bend before reaching the Gulf. Like Drewry's Bluff on the James, they were intended as impassable barriers. In fact, the Southerners considered them so strong they thought an attack on New Orleans would never come by way of the river and, for that reason, they wasted their energy in building land defenses nearer the city.[28]

These forts could have been models. Built years earlier—Fort Jackson by the Union's engineer officer General John G. Barnard and Fort St. Philip by the Spaniards—they were designed to take a terrific pounding from any enemy that might

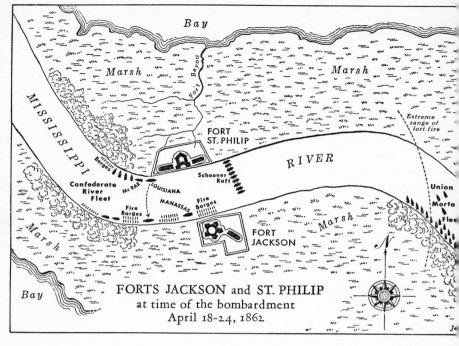

FORTS JACKSON and ST. PHILIP
at time of the bombardment
April 18-24, 1862

happen to make his way up the Mississippi. Fort Jackson, star-shaped, of stone and mortar, was armed with seventy-five guns; Fort St. Philip, considered the stronger of the two, was built of brick and stone covered with sod, and had fifty-two guns. Each was garrisoned by about seven hundred men, many of them Irish and German.

To support these formidable works, the Southerners stretched a heavy chain across the river near them, laying it in a line across the bows of six schooners. A raft of logs close to the west bank under the guns of Fort Jackson, arranged to permit passage of only one ship at a time, had been put in position the preceding fall. Although much time and effort had gone into its construction, this raft was a sort of Achilles' heel. The water beneath it was one hundred and thirty feet deep, and all efforts to anchor it to the river bottom failed. Lovell gave the reason in two sentences: "The difficulty of anchoring a heavy mass in the Mississippi arises from the fact that the bottom is a shifting

sand, and in high water the swift current soon cuts out the anchors or other obstructions placed on the bottom. In this manner
the raft began to sag by the drifting of the anchors, and the
whole weight was thrown upon the chains; and, when an immense amount of driftwood had accumulated above the raft,
these eventually parted." [29] High water several times threatened
to carry it away and, finally, in February, did.[30] A replacement
was quickly provided, but the situation remained unchanged.
As long as the Mississippi in time of flood could rise up and
spread out of its banks, nothing on its surface could be considered stationary.

While Farragut planned, factors other than high water and
the hapless raft were working in his behalf. Economic conditions in New Orleans, now a city cut off by the blockade from
its usual commerce with the outside world, were bringing hardships. There was no work except for carpenters, and the demand for them was mainly from the gunboats, which offered a
wage of four dollars per day, payable in Confederate notes,
honored only in certain stores. One tremor in the city, it was
estimated, would send the wealthy running, leaving the community a prey to vandals.

Porter's mortar fleet arrived at Ship Island March 11. The
journal of the U.S.S. *Richmond* made a dutiful record of the
occasion: "The great mortar fleet came in today. It was a beautiful sight to see so many vessels under sail. They came all together. There was a fine breeze in their favor. The bay is
crowded with the fleet, and they are all preparing for action.
The *Mississippi* is taking out coal and all unnecessary things to
lighten her." [31]

Barely had Porter's schooners dropped anchor when the
weather turned cold and rainy. But atmospheric conditions
had no effect on activities around Ship Island. Vessels came
and went in rapid succession, and in the late afternoon the mortar fleet started moving again and headed for the Mississippi.
"As far as the eye could reach out to sea we could see a line of
sails," it was recorded in the *Richmond*'s journal. Men on the

decks of these ships faced the future with confidence. "The attack will be made at once, and they say if we succeed it will end the war," wrote one of them.[32]

Four days later Farragut was able to report that the Head of the Passes was occupied in force. All of his flotilla was over the bar except the *Colorado,* and the struggle to bring her across finally was abandoned. This was after it was learned that the maximum depth they could expect at the bar was sixteen feet, requiring the removal of more than two thousand tons of weight before the ship could cross.

Attention was next centered on getting the assembled ships ready for action. Provisions were stored, and each day there was drill for the crews, including target practice. "At this time the energy and activity of the flag officer made themselves felt," John Russell Bartlett of the *Brooklyn* noted. "Farragut was about the fleet from early dawn until dark, and if any officers or men had not spontaneous enthusiasm he certainly infused it into them. I have been on the morning watch, from four to eight, when he would row alongside the ship at six o'clock, either hailing to ask how we were getting along, or, perhaps, climbing over the side to see for himself." [33]

Some days were so foggy that Farragut had difficulty making the rounds. Such weather brought a constant dripping from aloft, and the decks remained wet and slippery. On other days the weather was highly changeable, subject to the tricky squalls of spring. On March 21 the *Herald* correspondent reported: "For the last two days it has been blowing a gale of wind from the westward, with tremendous rain storms at night, accompanied with heavy thunder and very vivid lightning. The weather is so cold that peajackets are by no means uncomfortable." [34]

But even the handicap of weather did not stop the work. Each commander had the responsibility of preparing for the protection of his vessel and of the men on board. Heavy chains were swung from the sides of ships in such a manner that they provided almost a solid coat of mail to protect the engines and boilers. Hammocks, coal, bags of ashes and sand, clothesbags, and other items were stacked in position to keep shot from penetrating the boilers. Some vessels were covered with mud to make them less visible. Others whitewashed their decks, especially around the guns, to make objects more visible at night. "There is not on record such a display of ingenuity as has been evinced in this little squadron," Farragut reported to Welles.[35] Hospital space was provided in the hold. At the main hatch a cot was swung from davits so the wounded could be lowered to the forehold where the surgeon would set up his tables. Howitzers were placed in the foretop and maintop and, as a final precaution, a large kedge anchor was hung to the main brace bumpkin on each quarter, with hawser attached, to be used in case the ship had to be turned suddenly.[36]

Farragut was making the advance on New Orleans in the nick of time, for the Confederacy had converted it into a shipbuilding center. Several vessels were under construction, and two of them, planned as the most important factors in the defense of the city, were so formidable they might have overcome the entire Union squadron. These were the ironclads *Louisiana* and *Mississippi,* only days away from completion.

Having been started the preceding fall these two ships were originally scheduled to be ready February 1, but supply and labor troubles had delayed their completion.[37] The *Louisiana,* the more advanced of the two, had been hampered in the beginning by a strike of carpenters for higher wages. She was two hundred and sixty-four feet long and had a beam of sixty-four feet. Her hull was nearly submerged and was surmounted by a casemate protected by a covering of five hundred tons of railroad iron acquired from the Vicksburg and Shreveport Railroad, which in turn had bought it from the Government of Algiers. Into her had gone a million and seven hundred thousand feet of lumber, most of it procured from nearby Lake Pontchartrain and from forests along the New Orleans and Jackson Railroad.[38] Her engines were taken from the *Ingomar,* a river steamboat. Work on her was performed under contract to E. C. Murray, a practical shipbuilder who had been in the business twenty years.[39] She had a battery of sixteen guns, ranging from seven-inch rifles to nine-inch shell pieces. But there were faults in her design, and these would show up when she set forth to meet the enemy.

The C.S.S. *Mississippi* was the brain child of two Connecticut-born brothers, Nelson and Asa F. Tift, now after thirty years so much a part of the South that Asa had served as a member of his state's secession convention. Nelson had settled on a plantation in Georgia, while Asa had gone into the mercantile business in Florida. But they maintained close contact with each other and when Asa's property was seized by U.S. authorities, he fled to his brother's estate. It was there, in the quiet of rural life, that they planned the model of a ship, a ship that the Confederacy quickly adopted. The brothers were not engineers, yet they possessed ideas so novel that the harried Richmond government almost bowed at their feet. The innovations they had in mind were designed to circumvent the South's shortage of ship carpenters and joiners. They planned a vessel shaped like an ordinary house. Surfaces were flat, or in straight lines, doing away with the usual skeleton of futtocks, curved ribs, and crooked cross-knees, providing a type of construction that could easily be performed by the average house carpenter. Ends were pointed, and the sides were two feet thick and covered with three-inch iron plates. Overall, the vessel was two hundred and seventy feet long and fifty-eight feet wide, with a fifteen-foot depth of hold, making it rank in size with the U.S.S. *Colorado* and U.S.S. *Roanoke*. She had eight huge boilers and three engines, working three propellers of eleven-foot diameter, the one in the center having a shaft fifty feet long and the others, forty. Each shaft was nine inches in diameter.

The brothers, usually referred to in official records as "the Messrs. Tift," were appointed agents of the Confederacy—without compensation except for their traveling expenses—to construct the ship. So strongly was their idea endorsed that the drawings for the vessel were prepared by Lieutenant John L. Porter of the Norfolk Navy Yard, the same constructor who

had drawn plans for the alterations in the *Merrimack*. They had
to start from scratch. First a shipyard was opened on the side
of the Mississippi River immediately above the city limits of
New Orleans, next to the yard in which the *Louisiana* was being
built. Work then proceeded at record pace.[40] The Tifts operated
on a cost-plus basis and could pay what they liked for material
and labor. Some of the timber was brought from points seven
hundred miles away. The plating was procured from Atlanta.
In one hundred and ten days the woodwork was completed.
Then came delay, with the propeller shafts a major problem.
One of them, the largest, was fashioned at the Tredegar Iron
Works at Richmond from an old one out of the *Glen Cove,* and
there it lay for weeks before anyone bothered to ship it. Not
until April 9 did it reach New Orleans.[41]

Since March, Mallory had been trying frantically to get both
ironclads completed.[42] He recognized the emergency as so great
that he finally transferred Arthur Sinclair, Jr., son of an officer
in the old navy, from a special job at Norfolk to New Orleans,
instructing him to work with the Tifts and get the *Mississippi* in
the water without a moment's delay. He also wired authoriza-
tion to take the construction of the *Louisiana* out of the hands
of contractor Murray if this would speed the project.

Much misinformation regarding the Rebels' ship construction
activities at New Orleans came into the hands of the Federals.
A refugee reported in March that thirteen gunboats were under
way there, and that the *Louisiana,* armed with thirty guns, was
nearing completion.[43] General Halleck got word from a "pre-
tended" Unionist at St. Louis that the Confederates were building one or more ironclads like the *Merrimack*. He wired Secretary Stanton immediately: "This is a very serious matter, which
requires immediate attention." [44] This telegram brought together in the War Department at Washington a number of
Western boatbuilders.

March 25 a fleet of transports arrived at Ship Island. On
board were eighteen thousand troops under General Ben Butler. Farragut, after a conference with Butler, recorded: "He

does not appear to have any very difficult plan of operations, but simply to follow in my wake and hold what I can take. God grant that may be all that we attempt." [45]

Two days later, Lieutenant Colonel Edward Higgins, former lieutenant in the U. S. Navy and now commanding Forts Jackson and St. Philip, sent word to his superior at New Orleans, Brigadier General Duncan, that Union ships were crossing the bars and coming up the Mississippi in force. Duncan left for the forts immediately and, upon arrival, found them having trouble with high water. The river, swollen by spring freshets, was pouring in upon the parade ground and casemates at Jackson to a depth of from three to eighteen inches. The men's clothing and feet were constantly wet and, besides being uncomfortable, many were ill. Despite these conditions garrisons were worked by reliefs night and day. Sandbags were stacked higher at vulnerable points. Platforms were built on which to mount the twelve guns brought in after the evacuation of Pensacola and two seven-inch rifles transported from New Orleans. No sooner were the latter placed in position than, much to Duncan's disgust, one of them was ordered dismounted and sent back to the city for use on the *Louisiana*.

Floods created similar conditions elsewhere. Fearing an approach on St. Philip from the rear, General Lovell, the officer most responsible for the defenses of New Orleans, sent to that fort a company armed with shotguns, and dispatched two other companies, made up largely of sharpshooters and swamp hunters, to snipe at passing vessels from the riverbank. Night and day these men were in water nearly waist deep, so finally they were recalled. "The whole country became one vast sheet of water," Lovell reported.[46]

As the month advanced there was almost daily activity. A Rebel steamer slipped down the river and got close enough to attract fire from the Union vessels. Or Union vessels steamed up close enough to stir the two forts into action. Or a fire raft came floating down and gave the Unionists a scare until they could train water upon it and tow it ashore. Sometimes at night a bright light appeared against the clouds up the river, an ominous token of activity to the Federals. The invaders had many alarms from this source before they finally realized the light was the reflection of fires the Confederates kindled so they could see at night. The Southerners had telegraph lines all the way down to the Jump, or Wilder's Bayou, nine miles below the forts. After dark, blazing bonfires lit up strategic points, guard boats stood by on constant duty, and from dusk to dawn scouts in skiffs and pirogues threaded bayous and bays, each carrying alert Southerners assigned to watch enemy movements.

The French ship *Milan,* commanded by Captain George Charles Cloue, appeared and asked Farragut for permission to proceed up to the forts and telegraph the French consul at New Orleans. The flag officer consented, and the *Winona* was directed to escort the visitor to within two or three miles of his destination. It was emphasized that no flag of truce was to be hoisted. But the opportunity to get in a reconnaissance under the screen of diplomatic immunity provided by the neutral ship was too great to bypass and ambitious Commander John de Camp took advantage of it. No amount of remonstrance from fellow officers had any effect. He hoisted a flag and ran up toward Fort Jackson until a blank cartridge was fired at him. Then he got into his small boat and continued to advance, drawing another shot, this one live, the ball passing overhead. De Camp stopped. Soon a Rebel steamer with a flag of truce came out to him. After a conference, Confederate Lieutenant John Wilkinson, one day to set a record as a blockade runner, got into the boat with De Camp, and along with an Army officer and a civilian went on board the *Winona,* remaining there nearly an hour. The visitors were shown the battery of the vessel, and in return they reported that the South had gained a great victory at Corinth, resulting in the loss of four Union generals, thousands of men, and a number of gunboats. That was the end of the incident for the day. But next morning Cloue came storming to Farragut. The flag on the *Winona* had caused him to be imprisoned by the Confederates and to be given treatment not at all becoming to a neutral from a foreign country. A court of inquiry failed to find justification for De Camp's conduct. But Farragut, in announcing the verdict, was lenient and ordered no punishment.

Gradually the Confederate sharpshooters became so annoying to the Union ships that some of the vessels were sent up to shell the woods. This they did effectively, not only driving out the riflemen but breaking the telegraph communication below the forts. A lineman was sent to make repairs. He went, covered by Lieutenant T. J. Royster of the Twenty-second Louisiana Volunteers and fifteen men in pirogues, only to find that it was impossible to manage these awkward craft in the dense undergrowth of the swampy woods. The effort was abandoned.

On April 9 the attention of Farragut's sailors was diverted from their work by an unusual sight. The New York *Herald* reporter wrote: "A very large white eagle has been floating over our heads all day long, and its presence is hailed as a good omen. I do not know when I have seen such a sight. When first discovered he was right over our masthead, and just visible; slowly and gracefully he descended until within say eight hundred yards, when, sailing off southward for a moment, he suddenly darted upwards and towards the centre of the sun. Thus he sailed and winged until dark, when he was lost to our view." [47]

Whether as a result of this omen or not, two days later the current of the river became so swift that the moorings of the huge collection of logs were severed, and downstream the obstruction went, drawing cheers from the Federals.[48] It later lodged on shore, and David Porter himself, thrilled by the experience, superintended the placing of a fifty-pound charge of explosive that blew it to pieces.

On the 13th some of the Union vessels ran up toward the forts and let loose the first shells ever fired at Fort Jackson. While this was going on, three Coast Survey parties, the men who gave the Federal guns a chart of distances that accounted for their usually accurate fire, were escorted out to make triangulations. As the gig conveying one group neared shore, riflemen fired from the bushes, one bullet striking an oar. But the fire returned by the Federals drove the Southerners away, and three angles were taken one hundred yards from the spot where the smoke of their guns still hung above the undergrowth. Moreover, the other parties worked on undaunted, going within three miles of the forts and even observing the hoisting lines on the flagstaff at St. Philip. The mapping was completed the next day.[49] But hours later it was found that much of their effort was wasted. Rebels hidden in the bushes moved their markers, most of which had been posted in overhanging branches, and some of the work had to be repeated. In the end a thorough job was done, and Porter was given a map showing exact positions at which to place his mortar boats.

By the 15th, Farragut, moving ships up at a speed no greater than four knots, had the entire fleet assembled in the stretch of over twenty miles between the woods below the forts and the Head of the Passes—forty-six sail, carrying two hundred and eighty-six guns, plus twenty-one mortars. His big screw sloops were the *Hartford, Pensacola, Richmond,* and *Brooklyn.* Also there were the side-wheeler *Mississippi* and the screw corvettes *Oneida, Varuna,* and *Iroquois,* nine screw gunboats of five hundred tons each, the mortar flotilla, and numerous ferryboats and other craft. There they waited, the mightiest assemblage of vessels the nation had ever gotten together.[50] Each large ship was trimmed by the head, so that if she grounded it would be forward. In the swift current of the river, if one grounded aft, she would at once turn with her bow downstream.[51]

The fleet was anchored in no particular order along the winding course of the river, and nightly it was greeted by fire rafts sent down from above. While they were awesome sights, foreboding nothing but evil, like the fiery fuse of a bomb, the Federals got a thrill out of seeing them. "Sometimes of a dark night, when any of these fire rafts grounded on the opposite bank of the river or drifted down," the *Brooklyn*'s commander, Tom

Craven, wrote his wife, "the overhanging trees and bushes would catch on fire, and the effect of the bright flashes of light, in detached groups for sometimes a mile down the river, was beautiful, surpassing anything I had ever before witnessed in the shape of an illumination or bonfires." [52]

But these tactics of sending down incendiaries proved abortive. Some of the flaming barges drifted against the banks directly under the forts, firing the wharves and lighting up the fortifications.

At four o'clock on the morning of the 16th, however, one of these rafts threatened to break the perfect record its predecessors had established. It drifted in among the Union vessels, causing much excitement. Guns were fired at it, and steamers scuttled about to avoid its flaming tinder. Finally it was subdued, yet not until everyone within hearing distance had been awakened.

Later in the morning, Union gunboats ran up toward the forts for observation and were driven back by gunfire. Farragut had now received a supply of coal. The Rebels looked on from pirogues in the bushes, noting that the mortar fleet was anchored behind a point of woods below Fort Jackson, at a location that the Confederates had negligently failed to clear of trees. It afforded a screen for the mortars, and Federals, seeking perfection, trimmed the mastheads of their schooners with tree branches, doing such a fine job that, except when the vessels moved, all the men in the forts could see was a stationary front of green.

In the late afternoon of this day, a gunboat ran up the river and fired on the fort, providing cover for two mortar boats that sallied out behind them. These latter craft opened fire and continued it at a slow pace for an hour and a half, doing so mainly to find the range. Twenty times the Rebels fired answering shots, all without effect. Maybe their aim was a reflection of the consternation reported to exist so generally in the fort that night. This was caused by the threat to the magazine. Flames got so close that wet blankets were stacked against it to serve as a fire breaker.

The 17th was a day of organization for Farragut's squadron. It began at 4:30 A.M. with the appearance of a fire raft at a time when a fresh breeze was blowing up the river. This token from above was taken in tow and pulled ashore without damage. But other disturbances were in store that day. At 10:20 a Rebel gunboat fired at the fleet. It was followed in the early afternoon by several steamers, resulting in a brief exchange of fire, and that night another raft came down. A reporter on board the *Hartford* was thrilled by this second blazing message. After it was extinguished, an hour before midnight, he went below and wrote his newspaper:

I have just come from the deck, having witnessed one of the finest sights it has ever been my lot to see. The Rebels sent down a scow about one hundred feet long, filled with pine knots and well saturated with tar. The breeze was fresh from the southward, and it burned upwards finely, looking very much like a prairie fire. Signals were made for boats to tow the raft away from the shipping, and about forty boats were manned and sent away, each provided with grapnel and fire buckets. The picket boats *Kineo* and *Katahdin* worked around it and fired it, and then played a powerful stream of water on it. Now the boats found an opportunity, and went alongside and boarded the fire raft and commenced bailing water into it, and in twenty minutes they put the fire out. They then towed it ashore near where the one that came down in the morning was moored. While this was going on, the Rebels had small rowboats out watching the progress of their skill, and saw probably with regret their inglorious results and our high enjoyment.[53]

Between these interruptions day and night, attention was centered on details pertaining to passing the forts. Gunboats were separated into three divisions, the first to be headed by Captain Theodorus Bailey, the second by Farragut, and the third by Commander Henry Haywood Bell. The flag officer had chosen two distinguished career officers to share his responsibility. Both in their mid-fifties, they had grown up at a time when the nation was glorying in its naval victories over England. Bailey, second in command of the fleet, was the son of a United States Senator. He was a man with abundant hair and a modest handle-bar mustache that covered the corners of his mouth. A veteran of the Mexican War, he had had to transfer his flag from the *Colorado* after its unsuccessful attempt to get over the bar, and now he was on board the *Cayuga*. His acquaintances could easily enough tell when he was pleased, for on such occasions he had an invariable habit of slapping his thigh with his right hand. Bell, the fleet captain, was a North Carolinian who had become a midshipman at fifteen and had participated in much severe fighting during nearly forty years of sea duty.[54] His adherence to the Union surprised even his closest friends. He seemed to have the confidence of everyone except David Porter, who accused him of dreading responsibility, and described him as an officer with no mechanical ability and no confidence in himself.[55]

Commanders of the nine gunboats—*Sciota, Winona, Kineo, Wissahickon, Kennebec, Pinola, Itasca, Katahdin,* and *Cayuga* —this day were instructed to mark their smokestacks near the top with six-foot-high white identifying numbers. They also were ordered to patrol the river on watch for the vexatious fire rafts and to stand ready, with axes, hatchets, fire buckets, towlines and grapnels, to dispose of them, preferably by coaxing them ashore. Farragut issued a general order about them: "Fire rafts in such a current as this are easily managed if conducted with coolness and boldness." [56] Before midnight there was a chance to test this advice. Another raft, a roaring bed of flames, came floating down, but apparently there was not enough "coolness and boldness," for much difficulty was encountered in extinguishing it.

Some ships in the Union fleet spent much of the 17th coaling. At 1:00 P.M. two transports came up the river, their rails jammed with Massachusetts troops of Butler's command. Bands on board were playing "Dixie" and "The Star-Spangled Banner," and cheers in repeated volume rang across the water.[57]

The Confederates this day also were busy organizing, not without some confusion. A part of the mix-up was caused by an order from Secretary Mallory to send the *Louisiana* upriver to the aid of the squadron facing Foote. This was based on reasoning simply stated by Jefferson Davis: "The wooden vessels are below; the iron gunboats are above. The forts should destroy the former if they attempt to ascend." [58] But immediately there was protest from New Orleans against moving the ironclad. Governor Moore got off a telegram to Davis urging that she be left where she was, and adding: "Excitement among the people great on the subject." [59]

While Moore's protest was en route, the Tifts prepared to launch the unfinished *Mississippi*. Three steamboats were brought alongside and attached to her, and together they huffed and puffed until they broke their hawsers without moving her an inch. Investigation finally revealed she had been bolted to her bed "by some treacherous hand," and there was further delay before she could take to the water.[60]

At eight o'clock the morning of the 18th, Good Friday, ferryboats began towing the mortar schooners into position. Up the river they came, past the charred remains of the fire raft sent down the night before. Fifteen of the schooners were anchored along the bank next to Fort Jackson, behind the woods, and the other six on the opposite side, in plain view of the Confederates and at the extreme range of their heaviest guns. These were strange-looking craft, all bearing foliage on their upper rigging and some so daubed with mud that they were the color of the river itself. A sailor, staring up at the branches, dryly commented that they were lambs dressed for the slaughter.[61]

Some of this movement was watched from the forts, and at eight-forty the first shell was fired by the Confederates. It came from Fort Jackson, falling far short. Others followed, and a few minutes after nine o'clock the *Owasco,* lead ship on the western side, answered, firing on Jackson at a range of two thousand, eight hundred and fifty yards and on St. Philip at three thousand, six hundred—distances carefully calculated by the Coast

Survey party. In half an hour the bombardment was general, the Southerners bothered by lack of elevation and by inferior gunpowder. Even their nearest gun, a ten-inch seacoast mortar on a water battery anchored at the foot of Fort Jackson, failed to reach the target, though loaded with the heaviest charges.

The mortars on the Union vessels fired every ten minutes. On each, a man with a spyglass was stationed in the crosstrees, where he could observe the effect of the fire and tell the gunners on the deck below how to correct the elevation. Tiresome routine preceded each firing. After placing the loads, men scurried aft, running as far as possible and there standing on tiptoe, hands above heads and mouths open, to counteract the concussion.

The Confederates firing against these huge mortars worked their guns rapidly at first, and the shells they fired did damage mainly to the schooners on the eastern side of the river. Porter, noticing this, eventually ordered them across and behind the covering of trees.

The surface of the Mississippi was kept in constant turmoil by the exploding shells, and fish caught within range floated downstream, their white bellies skyward. More than fourteen hundred mortar charges were fired from the Union side, many of them wasted in the air owing to bad fuses. A thirteen-inch mortar in one of the forts was silenced by the "thirteen" jinx. On the thirteenth shot its bed broke in two, dropping the gun, where it lay for the remainder of the day.

As the bombardment continued, Lieutenant Francis A. Roe, executive officer of the U.S.S. *Pensacola,* took mental notes for his diary. "About six o'clock," he recorded, "the yards and mastheads of the ship were black with men and officers. As the fire became more and more accurate, their feelings could not be restrained, and at last they broke out in long, loud cheers, such as sailors only can give. The firing became magnificent, and presently the people from aloft shouted that Fort Jackson was on fire. A broad sheet of flame rose from the fort. As night closed in, the fire spread a broad glare all over the heavens."

This fire would destroy the citadel and all buildings connected with the fort, and it also would consume the bedding and clothing of many of the men and officers, adding further to their misery. When first seen by the Federals, there was much conjecture as to just what was burning. Some of the viewers thought a fire raft was on its way. But Porter settled the question by having himself rowed upstream in a small boat to a point at which he could satisfy his curiosity through the aid of a night glass. When he brought back the news, there was cheering from the entire squadron, and the band on the U.S.S. *Mississippi* struck up "Hail Columbia" and then "Dixie."

The signal to cease fire was given by the flagship at 6:30 P.M.[62] There would be wild estimates as to how many shells had been fired that day, and most of them would range into the thousands. "Thus ends the first day's bombardment of these grand, boasted forts!" diarist Roe chronicled as a finale.

The fire burned into the night. When the glare from the flames had abated sufficiently, Union officers stole up by small boat and examined the chain across the river.

As the day expired, there was little to cheer about on the Confederate side. Both forts were badly battered. Parapets and guns and casemates were damaged, and the men on duty were satisfied to settle down in the mud and dampness for a few hours of rest. At New Orleans there was some elation over the final launching of the ironclad *Mississippi,* but this, it later developed, would have no significance to what was going on down around the last great bend of the river where the two bastions were supposed to stop anything that came against them.

At daylight of the 19th, Fort Jackson was a sight to behold. All of the woodwork except a lone building behind the main fort had been destroyed. Walls had crumbled into a jumbled mass of earth. The parade plain, parapets, platforms, and casemates were badly damaged. Some of the men inside, poking around, found a shell buried five feet in the seven-foot wall over one of the magazines. "If that shell had exploded, your work would have ended," Ed Higgins, the commander, wrote

Porter a decade later.[63] Another had burst near the magazine door, opening the earth and burying two men under five feet of dirt. Still another had passed through into the casemate containing fixed ammunition. Five guns in the fort and two in the water battery were disabled.

Fire was resumed by the mortar fleet at 6:00 A.M. Looking on from the U.S.S. *Mississippi*'s maintop was artist William Waud of *Leslie*'s magazine. Occasionally gunboats came above the point behind which the mortars were concealed, and opened on Fort Jackson. Captain M. T. Squires, commanding at Fort St. Philip, aimed at them in the hope of drawing their fire away from Fort Jackson, and soon three of the mortars turned their guns on him.

Fort Jackson remained quiet throughout the early morning, and this was puzzling to Carpenter's Mate William M. C. Philbrick of the U.S.S. *Portsmouth*. He wrote in his journal: "Our mortars continued firing until about ten A.M., but we have called forth no response from Fort Jackson, but Fort St. Philip returns our compliments. We don't know what to think of it. We can see the Rebel flag flying, but as we hear no response from her (Jackson) we are all in hopes she is done for, as we saw the fire last night." At ten o'clock the gunboat *Iroquois* ran up within range of the forts and opened on them. Immediately from Fort Jackson came three flashes in quick succession, showing, as Philbrick put it, that "she had been playing possum."

In the midst of the excitement, a rifled cannon shot from Fort Jackson struck the mortar schooner *Maria J. Carlton,* wounding two men and leaving a large hole in her bottom. Porter, on a vessel close at hand, aided the rescue efforts. Under his direction the stricken ship was hauled onto the bank, enabling much of the stores and arms to be saved, but she soon slipped off into deep water and sank until only her upper rail was visible. Just before she slid toward the bottom, her mortar was fired at the forts for the last time.

At noon the mortar fire was kept up by divisions, two resting while a third worked. Even at this reduced pace a shell was lobbed over every minute and a half.

During the early afternoon a ten-inch columbiad shot struck the *Oneida* and bounced around, wounding nine men at one gun and nearly taking off the legs of a man at another. Shortly afterward a shot of the same size struck on the spar deck and tore up the trucks of a gun. Without further delay the vessel dropped out of range and anchored to make repairs.

Darkness failed to affect the mortar fire; it was kept up at a steady pace. Men in the crosstrees stared at the shells as they made their meteoric arcs through the night. At 11:00 P.M. a light appeared in the sky across the woods, and soon another fire raft could be seen coming down the river.

Throughout most of the night the bombardment continued. Even at an early hour it was evident the 20th was to be a different sort of day. Whipped along by a high wind, rain fell during the early morning. The Confederates, it was noticed, were firing more rapidly than usual, and they kept up the pace until 1:00 P.M., although doing little damage. This was the third day of mortar activity, and Farragut, who had no faith in such an attack, was becoming impatient. A deserter from the forts said the garrisons were still there, ready to man the guns when needed, despite the widespread destruction caused by the mortar shells.

Farragut was worried over the dwindling supply of essentials needed to carry on the campaign—shells, fuses, serge and yarn for cartridge bags, grape and canister shot, and even medical supplies. Moreover, he was assuming an I-told-you-so attitude toward the mortar bombardment, and even Porter himself was beginning to despair of success and to lose confidence in mortars.[64]

During the day Farragut gave evidence he planned to wait no longer. With his knee braced against the *Hartford*'s rail, he wrote a general order. "Conquer or be conquered," it read.[65] Then came an assignment of ships and gunboats—seventeen of them—by divisions, one of which he himself would lead.

Among other chores this day he began a report he never finished. "I expect," he wrote, "to destroy the raft and chain tonight, which duty is assigned to Commander H. H. Bell with two or three gunboats, whose masts I have taken out for the special purpose; and so soon as the weather is propitious I will attack the forts." [66]

At the same time the Southerners also were making decisions. Captain W. C. Whittle, commanding the naval station at New Orleans, ordered Commander John K. Mitchell, an officer who would see unusually active service in the Confederate Navy, to take command of the naval forces operating at the two forts. Native of North Carolina and resident of Florida, Mitchell was one of the most experienced men supporting the Confederacy. On resigning from the old navy at the start of the war, he had immediately been given responsibilities. But the assignment he now received was an impossible one and another example of the bungling both at Richmond and New Orleans. Too little time was left for preparation before Farragut would make his dash up the river.[67]

Mitchell accepted the new responsibility without complaint. But even the vessel that took him down the river was evidence he had two strikes on him at the start. It was the *Louisiana,* the ironclad that might be formidable when completed, but that now could do no more than float. As she was towed away from the wharf, fifty mechanics continued their work on board, striving desperately to get her into shape. Little about her was finished. Her propellers were not working. Iron plating had not yet been laid on her forecastle, forward hatch coamings, and upper deck. She was difficult to steer, and her rudders were powerless to control her. But ready or not, it was agreed her appearance alone would bring great encouragement to the men in the forts.

At nine o'clock that night, a dark and rainy evening with half a gale blowing downriver, Commander Bell appeared on board the *Itasca,* orders in his pocket directing him to proceed up to the chain and break it. With him he brought four kegs of powder, two lanterns, a box of matches, and some fuses. Standing by, ready to assist, was the gunboat *Pinola,* one of its passengers a man named Kroehl, widely hailed as a "petard man," or a specialist in setting off explosives.

Bell and his companions started up the river at 10:15 P.M. An hour or so later the behavior of the friends he left behind should have warned the Confederates that something out of the ordinary was taking place. The mortar fleet suddenly stepped up its bombardment, reaching a pace not even maintained during the daytime, and for what seemed an interminable period shells were rained upon the forts. Eyewitnesses counted as many as nine in the air at one time.[68] When the Southerners finally discovered what was happening, it was too late to do anything about it.

While Bell and his crew partially attained the objective, their operations that night were no model of success. To begin with, Kroehl threw a petard on one of the schooners supporting the chain, but before it could be exploded the *Pinola,* in backing off, broke the wire connected to it, and after that the expert on explosives was helpless.

The approach to the barrier had been made without mishap, the two gunboats, with their mastless low hulls, almost invisible in the night. Then, somehow or other, their presence was noticed by the Confederates. A rocket soared up from shore, and after that guns in both forts opened, sending their charges against an elusive target.

Bell worked desperately. Getting the *Itasca* alongside one of the schooners, he found the chain triced up a little above water by a short piece of cable wound around a windlass and hitched to a bitt. By using a chisel and hammer the hitch was unfastened, and the chain dropped to the bottom of the river. But suddenly the *Itsaca* drifted around and grounded hard, nearly opposite Fort Jackson. Desperately the *Pinola* tried to pull her free, and one after another three hawsers were broken in the attempt. Bell finally gave up hope and dispatched a man downstream in a small boat after a larger steamer. This effort was wasted, for soon the *Pinola* appeared again, out of the dark, this time with a heavier hawser, and the *Itasca* was pulled clear. As the gunboats steered toward the channel, they had an unexpected bit of luck. One of them, in running close by a schooner, struck a section of the chain and carried it away, opening all the passage needed to admit Farragut's ships.

It was 2:00 A.M. when the *Pinola* and *Itasca* dropped anchor near the flagship. The bombardment had returned to its pace of a shell every few minutes, but the Confederates were still disturbed. They continued to fire from the forts, and then at 3:00 A.M. they sent down the largest fire raft yet seen, a flatboat filled with pine knots. It was met by a tugboat and pushed ashore, and there it blazed until dawn.

Sometime during these hours when the river below was lighted by the burning raft, the *Louisiana,* relying heavily on towboats, floated into position below the Confederate fleet, at a point just above the water battery of Fort St. Philip, and there it was tied to the bank with her bow downstream, within effective range of what was left of the chain obstructions. Mechanics were still busy on her, frantically working around the clock. Little credit would they get in history for their efforts. But they deserved it, for they worked under the strain of knowing that at any moment war's destruction might burst in upon them.

Mitchell went at once to confer with the commander of the land forces, General Duncan, and between them passed words of friendly co-operation. Such would not be the case with all of those in command of the badly-divided Confederate defense. Standing by, armed, were the steamers *McRae* and *Jackson,* the ram *Manassas,* two launches, and the gunboats *Governor Moore* and *General Quitman,* the last two converted sea steamers owned by the State of Louisiana, all actually too slightly built for war purposes. There were also seven other steamers without guns and six steamers from what was known as the Confederacy's River Defense Fleet. These were the *Warrior, Stonewall Jackson, Resolute, Defiance, General Lovell,* and

R. J. Breckinridge, under command of Captain John A. Stevenson, commission merchant and secretary of the New Orleans Pilots' Benevolent Association, a man still burning from the wrong he thought the Confederate States Government had done him. Standing by to remind him of this alleged injustice was the ironclad *Manassas,* the old Massachusetts icebreaker *Enoch Train* that he had converted into an ironclad. Other men could testify that he had been pioneering in his effort, that he had arrived at Montgomery, Alabama, while the Confederate capital was still there and had spent days futilely trying to convince Stephen Mallory of the value of his far-sighted plan. Finally, after much buttonholing of members of the newly formed Congress, he went away disappointed but still determined. Working with desperation as his dictator, he raised enough money through private subscription to complete the conversion. But before his odd-looking "turtle-back" could take to the water an order came from Mallory directing him to turn over the vessel to the Government. He came down from her deck in tears, his dream of amassing a fortune as a privateer blasted and his allegiance to the South sorely tried.[69]

Perhaps it was the recollection of this upset in his personal affairs that led to the firm note Stevenson sent Mitchell soon after his arrival. It was in answer to an order from General Lovell directing him to place his entire command under Mitchell. "Every officer and man on the river-defense expedition," Stevenson wrote, "joined it with the condition that it was to be independent of the Navy, and that it would not be governed by the regulations of the Navy, or be commanded by naval officers. In the face of the enemy I will not say more. I will cooperate with you and do nothing without your approbation, and will endeavor to carry out your wishes to the best of my ability, but in my own way as to the details and the handling of my boats. But I expect the vessels under my charge to remain as a separate command. All orders for their movements addressed to me will be promptly executed, if practicable, and I undertake to be responsible for their efficiency when required." [70]

Mitchell immediately notified Duncan and Lovell that he would not be responsible for the vessels in the River Fleet. In a later report he would say of Stevenson: "His attitude with respect to my authority was one of absolute independence of action and command, and very embarrassing in the face of the enemy." The River Fleet captain was in no mood to co-operate. When Mitchell asked him to keep one or two gunboats on guard below the chain at night, he refused with the explanation that he did not have confidence enough in the fitness of his commanders for the service.[71]

Sight of the *Louisiana,* a giant and fierce-looking mass of iron and wood tied up to the bank, did seem to have its effect on the men in the forts the morning of the 21st. Their fire was the heaviest laid down by them so far, and it was troublesome to the Federals. In an hour and a half, one hundred and twenty-five shots fell close to the mortar fleet, cutting up rigging and masts and causing some change in positions. The crews of these vessels by this time were starved for both food and rest. Not since the 17th had they had much of either. So fatigued were officers and men that they could lie sound asleep on the deck of a schooner while only a few feet to the side a mortar was thundering away with blasts that shattered windows miles distant.

April 22 was only an hour old when the Confederates, up to their old tricks of disturbing the repose of their enemies, sent down a fire raft. The wind that had been sweeping the river for days was still blowing, and the Federals had some difficulty beaching the flaming torch.

The bombardment continued and at times grew heavy. At daylight the fire from the forts was concentrated on the point of woods behind which was anchored the mortar fleet, and some of the shells were finding their mark. One of these struck the smokestack of the unfortunate *Oneida,* passed through the deck and exploded, taking off the left arm and leg of the signal quartermaster, splintering a gun carriage, and tearing the rammer of a gun into small bits. For a time there was so much smoke the crew rushed about with fire buckets, sure the ship was aflame.

The Federals, from their direction, continued to batter Fort Jackson, although Fort St. Philip again tried to distract the fire, hoping to give the men in the other fortification time to make repairs. Seeing the effort was wasted, Duncan offered a suggestion: send the *Louisiana* below St. Philip and tie her to the bank where she could shell the mortar boats and still be under the protection of the forts. This would give the Southerners three direct cross fires upon the enemy's approach. Mitchell refused to consent, and Duncan appealed to Lovell, who in turn called upon Whittle, inducing him to wire Mitchell to "strain a point to effect this."

Under pressure from New Orleans and upon receiving a second request from Duncan, Mitchell made a reconnaissance, and then called the officers around him into conference. Present were his aide, Lieutenant George S. Shryock, Commander Charles F. McIntosh of the *Louisiana,* Lieutenant Thomas B. Huger of the *McRae,* and Lieutenant Alexander F. Warley of the *Manassas.* They agreed that Duncan's suggestion was unwise. To move the *Louisiana* below would place her under the direct fire of the entire Federal fleet, while she in turn would be unable to reach the enemy with a single shot because her ports would not allow a gun elevation of more than five degrees.

As the bombardment continued, the Confederates became more and more convinced the main attack was nearing. Duncan appealed to Mitchell in alarm. Mitchell replied that he had ordered a fire to be built on the beach below Fort St. Philip after dark and that a fire raft would be held ready at Fort Jackson to be turned adrift at the first alarm. He also said he would direct all vessels to keep a vigilant lookout.

Actually, Farragut's advance up the river might have come that night. During the afternoon all his ship commanders had been called to the flagship for a conference, and there he laid before them his plan for passing the forts. The officers were

opposed to risking the fleet until the forts had been further reduced, but Farragut explained he was facing an emergency,
that Porter was using up his ammunition, the mortar schooners
were badly shaken from the constant concussion, and the men
firing the mortars were fagged out. For these reasons, he said,
he had decided to attack at once. But the carpenters' crews of
two of the vessels were found to be at work farther down the
river, and the captains of these ships objected to moving without
them. A delay of twenty-four hours was called.

At the customary hour of one o'clock, almost on the dot, a
fire raft came floating down the morning of the 23rd, giving the
Federals another flurry of excitement and further disturbing
their rest. Until dawn it burned, and then died out in the growing
light of a day that broke warm and clear and cloudless. At an
early hour Duncan sent Lovell a telegram: "A heavy, continued bombardment has kept up all night, and is still progressing. There have been no further casualties except two men
slightly wounded. God is certainly protecting us. We are still
cheerful, and have an abiding confidence in our ultimate success. We are making repairs as best we can. Our best guns are
still in working order. Most of them have been disabled at
times. Twenty-five thousand thirteen-inch shells have been fired
by the enemy, thousands of which fell in the fort. They must
soon exhaust themselves; if not, we can stand as long as they
can." [72]

An additional force of mechanics for the *Louisiana* arrived
from New Orleans that morning. Mitchell sent them to the
assistance of the weary crew that had been working night and
day since the 20th, and his hopes immediately soared. He believed the ship could be got ready by the night of the 24th.

At noon the bombardment from the mortars slackened noticeably, and Duncan took it as an indication that the Federals
doing the firing were reaching the point of exhaustion, a development that would force the enemy to change its tactics and
to attack with broadsides from the larger vessels. He passed on
this view to Mitchell and again urged that the *Louisiana* be

placed lower down, but Mitchell, supported by the ship commanders under him, remained adamant. Not once during the day had the Southerners fired a gun.

As the afternoon advanced, excitement increased among the men on the Union ships, for word began to get around that Farragut planned to attack that night. This rumor seemed rather vague to some until 4:00 P.M. when the flagship made a signal for the fleet to form in line, the large vessels on the port side, the small ones on the starboard. This movement the Confederates inside the forts were not aware of, but shortly before sundown they got a clear indication that something was in store. Aided by heavy mortar fire, a few men in a small boat rowed up from below and planted a series of white flags on the St. Philip side, beginning at a point three hundred and fifty yards above a lone tree standing along the bank. Duncan notified Mitchell of this development, and added: "Please keep the river well lit up with fire rafts tonight, as the attack may be made at any time." [73]

Late in the afternoon, Mitchell called his ship commanders together for a consultation. It was agreed that each should act at his own discretion and make every effort to oppose the passage of the enemy. Steam was to be kept up as usual. Each river-defense gunboat would have a fire raft tied to it, ready to be towed into the river and fired. There was also talk of stringing enough of these together with chains on the morrow to extend entirely across the river.

Mitchell sent for Acting Master C. B. Fairbanks, stationed the night before with a crew of twenty men in one of the launches to keep a fire burning on the riverbank below St. Philip so the approach of the enemy fleet could be seen. When this officer appeared, he was ordered to repeat this duty and to keep up a good fire and a vigilant lookout, to give alarm by firing his howitzer and discharging rockets if he noticed any suspicious movements of the enemy, and not to leave his station before daylight.

At nine o'clock that night Lieutenant Shryock came on shore

to inform Duncan that the *Louisiana* would be ready for service the next evening. Duncan was in conference with Ed Higgins when Mitchell's aide appeared, and he commented, in answer to the announcement, that tomorrow in all probability would be too late. Higgins agreed, remarking that the major attack would come within a few hours. Shryock left with a promise that fire barges would be sent downriver every two hours.

After dark the Federals made their final reconnaissance before attack. Lieutenant Charles H. B. Caldwell of the *Itasca* was rowed in a ten-oared boat up to the chain to be sure the barrier had not been restored by the Confederates. He was pulled up to a point where he could hear the voices of men at Fort Jackson engaged in some outside work. A watch fire blazing on the Fort St. Philip side lit up part of the river, but not enough to reveal what was happening along the opposite shore. The Federals found the outside schooner riding head to the current, with a number of chains hanging from its bow. They passed, leaving her fifty yards to port, and dropped over a deep-sea lead, paying out up to twelve fathoms of line. Then they lay on their oars and drifted downstream, feeling no obstructions. Next they rowed across and tried the same thing on the outside schooner on the east bank, with identical results. Caldwell, now convinced the channel was clear and that the whole fleet could pass, whispered the order to start the return.

During the day Farragut had sent a notice to each mortar-vessel commander, cautioning him to be careful of his firing and to watch out for the movement of the fleet. Then he issued a general order: "The *Colorado*'s distinguishing signal, two perpendicular red lights, will be hoisted at the peak of this ship when I wish the fleet to get under way, and when under way to proceed up the river." [74]

Lieutenant Roe of the *Pensacola* wrote faithfully in his diary before crawling into his hammock for an hour or so of rest. His thoughts were solemn: "These may be the last lines I shall ever write. But I have an unflinching trust in God that we shall plant the Union flag upon the enemy's forts by noon tomorrow. I trust in Almighty God for the results. If I fall, I leave my darlings to the care of my country." [75]

Men on both sides were having similar reflections as the hours stretched past midnight into the first hour of April 24. It was a clear night, with a moderate breeze blowing from the south. What would happen just before dawn at this point along the river would be talked about and written about for generations. There would be fighting in the swampland off Richmond, death and daring along the mountain ridges that sheer into the South from Pennsylvania, and immortal charges up the inclines of Gettysburg. But the war of the Sixties would have only one Battle of New Orleans.

Hammocks were stored on the *Hartford* at midnight, and cooks got coffee and hardtack ready for serving at 1:00 A.M. At approximately 2:00 A.M.—the men who should have known best were never quite sure whether it was exactly that hour or five minutes before or after—two red lanterns were pulled to the peak of the flagship. Lights like these often had been seen before, flashing identification of the *Colorado* now on blockade off the mouth of the Mississippi, but never were they so startling and tragic and foreboding. This time they meant a brutal, all-out, desperate assault on the Confederates standing as the protectors of the South's largest city. Because these lights burned, men would die and men would be maimed, and others would go unscratched to carry on a war that day by day was becoming tougher and more suicidal and more ruthless. But fate stops not for reflection. Grim were the faces turned upward toward the two red beacons, rubies of destiny, twinkling high in the air on a night so dark the shores of the river eight to nine hundred yards apart were totally obscured from each other.

Among other reactions, the silent signal from the lights set in motion the gunboat *Cayuga*, but she, like the other vessels, was late getting under way. Standing on her bridge, the twinkle in his eye traitor to the grimness of his lips, was Theodorus Bailey, the thigh-slapper and Farragut's choice to lead the column of ships now heading toward New Orleans. He realized he was lucky to have a part in this great adventure, for the vessel he was originally intended to command on the dash past the forts was the *Colorado.* Just twelve days past his fifty-seventh birthday, he could look back on forty-four years of sea duty, duty filled with action and danger and suspense. Born in New York and a midshipman at thirteen, he had sailed around the world in days when such a venture was looked upon as the gravest of risks. The Mexican War had brought him distinction. And the present war had found him at Pensacola, ready to take part in the opening hostilities. Both his manner and his appearance invited confidence. He had a beer-barrel nose, a miniature walrus mustache, and hair that curled and looked always as though it needed combing. Those who knew him agreed that Bailey was all man, with a smile and sense of humor rare even among the Irish.

As the engines of his ship roared, Bailey stared ahead into the darkness. He was leading the right or Red column. Behind him—a part of his division—came the *Pensacola,* Captain Henry W. Morris; *Mississippi,* Commander Melancton Smith; *Oneida,* Commander S. P. Lee; *Varuna,* Commander C. S. Boggs; *Portsmouth,* Commander Samuel Swartout; *Katahdin,* Lieutenant Commander George H. Preble; *Kineo,* Lieutenant Commanding George M. Ransom, and *Wissahickon,* Lieutenant Commanding A. N. Smith. Advancing up the opposite side and to his rear was the Blue column, made up of the *Hartford,* Commander Richard Wainwright, with Farragut on board; *Brooklyn,* Captain Thomas T. Craven, and *Richmond,* Commander James Alden; and immediately behind it the third column, the Red and White, composed of the ships *Sciota,* Lieutenant Commanding Edward Donaldson; *Iroquois,* Commander John de Camp; *Kennebec,* Lieutenant John H. Russell; *Pinola,* Lieutenant Commanding Peirce Crosby; *Itasca,* Lieutenant Caldwell, and *Winona,* Lieutenant Ed T. Nichols.

The vessels, all without lights, moved much slower than usual in the dark. As Bailey advanced, he veered to starboard to make room for the other divisions. Off to the right the moon slowly climbed above the horizon, coming finally to hang like a giant orange ball in the sky.

Bailey was scarcely above the point where the chain had been located before he was discovered. It was 3:45 A.M. "We could bring no gun to bear, but steered directly on," he reported. "We were struck from stem to stern. At length we were close up with St. Philip, when we opened with grape and canister. Scarcely were we above the line of fire when we found ourselves attacked by the Rebel fleet of gunboats; this was hot, but more congenial work." [76] Fifteen minutes had elapsed.

Somehow men in Fort St. Phillip had sensed that the attack was about to come, and they were kept ready and standing at the guns.[77] They were there at three-thirty, looking out into the dim moonlight. "No vessels were to be seen," reported their commander, Captain Squires, "and the first notice of an enemy nearing us was the reply to the shots from Fort Jackson, and the gunners were ordered to fire by the flashes of the enemy's guns, which was done, but the fire was entirely too high and passed over them. Immediately after this a vessel came in sight, and they followed each other in rapid succession, seemingly in pairs, one of the two keeping back far enough to enable her to deliver her fire from her broadsides." [78]

Fort St. Philip gave the alarm. A rocket flared up from its ramparts into the night, silently demanding action, and a rifle shot re-echoed sharply across the water, breaking the stillness and sounding the tone for what was to come.

Before the alarm from Fort St. Philip was given, General Duncan had known of the approach of the Union fleet. So had Higgins, who had sent three verbal communications that the enemy was stirring. Both were still greatly disturbed because Mitchell had refused to move the *Louisiana*, and at three-thirty Duncan dispatched a note to him saying: "As I anticipated and informed you yesterday, the enemy are taking up their position at the present moment with their large ships on the Fort St. Philip shore, to operate against Fort Jackson. They are placing themselves boldly, with their lights at their mast-heads. You are assuming a fearful responsibility if you do not come at once to our assistance with the *Louisiana* and the fleet. I can say no more." [79]

Just before the alarm from Fort St. Philip set off the excitement, a river steamer from above drew up near the point where the *Louisiana* was moored. On board the newcomer was General Lovell, just down from New Orleans. As soon as the attack began, he started back to the city, believing it could not be held more than twenty-four hours. "I was well aware," he confessed, "that my batteries of thirty-two-pounders at the lower levees, manned by inexperienced troops, could not detain for any length of time the heavy ships of war of the enemy armed with nine- and eleven-inch guns." [80]

As the excitement spread along the river, strangely silent were Acting Master Fairbanks and his launch crew. These men failed in their duty completely. No fire burned, no howitzer was fired, and no rockets were discharged. After the action it would be learned that their movements were indeed mysterious. On discovering the Union ships in motion, they brought the launch, without so much as a shout or a pistol shot by way of warning noise, to a point on the bank near where the *Louisiana* was tied up, and from there escaped to the swamps. [81]

Captain Craven of the *Brooklyn* advanced with his eyes on the moon. "As we passed her disk," he reported, "our vessels were plainly seen by the enemy, who immediately commenced hailing shell and shot upon us in the most lively manner, and that, too, long before we were able to return the compliment, for we were steaming head on to the fort, and every shot from them was a raking one to us." [82]

A nine-inch shell fired by the *Louisiana*, just above the fort, struck on the starboard side of the *Brooklyn* a foot above the water and buried itself in her timbers. Later, when it was dug out, the men on board realized what a narrow escape they had had. But for the failure of the Confederates to remove the lead patch from its fuse, it might have blown the whole bow off the ship.[83]

But the reflection of the moon was soon nullified as the battle developed. "The fog and smoke rendered it difficult to see a ship's length ahead," wrote one historian.[84] "The enemy's fire was returned with vigor as the fleet pressed forward. The explosion of powder and shell soon became terrific, and by 4:00 A.M. the battle became an incessant and awful roar. The darkness was so dense that one boat could not see another, being guided only by the flash of each other's guns and the guns of the forts. The enemy were continually sending down fire rafts, altogether making the scene at once magnificent and terrible." Farragut, looking on, took in the scene so graphically that this was the description he subsequently put in the record: "The smoke was so dense that it was only now and then we could see anything but the flash of the cannon and the blaze of the fire rafts. The passing of Forts Jackson and St. Philip was one of the most awful sights I ever saw."

The *Hartford* fired her first broadside. A news correspondent on board ran forward to see how things were going, and the wind from a huge rifle shell knocked off his hat. "It was a time of terror," he noted for his newspaper.[85]

Craven, trailing the *Hartford* in the *Brooklyn,* lost sight of her in the smoke, but kept on in the line of what he thought to be her fire, and suddenly found his ship running directly over one of the large hulls moored in the river to support the chain barrier. The hulk was completely crushed, and then appeared another obstacle in the shape of a large raft. This the *Brooklyn* ground over, and Craven heaved a sigh of relief, thinking there was nothing ahead, when his ship suddenly stopped. Investigating, he found one of the anchors hanging at the starboard quarter had caught in the wreck of the crushed hulk and was now way out astern. The cable was quickly cut, and the vessel steamed on up the river. Again she was steered in what was thought to be the *Hartford*'s trail, only to wind up within sixty yards of Fort St. Philip. Three broadsides were fired into the fort as she veered away. Her guns were reloaded, and again they blazed in unison, sending their charges this time into the sides of the Rebel *Warrior*, floating by aflame.

Men on the *Pensacola* were directed to lie flat on the deck until their ship's guns were in range. The lieutenant who ordered this, Francis A. Roe, the faithful diarist, later would congratulate himself on the strategy, citing that he had saved many valuable lives, as well as much ammunition.[86] But not everyone escaped. Thomas Flood, a boy serving on the bridge, was swept away by a shell that took off the leg of Signal Quartermaster George Murray. Finding himself unhurt on the deck below, the boy assisted the injured man to the surgeon's table and then calmly returned to his post beside the executive officer.

Roe, by his account a man with a charmed life, found the bridge on which he was standing a special object of the Confederate gunners. "The gun's crews, right under me, were decimated," he later recorded. "The groans, shrieks, and wails of the dying and wounded were so horrible that I shudder now at the recollection of it." [87] At daylight he found the right leg of his pantaloons and drawers cut away at the knee and the skirt of his coat cut into strips, yet his body was untouched.

Back down the river around the bend made by the wooded point the mortar fleet was keeping up a terrific bombardment of Fort Jackson, firing as rapidly as at any time since it first had opened on the 18th. "Such a fire I imagine the world has rarely seen," attested Farragut. Standing ready to run up behind the advancing flotilla and to shell the forts were the *Portsmouth* and the steamers assigned to the mortars.

The *Oneida* blazed away with eleven-inch shrapnel heavy with sulphur. The Confederates, seeing the bright flames, immediately came to the conclusion the Federals were using Greek fire.

This vessel ran in under the fire from Fort St. Philip and swung over toward the Fort Jackson side. Its steersman got lost in the darkness and smoke. A flash from the guns revealed the ram *Manassas* gliding down her portside, passing too near and too swiftly for guns to be brought to bear on the ironclad. Next came a gunboat, quite near, crossing the river in the opposite direction, and the *Oneida* rammed it with full head of steam, cutting it down with a loud crash on its starboard quarter, but failing in the darkness to learn its identity. Then she chugged slowly along, firing right and left into passing vessels and, fearing they were friends, ceased fire when they made no return.

No embarrassment during the battle could have been greater than that of Farragut when he found his ship the victim of a fire raft. It was at 4:15 A.M. The man at the helm, blinded by smoke, grounded the vessel on a shoal near Fort St. Philip. In the excitement, one of the rafts was allowed to get close to the *Hartford*, and the flag officer's final cry of "Hard-a-port!" was too late. The vessel sheered, edged by the current, and her bows sank into the mud of the bank. The saucy little Rebel tugboat *Mosher,* under command of a river-boat captain named Horace Sherman, seized its chance, nosed the raft into the flag-ship's portside, and in moments her hull and rigging were in flames.

"We were so near to the shore that from the bowsprit we could reach the tops of the bushes," wrote one of her crew.[88] "On the deck of the ship it was bright as noonday, but out over the majestic river, where the smoke of many guns was intensified by that of the pine knots of the fire rafts, it was dark as the blackest midnight. For a moment it looked as though the flagship was indeed doomed. . . . The flames, like so many forked tongues of hissing serpents, were piercing the air in a frightful manner that struck terror to all hearts."

The *Brooklyn,* seeing the threat to the *Hartford,* stood by to offer help, undergoing the intense fire of Fort Jackson. It was a brave act for which she would get no credit from newspaper correspondents, even though sixteen shot tore into her sides, for her captain, Tom Craven, was old-fashioned to the degree that he would allow no reporters on board.

While the emergency was gravest, Lieutenant Albert Kautz crossed from starboard to port. In so doing he passed close to Farragut, and saw the flag officer clasp his hands high in the air and heard him exclaim, "My God, is it to end this way!"

But the *Hartford* was not to "end this way." Farragut himself was to see to that. While he stood in doubt as to the fate of the flagship, he shouted above the noise of battle: "Don't flinch from that fire, boys! There's a hotter fire for those who don't do their duty!" As if in answer, firemen pushed in with yards of hose and buckets of water, and eventually it could be seen that their efforts were checking the blaze. "I shall always be ready to bear testimony to the good conduct of Commander Wainwright and his first lieutenant, whose good organization of the fire department saved this ship," Farragut would write.[89] And he would praise in unstinted terms the ship's chief engineer, James B. Kimball. When the flag officer ordered the burning vessel "backed with all speed," it was Kimball who complied in such a manner that she slid free, at the same time throwing the raft and the *Mosher* on shore.

A New York *Herald* reporter, standing by during all this excitement on board the *Hartford,* ran below to write, whenever he could tear himself away. "It defies the powers of my brain to describe the scene at this time," he said in his report. "The river and its banks were one sheet of flame, and the messengers of death were moving with lightning swiftness in all directions. . . . Our ship had been on fire three times, and she was riddled from stem to stern. The cabin was completely gutted, the starboard steerage all torn up and the armory all knocked into 'pi.' My clothing was strewn abaft decks, and I was obliged to pick it up piece by piece. The manuscript of the bombardment came near to destruction by a rifle shell, which tore up my room and killed one man." [90]

At the first alarm the Confederate *Manassas*, a slow ship hard to handle, had moved out from the bank above Fort St. Philip and headed down the river. She had on board thirty-six officers and men, a thirty-two-pounder carronade, four double-barreled shotguns, three muskets, some pistols, twelve cane knives, and twenty charges of powder. Seeing a vessel coming up, her commander, Lieutenant Warley, gave orders to ram, and she had just straightened out ready for the attack when the C.S.S. *Resolute* ran into her. Warley backed to clear, and the vessel coming up ran by, pouring a broadside into the *Resolute*.

The *Manassas* again got started, pointing for a heavy ship standing across, but this vessel eluded the ironclad, and Warley swung about and headed for a side-wheel steamer, the *Mississippi,* striking her on the quarter. The Rebels at the same time used their carronade at short range, sending a ball through the enemy ship's cabin. The Federal steamer fired a broadside, stood free, and headed up the river.

Warley next saw a large ship, later identified as the *Pensacola,* and dashed at her. She avoided the collision and fired her stern pivot gun close on the Confederate, cutting away her flagstaff. Warley was then almost down to the chain, and both forts opened on him, the shots from Jackson striking the vessel and passing through her as though she were not ironclad. Turning back, he made out a ship-rigged vessel lying across the stream. Resin was thrown into the furnaces to put on extra steam, and the "turtle-back" went driving at her enemy with everything open. The collision came amidships with such force that everybody on the ironclad except the man at the wheel was knocked off his feet. Her carronade was jolted from its fastenings and turned over, there to remain with a charge in its breech ready to fire. Warley backed clear, not able to see in the dark that he had just rammed the *Brooklyn,* leaving a tear that extended five feet under water.

Tom Craven of the *Brooklyn* described the situation in which he found himself: "I was too near the shore to get out of her way, and could only hope to lessen the blow by giving the order to 'port the helm hard.' But she was too close, and the next moment, as she was within ten feet of us, a flash from an up-and-down pair of port shutters, the report of her gun, and then her butt in our side, jarred the *Brooklyn* fore and aft. At

first I thought, as a matter of course, that we must sink, but on
sending the carpenter down to ascertain what damage we had
sustained from the shock, he soon after returned, saying, 'All
right, sir; no harm done.' Meanwhile the black, whale-like looking beast dropped alongside and fell astern of us, and as she
was doing so the leadsman in the chains threw his lead at a
couple of persons who were standing in a scuttle just forward of
her smokestack and knocked one of them overboard." [91]

Warley's attention now was focused on a heavy gunboat, the
Iroquois, but she spied him, put on steam, and left him as if
he had been at anchor. Two other gunboats went by, firing as
they passed.

By this time dawn was beginning to creep in, and Warley
saw the *McRae,* armed with eight guns, fighting four gunboats
at short range.[92] He stood to her assistance, after hearing her
fire bell ringing as he passed. On his approach the gunboats
hurried off upriver. Warley followed until he saw two of the
heaviest in the lot heading toward him. "I was too near them
to effect a retreat," Warley later explained. "My gun was disabled; my vessel was shot through, as well in the bows as amidships. I considered that I had done all that I possibly could to
resist the enemy's passage of the forts, and that it then became
my duty to try and save the people under my command." He
ordered the delivery pipes cut, ran the vessel bows onto a steep
part of the bank, and he and the crew escaped from the bow
port into the swamp. As they fled, the Union gunboats behind
them fired grape into the bushes and continued to do so for an
hour and a half. Hours later these men would show up on
shore near Fort St. Philip and go on board the *Louisiana.*

The *McRae,* which the *Manassas* tried to help, had been
having a hard time. Before she was long away from her moorings, her engines became hot and she had to be stopped. Soon
after starting out again a shell exploded in her sail room and
set her afire, causing the fire alarm the men on the *Manassas*
had heard. After this was extinguished, she went into the battle,
and an eleven-inch shell tore through her amidships, wounding

her captain, Thomas B. Huger, and taking off part of the head
of First Class Fireman George Kendricks.[93] When Huger was
taken below, into his place stepped twenty-three-year-old Lieutenant Charles William Read of Mississippi—"Savvy" Read
he had been to his classmates at Annapolis—a brown-haired
and brown-whiskered man of narrow face and slight frame.
He had finished last in the 1860 class at the Academy, but the
Union would hear much of him before the war ended. He directed the vessel up the river to the first bend above the forts,
firing the starboard guns as rapidly as possible. When he
rounded the bend, he saw eleven enemy ships and, "not deem-
ing it prudent to engage an enemy so vastly superior," turned
back to the forts. But before he had gone far, the tiller ropes of
the *McRae* parted and she ran into the bank. Just above where
she lay Read saw the C.S.S. *Resolute*, hard ashore and flying a
white flag. He sent eleven men to haul down the flag and man
her guns as long as possible. Later in the day, after the battle
had ended, he would appear on board the U.S.S. *Mississippi*,
frantically appealing for his dying commander to be transported
to New Orleans.[94]

Over on the *Louisiana* as the battle waged, another prominent Confederate received a mortal wound. In a close exchange
with the enemy, her captain, Charles F. McIntosh, fell in a
pitiful condition, disabled in both arms and legs.

Back at the mortar fleet Porter was in the crosstrees staring
in fascination. "The sight of this night attack was awfully
grand," he wrote. "The river was lit up with rafts filled with
pine knots, and the ships seemed to be literally fighting amidst
flames and smoke." [95]

This battle would be the last for the C.S.S. *Governor Moore*.
As she rounded a point, her commander, Beverly Kennon,
spied in the growing dawn an enemy ship ahead, running rapidly upstream. He noticed that shots fired at her got none in
reply, and that attracted his attention. She was burning black
smoke and wore at her mastheads red and white lights, while
those of his squadron were blue. He saw that she was schooner-

rigged, had a white smokestack and long, white hull. His own blue light had been shot away, so he knew he could close on her without being recognized.[96] He steamed after her and when he opened fire this time, it was returned. For two miles or more they raced, firing occasionally. She was continually sheering so as to rake the Confederate with her broadside guns, but the pursuer watched her helm and, by staying in her wake, was able to prevent it.

Finally the Confederate vessel drew close, and Kennon was able to see her name, *Varuna*, spelled out in large letters on her side. Her fire of grape, shrapnel, case, and canister had been deadly on his men, especially those forward on the spar and main decks, and so many powder and shell passers had been shot down that Kennon had to aid with their duties. He got to within yards of her and found it impossible, because of the height of his vessel, to depress his bow gun enough to rake her. There was no time for delay. He himself pointed the gun and fired through the deck of the *Moore* in order to strike the enemy. A second shell was fired the same way.

"The smoke was now very thick and the ships ten feet apart," Kennon related in his report. "She raked us with her after pivot, sheered so as to give us her starboard broadside, but I was now on top of the hurricane deck and could see her mastheads above the smoke. As quick as lightning our helm was hard aport, and in the twinkling of an eye the crashing noise made by her breaking ribs told how amply we were repaid for all we had lost and suffered."

Twice the *Moore* rammed the *Varuna*. And then on the scene suddenly appeared another Rebel steamer with an iron-clad prow, the *Stonewall Jackson*, and she too rammed, doing considerable damage; then, backing off, struck again. But this time as her new antagonist swung around, the *Varuna* was able to fire five eight-inch shells into her side, driving her ashore in flames.[97] Commander Boggs of the Union vessel realized all at once that his own craft was sinking, too, and he ran into the bank, let go the anchors, and tied up to the trees.

As the *Governor Moore* turned away from the scene, Kennon noticed seven enemy vessels coming down upon him. Before he could escape, they opened fire, riddling his ship so badly that he quickly drove her ashore. Forty or fifty shot and shell, he estimated, ripped into her, tearing out her rigging and filling her sides with holes. He gave the order: "Set fire to the ship!" Hearing it and realizing it meant the end, all the crew except two, the pilot and a seaman who had been ill, grabbed life preservers and jumped overboard. Kennon ran about looking for the wounded, toting and dragging them to the gangway. Sixty-four of the ninety-three who had set out with him that morning were dead or wounded.[98] Then he got the lamps from the engine room, poured oil on the bedding, and set beds and mosquito bars on fire. Later, a prisoner on board the *Colorado* along with five of his crew, he wrote:

"The flames that lit our decks stood faithful sentinels over their halyards until they, like the ship, were entirely consumed. I burned the bodies of the slain. Our colors were shot away three times. I hoisted them myself twice; finally every stripe was taken out of the flag, leaving a small constellation of four little stars only, which showed to our enemy how bravely we had defended them. The wounds by the grape and shot were terrible, the men in all cases being horribly mangled. Many poor fellows bled to death before assistance could be rendered them; others were killed when being taken below, and in some cases the men who took them. One man, Oberhartz, lost both legs, and after this, the upper part of his breast, both arms and his head. I recognized what was left of him by his dress." [99]

The *Pinola*, a dead-eye target for the Confederates, was having a time of it. The first shot that struck her killed Thomas Kelly, captain of the forecastle. The second cut away the launch's after davit, entered the starboard quarter, cut away part of the wheel, and wounded William Ackworth, quartermaster. The third cut away the top of the steam escape pipe. The fourth clipped off the cable attached to the anchor, entered the starboard bow, passed through the yeoman's room, and lodged in the portside. The fifth struck the topgallant fore-castle and carried away part of the rail. The sixth passed through the plank-sheer abreast of the eleven-inch pivot gun. The seventh struck a barricade of hammocks on the fore hatch. The eighth cut away one of the deadeyes of the starboard forerigging. The ninth cut a bucket from the hands of Acting Master's Mate Gibbs. The tenth cut a rammer from the hands of the first loader of the pivot gun. The eleventh passed entirely through the hull, directly over the magazine. The twelfth entered the starboard and lodged in the portside of the berth deck, killing two and wounding five.

Arriving abreast of Fort Jackson, the *Itasca* was met by a hail of shot from both sides of the river. Fourteen times she was hit. A forty-two-pound ball passed through the portside coal bunker, through an iron-plate bulkhead, and wound up in the boiler, making a large hole. Steam burst forth in a dense cloud, filling the fire and engine rooms and driving everyone up from below. Charles Caldwell, the captain, directed every man to throw himself flat on the deck, ordered the steersman to put the helm hard astarboard, and waited breathlessly as the vessel floated back downstream. But not again was she struck. She drifted with the current to a point below the mortar fleet, and there she was run ashore with her deck several inches under water.

In the push up the river, the *Winona*, not far to the rear of the *Itasca* and following her red light, found herself in a mass of logs and driftwood held by the chain and moorings of the hulks, and for half an hour or so she was delayed as she fought to back clear. When she finally got free and proceeded on her way, day was breaking and the vessel was brought out in bold relief against the brightening sky. Fort Jackson fired at her, kill-ing one man and wounding another with the first shot. The third shot killed every man at her rifle gun except one. Edward Nichols, her captain, veered away, misjudging his distance, for Fort St. Philip suddenly opened on him at less than point-blank range. He sheered off and shot across the river toward Fort

Jackson and, in the smoke and confusion, found himself so close to shore that he could not turn her head upstream. Ordering his men to flatten themselves on the deck, he allowed the vessel to drift with the current. She had been hulled several times, and he noticed that her decks fore and aft were wet from the spray of falling shot.

At early dawn Bailey found himself in the clear and pushed on up the river. The *Cayuga* had been struck forty-two times. Both masts were so riddled they were useless, and the smokestack was peppered with holes. But he was still able to make progress. Presently, seeing a Rebel camp on the right bank of the river, he anchored and shouted across the water for the officer in charge to pile his arms in sight on shore and to come on board. It was the camp of Louisiana's prized Chalmette Regiment, commanded by Colonel Ignatius Szymanski. He was captured, along with his men, the regimental flag, tents, and equipage.

The firing at the forts ended at 5:30 A.M. Fourteen of the eighteen Union vessels in Farragut's fleet had succeeded in passing them.

The Confederate fleet was annihilated. Shortly after daylight Carpenter's Mate Philbrick sat on the crosstrees of the *Portsmouth* and watched an object floating downriver. Smoke was pouring from it. When it got nearer, he recognized it as the *Manassas*. "She was what we called played out," he wrote. "Just before she got to us the fire broke on board of her. It burst out through the hatchway and shot holes. Just as she got abreast of us, the only gun she had went off, caused by the heat. About one minute after, down she went to the bottom." David Porter was watching her also and described her end in one of his reports: "Like some large animal, she gave a plunge and disappeared under the water." [100]

Few vessels escaped damage. The *McRae* was badly cut up by shot and grape. The *Resolute* was run on shore and subsequently wrecked and burned. The *Warrior* was jammed against the bank and set afire. So also destroyed were the

Mosher, with her crew on board, the *Music, Belle Algerine,* and *Star.* The *Stonewall Jackson, Governor Moore,* and *General Quitman* were missing.[101]

Noticeably lacking from the Confederate standpoint throughout the battle was the light that was supposed to have come from bonfires along the banks of the river.[102] Fort St. Philip's guns had roared constantly. Seventy-five times they fired on the *Manassas* alone, mistaking it for a disabled Federal vessel, but all of these shots went astray.[103]

Five miles upstream, at the Quarantine Station, Farragut slowed up long enough to capture between three and four hundred prisoners. They surrendered, and he paroled them not to take up arms again, knowing he could not take them along with him.

"We had a rough time of it," Farragut wrote back to Porter as his ship steamed on upstream. "I intend to follow up my success and push for New Orleans and then come down and attend to the forts; so you hold them in status quo until I get back." [104] He had lost forty-four killed and one hundred and sixty wounded, compared with seventy-four killed and seventy-two wounded among the Confederates.[105]

In a few hours Porter sent back a reply: "I congratulate you on your victory. I witnessed your passage with great pleasure." To this he added a report of what the Confederates left at Forts Jackson and St. Philip were doing: "They are moving all their heavy guns upon the riverside. You will find the forts harder to take now than before, unless their ammunition gives out. I threw bombs at them all day, and tantalized them with rifle shot, but they never fired a gun. I hope you will open your way down, no matter what it costs." [106]

This had been a great day for Farragut. No other naval officer had received from Ben Butler the congratulations the general penned immediately after the battle: "A more gallant exploit it has never fallen to the lot of man to witness." [107] The victory was not yet complete, but the most dreaded barriers on the route to New Orleans had been passed.

5

New Orleans:
"through the gates of death"

MARCH-APRIL 1862

Perhaps never again would Louisiana's "Crescent City" be seen as Farragut saw it when he rounded a turn and steamed toward it the morning of April 25. Destruction was crackling in a bedlam of smoke and flame on both sides of the river. Over a wide sweep of the wharf and warehouse area and along the streets extending through the center of water commerce it raged, a general acceptance of havoc reflected by a howling mob of men, women, and children jammed into a writhing mass on the levees. Ships, cotton, coal, and other items were going up in a common blaze, the Southerners' answer to overwhelming force and their own lack of preparation. Resistance was out, as signified by another salute blazing before the custom house on Canal Street: a huge bonfire of gun carriages, caissons, and other munitions of war. New Orleans was expressing its derision and disdain of the approaching enemy.

It was noon when Farragut's fleet came to anchor before the city. As the vessels slowly drew to a stop, the people on the banks made faces, shook their fists, flourished knives and pistols, and yelled out a vile assortment of names.

Thrilling to the moment, a lad stood near the front of the crowd, panting wildly as a result of the run from the store where he worked. In later years, as a famous novelist, George W. Cable would describe the scene: "What a gathering! The riff-raff of the wharves, the town, the gutters. Such women—such wrecks of women! And all the juvenile ragtag. . . . The crowd on the levee howled and screamed with rage. The swarming decks answered never a word; but one old tar on the *Hartford*, standing with lanyard in hand beside a great pivot gun, so plain in view you could see his smile, silently patted its big black breech and blandly grinned."

As the ships dropped anchor, an accumulation of refuse, saturated with oil, alcohol, whiskey, and other flammables and set afloat, floated past them on the surface of the river. Vessels, from schooners to steamers, trailed clouds of smoke that told of the flames gutting their insides. Bales of cotton bobbed up and down on the water, looking like little boats puffing their individual way. Flatboats drifted by, stacked high with cotton from the lowlands, all roaring as the fire climbed up in a funnel of smoke that curled toward the peaceful skies. Working instruments of all sorts, especially those for use in shipyards, added to the conglomeration. Dwarfing everything, eventually appeared the house-shaped ironclad the Tifts were building to stop the very fleet now advancing to take over the city. Her insides were an inferno.

Farragut's sailors looked on with awe. Never before had they seen such vandalism and destruction, but they might have expected it from the reflection in the sky the night before. Their trip up the river from the forts was a victory parade. Waving from houses along the banks they could see white flags and now and then a tattered and torn United States flag. People were riding back and forth on horseback in great haste. Occasionally they came to huge plantations spread in beauty along the levees, and at these points Negroes left their labors and hurried to the water's edge, screaming, shouting, and jumping up and down in ecstasy. At one of the plantations, identified as "Mag-

nolia," thirty teams were plowing in the fields, but all at once
the horses were left standing in the furrow as the rush toward
the river began. From the ships the men stared toward New
Orleans, where, as they advanced, they could see the smoke
growing in density. That night at eight o'clock, when they came
to anchor eighteen miles below the city, a reddish glow, hellish
and chilling in its implication, flared out in the sky.

This glowing blaze finally rose above the trees so brightly
that another visitation from fire rafts was feared. The fear grew,
and became so overpowering that soon after midnight the ships
got under way and remained expectantly alert until dawn. Then
they struck out up the swollen stream.

Not until they reached Camp Chalmette at the English Turn
was there resistance. Approaching this spot four miles below
the city, where Andrew Jackson gained renown in an earlier
war, they were fired at by batteries on shore, and they slowed
up to let loose several broadsides. The exchange was brief, for
the Confederates were short of powder, after which, according
to Farragut, they scurried in every direction.

As the firing died out at Chalmette, the mayor of New Orleans, John T. Monroe, a self-made man, waved from the street
in front of City Hall to his private secretary, ex-news reporter
Marion A. Baker, waiting expectantly on the roof of the building. At the signal, Louisiana's state banner was raised to the
top of a flagpole. Standing by in approval were members of a
Committee of Public Safety. It had been hastily formed by the
Common Council to aid in the defense of the city. Sixty-eight
prominent citizens were included in the membership, among
them John A. Stevenson, the creator of the *Manassas*.[1]

But there were other reactions to the enemy's approach,
some centering on General Lovell. After leaving the area of
the forts at the beginning of the attack the morning before, he
had hurried back to New Orleans to get the public property in
readiness for wholesale evacuation. Here was a man of much
greater ability than his war record would reflect. Lithe, brown-
haired, forty-odd, he had an attractive figure shaped for activ-

ity. A showy horseman, visibly fond of the animal he rode, his stirrup leather was so long he seemed to be standing up in the saddle. Folks liked to watch him ride about the city, for at times he cut capers, even to guiding his mount up the gangplank onto the deck of a ship.

Lovell's helpers were largely ninety-day military volunteers called out by the Governor—three regiments and a few companies—for most of the men loitering about the city refused to work. Some were afraid of the punishment they might bring upon themselves when the Federals arrived, while others shunned the Confederate currency offered as pay. Nearly every Confederate soldier in the area had been hurried off to Virginia in March, or to help Beauregard fight at Corinth. A part of one regiment remained—the Confederate Guards, made up of men too old to go to war. Their camp was in Lafayette Square, and their tents were luxuriously furnished. Meals were supplied from the best restaurants. When called on to fight at the city's outskirts, they fought well, but the approach of the enemy and the threat of bombardment shattered their ranks.[2]

The fall of New Orleans would cause Lovell to be much maligned. "A most worthless creature was sent here by Davis to superintend the defense of the city," a woman resident wrote. "He did little or nothing, and the little he did was wrong." [3] But such evaluations were not even casually fair. Lovell, a graduate of the U.S. Military Academy and a Mexican War veteran twice wounded, was backed by experience in municipal affairs and in large-scale organizing, having served prior to the war as deputy street commissioner of New York City. He recognized the task he faced, although every move he made was one of desperation. When it was suggested that a sufficient number of bold men could board the Union vessels and carry them by assault, he fell in with the plan, but a call for one thousand brought only one hundred, so the undertaking was abandoned. Meanwhile every move was aimed at clearing the city of military items.

Lovell knew that the enemy could anchor a ship at nearby

Kenner and command the railroad toward Jackson, Mississippi, one of the points toward which he planned to evacuate, so
steamers were ordered held in readiness in Lake Pontchartrain,
just in case. But this possibility failed to develop and, under his
direction, property was hauled away by rail and water as the
Union vessels approached. The militia at his service, about
three thousand men, twelve hundred of them armed with muskets and the remainder with indifferent shotguns, were directed
to Camp Moore, seventy-eight miles distant. Out of the city went
a vast amount of public stores—light artillery, shot and shell,
clothing, shoes, blankets, medicine, commissary items, machinery, leather and harness, wagons, and many articles of camp
equipage. As later reported, nearly everything was taken away
but some heavy guns along the levees.

A short distance upriver at the shipyard where the *Mississippi* was being built, her commander, Arthur Sinclair, Jr., the
engineer sent from Virginia to speed her progress, strove frantically to save her. Taking her out of the hands of the Tifts,[4] he
rounded up gangs of nearly five hundred laborers to freight her
with machinery, tools, and the various items needed for her
completion, and then he began to look about for a way to get
her up the river. Only two steamers, the *St. Charles* and the
Peytona, could be found to tow her, and these were not brought
until eight o'clock the evening before, having been delayed by
a lack of engineers and hands. Throughout the night they tugged
unsuccessfully in an effort to buck the strong current sweeping
down in a spring freshet, but they lost ground instead of gaining.
During the early morning, Sinclair, desperate now, tied up the
vessel and hurried off to New Orleans in the *Peytona*. Behind,
with instructions to burn the ship if the Federals appeared, he
left Lieutenant James Iredell Waddell. In this young man, formerly of the U.S. Navy and destined to make a much more
prominent name in the Confederacy, he had a capable
assistant.

At the city Sinclair found available steam vessels, but they
had no crews, and he could get no one to man them. He hurried

back, but before he had covered a fourth of the distance he saw smoke rising from her and knew that Waddell had seen the enemy. In sadness he watched her burn. "She was a formidable ship, the finest of the sort I ever saw in my life," he later testified during a court of inquiry. "She would, in my opinion, not only have cleared the river of the enemy's vessels, but have raised the blockade of every port in the South." [5] The Tifts also stared sadly while she drifted away. They thought they could have finished her in two or three more weeks. Others on her disagreed, for two of her propellers were still lying on the wharf, some of the iron on her shield had not been bolted down, her rudder was not on, and her ports were not completed; July 1 would be more likely the actual completion date, they now estimated.

As the Union squadron dropped anchor abreast of the custom house, a pouring rain started. It pockmarked the surface of the river, splattered the decks of the ships, and fell in such torrents that the section of the city most distant to the wharf was blocked from view. But the crowd remained, rooted by excitement, and continued to shout and jeer. It was still there at one-thirty in the afternoon when a boat was rowed from the *Cayuga* to the foot of Laurel Street. A reporter for the New Orleans *Democrat* was on hand to describe the scene:

"Out of the boat stepped an elderly, corpulent officer with a very red face, a grave expression, and an air of command. He wore his sword, and was accompanied by a young and handsome naval officer. They asked the way to the mayor's office. . . . They were told to find their own way. . . . At last two venerable and much respected citizens—William Freret and L.E. Forstall, a member of the City Council—made their way through the crowd, which was threatening the officers with speedy destruction and, each seizing the arm of one of the officers, conducted them in safety to the mayor's office."

The red-faced officer was Theodorus Bailey, and his handsome companion was his lieutenant on the *Cayuga*, George Hamilton Perkins. History would record their mission as one of the daring acts by Americans who know not the meaning of the word fear. Farragut had chosen them to bear a message to the mayor, calling for unconditional surrender of the city, the hoisting of the U.S. flag on the custom house, post office, and mint, and the lowering of the flag the mayor's secretary had hoisted above City Hall.

"They were all shouting and hooting as we stepped on shore," Perkins remembered. "As we advanced, the mob followed us in a very excited state. They gave three cheers for Jefferson Davis and Beauregard, and three groans for Lincoln. Then they began to throw things at us, and shout, 'Hang them! Hang them!' We both thought we were in a bad fix." [6]

Young George Cable was there, in the front of the mob, yelling "Hurray for Jeff Davis!" It was an experience he never forgot. "About every third man had a weapon out," he remembered. "Two officers of the United States Navy were walking abreast, unguarded and alone, looking not to right or left, never frowning, never flinching, while the mob screamed in their ears, shook cocked pistols in their faces, cursed and crowded, and gnashed upon them. So through the gates of death those two men walked to the City Hall to demand the town's surrender. It was one of the bravest deeds I ever saw done."

Fate would never throw together a more unusual pair. Bailey was like a bulldog as he strode through the streets. Gone from his face was the exuberant good humor so characteristic; now eyes and lips were grim. Beside him, walking with quicker step and touching elbows with the older man at times, the thirty-year-old Perkins was so much his junior that they might have been father and son. Between them they had a sole thought that nerved them: they knew Farragut would bombard the city if they were harmed. And they knew the New Orleans residents were aware of this, too. But even in that there was not too much consolation. The shells that destroyed the community might destroy them at the same time.

With the crowd at their heels, they reached the City Hall, and there they were conducted into the chamber of the mayor.

This official shook hands with them, introduced them to other men seated around the room, and stood patiently listening to Bailey's message, orally delivered, from Farragut.

"I am not the military commander of the city," the mayor replied. "I have no authority to surrender it, and would not do it if I had. There is a military commander now in the city who is charged by the Confederate States with its defense. To him your command must be addressed. I will send for him if you desire." [7]

A messenger was hurried away to summon Lovell, and in half an hour the General appeared. By this time the crowd had grown larger and more boisterous, and a loud roar went up as the General climbed the stairs to the mayor's office. Inside, his manner was brusque, and his actions were such that Perkins wrote home that "he is a perfect snob." [8]

Bailey repeated Farragut's demands, adding that he was instructed by the flag officer to express his regret over the destruction of private property in the city.

Lovell spoke curtly: "In reply to his demand, say to Commodore Farragut that I decline to surrender the city, nor will I allow it to be surrendered; that, being unable to fight him on water, I have sent my troops out of the city; that there are now no armed troops in the city, nothing but women and children, and if he desires to shell them he can do so on his own responsibility." [9]

A moment later, reflecting more seriously, he added that he would retire and leave the city authorities to pursue their own course in the matter. As for himself, he said, he would go back to his army and would be glad to meet the invaders in fair and equal combat.

Bailey, ignoring the challenge, repeated Farragut's regrets over the widespread vandalism.

"It was done so by my orders, sir!" Lovell snapped.

Seeing that nothing further could be gained by the interview, Bailey asked for an escort to take Perkins and himself back to their boat. While they had been in conversation, the mob out-

side was growing louder and more unruly. Several times someone kicked the door of the mayor's chamber.

The Southerners in the room realized the emergency at hand.
The temper of the mob, judging from the noise it made, was
now uncontrollable. To allow the two officers to go back into
the throng might lead to acts for which they would all be sorry.
The situation called for strategy. It was decided two men should
lead Bailey and Perkins out of the rear of the building, while
others made an effort to distract the attention of the mob in
front. This latter responsibility fell upon Pierre Soulé, now nearing his sixty-first birthday, one of the most influential men in
New Orleans and among those gathered in the mayor's chamber
when the officers arrived. His career was one Americans ad-
mired. As a young man, he had escaped from France after
imprisonment for writing revolutionary articles and had come
to Baltimore. Later, in Kentucky, working as a gardener, he
learned English and then took up the study of law. His years
since then, both in Louisiana and elsewhere, were a story of
success. Twice he had been elected to the United States Senate,
and for two years he had served as minister to Spain. A foe of
secession, he buried his sentiments and remained faithful to
his adopted state.

One characteristic about Soulé would be of use to him as he
faced the mob: he had a hypnotic finger. James Morris Morgan,
native son, was there and joined in the cheering when the
Frenchman crossed the portico and mounted to the head of the
City Hall steps: "He raised his arm and that magic forefinger
commenced to tremble, and there was instant silence. I thought
the finger would never stop trembling, but it was evident that
as long as it did so it fascinated the attention of the crowd. I
don't remember what he said, but I do recollect that he commenced his speech with the words 'Sons of Louisiana,' when at
last he broke the silence with his wonderful and sonorous voice,
which had a strong French accent." [10] Long before he finished
talking, Bailey and Perkins had been spirited through the streets
in a closed carriage and were back in their boat at the wharf.

At six-thirty in the evening the City Council convened in emergency session. The day had been hectic. Not for a moment did the noise along the wharf, where the mob was still hurling epithets at the Federal squadron, quiet, and in the French Quarter at one period a disturbance broke out with such violence that a body of militia fired a volley into the crowd.

Most of the afternoon Mayor Monroe remained at work in his office. When the Council assembled, he was ready with a message. In clear, direct sentences he reviewed the developments of the day, and suggested simply that the city had no protection and could offer no resistance to its occupation. At the conclusion he said, "We yield to physical force alone, and we maintain our allegiance to the Government of the Confederate States." [11]

The Council, none too friendly with the mayor even in normal times, listened, but refused to take action hastily. After some deliberation, it adjourned in a hubbub, with announcement that it would reconvene at ten o'clock next morning.

At his home later in the evening the mayor took a step on his own responsibility. He instructed his secretary to go off to the *Hartford* as early as possible next morning, to inform Farragut that the Council would meet at ten, and that a written reply to his demands would be sent as soon as possible after that hour.

While New Orleans seethed in turmoil and excitement that night, with fire bells ringing continually, things were alarmingly quiet seventy-five miles downstream at the forts. Schooners were successively burned out in the river by the Confederates in order to provide illumination for them to see what their enemies were doing, but there was no gunfire.

During the day the Southerners in the two forts had taken advantage of the silence from the mortar fleet to rearrange their guns. Some of the biggest of these were placed so they could be swung about in full circle, and some of the twenty-four-pounder barbette guns at Fort Jackson were replaced by ones of heavier caliber.

Porter, an alarmist by nature, was busy getting off messages from the Head of the Passes, where he had hurriedly gone.[12] One went to Flag Officer William W. McKean, commanding at Key West. "The squadron, in the dark," it stated, "left behind them an enemy that is going to give us some trouble here, and we have not, I fear, force enough to contend with it. I mean a powerful ironclad battery of ten or sixteen guns; the enemy are working night and day to get it under way. I ask all the assistance you can give us in the shape of steamers with heavy guns and solid shot. There is no time for delay; we may otherwise meet with disaster." [13]

A similar message went to Welles: "The matter of the floating battery becomes a very serious affair, as they are hard at work at Fort Jackson mounting heavy rifled guns on it, which are of no further use to them in the fort. She mounts sixteen guns; is almost as formidable a vessel as the *Merrimack*, perfectly shot-proof, and has four powerful engines in her. I shall at all events take such steps as will prevent her from destroying anything, and we may still hold her in check with the steamers, though they are rather fragile for such a service. This is one of the ill effects of leaving an enemy in the rear." [14]

Porter's fears about the *Louisiana* might have been well founded. The Confederates actually had planned to move her into action, but unexpected interference prevented. The crew of the little steam tender, *W. Burton*, scheduled to do the towing, got so drunk the undertaking had to be postponed.

Excitement at New Orleans started early on the morning of the 26th. Well before sunrise a boatload of desperate sailors from one of the Union ships rowed ashore and planted a United States flag on the mint. There it remained while the city's populace was working up its nerve to tear it down.

At an early hour that morning, Baker, as instructed the night before by the mayor, set out for the *Hartford*, accompanied by the chief of police.[15] With a handkerchief tied to a walking stick as flag of truce, they were rowed to the flagship and there escorted to the cabin. They found Farragut seated with two of his commanders, Bailey and Bell. Farragut, recognizing the secretary as a friend he had known for years, received the visitors kindly and, when the mayor's message was delivered, answered questions about the battle at the forts. With almost boyish enthusiasm, he took the two men from the city over the ship and showed them the scars with which she had emerged. While standing at the very spot where he had stood during the passing of the forts, he described incidents of the conflict. "I seemed to be breathing flame," he said, perhaps having in mind the fire raft the little *Mosher* had pushed against the *Hartford*'s side.

It was eight o'clock that morning before Baker and the police chief returned to the mayor's office to report. While there, Pierre Soulé appeared with his son and excitedly reported that two men, traitors beyond doubt, had been seen to leave one of the ships and to land at the levee. The Frenchman's fears were quickly quieted.

At the appointed hour the City Council convened and requested a second reading of Monroe's message of the night before. After listening to it again, the body adopted a resolution approving the sentiments of the mayor and declaring that no resistance would be made.

But the mayor had another ace up his sleeve. During the night and early morning he had been at work with Durant da Ponte, editor and one of the proprietors of the New Orleans *Delta*, the newspaper with which Baker had worked as a reporter before becoming secretary to the mayor, and between them they had prepared a letter addressed to Farragut. It was read to the Council. Baker, who did the reading, was convinced it was well received and entirely satisfactory. But soon the mayor was called back. The councilmen had another letter they liked better. It had been prepared by Pierre Soulé. Monroe, desiring to placate the somewhat hostile chamber, consented to the substitution.

Before the letter could be readied for transmission to Farragut, shouts sounded out in the streets, and the uproar grew louder, a repetition of the day before. Soon two Union naval officers were escorted into the Council chamber. They were Lieutenant Albert Kautz and Midshipman John J. Read of the *Hartford*, and they had brought another message from Farragut, this one written.

Their trip through the streets had been much on the order of that of Bailey and Perkins. With a Marine guard of twenty men, they landed on the levee in front of a howling mob. Before leaving, Farragut had told them he would level the town if a shot were fired at them. Kautz drew the Marines up in line on shore and attempted to reason with the mob, but he was shouted down. At that moment a militia officer pushed through the crowd and took charge. He told Kautz to leave the Marines at the wharf and to come with him. The Union officer, retaining one man with a musket, sent the remainder back to the ship. Before starting up the street, he fastened a white handkerchief to the bayonet of the musket, and with this badge the three men moved in safety, but still with such tenseness that Kautz failed to remember the name of the militiaman who had come to his aid. As they strode along, they were cursed and jostled, but were spared actual violence.

Farragut's message was one more of reasoning than of threat. He reminded them that he, a naval officer, could not assume the duties of a military commandant. He had come, he said, "to reduce New Orleans to obedience to the laws of and to vindicate the offended majesty of the Government of the United States." Consequently, he added, he now demanded the unqualified surrender of the city. In closing he warned: "I shall speedily and severely punish any person or persons who shall commit such outrages as were witnessed yesterday—armed men firing upon helpless men, women and children for giving expression to their pleasure at witnessing the old flag." [16]

This message was read to the Council. Mayor Monroe added to the Soulé letter a single paragraph promising to prepare an answer by noon if possible. He then hurried it away in the hands of Baker. It was couched in flowery language, and it did nothing to help the situation:

> I have, in concert with the city fathers, considered the demand you made of me on yesterday of an unconditional surrender of the city . . . and it becomes my duty to transmit to you the answer which the universal sentiment of my constituency, no less than the promptings of my own heart, dictate to me on this sad and solemn occasion. . . .
>
> It would be presumptuous in me to attempt to lead an army to the field if I had one at my command, and I know still less how to surrender an undefended place, held as this is at the mercy of your gunners and mouths of your mortars.
>
> To surrender such a place were an idle and unmeaning ceremony. The city is yours by the power of brutal force and not by any choice or consent of its inhabitants. It is for you to determine what shall be the fate that awaits her.
>
> As to the hoisting of any flag than the flag of our own adoption and allegiance, let me say to you, sir, that the man lives not in our midst whose hand and heart would not be palsied at the mere thought of such an act; nor could I find in my entire constituency so wretched and desperate a renegade as would dare to profane with his hand the sacred emblem of our aspirations.
>
> Sir, you have manifested sentiments which would become one engaged in a better cause than that to which you have devoted your sword. I doubt not but that they spring from a noble though deluded nature, and I know how to appreciate the emotions which inspired them.
>
> You will have a gallant people to administer during your occupation of this city; a people sensitive of all that can in the least affect its dignity and self-respect. Pray, sir, do not allow them to be insulted by the interference of such as have rendered themselves odious and contemptible by their dastardly desertion of the mighty struggle in which we are engaged, nor of such as might remind them too painfully that they are the conquered and you the conquerors. . . .
>
> You may trust their honor, though you might not count on their submission to unmerited wrong.
>
> In conclusion, I beg you to understand that the people of New Orleans, while unable at this moment to prevent you from occupying this city, do not transfer their allegiance from the government of their choice to one which they have deliberately repudiated, and

that they yield simply that obedience which the conqueror is enabled to extort from the conquered.[17]

Farragut was again friendly to Baker. During their conversation the secretary pointed to the flag waving over the mint. The flag officer commented that it had been placed there without his knowledge, that he could not order it down, even though negotiations were still under way, because of the mood of his men. He explained that they were flushed with victory and much excited by the taunts and gibes of the crowd, and that, if the flag were hauled down, it would be impossible to keep them within bounds.

At eleven o'clock the church pennant was hoisted on every vessel in Farragut's fleet, and crews were assembled in humility and prayer "to return thanks to Almighty God for His great goodness and mercy in permitting us to pass through the events of the last two days with so little loss of life and blood." [18] While the sailors were assembled on the quarter-deck with bowed heads, a lookout in the maintop of the *Pensacola* shouted, "The flag is down, sir!"

For a few minutes religious services were interrupted, and there was great excitement on deck, but it was insignificant compared to that around the mint. There a howling mob dragged through the streets the flag taken down from the roof of the building. At City Hall the banner was torn into shreds and thrown through the window of the room in which Kautz and Read were talking with the Council members.[19]

Baker returned to find the mob in a frenzy. Its mood was so violent that the mayor had ordered the City Hall's heavy doors closed. The next worry was that of getting the officers back to their ship. This time Monroe kept the crowd occupied in front while the secretary spirited them through a rear entrance to a closed carriage waiting at Carondelet and Lafayette Streets. They were seen, and a chase developed, but they managed to escape without violence.

Seeing that the police force was inadequate, the mayor now proclaimed martial law and called to his assistance the European Brigade, made up of foreign residents who had offered their services for the thrill of it. In and out of City Hall they paraded in gorgeous uniforms, set off by much gold lace, their swords clanking on the marble floors. Night patrols were ordered, and a military court was organized. Farragut approved. He sent notice he had no disposition to interfere with this "foreign police guard." [20]

At the forts during the day matters were not completely quiet. The *McRae*, escorted by a gunboat with a white flag and loaded with wounded—exclusive of Charles F. McIntosh who refused to be moved—set out for New Orleans in an atmosphere of quiet. Because of the holes inflicted in her smokestack during the battle, she steamed poorly and had to be tied up to the bank frequently to wait until steam could accumulate.

Shortly before noon, Porter, back from the Head of the Passes, sent up Lieutenant John Guest from the mortar fleet under flag of truce to demand a surrender from the forts. Duncan received him at Fort Jackson, heard him out, and politely declined. The mortars had been quiet all morning, but now they opened in a fierce bombardment.

During Sunday the 27th, two developments took place at the forts that became a threat to the Confederates. At dawn a steamer was seen working its way up the back bays behind Fort St. Philip, and soon it was landing troops in small boats a few miles up. During the day the wives of some of the men in Fort Jackson arrived for a visit, and during the time they were there the strain of the last four days was broken.

But the 27th was largely a day of routine. At noon a boat came up under flag of truce from Porter to present another demand for surrender, and this also met with refusal. The situation in and about the forts, with the exception of the land forces accumulating behind St. Philip, looked not at all pessimistic. The men seemed in good cheer, and the work on the *Louisiana*, still in the same spot where she had remained during the battle, was so far advanced that she was expected to be given a trial next morning.

Under these circumstances the officers in Fort Jackson were caught by surprise when at midnight the garrison revolted *en masse,* seized the guard, reversed the fieldpieces commanding the gates, and commenced to spike the guns. When officers tried to interfere, they were fired at. This was a reaction that had been feared, but not necessarily expected.[21] The lull since the 24th and the fatigue duty of repairing damages to the fort amidst a rumor that New Orleans had surrendered was too much for a group made up largely of foreign enlistments who had no great interest at stake in the outcome of the campaign. Efforts to keep up their morale had failed. Couriers sent to the city for information failed to come back. As a last resort, Duncan issued on the 27th a charge, urging the men to stay at their guns and said: "You have nobly, gallantly, and heroically sustained, with courage and fortitude, the terrible ordeals of fire, water, and a hail of shot and shell, wholly unsurpassed during the present war." [22]

As the mutiny developed, a wholesale massacre of officers was threatened. Whenever they appeared, they were fired at, and the sergeants of companies, acting as emissaries, said the mutineers would hold out as long as they had food unless they were permitted to leave unmolested. The Reverend Father Nachon, moving among them, found they had been talking about revolting for two days and that signals had been exchanged with Fort St. Philip. It was their conviction that since New Orleans had fallen, the enemy was now about to attack on three sides at once and continued resistance at the forts would lead only to butchery.

So about half the garrison left with their arms. Included were men from every company except Captain Florion O. Cornay's St. Mary's Cannoneers, a band of Irishmen who drew the warmest commendation in official reports. "They are an honor to the country, and well may their friends and relations be proud of them," wrote one officer.[23]

But the fight was gone from Fort Jackson, and the officers stationed there knew it. At midnight on the 28th General Duncan sent a messenger to the *Harriet Lane* to inform Porter that he was ready to capitulate.

Next morning a small boat, overlooked by the mutineers, took the post adjutant over to Fort St. Philip and the *Louisiana* to report on developments at Fort Jackson. Captain Mitchell and Lieutenant Shryock soon appeared on shore and discussed the situation in detail, leaving with a remark that they would return to the *Louisiana* and endeavor to get her up the river for an attack on the enemy at the Quarantine Station.

Later in the morning four[24] gunboats came upriver under flag of truce and anchored, and soon a small boat was on its way ashore to convey General Duncan and Colonel Higgins to one of them, the *Harriet Lane*, for a discussion of surrender terms. Porter, meeting them at the gangway, greeted them cordially, but noted that their manner was one of victor rather than vanquished. He knew nothing about the mutiny and he was not too well posted on developments at New Orleans, so he was understandably anxious to gain control of the forts as quickly as possible.

The terms of surrender were not unconditional: Porter observed the next day that they should have been. All prisoners were to be paroled, and officers were to be permitted to keep their side arms. As the men in the assembled groups were about to sign the papers, Porter realized suddenly that the *Louisiana* and two other Confederate vessels left at the forts were not included. Duncan explained that he had no control over them, that in fact the military authorities had been set in defiance by Mitchell who commanded them. Porter waived the point, assuming they would be at his mercy after he gained possession of the forts.

Porter signed. So did Commander William B. Renshaw of the *Westfield*. Lieutenant Commanding Wainwright of the *Harriet Lane* was in the process of signing when an officer entered and informed him he was wanted on deck. He got up from the table and answered the summons immediately, returning a few minutes later with the announcement that the *Louisiana*, in flames, was drifting downriver toward the little fleet of Union ships gathered at the forts.

Before coming below, Porter had noticed the ironclad above the forts, apparently in motion, but assumed she was included under the flag of truce. He now turned on Duncan and asked if she had powder on board or if her guns were loaded. Duncan shrugged. He could not undertake to say what the Navy officers would do, he replied.

"He seemed to have a great contempt for them," Porter later reported.[25]

The mortar-fleet captain dismissed the subject with the remark, "This is sharp practice, but if you can stand the explosion when it comes, we can. We will go on and finish the capitulation." [26]

But before they turned their attention again to the papers before them, Porter told Wainwright to hail the nearest vessel and have it pass on to the others word that he did not want them to leave their anchorage. Instead, they were to veer to the end of their chains and be ready, by using steam, to sheer out of the *Louisiana*'s path if necessary when she drifted past. When that had been attended to, the pen was handed to Duncan, and next to Higgins. Both coolly signed their names as though things in the area were as peaceful as the terms agreed to in the ink they had just spread.

As they proceeded with the capitulation, the report of a cannon came to their ears. Then another, and another, and they knew the fire on board the *Louisiana* had at last reached her loaded guns. Finally a violent explosion jarred the very seats on which they sat and threw the *Harriet Lane* well to port. Porter wrote Welles about it: "Had the *Louisiana* blown up in the midst of our vessels she would have destroyed every one of them. As it was, good fortune directed her toward Fort St. Philip, when she exploded with great force, scattering fragments all over the work, killing one of their own men in the fort, and landing a large beam close to the tent of Commander McIntosh, who was lying with one arm blown off, another broken, his kneecap shot away, and a leg broken. . . . The explosion was seen and heard for many miles, and it was supposed that the forts were blown up."

When Porter and the others hurried above after the explosion, the water around them was slowly settling down, and the only traces they could see of the *Louisiana* were bits of timber and debris floating on the surface.[27]

At 3:00 P.M. of the 28th the United States flag was raised above the fortifications,[28] and an hour later the prisoners from Fort Jackson were ordered on board the gunboat *Kennebec* which started toward New Orleans. Those from Fort St. Philip would follow the next day. But the men taken after they hurried ashore from the *Louisiana* before she exploded faced months in prison. Porter sent them North along with a message to Navy Secretary Welles, informing him "of their infamous and perfidious conduct in setting fire to and blowing up the floating battery *Louisiana* and sending her adrift upon the four vessels of ours that were at anchor while they had a flag of truce flying." [29] He said: "These persons have forfeited all claim to any consideration."

Carpenter's Mate Philbrick, the diarist on board the *Portsmouth,* heard about the surrender of the forts and made an entry about them that, in view of the way in which the story of the war was told in biased favor of the Army, would appear to have been prophetic: "Came the glorious news of the surrender of both forts. Flags were displayed and we gave some rousing cheers. The forts are being occupied by Major-General Butler's troops. Sailors done *all* the work. See who gets the credit, seamen or soldiers." [30]

The Sabbath, when the revolt in the forts was developing in the minds of the mutineers, had been relatively quiet at New Orleans, but the 28th went into the records as a different day. The *McRae,* after many stops en route to wait until steam could be generated, reached the city during the morning, and the wounded on board were unloaded off Julia Street. Her captain, Lieutenant Charles William Read, agreed to depart by

10:00 A.M. next day, a promise that was destined never to be fulfilled. By nightfall she was found to be leaking, and within a matter of hours, despite all efforts at the donkey and bilge pumps, she settled to the bottom of the Mississippi.

By the morning of the 28th, Farragut was boiling. A Louisiana flag still waved from City Hall, and there was no evidence that the Southerners were not as defiant as ever. He had taken no action on the 27th, apparently in respect of the Sabbath, but he now put the decision as to his next step up to the populace. In a brief message to the mayor and City Council he expressed "deep regret" that the flag had not been hauled down, and even took credit for raising on the mint the United States flag that had been lowered by the mob and dragged through the streets. He warned that the fire of the fleet might be drawn upon the city at any moment, bringing distress to the population which he had assured he wanted to avoid. "The election is therefore with you," he concluded, "but it becomes my duty to notify you to remove the women and children from the city within forty-eight hours if I have rightly understood your determination."

Mayor Monroe transmitted the message to the Council. Along with it went further sentiment against taking down the state flag, under the reasoning that the city was no longer a military post and that Farragut would not dare shell it and bring down "the universal execration of the civilized world."

The reply sent Farragut later in the day repeated the city's attitude of defiance and was worded in part in the fluency of Pierre Soulé. It first scored Farragut for assuming the responsibility of raising the flag over the Mint, citing that such an act was a violation of the courtesies granted in a time of surrender negotiations. It then turned to the demand for the city's evacuation:

Sir, you can not but know that there is no possible exit from this city for a population which still exceeds in number one hundred and forty thousand, and you must therefore be aware of the utter inanity of such a notification. Our women and children can not escape from your shells if it be your pleasure to murder them on a question of mere etiquette; but if they could, there are but few among them who would consent to desert their families and their homes and the graves of their relations in so awful a moment. They would bravely stand the sight of your shells rolling over the bones of those who were once dear to them, and would deem that they died not ingloriously by the side of the tombs erected by their piety to the memory of departed relatives.

You are not satisfied with the peaceable possession of an undefended city, opposing no resistance to your guns, because of its bearing its doom with something of manliness and dignity; and you wish to humble and disgrace us by the performance of an act against which our nature rebels. This satisfaction you can not expect to obtain at our hands.

We will stand your bombardment, unarmed and undefended as we are. The civilized world will consign to indelible infamy the heart that will conceive the deed and the hand that will dare to consummate it.[31]

Farragut by this time had worked out a signal system for exchange of messages—a hoisted square flag with a diagonal red cross on an exchange from ship to shore, and a handkerchief held by two corners on the riverbank for the reverse—and later in the day it was needed, for other communications were directed to him, some from the foreign consuls in New Orleans. He had warned them to remove their families to a place of greater security, and they protested on the ground that this meant moving upwards of thirty thousand persons. The French steamer *Milan*'s Captain Cloue even scoffed at the forty-eight-hour ultimatum for the evacuation and demanded sixty days.

Present when the Council went into session that day was Lovell's volunteer aide-de-camp, Major Samuel L. James, a young man greatly disturbed over a growing sentiment that the general had been rather hasty in hurrying his troops away and leaving the city without protection. After listening to the councilmen he wired Lovell about it, and promptly got back a telegram of reply:

"If the people are willing to stand the result I will bring

about four thousand, five hundred men down as soon as I can give them arms and powder, and stay as long as a brick remains. It is their interest I am endeavoring to consult, not the safety of my men. I have nothing but infantry and two batteries of field artillery, which would be of no use against ships. I will come down myself if they wish it, and bring the men along as fast as ready. They are newly raised regiments, and are being now armed and equipped as you know. Can begin to bring them down tomorrow, if that is the desire of the citizens. Shall I come down myself tonight? Will do so if I can be of any assistance, and leave General Smith to complete the organization and bring down the five regiments when ready. The citizens must decide as to the consequences. I will come, if it is wished, cheerfully." [32]

James hurried to the City Council, was recognized, and read the telegram. But no one—mayor, councilmen, or Pierre Soulé —approved of Lovell's bringing troops back to the city. Instead, they thought he should return alone and see the situation for himself.

The aide-de-camp telegraphed this opinion to Lovell. Back came a brief wire: "I shall start down myself with an aide now, and am perfectly ready, if it is the desire of the city, to hold it to the end. It is for them to say, not me." [33]

Lovell arrived in the city that night and, with James and the aide he had brought with him, went to see the mayor at his home. There the general repeated his offer to bring the troops back in twenty-four hours, again explaining that he had removed them in order not to draw fire upon the residents while they were making up their minds about a surrender.

By this date the mob had worn itself out and no longer created a threat along the streets. Even the French Quarter had returned to almost normal, and the night passed without the clanging of fire bells.

On the morning of the 29th, Farragut sent Mayor Monroe his shortest message of all their exchange of communications to date. It said simply that the mayor was required as the sole representative of authority in New Orleans to haul down all ensigns and symbols of government, and added: "I am now about to raise the flag of the United States upon the customs house, and you will see that it is respected with all the civil power of the city." [34]

True to his promise, a battalion of about two hundred and fifty Marines soon was disembarked and marched to the custom house. There they occupied the building and hoisted a flag. Shortly afterward two howitzers were brought to that point and manned.

Mayor Monroe, thoroughly alarmed, sent a policeman to find Major James. When the aide-de-camp appeared at his office, the city official asked him "for God's sake" to get General Lovell out of town, explaining that if he were found in New Orleans by the Federals there might be some hangings.[35]

But all developments during the day were peaceful. General Butler arrived, and arrangements were made to bring his troops up to the city. Captain Bailey also appeared, bringing news of the surrender of the forts, as well as the men and officers captured in Fort Jackson. On shore, General Lovell waited until nightfall for a reply from either the mayor or City Council and, receiving none, set out on his return to Camp Moore.

The 30th was a day of much the same order. The paroled Confederates from Fort St. Philip arrived during the morning. Porter got off a message to Welles: "Truly the backbone of the rebellion is broken." [36] And Farragut answered Mayor Monroe's last correspondence with a note worded as though his feelings were hurt:

I informed you in my communication of 28th of April that your determination, as I understood it, was not to haul down the flag of Louisiana on the city hall, and that my officers and men were treated with insult and rudeness when they landed even with a flag of truce to communicate with authorities, etc., and if such was to be the determined course of the people, the fire of the vessels might at any moment be drawn upon the city.

This you have thought proper to construe into a determination on my part to murder your women and children, and made your letter so offensive that it will terminate our intercourse, and so soon as General Butler arrives with his forces I shall turn over the charge of the city to him and assume my naval duties.

He was preparing to leave this area where his fame had been established. Before going to bed that night he wrote a letter home:

We have destroyed, or made the enemy destroy, three of the most formidable rams in the country. Arthur Sinclair declared that the *Mississippi,* which he was to command, was far superior to the *Merrimack.* But we were too quick for them. Her machinery was not in working order, and when I sent after her they set her on fire, and she floated past us, formidable even in her expiring flames. Mitchell commanded the other as flag-officer. Poor Charlie McIntosh was her captain, and is now going on shore in a dreadful condition. It is not thought he will live, but he had a good constitution, and that will do a great deal for him. . . .

I am now going up the river to meet Foote—where, I know not— and then I shall resume my duties on the coast, keep moving, and keep up the stampede I have upon them.[37]

The windup at New Orleans came May 1. On that date Butler took formal possession of the city.[38] Into the custom house, City Hall, mint, Lafayette Square, moved Massachusetts, Wisconsin, Connecticut, and Vermont troops, and across the river at the little town of Algiers was stationed the Twenty-first Indiana.[39]

"On landing," Butler reported to Secretary of War Stanton, "we were saluted with cheers for 'Jeff. Davis' and 'Beauregard.' This has been checked, and the last man that was heard to call for cheers for the Rebel chief has been sentenced by the provost judge to three months' hard labor at Fort Jackson, which sentence is being executed. No assassinations have been made of any United States soldiers, with the exception of a soldier of the Ninth Connecticut, who had left his camp without orders in the night and was found dead the next morning in an obscure street, having probably been engaged in a drunken brawl." [40]

Men were still to die as a result of the seizure of New Orleans. There in a bed, where he had been placed after his arrival on board the *McRae,* lay the handsome widower and Charleston patriot, Thomas Bee Huger, his deceased wife a sister of Union General George G. Meade. A Baton Rouge lady got a report of his condition from a sister, newly arrived from New Orleans, and wrote: "Captain Huger is not dead! They had hopes of his life for the first time day before yesterday. Miriam saw the ball that had just been extracted. He will probably be lame for the rest of his life. It will be a glory to him. For even the Federal officers say that never did they see so gallant a little ship, or one that fought so desperately, as the *McRae.* Men and officers fought like devils." Her optimism was based on misinformation.[41] Tom Huger was dying, and would be dead by May 10, while a certain lady in the Crescent City's Jackson Square wept with her lips pressed to an engagement ring.[42]

Shortly before Union troops pushed in to take over New Orleans, three men engaged in a unique project departed. They were Captain H. L. Hunley, Captain James McClintock, and Baxter Watson. For months, as spies and others had reported in the North, they had been at work on a submarine in the city's New Basin, and the result of their labor now lay below several feet of water, scuttled in its unfinished condition to keep it away from the enemy. Rededicated and determined, they were on their way to Mobile, there to start work all over again.

News of the victory at New Orleans was en route to Washington meanwhile in an official report from Farragut to Welles. It was carried by Theodorus Bailey, so pleased he was slapping his thigh more frequently than usual. At the Union capital he would find himself in an embarrassing situation, victim of a cruel circumstance. In his account of the passing of the forts, he told that he had led the squadron, but Farragut made no mention of this in the written version. Just as the Congress was in the act of eulogizing Bailey in his presence, a note citing the discrepancy of accounts arrived from Welles, a stickler for accuracy, and the action was canceled. No amount of explaining at this time would clear the embarrassed Bailey, now more red-faced than ever. It was seven years later, in an exchange of correspondence with Farragut, before he was able to clear himself.[43]

"Unpleasantly warm"

APRIL-JUNE 1862

General David Hunter, commander of Union forces besieging Fort Pulaski off the coast of Georgia, in the Port Royal area, was a Methodist preacher's son who would never ingratiate himself with his Virginia cousins siding with the South. How they must have appreciated the classic rejoinder thrown back at him on demanding, the nights of April 10-11, 1862, surrender of Fort Pulaski to avoid "the effusion of blood which must result from the bombardment and attack now in readiness to be opened." [1] The answer came from the leader of the Confederates, Colonel Charles H. Olmstead, First Volunteer Georgia Regiment, who spiritedly replied: "Sir, I have to acknowledge receipt of your communication of this date, demanding the unconditional surrender of Fort Pulaski. In reply, I can only say that I am here to defend the fort, not to surrender it." [2] The bombardment went on for hours before the Southerners capitulated.

Despite scattered activity along the Atlantic and Gulf coasts, public attention at this period remained focused on the Mis-

sissippi River. Foote was pushing downstream to meet Farragut. The reputations of these two leaders, strangely similar
in many respects and perhaps the most determined and relentless the Southerners would meet, were rising, but that of Foote
less consistently. At least one person was dissatisfied with the
manner in which he had captured Island No. 10. Charles W.
Wills, an Illinois soldier moving with Pope's army, wrote his
sister: "It don't sound like Foote's fighting." And to this he
added: "Don't it look that, if Grant and company can whip
them out at Corinth, we'll have all the forces at Memphis and
intermediate points to put Island 10 in a bag? If they run it
will be into Arkansas, and they can take nothing with them
but what their backs will stand under. Seems to me that the
plans of the campaign are grand from the glimpses we can get
of them and have been planned by at least a Napoleon. Certain it is we are checkmating them at every point that's visible.
I firmly believe the summer will see the war ended. But it will
also see a host of us upended if we have to fight over such
ground as this. It is unpleasantly warm already in the sun." [3]

As Wills implied, the Southern climate was beginning to have
its effect on the soldiers from the North. By the time Island
No. 10 was captured, at least a third of the men in Foote's
flotilla were unfit for duty.[4]

Foote wasted no time before moving south again. On April
11, he advanced to New Madrid. His goal was Fort Pillow,
"or any place where opposition is made to our progress toward
Memphis." Pope caused him some delay, trying to get the army
in readiness to go along, but Foote finally became impatient
and proceeded without it. He knew the Rebel fleet was waiting downstream at Fort Pillow, although he did not expect it
would make a stand.

Fort Pillow, Foote's spies had told him, was a strong point
on the First Chickasaw Bluff eighty miles above Memphis.[5] It
consisted of a long line of fortifications stretching seven miles
along the bank of the river and on cliffs high enough to prevent an attack from the front. According to his information,

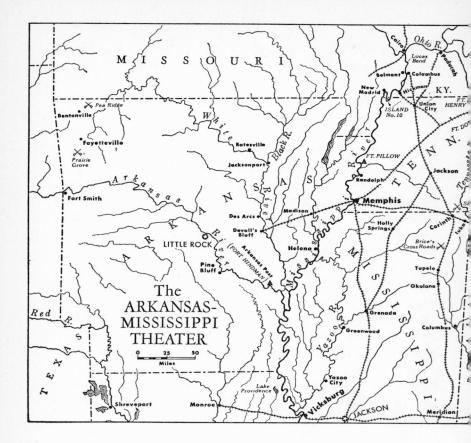

The
ARKANSAS-
MISSISSIPPI
THEATER

0   25   50
Miles

at least forty guns were in position there, and a gang of twelve hundred Negroes was engaged in strengthening the earthworks surrounding them. Later he learned that the position was commanded by Brigadier General John B. Villepique, a New Orleans Creole and West Point graduate considered second only to Beauregard as a military engineer.

The night of April 12 was soft and balmy. A light southerly wind gently caressed the watch on the decks of Foote's vessels, and the men who felt the romance of its fingers stood at their posts and looked off into the distance, seeing the stars but not thinking of stars. Through their minds passed visions of home and of other nights like this when there was someone close who might share the beauty of the starry heavens. Until dawn they could enjoy this reverie, and then confusion would take over as Pope's army of twenty thousand began to arrive in transports at a point just below the Arkansas line, fifty miles from New Madrid.

Foote waited until the last troop-bearing vessel arrived, and then ordered the entire squadron to resume its journey. A New York *Herald* reporter on the flagship described the scene as the little fleet swung out and headed downstream: "The day was clear and beautiful, and we steamed lazily along—the sluggish pace of the gunboats, behind which all other boats were compelled to remain, not admitting of much speed—winding among the bends and turns of this proverbially crooked river. The sight was one of the most beautiful imaginable. At every settlement and dwelling along the shore the people were all out to see the novel spectacle. Frequently these people greeted the passing vessels with shouts and cheers, waving of hats, handkerchiefs, and sometimes an enthusiastic individual, in default of anything better, would pull off his coat and swing that. . . . At other places the people were out in force to see the sights, but were very glum and downcast." [6]

Toward noon the vessels in the lead steamed around a bend above Flower Island, No. 33 in the chain, expecting to meet the enemy fleet at any moment, and suddenly there it was, five gunboats moving steadily upstream. Foote reversed his course and hurried away, watching the splash from three Rebel shots that had passed harmlessly overhead. But, sensing the situation, he abruptly turned about, and so did the Confederates, the latter taking the lead in a chase that continued for thirty miles to Fort Pillow. To within a mile of the fort Foote followed, and there stared through his glasses while the enemy shot fell near. He then ran back upstream and tied to the Tennessee shore, out of range.

Gradually matters settled down for a peaceful evening. Before dark Foote called a conference on the flagship. Pope and Assistant Navy Secretary Scott both were there. In this discussion it was decided that troops should be landed at a point five miles above, in an attempt to get to the rear of the fortifications, while Foote kept the Southerners occupied from the river side.

Next day Foote ordered the mortar boats to begin shelling the fort, assuming Pope's army in the meantime was on its way from the rear. But Pope returned during the afternoon and reported failure. He had been unable to reach the fort from above. This called for a new conference, and now it was proposed to do the same thing that had been done at Island No. 10: cut a canal across the peninsula formed by the bend of the river and thus get gunboats below so the approach could be made from that direction.

Foote kept up a continuous bombardment while he watched in depressed mood from the flagship. He was suffering more than ever from the inflammation and swelling in his foot and leg, but determined to capture the fort before giving the limb the attention and rest it required.

By the 15th, ten mortar boats were training their fire on Fort Pillow. Pope's fleet of transports was spread out along the Arkansas side of the river. The Confederates in the meantime were cutting the levee in four places to keep the troops from marching overland. The scene thus created was described by the *Herald* correspondent: "The water poured through the cuts in torrents, deepening and widening them constantly, until the inundation not only of this point became a certainty, but of the bottom lands of the whole eastern portion of Arkansas. Their object was doubtless to prevent anticipated operations at this point by our army. The result will be the loss of immense amounts of property to the planters along the river." [7]

Foote was suffering acutely from his injured limb. During the day a message arrived from Halleck that shocked him: it announced that Pope's army was ordered to move to Pittsburg Landing, leaving the flotilla to continue the bombardment of Fort Pillow.

Such a sudden change of plans was a serious blow to the ailing Foote. Halleck had made some concessions, announcing that two strong regiments—"sufficient to garrison Fort Pillow when it is evacuated"—would be left by Pope. But Foote was not so confident that the situation on his front was in hand. Two deserters had informed him that the Confederates he was facing were headed by the veteran Hollins, experienced fleet leader, and by other capable men, most of whom had seen service in the old navy.

Foote was so upset that he wrote Halleck immediately after Pope left that his departure "has frustrated the best matured and most hopeful plans and expectations thus far formed" on his expedition. By joint operations, he believed, Fort Pillow would be taken in four days and Memphis in two more. He revealed further that he was informed the Rebels were increasing their fleet, that Hollins had left on the 13th to bring up the heavy gunboat *Louisiana,* said to be building at New Orleans and the only vessel on the Confederate side he feared.

Stumping about on deck, his green goggles now more frequently in use than ever, Foote had other worries. The two regiments left by Pope were under Colonel Graham N. Fitch, commanding the Indiana Brigade, a soldier who endorsed the Army's attitude of running its own show. He was under orders from Halleck, so he promptly let Foote know that he was operating independently and in no way under the naval leader's command.[8]

Soon after assuming his new role, Fitch found a bayou by which small boats could be taken below Fort Pillow. But this was not enough for Foote. He still hoped to locate a bayou leading into a lake with sufficient water for the gunboats to pass through. The ailing leader was greatly exercised about his position, realizing he was facing forty heavy guns in Fort Pillow, six thousand troops, and nine armed vessels, three of them ironclads. Against these he had seven ironclads and one wooden gunboat, sixteen mortar boats—"only available in throwing shells at a distance and even worse than useless for defense"— and a land force of two regiments totaling fifteen hundred troops.

Little progress had been made by April 23. Much of the time it rained, the downpour continuing so heavily that the mortars had to stop firing because they recoiled dangerously on their wet platforms. The *Herald* newsman, looking up at the weeping heavens and out across flooded fields, wrote his newspaper:

Rain, rain, rain; water everywhere as far as the eye can reach, covering cornfields, filling the woods, surrounding dwellings and flooding the whole country; and still it rains and still the water rises. A flood in the Mississippi is an event of annual occurrence, yet one that invariably brings its apprehensions to residents along its shore, and destroys an incalculable amount of property. The present flood is greater than any that has swept through the valley for a number of years, and, owing to the cutting of the levee on the west side of the river, will prove the most desolating and destructive probably that ever occurred. On every hand water covers the entire face of the earth, increasing the width of the river from a mile and a half to thirty or forty miles. As we lay moored to the trees that were once on the channel bank, but which now are in the middle of the vast expanse of water, buildings, cattle, houses, lumber and huge rafts of debris of all manner of property floated by, showing the desolating work of the mighty torrent. The scene is a grand yet a terrible one. Attempts to picture it are utterly futile. It challenges the descriptive powers of the ablest pen. And yet the rain descends in torrents, and the water rises higher and higher. God only knows when it will stop.

In the midst of this watery chaos the fleet remains quiet, undisturbed and uninjured by the rolling, surging tide. Nothing, apparently, is doing. Everybody has ample time to see the grand sight the waters afford, and everybody wearied in the contemplation. The vocation borders on the montonous. . . . With no variety to give interest to the spectacle, the flood—in itself grand, imposing, sublime—becomes a stale monotony from which the eye vainly turns for a change.[9]

More disheartening news for Foote was the information that the Confederates now had thirteen gunboats lying near, seven of them mere river steamers with boilers and machinery sunk into the hold for protection, but all armed with from four to eight heavy guns, some rifled. The other six vessels were iron-plated or protected by cotton bales stacked on their decks. The *Louisiana* still had not arrived, but was expected daily.

Perhaps moved by the treatment he was receiving from the War Department, Foote wrote Welles a private letter at this period in which he said: "The Rebels in person and in their papers speak with great respect of the gunboats. An army major told me that we were purposely held back from Nashville that General Buell might take it, although that officer sent for a gunboat, which went off Nashville before he entered the city. General Halleck refers to General Smith taking possession of Clarksville and says not a word about gunboats, whereas three days before I took possession, hoisted our flag on the forts, and issued my proclamation." [10]

Another depressant for Foote at this time was news of the advance on New Orleans. He was well aware that Farragut was pushing up the Mississippi to meet him, and he was impatient for his flotilla to show some progress, to push on past Memphis, and to meet the other fleet before it got past New Orleans.

Obviously goaded by Farragut's success, Foote wrote Welles on April 30 that he favored taking the initiative and running past Fort Pillow some dark night. He reminded the Secretary that his position at the moment was bad, because his slow steamers would be unable to grapple with the enemy and at the same time keep the current of the fast-flowing Mississippi from taking him under the guns of the fort.

By early May, Foote's physical condition had become pitiful. The correspondent of the *Herald* recorded: "The mortars below continue firing at Fort Wright, at intervals of ten minutes. Commodore Foote is preparing for a general attack on the Rebel works. The river is stationary, and eight inches higher than ever before known." [11] He was right about the river, but wrong about Foote. The veteran was in such constant pain and his foot so inflamed he was unable to move about at all, and he finally reached such a state of misery that he could not concentrate on military matters. Only then would he listen to his doctor's advice. On May 9 this entry was made in the log of the *Benton:* "Flag-Officer A. H. Foote took leave of his officers and men. At four P.M. Flag-Officer Foote went on board the transport *De Soto.* As the *De Soto* was leaving the U.S. gunboat *Benton,* the officers and men gave three cheers for Flag-Officer Foote."

The veteran was visibly shaken by the applause that rang over the water. Seated in a chair on the guards of the *De Soto,* he held a large palm-leaf fan over his face to hide the gushing tears. The sadness of the occasion was justified, for Foote was taking final leave. He would see brief service later as head of the Bureau of Equipment and Recruiting at Washington, but in little more than a year he would be dead of complications brought on by the wound received at Fort Donelson. His end came just after he had been appointed commander of the South Atlantic Blockading Squadron but before he could assume his new duties.

Before leaving the *Benton,* Foote had had the privilege of recommending a successor. His choice was the one-time Harvard student, Charles Henry Davis, a Bostonian only four months his junior. This officer, captain in rank, had only been with the Western Flotilla since the latter part of April. His service in the early months of the war had been distinguished, but only from behind a desk, as junior member of the Board of Detail, an agency created by the Navy Department and assigned the responsibility of determining the best way for the Union to recapture the forts and harbors taken over by the Southerners. Its decisions led to the Hatteras and Port Royal expeditions, deliberations that brought credit to its members. But Davis fidgeted at the inactivity of duty in a Washington office, and finally managed to get himself detached and made fleet captain of the South Atlantic Blockading Squadron, under the veteran Samuel F. du Pont. With Foote's failing health Davis was transferred to the Western Flotilla.[12]

Captain Davis was not a handsome man. He had a large nose and bushy mustache. His hair, swept back from a high forehead, was curled in copious rolls over the ears. The heavy whiskers on his face and under his chin resembled a bearskin. He joined Foote on the *Benton* the night of May 8, at a time of high excitement. During the morning, just as daylight was beginning to creep in, smoke had been seen rising above the trees around the nearest bend down the river, and soon three Rebel gunboats steamed into sight. The log of the *Carondelet* recorded what followed: "One of these steamed up to the place where our mortars were in the habit of firing, during the day, evidently with the intention of capturing them. Our flotilla on the Arkansas shore opened fire on one of the boats that was advancing up the river, but all their shots fell short about half the distance. . . . The enemy, not finding the supposed object of their search, returned to Fort Pillow. . . ." [13]

Foote was bedridden and unable to share in the activity during the day. Davis wrote his wife about the condition in which he found the flag officer: "I came down last night, as I said I should in my note of yesterday, and breakfasted with Foote on board this vessel this morning. He was in bed when I came on board, and he was so overpowered at the sight of me he was unable for some moments to speak. The scene was very touching; the pleasure of meeting was not without a badge of bitterness. We both shed tears. I find Foote very reduced in strength, fallen off in flesh, and depressed in spirits. His foot is painful and requires rest; his digestive organs are deranged by the disease of the climate. . . . It excites a very deep sentiment to look back to our early association as boys in the frigate *United States,* where we became intimate and studied together for our examination of midshipmen. . . . We often say that we wrote the first book of seamanship that was ever written in the service. Foote leaves me a mosquito net and a straw hat. We had for breakfast this morning venison, ortolans, and squirrel; we have for dinner wild turkey, and our table is constantly supplied with game." [14]

Foote's departure seemed to be an invitation to the Southerners to attack, for it was followed immediately by the war's

largest strictly naval engagement to date.[15] Actually the close-
ness of the two developments—Foote's departure and the Rebel
offensive—was a coincidence. For two days the Confederates
had been taunted by the sight of the U.S. gunboat *Cincinnati,*
standing alone on guard while mortar boat No. 16 lobbed
shells over on Fort Pillow.

On the afternoon of May 9 a small steamer came up the
river from Fort Pillow, bearing a flag of truce. On board were
two Union surgeons captured in the battle of Belmont, Missouri, who were now offered for exchange. "By this *ruse de
guerre,* or timely movement," it was recorded in the *Carondelet*'s log, "the enemy obtained a perfect knowledge of the position of our fleet and mortar boats."

That night, only a few hours after Foote had tearfully set
out upriver, a council of war was held by the Southerners. All
of the fleet captains were present, and so was Brigadier General
Jeff Thompson, commanding the troops at Fort Pillow. Hollins
was absent. In his stead sat J. E. Montgomery, former Mississippi River steamboat captain and now senior officer commanding the River Defense Service. It was at his suggestion mainly
that the Confederate Government early in the war had seized
fourteen river steamers. These made up the river-defense fleet,
their bows plated with one-inch iron and their machinery protected by pine bulwarks and cotton bales. The decision reached
by these leaders was unanimous: attack.

At six o'clock on May 10, a hazy morning, mortar boat
No. 16, under Acting Master Thomas B. Gregory and his experienced crew, started its daily chore of lobbing shells at Fort
Pillow. It had fired only five when a dull confusion sounded
downriver, and around a curve three-quarters of a mile distant
appeared the Rebel squadron. Davis counted eight steamers,
four of which, he could see with his glasses, were fitted as
rams. His own vessels numbered seven, three tied along the
eastern bank and four along the western.

Gregory trained his mortar upon the advancing ships and
fired, the shell bursting directly overhead. Ignoring it, the Rebels

steered their gunboats steadily toward him. The nearest Federals on that side of the river, the *Cincinnati* and the *Mound City,* hurried to his support, and the Confederates closed in, repeatedly striking with their rams.

During the next hour the Mississippi was the site of a battle such as had never before agitated its surface. There had been fighting somewhat on this order at Forts Jackson and St. Philip the morning of April 24, but it was confused and its ferocity was limited by poor visibility due to smoke and fog. Here, sight was clear. Around and about, at a cumbersome and awkward pace so unlike most things which travel by water, the vessels circled and zigzagged and lunged in a vicious struggle, but one surprisingly free of casualties. The lighter steamboats of the Southerners had the advantage of speed over the heavier, better-armored ships of the Federals. Both sides fought with determination. Here was the conflict the North had expected.[16] It could spell the end of progress for the Union's Western Flotilla and, equally so, it could quash the hopes of the Rebel fleet so desperately and hurriedly put together under command of the dauntless George Hollins.

One after another the vessels joined in the action. The U.S.S. *Carondelet*'s commander, Henry Walke, noticed a Confederate ram, the *General Bragg,* heading for the *Cincinnati* and opened fire against it at a distance of three-eighths of a mile. The ram kept on, striking the *Cincinnati* on the starboard quarter as she attempted to avoid the blow, and firing broadside and bow guns before and during the collision. With muzzles touching the Rebel boat, the *Cincinnati* poured a broadside into her foe—at ten feet distance, the report said—causing, as Commander Phelps of the *Benton* described, "a terrible crashing in her timbers." [17] Then both turned, the Union vessel heading upstream and the Confederate down, the latter on its way out of the battle because of a severed tiller rope.

The *Sumter* and the *General Earl Van Dorn,* Rebel gunboats, came after the *Cincinnati,* and the *Carondelet* now turned her attention to them. She fired a fifty-pound rifled shot which apparently struck the boilers of one of the Confederates, for they exploded with a great outburst of steam and the vessel immediately dropped downstream. But before leaving, her sharpshooters poured effective volleys into the Federal. One bullet struck Commander Roger N. Stembel just above the shoulder blade on the right side and, passing through the neck, came out directly under his chin. Another inflicted a wound upon Acting Master G. A. Reynolds that would cause his death within forty-eight hours. A third struck a seaman in the leg.

The *Van Dorn,* steering away from the *Cincinnati,* ran to within twenty yards of the mortar boat and fired into it. Then she backed off, looking for larger game, and rammed the *Mound City.* In veering away after the collision and before she could right her course, the *Van Dorn* ran ashore. There for several minutes she sustained a terrific cannonade until she could back off. As she came away, splinters on her iron bow indicated she had torn a hole in the *Mound City.*

Next in line, the *Sterling Price* struck the *Cincinnati* a little aft of her starboard midship and carried away her rudder, stern post, and a large piece of her stern, receiving in return several point-blank shots. This threw the Union vessel's stern toward the *Sumter,* and this gunboat struck her running at full speed. The *Beauregard, Colonel Lovell, Jeff Thompson,* and *Little Rebel,* unable to get into the fight because of the narrowness of the channel, stood off and kept up a constant fire from the guns.

The *Benton* pushed in, her guns blazing. "By this time we were in their midst," Phelps reported, "and I had the satisfaction to blow up the boilers of the ram that last hit the *Cincinnati* by a shot from our port bow rifle. I fired it deliberately with that view, and when the ram was trying to make another hit. Another ram had now hit the *Mound City* in the bows, and had received the fire of every gun of that vessel in the swinging that followed the contact. We interposed between another and the *Mound City,* and the rascal, afraid to hit us, backed off, when he also blew up from a shot I fired from the same rifle, hitting only a steam pipe or cylinder. All their rams drifted off disabled and the first one that blew up could not have had a soul remaining live on board, for the explosion was terrific." [18]

Phelps, more than anyone else, saw the battle in a victorious light for the Federals. "The loss of the Rebels must be very heavy," he wrote. "Their vessels were literally torn to pieces, and some had holes in their sides through which a man could walk. Those that blew up—it makes me shudder to think of them." He mentioned that the *Mound City* had her bow "pretty much wrenched off" and was run ashore, and that the *Cincinnati,* receiving a blow on her starboard quarter that opened her clear to her shell room, sank in eleven feet of water, but he failed to report that both were so badly damaged they would have to be taken to Cairo for repairs.

Vessels fired in rapid succession. Fragments from the U.S.S. *Pittsburg* struck the *Carondelet* amidships, some of the shot passing overhead, and the latter for a time was more in dread of her shot than that of the enemy. The Rebel gunboat *Sumter* ran up to within sixty feet of mortar boat No. 16 and fired two thirty-two-pound shot through its iron blinds, following them up with harmless volleys of musketry.

There was no chasing by either side when the fight ended. The Federals stood upstream and the Southerners down, past the stretch of the river covered by the guns of Fort Pillow. Both sides would claim victory. Captain Montgomery wrote in his report: "I perceived from the flagboat that the enemy's boats were taking positions where the water was too shallow for our boats to follow them, and, as our cannon was far inferior to theirs, both in number and size, I signaled our boats to fall back." [19]

The exact damage on the Confederate side would not be made clear by the records. Davis, a diligent diarist, recorded after the fight: "I can not tell what damage I did to the Rebel fleet. Two of their vessels dropped out of action, enveloped in steam and smoke, in the first fifteen minutes, and one appeared to sink as she rounded the point. The information given by the refugees (who are numerous) is that she was kept afloat twenty-four hours and then sank, and that we killed one hundred and eight of the Rebels. This is the least estimate; others give more." [20]

General Thompson, who had divided his troops among the fleet and had looked on from the *General Bragg,* reported two men, a steward and a third cook, killed, and eight or ten wounded.

The Federals later correctly concluded that the attack was not planned as a general one, but merely to sink the *Cincinnati* guarding mortar boat No. 16, so the latter could be cut loose and allowed to drift down with the current into the possession of the Confederates.[21] Whether it was to be repeated remained in doubt. The Southerners were said to be repairing the damage to their fleet. And they also were reported to be preparing to strengthen it with a "great craft" they had been building at Memphis but had taken up the Yazoo to complete, possibly within the next fifteen days.[22] This vessel was rumored to have been named the *Arkansas* and was described as the mightiest machine of war ever to appear on the Mississippi. "We must catch her there before she can be fitted out," Phelps wrote Foote.[23]

Ten quiet days followed the river fight, except for an occasional shelling from the mortar boats. Then, on May 21, the Union steamer *Kennett* went downstream under flag of truce with a number of prisoners to be exchanged. When she returned, her crew reported no signs of life were visible at Fort Pillow. It was the general impression that the Confederates had fallen back twelve miles to Fort Randolph.

But Davis was cautious: he still expected the Rebel gunboats to come up again. On May 12, only two days after the river fight, he sent a message to Gideon Welles: "If there are rams, as I understand there are, being fitted up under direction of the War Department, at Pittsburgh, Cincinnati, or elsewhere, for service in this river, now is the time to make them useful." This call was forwarded to Colonel Charles Ellet, one of the ablest engineers in the Union Army and one of the fathers of steam rams. He also had been a strong advocate of ironclad ships and wrote pamphlets urging the Federal Government to build them as one of its most important means of protection. But Ellet could get nowhere with the Navy Department. When he suggested building rams for use on the Mississippi, his plan was rejected. He then proffered it to the War Department, which accepted it and gave him military rank.

Ellet started building the rams at Pittsburgh late in March. "They will be only off-hand contrivances at best, mere substitutes for rams," he wrote Halleck, "but if we find a few brave pilots and engineers to man them I think we can make them do the work." [24] He received in reply a telegram urging him to "lose no time" and informing him of the *Arkansas* the Rebels were building as a ram at Memphis.

Ellet began by acquiring coal towboats, a strong type of craft that could make good speed in traveling down the Mississippi. These he directed to be strengthened by removing their upper cabins and filling in their bows with heavy timbers. He knew he could not wait to put on iron. Nine boats of this class were chosen and sent to four different cities—Pittsburgh, Cincinnati, New Albany, and Madison—so mechanics and supplies of materials would not be too heavily taxed in any one locality. The work went on rapidly. Three solid timber bulkheads from twelve to sixteen inches thick were run fore and aft from stem to stern. Boilers and machinery were fastened by iron stays and covered by two-foot thicknesses of oak timber.

By the middle of May, Davis was expecting Ellet's rams any moment. They came in on the 25th, bearing such imaginative names as *Mingo, Lioness,* and *Samson.* Ellet had done a speedy and economical job in building them. In forty days from the time he left Washington he had them ready—nine rams and two floating batteries at a cost of something less than three hundred thousand dollars. The task that awaited him along the river ahead was clearly understood by him. "What we do with these rams," he wrote the Secretary of War while working on them, "will probably be accomplished within a month after starting the first boat. Success requires that the steamers should be run down below the batteries, after which they will be isolated, unable to return, and compelled to command the Mississippi or be sunk or taken. I think if I can get my boats safely below Memphis I can command the river." [25]

Immediately upon arriving above Fort Pillow, Ellet proposed joint action—a dash past the fort in the daytime and an attack against the Confederate fleet, wherever found. Davis promised to give the matter consideration. Ellet repeated the suggestion three days later, and again he was promised a reply. On the fifth day he wrote the Secretary of War that he was going to inform Davis of his readiness to move alone on Monday morning.[26]

Deserters coming into Fitch's lines on May 31 reported that Fort Pillow was about to be evacuated, either that day or that night. The Confederates, they said, were suffering from lack of food, and were disgusted and disappointed. But no action followed, and next morning Ellet again wrote Davis that he planned to run his fleet downstream. He reminded him that he had postponed the expedition from day to day in the hope of getting at least one armed vessel to accompany him, and added: "But should you not deem it expedient to allow even one gunboat to share this enterprise, permit me to say that I would be very much gratified to have on board my vessels, as volunteers, the company of a few of the gallant gentlemen and brave men of your command, for the sake of the example alone which all connected with the Navy are sure to offer whenever the opportunity is presented to them to engage in a daring and patriotic enterprise." [27]

This brought a sharp note from Davis: "I decline taking any part in the expedition which you inform me you are preparing to set on foot tomorrow morning at early dawn. I would thank you to inform me how far you consider yourself under my authority; and I shall esteem it a favor to receive from you a copy of the orders under which you are acting." [28]

Two letters of explanation from Ellet came back, one conveying copies of his orders, but in neither did he show anger. He said he had come to do good service, with the approbation of the naval commander. "No question of authority need be raised," he wrote. "It is my intention to continue, as I have done, to communicate all my plans to you in advance, and to keep prepared to aid in the execution of all yours as soon as you deem it proper to intrust me with them; to do nothing contrary to your wishes, but to move against the enemy the moment you intimate that you are yourself ready, or that my advance will not interfere with your own program." [29]

Ellet's co-operative attitude brought a concession from Davis. "I have no desire to oppose or circumscribe your movements," he replied. "My opinion is unfavorable to your attack, as I understand it, but your mode of warfare is novel, and the service is peculiar; and under the circumstances of the case I willingly defer to your judgment and enterprise." [30]

A Rebel gunboat lying in plain view off Craighead Point under the guns of Fort Pillow began to worry engineer Ellet. On the night of June 2 he sent a small party on reconnaissance under command of his brother, Lieutenant Colonel Alfred W. Ellet, whom the War Department had boosted in rank from a captaincy to give proper stature with the ram fleet. This party came back with a report that the gunboat had gone. But the venture was not considered a failure. Two of its members had managed to get so close to the fort they could see beyond question that it was being evacuated.

While Ellet was thus engaged in reconnoitering, Davis was shaken by an incident on one of his mortars. He wrote his wife about it: "A man was killed in the mortar fleet this morning in a curious way. He had a cylinder of loose powder over his shoulder and a lighted cigar in his mouth. His head was blown off. These mortar men are said to be very careless." [31]

Refugees lining the banks of the river became more numerous as word spread that Fort Pillow was to be evacuated. There was also a report that Corinth, another important Rebel stronghold, had fallen. Union scouts stepped up their efforts to learn the truth, and in the meantime Davis sent a steamer upriver to evacuate the contraband or Negro families in worst distress.

On the 3rd, seeing the Rebel gunboat again lying around Craighead Point, Ellet ran down with two of his rams to capture it. Before he could get there, the Confederate steamer slipped her lines and escaped. Ellet ran on undaunted. The firing from the fort when he came within range was brisk, but he estimated it came from only seven or eight guns. He also learned that the Rebel fleet of rams and gunboats was larger than his own, with eight at Pillow and four at Randolph, and he came back and wrote Secretary Stanton a report that concluded with the paragraph: "Commodore Davis will not join me in a movement against them, nor contribute a gunboat to my expedition, nor allow any of his men to volunteer so as to stimulate the pride and emulation of my own. I shall therefore first weed out some bad material and then go without him." [32]

In drawing the fire of the fort on this venture downstream, Ellet unknowingly upset the plans of Colonel Fitch. Through careful reconnaissance, the Indiana officer had learned of a way to get his infantry within thirty yards of an unguarded point of the enemy's outer works, which had been laid open when the water fell. By opening a road and building a bridge across a creek, which could be done under cover of the heavy woods, a rear attack could be made on a crescent battery on a bluff above, after which other batteries would be exposed to the fire of his riflemen. Three companies of men began work on the project the morning of the 3rd. They labored diligently, concealed by the trees, but suddenly they had to throw down their tools and flee, for Ellet's pursuit of the Rebel gunboat was causing shells to fall in their vicinity.

So it was the next day, the 4th, before the road could be completed. That night plans were made for a combined attack. Troops were ordered on board the transports, ready to move over the road and storm the fort. Gunboats and mortars and rams stood by, awaiting the word to drop down and begin a concerted bombardment. But a deserter brought the news that they were wasting their time—the Confederates had already departed.

From the appearance of the fort, Colonel Fitch gained the impression that the deserter was telling the truth, and he changed his plans. Instead of marching over the hastily prepared route through the forest, he dropped down in a transport, preceded by men in open rowboats. It was three o'clock the morning of the 5th when they touched shore and moved into the fort, finding it had been abandoned hours earlier. The delay Ellet had caused by drawing fire on the road crew gave the Confederates time to escape. With them went everything of value.

★ 7

"Foot by foot"

APRIL-JUNE 1862

As the two Union fleets pushed toward each other on the Mississippi River, one thought was uppermost: the "great craft" the Rebels were said to be building under the name of *Arkansas.* They knew it was somewhere between them. But exactly where was it? And how much should it be feared? These were questions spies and deserters were unable to answer. They had heard rumors that it was patterned after the *Louisiana* and the U.S.S. *Mississippi,* and that it was stronger than any other vessel along the entire stretch of the river and its tributaries.

The Federals were justified in fearing this mysterious craft, for it actually was another great effort on the part of the Confederates to bring out a ship that would offset the more numerous vessels in the Union fleets. Work on it had begun the previous fall, more than two months after Jefferson Davis, in a special message to Congress, asked for one hundred and sixty thousand dollars to build two ironclads with which to defend the Mississippi. The request was approved by the Confederate Congress on August 24, and shortly afterward Secretary Mallory awarded a contract for their construction to a Memphis builder, John T. Shirley, who had been strongly recommended by congressmen and military leaders.

Shirley hired as his construction boss, Prime Emmerson, a man accustomed to doing things the casual way. With Prime, speed was not an essential, and he seemed to have little aptitude for cutting corners. A call for ship carpenters which Shirley sent out to New Orleans, St. Louis, Mobile, Nashville, and even as far away as Richmond and Baltimore, received weak response. He then applied to military commanders for men, and in most instances was refused. General Leonidas Polk, ignoring two letters from Secretary Mallory, assigned Shirley six or eight men when he had asked for one hundred.[1]

Under Emmerson's direction two sawmills were rebuilt in the neighborhood, and the stocks for the vessels were erected at Fort Pickering, near Memphis. There in October the hulls were begun. Pine timber for them was cut one hundred and four miles away in virgin forests and hauled by ox teams to the mills. Hardwood came from five different mills, one of them twelve miles distant. Railroad iron was bought in Memphis and in Arkansas. Bolt and spike iron came from many directions, in lots of ten to one hundred pounds—church bells, parts of locomotives, buggy-wheel rims, anything that could be melted and made into needed items—and was rolled at Nashville. A foundry in Memphis was taken over and set to work on two low-pressure engines capable of four hundred and fifty horsepower. Propellers were pounded out by hand, while local residents looked on with interest, for no vessel of war had been built in the area since the canoe.[2]

According to contract, the ships were to be ready in December '61, and most people thought they would be, knowing Shirley's reputation for energy. But by that date they were no more than skeletons. The builder at one time had difficulty supplying thirty-four thousand dollars which he had to put up himself before he was entitled to it from Congress under stipulations of the contract. But he mortgaged his home and continued work, feeling it was no more than his duty, for Secretary Mallory, in his opinion, had been generous in advancing money.

Finally the day came when the *Arkansas,* given priority over the *Tennessee,* could be floated. The stocks were knocked out from under her, and she drifted beautifully, her hull fourteen feet down in the water. But there was still much work to be done on her. From twenty to one hundred and twenty men, including house carpenters as well as ship carpenters, labored on her, although never at night or on Sundays.

Thus matters stood the day word arrived that the Union fleets were approaching. The first scare was created the moment three gunboats passed Island No. 10 on April 10, but the clincher came when Farragut successfully passed the New Orleans forts. Shirley at the time had the supply situation well in hand, but had fallen behind on construction. All the lumber needed for the vessels was on the building site except two lots at the Memphis & Charleston Railroad depot in Memphis, and all the iron was there except a purchase made across the river in Arkansas. But the ships themselves were far from ready. The *Tennessee's* frame had been completed, and she was receiving her planking. On the *Arkansas* the woodwork had been finished, with the exception of the cabin, but the iron plating still had to be added.

Here was an emergency in shipbuilding similar to the one at New Orleans, but in this instance the Rebels found a partial solution. The *Arkansas* on April 25 was floated three hundred miles down the Mississippi to the mouth of the Yazoo, and then towed up that stream two hundred miles to its head at Greenwood, Mississippi. Meanwhile work continued on the *Tennessee* until the day before Union ships arrived at Memphis, and then, on order of Secretary Mallory delivered through the provost marshall, she was burned on the stocks to keep her from falling into the hands of the Federals.

At Greenwood, construction of the *Arkansas* continued slowly under the casual eye of Prime Emmerson. At times only five carpenters, with two hammers between them, crawled around her decks, and on land a single blacksmith forge smoked lazily, seeming to frown at the sparks of industry. This trifling finally was changed by direction from Richmond. Secretary Mallory, spurred by the squeeze of the two Federal fleets moving toward each other, ordered Lieutenant Isaac Newton Brown "to assume command of the *Arkansas* and finish the vessel without regard to expenditure of men or money." This was one of the wisest moves Mallory ever made, for in Brown the South had an efficient and loyal servant. Born in Kentucky, son of a Presbyterian minister, he received appointment to the U. S. Navy in 1834, and thereafter his career was lively and successful. He fought in both the Seminole and Mexican wars. Twice around the world his course took him. When Japan was opened, he played an active role, and he served as executive officer on the ship that brought the first Japanese envoys to the United States. But in early June of '61 he resigned his commission, deserting his promising future in the field he had chosen, and joined the Confederate Navy. The fall of New Orleans found him, with the rank of lieutenant, working on ironclad gunboats at Algiers, across the river from that city. From there he fled with the military forces led by Lovell. But not for long was he without duties. Mallory's telegram assigning him to the *Arkansas* overtook him at Vicksburg. It came as a surprise. He had heard there was such a vessel under construction, but he had not been told of its escape ahead of the Union advance.[3]

Brown arrived at Greenwood to find his new command four miles from dry land. It was the season of floods, and the Yazoo had escaped its levees and was lashing at the soil of Mississippi plantations. Nothing he saw was encouraging, and the men with whom he was to work were hostile. "In the beginning I have had to assume extraordinary powers both with workmen and officers," he wrote General Daniel Ruggles. "The lukewarmness of inefficiency of the commander whom I relieved amounted to practical treason, though he meant nothing of the kind. I have got rid of him, but in doing so have placed myself inside the mutiny act. I came near shooting him, and must have done so had he not consented and got out of my way. He has gone to Richmond to denounce me, no doubt, but I care not what they say of me there so long as it is evident here that I am trying my best to get ready to strike the enemies of my country and of mankind." [4] Because of the resentment Brown found on first arriving, he asked for twenty armed volunteers and a lieutenant to act under his orders, but this request later was withdrawn, after he found the citizens in the neighborhood would sustain him. "Great deception has been practiced by some party or other regarding the forwardness of the *Arkansas'* equipment," he observed, "or else the Department of the Navy, as well as the public, have gratuitously concluded that the vessel was much more nearly ready than it is." [5]

The ship itself presented a picture of discouragement. Iron still had to be put on her sides. The cabin was incomplete. Engine parts were scattered about her hold. Guns without carriages lay on her deck. And down at the bottom of the river was a barge laden with four hundred bars of railroad iron that had sunk the day it arrived from Memphis. He immediately fished up the barge and moved everything downstream to Yazoo City, within fifty miles of the Mississippi, at the first point where the hills reached the river.

On arriving at Yazoo City, Brown sent out a clarion call for help. Plantation owners were summoned: from them must come blacksmith forges and blacksmiths. Laborers were called from the streets, saloons, and the nearest military posts. Using every means of argument and persuasion, he soon had two hundred men and fourteen forges busy, while drilling machines on the steamer *Capitol,* drafted into service, worked night and day fitting the railway iron for the bolts which would fasten it to the ship's sides. The trees from which carriages for the guns were to be made were still standing, but this presented no serious problem. A contract was arranged with two men at Jackson, Mississippi, to prepare these necessary items, and one day Brown brought the carriages in by ox cart.

Nothing was allowed to stop the work on the *Arkansas*. For five weeks it went on without interruption while Brown alternately encouraged, scored, applauded, and ranted. Loitering was strictly prohibited. Men worked or they had to leave. The scene was a constant beehive of activity. No act or deed that would throw things behind schedule was permitted. Thus went the routine while a hot Mississippi sun by day beat down on the backs of the workmen, and then by night gave way to cruel swarms of indefatigable mosquitoes and swamp bugs. Brown was constantly on hand, speaking in a commanding voice and pointing to the level of the river. The *Arkansas* must be away from there before the water fell and went into its summer sluggishness.

The Confederate action in moving the ship from Memphis was none too soon. Early in May, Farragut sent seven vessels up the Mississippi from New Orleans "to keep up the panic as far as possible." He planned for the larger of these—the *Richmond, Oneida,* and *Iroquois*—to go at least as far as Baton Rouge, and for the smaller to get up as high as Vicksburg and there cut off the South's supplies from the West. This meant that the Union Navy at last was plunging toward one of the most vital parts of the Confederacy. From Vicksburg a little railroad ran over to Monroe, Louisiana, on the Ouachita River, a stream that emptied into the Red River and watered some of the richest lands in the Deep South. The Red flowed into the Mississippi between Natchez and Port Hudson. Thus, supplies from the Red River Valley bread basket were moved up the Ouachita to Monroe, thence by rail to Vicksburg, and eastward from Vicksburg by rail to Demopolis, Alabama, on the Tombigbee River, which conveyed them south to Mobile and open water.

Farragut's advance up the river was against his better judgment. He believed that Vicksburg could not be taken by naval strength alone and, besides, this move stretched too thin his lines of communication. He thought it would be better to build up the blockade in the Gulf and to wait until such a stemming of the South's supply lines brought effect. But the Navy Department at Washington—especially Gustavus Fox—was on his neck, and there was little else he could do but act. Fox, taking upon himself much of the glory for the capture of New Orleans, was convinced "the rebellion seems caving in all around" and that what lay ahead was largely the task of mopping up. Farragut, looking on from the scene of action, of course felt differently.

No matter what strategy the flag officer had in mind, his instructions from Washington were specific, and they were emphasized and repeated. A part of this concern had been created by Theodorus Bailey upon his arrival at the Union capital. Asked how many ships Farragut had sent up the river, he replied, "None," speaking to the best of his knowledge, for the fleet had been at New Orleans when he left. Fox gasped: "Impossible; the instructions were positive and founded upon the probability of a condition of things which has happened exactly as anticipated, and the carrying out of which will be the most glorious consummation in history." To this Bailey answered that he thought Farragut had forgotten his orders. More consternation! Fox sent two ships in quick succession to notify Farragut that he must go up the river and get in the rear of Beauregard. "Mobile, Pensacola, and, in fact, the whole coast sinks into insignificance compared with this," the Assistant Secretary ranted.[6]

Farragut's ships were already on their way when Fox's messages arrived. Reports soon were received from Baton Rouge, capital of Louisiana, a short run above New Orleans. They were sent by Captain James S. Palmer, one of the calmest men in the Navy, an officer who could go into battle slowly pulling on the white gloves customarily a part of his uniform. But after thirty-seven years of ardent naval service, he was momentarily escaping from embarrassment suffered at the hands of the Confederate raider Raphael Semmes. Though slowly relenting, the Navy Department was still frowning at him over what had happened off the coast of Martinique.

There he had been sent after the C.S.S. *Sumter,* and there he had found his quarry tarrying until a supply of coal could be loaded. Nine days and nine moonlit nights Palmer lay out in international waters, keeping an eye toward the shore for prearranged signals that would tell him when the Southerner was moving. Then came the first dark night, and so also the signals. Palmer steamed to make the capture, and Semmes, sensing what was happening, reversed his course and escaped without so much as a random shot in his direction. The Federal officer's command was taken away from him, and only after Farragut's ships had passed the forts below New Orleans, with Palmer's vessel one of them, was it returned to him.

As senior officer of the little fleet moving up the Mississippi, Palmer relayed word of the surprise that had awaited him at Baton Rouge. There his written demand for surrender of the city brought a prompt reply from the mayor: "This note has been submitted to the board of selectmen, and I am instructed to say that the city of Baton Rouge will not be surrendered voluntarily to any power on earth. We have no military force here and are entirely without any means of defense. Its possession by you must be without the consent and against the wish of the peaceable inhabitants." Palmer promptly raised the U.S. flag over the arsenal on the outskirts of the city, and then wrote Farragut: "Here is a capital of a State with seven thousand inhabitants, acknowledging itself defenseless, and yet assuming an arrogant tone, trusting to our forbearance." [7]

More arrogance awaited him up at Natchez, Mississippi, a trading community half a mile or so back from the landing. He sent in a note demanding its surrender, but no one would accept it. Palmer quickly seized a ferryboat on the opposite side of the river, loaded it with seamen and Marines and a couple of howitzers, and directed it across. This time two members of the Common Council, bringing an apology from the mayor, received it and disappeared. In time a reply was returned that cooled Commander Palmer's zeal with the suddenness of a dash of cold water: "An unfortified city, an entirely defenseless people, have no alternative but to yield to an irresistible force, or uselessly to imperil innocent blood. Formalities are absurd in the face of such realities." [8]

Arrogance repeated was the greeting at Vicksburg. In answer to a demand for surrender, Military Governor James L. Autry wrote: "I have to state that Mississippians don't know, and refuse to learn, how to surrender to an enemy. If Commodore Farragut or Brigadier-General Butler can teach them, let them come and try." [9] Next, General Martin Luther Smith, commanding the post, responded: "Regarding the surrender of the defenses, I have to reply that, having been ordered here to hold these defenses, it is my intention to do so as long as in my power." And to this the mayor added: "Neither the municipal authorities nor the citizens will ever consent to a surrender of the city."

Farragut himself soon came up the river, and on arrival at Vicksburg realized the task ahead would not be easy. The Confederates were digging in, and some of their batteries could be spotted on the brow of the cliffs along the water front. But others could not be seen. They were cleverly concealed in queer places: some inside the railroad depot, one in the engine house, and some behind carts turned up on their sides. At almost any time during the earlier months of 1862, Vicksburg, referred to as "the key to the Mississippi," might have been taken without a siege, but since the arrival of Martin Luther Smith, with his notions about defending a city that was by nature defended, the situation had changed. Vicksburg, spread along the banks at a hairpin turn of the Mississippi, was no Baton Rouge or Natchez. Sheer walls and the mile-wide river protected it on the west. More bluffs and hills covered it on the south. And swamps, bayous, and old river beds lay as an impediment on the north. Only from the rear, toward the east, could an enemy force its way in, and that meant land forces. [10]

Never would the world see a more determined defiance than came from Vicksburg. Military leaders reported that the inhabitants, "inspired by a noble patriotism," were determined to devote the city to destruction "rather than see it fall into the hands of an enemy who had abandoned many of the rules of civilized warfare." Van Dorn wired: "Foot by foot the city will be sacrificed. Of course, citizens proud to do so." [11]

By the end of May, Farragut was back in New Orleans. His return was not without the advice of the officers at his side, and it was not before he had tried bombarding Vicksburg. On the afternoon of May 26 his ships opened fire and kept it up for two hours, apparently trying to get the range. The Southerners merely looked on, Martin Luther Smith feeling confidence in the defenses he had arranged.

Farragut's officers, called into conference, advised abandoning the attack. The flag officer was quite sick at the time, and he submitted to their judgment. Sound reasoning lay behind the decision. His ships were battered from the New Orleans campaign, and in no condition to contend with Confederate ironclads coming down with the current. Another factor was the problem of supplying coal and provisions in a hostile area. But nothing, in his opinion, compared to the evils of the river—the danger of running aground, of ships colliding with one another, and of their frequent experience in losing anchors. "The more you do the more is expected of you," he wrote in private letters. "They will keep us in this river until the vessels break down, and all the little reputation we have made has evaporated. The Government appear to think that we can do anything. They expect me to navigate the Mississippi nine hundred miles in the face of batteries, ironclad rams, etc., and yet, with all the ironclad vessels they have North, they could not get to Norfolk or Richmond." [12]

But no matter how much Farragut ranted, Washington was the controlling factor. Lincoln saw the Mississippi as the backbone of the rebellion, "the key to the whole situation."

Attention was now centered on the fleet that Charles Henry Davis was bringing down from Fort Pillow. After the fall of that stronghold on June 4, he headed for Memphis, arriving

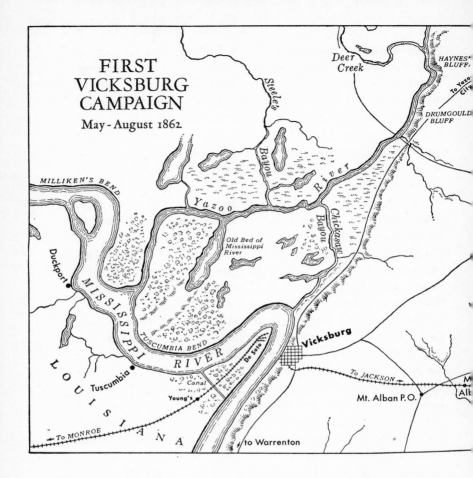

FIRST
VICKSBURG
CAMPAIGN
May - August 1862

Deer Creek

HAYNES' BLUFF

To Yazoo City

DRUMGOULD BLUFF

Steele's

Bayou

MILLIKEN'S BEND

Yazoo

River

Chickasaw Bayou

Duckport

Old Bed of Mississippi River

MISSISSIPPI

TUSCUMBIA BEND

Vicksburg

To JACKSON

M

Alb

LOUISIANA

Tuscumbia

RIVER

De Soto

Canal

Young's

Mt. Alban P.O.

To MONROE

to Warrenton

there the following day. Confederate General Villepique was there ahead of him, along with most of the troops he had commanded higher up the river, and General Ruggles soon would be on hand. The steamer *Golden Age* brought in six hundred Confederates from above, to join two hundred already on duty, and public meetings were held daily, with great exhortations, especially from the military commanders.

Into the wharf at Memphis at noon of June 5 drifted Confederate Captain J. E. Montgomery and what was left of the River Defense Fleet. These boats had been as well reinforced as the supplies of the South would permit. Their machinery was protected by an inner bulkhead of twelve-inch-square timber, bolted together every eighteen inches, and an outer bulkhead of six-by-twelve-inch timber, similarly bolted, with the space between filled with compressed cotton bales. A coating of one-inch railroad iron was fitted over the outer bulkhead. Strength was added to the bows of the vessels by bolting twelve-inch-square timbers together and sheathing them with four-inch oak plank and one-inch iron.

Montgomery would have preferred to take his fleet on to Vicksburg, but only one of his vessels had coal enough to advance that distance. In this emergency he sent out a plea for more fuel as soon as he dropped anchor at Memphis, and it came in driblets—wagonloads from factories and wheelbarrow loads from private homes.[13] By nightfall all of the vessels had at least a partial supply.

Memphis went to bed that night in tingling expectancy of what would happen at dawn. It was generally known that the Union fleet had come down the river before bedtime and had anchored a few miles above the city near a series of little islands known as Paddy's Hen and Chickens. Moreover, Montgomery had let it be known that, thanks to the co-operation of the townspeople in giving up their coal, he would fight instead of destroying the fleet. To guard against surprise, the tug *Gordon Grant* was sent up the river to watch the enemy, and in the darkness it ran aground and had to be burned. It flared up like a torch, an evil omen of what would await the Confederates at dawn.

Union gunboats—the flagship *Benton,* the *Louisville, Carondelet, Cairo,* and *St. Louis*—and the rams *Queen of the West, Monarch, Lancaster,*[14] *Mingo, Lioness, Switzerland, Dick Fulton,* and *Horner*—were astir at five-thirty on the morning of the 6th. Soon the heavens were a solid cloud of black smoke. At six o'clock Montgomery swung his fleet—eight rams and gunboats—out into a double line opposite the city and ordered two of them, the *Jeff Thompson* and the *Colonel Lovell,* to start the action. From rooftops and along the bluffs skirting Memphis thousands of spectators, torn from their beds before dawn, looked down. Many of them were soldiers, aware that they were eyewitnesses to a battle in which land forces, other than sharpshooters along the banks, would have no part.

The current of the Mississippi at Memphis ran close to the Tennessee side, and rushed by "like a strong man in a race." [15] Into this the *Thompson* ran, slowed up, and swung around. At that moment the *Little Rebel*'s bow pivot gun blazed away at the *Benton,* flagship against flagship. It seemed to be a signal, and a newspaper correspondent looked at his watch and noted it was twenty minutes after six. In a matter of moments the firing became general, shells bursting in the early dawn, and smoke belching forth over the rippling water and drifting ashore as though fleeing the scene of battle. Past the advancing Union fleet rapidly pushed two vessels. They were the *Queen of the West* and the *Monarch* from Ellet's rams, and they steamed on into the first line of Confederate boats.

The *Lovell* ran directly toward the *Queen of the West,* the vessel Ellet was commanding, and then all at once drifted helplessly, one of her engines out of order. The ram closed in and struck her amidships, with disastrous effect. A moment later another ram struck her on the other side. The captain and most of his crew were seen to dive overboard and swim ashore, leaving behind those who could not swim. Her pilot lying dead and with blood splattered around her decks, she seemed to welcome the waters which closed over her.

The Confederate *General Price* rammed the Federal *Lancaster* and sank her. Then the Rebel swung about and headed for the *Eastport.* Coming downriver from the opposite direction, with the same object in mind, was the *General Beauregard.* As they closed, the Union ram, more easily handled, backed out from between them, and they ran together. Before they could straighten out, several rams forged in and struck, sinking both Confederate vessels. Before the *Beauregard* went down, the Federals were able to capture from her a book supplying them with a complete set of the signals used by the River Defense Fleet. For day use the semaphore was by flag— "Lights, show none tonight," "Smoke, I see ahead; get ready for action," or "Take me in tow, I am disabled." By night, it was in lights—a single red, "Action, prepare for tonight"; a single blue, "Captain come aboard," or a red over a blue, "Get everything ready to attack tonight." Forty-seven messages in all were involved.

Off at one side the Rebel flagship *Little Rebel* was rapidly sinking: a cannon ball had struck below the water line and passed through her boilers. Montgomery and most of the crew swam ashore.

On a sand bar the *Sumter* and *General Bragg* lay helpless, both aground. Over their sides men scurried like bees, striking the water and heading for shore, among them the *Sumter*'s captain, W. W. Lamb, the blood streaming from a finger just torn off by a bullet. The *Thompson* lay on the bank burning, her captain shot in the arm.

A constant patter of small arms from shore was so bothersome at times that the Union ships turned their guns and blazed away at the trees with grape.

The *Queen of the West,* her artillery roaring, headed for a Confederate ram. "The crash was terrific," Ellet reported. "Everything loose about the *Queen,* some tables, pantryware, and a half-eaten breakfast, were overthrown and broken by the shock. The hull of the Rebel steamer was crushed in, and her chimneys surged over as if they were going to fall over on the bow of the *Queen*." [16]

Ellet had been in the pilothouse at the time of the collision. After the impact he ran on deck, and there he was spotted by a signal quartermaster on one of the Confederate vessels. The Southerner raised his gun and fired, and the bullet found its mark, tearing into Ellet's knee, a simple wound, but one that in a few days would develop blood poisoning and prove fatal.[17]

The *Monarch,* near at hand, singled out a Confederate gunboat and rammed her. The wounded Ellet was on his way below, but he heard the noise of the crash and looked to see what was happening. "The blow of the *Monarch* was so severe," he related, "that piles of furniture were precipitated from the Rebel steamer upon the forecastle of the *Monarch,* and were found there in large quantities after the action." [18]

For an hour and ten minutes the battle raged, and then off down the river went the Union fleet, chasing the only two Confederate boats to escape. They were the *General Earl Van Dorn* and the little storeboat *Paul Jones,* the latter carrying a large amount of powder, shell, cannon balls, and commissary stores evacuated from Fort Pillow. With them went nearly all that was left of the Confederate naval power on the Mississippi.

A little later in the day the *Lioness* pulled up to the wharf at Memphis. On board were Ellet's son, Charles Rivers Ellet, a medical cadet, and two soldiers, each with a folded flag under his arm. It was New Orleans repeated. To the accompaniment of pistol shots and angry threats they raised one of the flags over the post office. The other was seized by the mob that trailed the landing party and torn to bits.

In this battle Ellet's rams seemed to have proved their value to most everyone but Lieutenant Phelps. In a gossipy letter to Foote he reported: "The *Queen of the West,* failing to hit the *Beauregard,* made a pass at the *Colonel Lovell,* cutting her through, and that vessel sunk in a few minutes, many of her crew going down with her, and she is entirely out of sight. This is all the rams did, except the confusion created by them gave us better chances at the Rebel craft." It was his opinion that the most damage was done by the shells from the Union vessels that penetrated the boilers of the Confederate boats.[19]

Memphis' alert newspaper, the *Argus,* Union in sympathy, appeared that afternoon with flaming headlines. "One sixty-four-pounder from the Federal gunboats," it reported, "struck the residence of N. Cavelline, Esq., in South Memphis, which passed through the chimney, knocking it down and completely covering up with bricks a little boy lying in bed. It was a shell, and did not explode, and, strange to say, the little boy escaped unhurt. A shot struck the city icehouse, doing no very serious damage. One large shell fell near a crowd on the bluff, in front of the Gayoso, but did not explode, and no damage was done. . . . Many of the ladies were seen with the tears trickling down their cheeks, humiliated at the triumph of the Federal boats. All the stores, with few exceptions, were closed, business of every kind being suspended. Not less than five thousand persons were on the wharf. The train which left on the Mississippi & Tennessee road was jammed and crammed by our citizens, many of whom remained until the last opportunity to get away."

It was also reported that General Jeff Thompson, the Confederate officer the Federals considered a guerrilla leader, sat his horse, a spectator, until the boats disappeared down the river. Then, muttering "They are gone and I am going," turned his mount about and "disappeared for a more auspicious field of action."

The two Union fleets assigned the task of opening the Mississippi River now pushed closer together. On the 9th two of Farragut's ships, the *Wissahickon* and *Itasca,* were roughly handled by rifled Confederate guns mounted in a battery on the bluffs at Grand Gulf, Mississippi, receiving a total of forty-one shots, with several fatalities on board. Farragut, at Baton Rouge, made his plans to advance on Vicksburg.

The battle of Memphis was only two days old when the Navy had an urgent call from the Army. General Samuel R. Curtis, Halleck wrote Welles, was out in Arkansas trying to raise two regiments of infantry and had been so hard pressed by the Confederates that he was forced to fall back behind the White River. There he found himself in an emergency, for the roads in Missouri were so bad it was almost impossible for aid to reach him by land. Could the Navy send gunboats down the Mississippi and up the White to aid him? Welles shifted the burden to Charles Henry Davis, and Davis answered by dispatching three vessels—the *Mound City, St. Louis,* and *Lexington*—under Commander A. H. Kilty.

Along the way this little fleet found all sorts of obstructions, including rafts of wet and heavy timber, but it forged along. On the morning of the 16th it was overtaken by the *Conestoga* and two transports bearing provisions and Colonel Fitch's Indiana regiment. That night anchors were dropped five miles from St. Charles, Arkansas, where the first bluffs along White River appeared.

The Confederates at St. Charles, not sure of the size of the force confronting them and not knowing when the attack would come, worked frantically throughout the night. The *Maurepas,* a gunboat rescued from Hollins' fleet at Island No. 10, swung across the stream and prepared to fight. But when the Federal ships failed to come up before dark, Lieutenant Joseph Fry, senior officer on hand, began landing guns from this vessel and from the *Pontchartrain,* still higher up, and placing them along the bluffs.[20] He had a force of one hundred and fourteen men, including thirty-five sharpshooters under Captain A. M. Williams of the C. S. Engineers and seventy-nine sailors from the two gunboats, to face Fitch's Indiana regiment and four gunboats, two of them ironclads.

At five-thirty next morning men on the Union ships watched several bales of cotton float past.[21] These were from the deck of the *Maurepas,* scuttled before dawn to block the channel at St. Charles. Soon the fleet got under way, led by the *Mound City,* carrying Commander Kilty. A mile or more up the stream enemy pickets were encountered, sniping busily from the trees, and the boats opened fire. Fitch in the meantime landed his regiment and began driving the Confederates back. A little farther up, the fleet came to a bend in the river about a mile in length, at the upper end of which three vessels had been sunk—the gunboat *Maurepas* and the river boats *Eliza G.* and *Mary Patterson*. Abreast of these obstructions was a bluff, on which the Federals imagined there were batteries, although no guns could be seen because of the trees.

The gunboats stood boldly on, firing as they went. Soon a

battery answered from the bluff, and the Federals stepped up their cannonading to a terrific pace. The *Mound City,* still in advance, was only six hundred yards from the Confederate guns when a shot penetrated her port casemate a little above and forward of the gun port, killing three men in its flight and exploding her steam drum. Immediately, amidst a great cloud of steam that seemed to come from every part of the ship, her crew began leaping through her portholes into the river. Before they could swim to shore, sharpshooters rushed down from the bluffs and began firing at them.[22]

Ten minutes later Fitch signaled for the firing to cease and, when it did, he pushed in against the batteries. Facing his thousands were one hundred and fourteen Southerners, who quickly spiked their guns and retreated, with a loss of six dead, eight missing, and one wounded, the last their commander, Joseph Fry, formerly of the U.S. Navy and a man respected by both sides.

But no captures could compare with the disaster to the stricken ship. "The loss of life on board the *Mound City* by the explosion of the steam drum is frightful," Lieutenant Wilson McGunnegle of the *St. Louis* reported. ". . . To endeavor to describe the howling of the wounded and the moaning of the dying is far beyond the power of my feeble pen. Among the scalded and suffering was the brave Commander Kilty, who but a short time before I had seen proudly pacing his deck with the enemy's balls whizzing past him." [23] When the steam permitted a view, men could be seen tearing the clothes from their scalded bodies.

Even as she drifted helplessly the *Mound City* spelled trouble to the fleet. One of her bow guns was loaded with grape, cocked and primed, the lock string lying on deck. In the confusion one of the wounded men rolled on the string and set off the piece, a part of its charge passing through the steampipe of the nearby transport *New National.*

Only two officers, the first master and the gunner, escaped

injury. Fifty-nine of the crew were interred in a common grave. Many of them had been killed by enemy bullets while struggling in the water.

The record of the Union Navy personnel that day was not without blemish. First Master John A. Duble of the *Conestoga,* assigned to temporary command of the *Mound City,* told of it in his report: "I beheld with extreme disgust a portion of the few men who were uninjured, drunk. A portion of the crew of the *St. Louis,* a portion of the crew of the *Conestoga,* also some of the soldiers of the *New National* were in the same beastly condition, and acts most scandalous were perpetrated on board. Rooms were broken open, trunks, carpet sacks, etc., pillaged, and their contents scattered around and destroyed. Watches of the officers were stolen, and quarreling, cursing, and rioting, as well as robbing, seemed to rule. Liquor was put in water casks, with water and ice, for the relief of the wounded, but these men had buckets full, pure, who drank for the purpose of debauch."

The *Mound City* was tied up ashore, and there she lay with much less confusion on board after her command was taken over by the righteous Duble. But developments around her would not let her forget her disaster. At three o'clock in the afternoon the body of one of her crew, risen from the bottom, drifted past, a bullet hole in his forehead. At nine o'clock next morning the body of a fireman, Allen Wood, rose up out of the water at the side of the ship.

Davis sounded a sad requiem in his report of the expedition: "The victory at St. Charles . . . would be unalloyed with regret but for the fatal accident to the steam drum and heater of the *Mound City.* . . . Of the crew, consisting of one hundred and seventy-five officers and men, eighty-two have already died; forty-three were killed in the water or drowned, twenty-five are severely wounded and are now on board the hospital boat." [24]

On board his flagship Davis kept a journal, in which he

daily recorded developments by writing letters to his wife. After the affair at St. Charles he made two entries:

"Our expedition to White River is in some measure a failure, owing to the shallow stage of the river. The boats have returned to the mouth of the river, having grounded several times and run the risk of being detained all summer. . . .

"Since finishing the enclosed letter I have received a message from Farragut asking me to come down and help him take Vicksburg. I am getting ready to go now." [25]

★ *8*

"Glorious even in death"

JUNE-AUGUST 1862

Union sailors floating down the Mississippi with Davis' fleet had reason to believe the world was on fire, for at times both sides of the stream were an inferno. Tongues of flame licked into the air, a symbol of fright and desperation and somehow a token of defiance: the Southerners were burning their cotton to keep it out of the hands of the enemy. Each spark, each wisp of smoke was an omen of defeat for the Confederacy. Into ashes was going the staple that would have bought more ships in England, that would have supplied a valuable exchange in any foreign market, that would have kept busy the mills of other nations, some of them already idle and surrounded by starvation. But the South's leaders had been stubborn about their "white gold," the big stick they believed they held over the rest of the world, and now thousands upon thousands of bales were disappearing under the torch.

Vessels moved slowly, drifting with the current, for smoke lay like a screen over land and water. By day, great bonfires of cotton, crackling and dancing in the sun; by night, hot, sticky, smoky hours—the same fires throwing a sickening yellow glow against the darkened heavens, spreading an awning of terror beyond the horizon, and announcing to planter, sharecropper, and slave that the enemy had come. Here and there were ruins of cotton gins, cotton presses, and raw materials in bulk and in bale. Riverbanks were white with cotton flocks caught on roots of trees and on stranded drift. A newspaper correspondent observed: "There were white masses floating in the channel, as if there had been a tremendous wash of dirty clothes somewhere, with no end of soap suds. No toiling field hand on the richest Mississippi plantation, with the millions of bolls bursting with the snowy fibers, ever saw such a glorious chance to fill a basket, not only a basket but a cart, or a house, or a big New England barn. Not all floating, but some trampled in the dirt, or smoldering in the numerous fires along the fields."

The U.S. ram *Lancaster* learned of a barge laden with one hundred and fifty bales of cotton concealed up the St. Francis River and ran fifty miles off course to investigate. Finding the craft had been burned to the water's edge, she returned to the Mississippi and approached Island No. 98 in late afternoon, the attention of her crew centered on a great cloud of smoke rising to the left of the island. Investigation revealed two hundred bales on fire.

But not all the smoke was from cotton set ablaze by the Southerners. There were other causes. Farragut, coming up the river, was adding to it. When his ships were fired on as they passed the little town of Warrenton, twelve miles below Vicksburg, he whirled about and burned the community. The same was done to Grand Gulf. Two Federal rams running up the Yazoo noticed oil floating on the water. A man picked up from a skiff a short time later said it came from boats higher up the river that had been oiled and tarred in readiness to be set on fire. Twenty miles farther and the Union vessels rounded a curve to see ablaze and drifting down upon them almost all that was left of the Confederacy's River Defense

Fleet—the *Van Dorn, Polk, Livingston,* and *General Clark.* But the Federals could not keep their attention on the burning ships. A little higher up a huge raft was blocking the river, and beyond it the unmistakable shape of the *Arkansas.* They looked on, and then turned downstream to avoid the destruction floating toward them.

The rams assigned to Davis' fleet began to reach Vicksburg a few days before Farragut showed up from below with an army of thirty-two hundred men under General Thomas Williams, West Point graduate, Mexican War hero, and now commander of the Second Brigade, Department of the Gulf. These vessels were the responsibility of Alfred W. Ellet, brother of Charles, by that time in his grave. On June 26 the advance of Farragut's fleet began to arrive, and soon the mortar boats were taking position to begin bombardment. That night a detail of four men, including Charles Rivers Ellet, son of the deceased ram expert, and Edward C. Ellet, Alfred's son, all dressed in civilian attire and armed with Navy revolvers, set out to try and reach Farragut. They were gone all night on a junket they would long remember, a trek through swamps and sloughs, part of the time up to their waists in muck. Next morning they were back with an account of their reception, which turned out to be far from what they expected. When they arrived, Farragut was absent from his flagship and the officers who confronted them were highly suspicious, believing they were spies. But three hours later the flag officer returned and gave them a more gracious welcome.

Charles Ellet was carrying a letter from his uncle to Farragut, announcing that the Mississippi was free of obstructions from Cairo to Vicksburg and that the ram fleet was ready to co-operate in clearing it all the way down to the Gulf. In reply Farragut said that rams would be of no value to him in the attack he was planning, but that, "if Commodore Davis' ironclad gunboats could be present, they would add greatly to the chances of success without much loss of life, which is always desirable in such cases." [1] When this message was delivered to

Alfred Ellet he immediately sent it to Davis by the tender *Dick Fulton.*

While this was going on, Gideon Welles passed on to Davis by telegraph an idea that would be defeated by the dry season and the lazy old Mississippi. Maps showed a narrow neck of land made by the winding bed of the river across from Vicksburg, at times only three-quarters of a mile wide. The water sometimes overflowed this neck, and the Secretary suggested that a canal be opened across it that would obviate the necessity of passing Vicksburg. The plan was adopted at once, and crews from Williams' army were assigned to its execution.

On June 26, Farragut wrote a letter to his wife, in which he revealed some of his unspoken thoughts: "Here we are once more in front of Vicksburg, by a peremptory order of the Department and the President of the United States, 'to clear the river through.' With God's assistance, I intend to try it as soon as the mortars are ready, which will be in an hour or two. The work is rough. Their batteries are beyond our reach on the heights. It must be done in the daytime, as the river is too difficult to navigate by night. I trust that God will smile upon our efforts, as He has done before. I think more should have been left to my discretion; but I hope for the best, and pray to God to protect our poor sailors from harm. If it is His pleasure to take me, may He protect my wife and boy from the rigors of a wicked world." [2]

In the late afternoon of June 26, mortars began bombarding Vicksburg. They fired until dusk. At sunrise next morning they resumed, and were answered occasionally from batteries in the city. At times during the day two of the Union ships, the *Westfield* and *Octorara,* joined in with a few shots. The roar was continuous. Loud explosions shook the city to its foundations, and men, women, and children fled eastward into the open country for safety. The air seemed filled with shells. They tore through trees and walls, and scattered fragments in all directions, one of which bore into hard, compact clay and failed to explode. S. H. Lockett, chief engineer of the city's defenses, dropped a line into the hole and found it seventeen feet deep.

On the 27th the furor of the bombardment increased. The mortar fleet was divided into two squadrons, one on each side of the river, their masts again, as at the New Orleans forts, covered with tree branches. The pace of the firing grew more rapid in the late afternoon and early evening, but by 9:00 P.M. all was quiet again, and the Union sailors went to their hammocks for a few hours' sleep. But darkness meant added work for the Coast Survey. Its crews had been busy during the day making triangulations to guide the gunners, and at night they stole in to plant stakes on shore, attaching to each a lantern darkened on the side next to the city.

Inside Vicksburg as the day's bombardment ended there was some cause for rejoicing: houses had been perforated by shells, but none had burned.[3]

At 1:45 A.M. on the 28th the sailors in Farragut's fleet were roused, and fifteen minutes later were at breakfast. A hushed excitement lay over each ship. It was commonly known that the veteran flag officer was planning another run past a concentration of Confederate batteries.

Except for the fact that Theodorus Bailey was not leading the column of ships and that there were no Confederate vessels to oppose them, this run past Vicksburg was a repetition of the previous operation. It was accomplished in the gray of dawn, while the mortar fleet resumed its bombardment with a mad uproar, and a couple of hours later Farragut was writing Welles a message from above the city. Three of his boats, the *Brooklyn, Kennebec,* and *Katahdin,* had failed to get past, why he knew not. He had been much impressed with the way the Southerners handled their guns, running away from them when the enemy ships got abreast, and then returning to send a raking fire on the vessels after they had passed. "I am satisfied," he wrote, "that it is not possible for us to take Vicksburg without an army force of twelve thousand to fifteen thousand men."[4]

But his orders were peremptory: he had to do all within his power to free the river of impediments. And that before the stream got so low his ships became stuck in the mud.

Soon after running past Vicksburg a disturbing message reached Farragut. It urged him to send the mortar fleet to bomb Fort Morgan at Mobile. This move he opposed in an immediate letter to Welles, citing that the vessels would have no protection at Mobile and that they would be in danger of destruction by ironclad rams. "I fear the Department is misinformed in relation to ironclad rams," he explained. "The Rebel gunboats can not stand before ours, but what they dignify by the name of ironclad rams is an article entirely different, and had they succeeded in getting any one of those on the Mississippi finished before our arrival, it would have proved a most formidable adversary. We have one now blockaded up the Yazoo River, and hope to prevent her from ever getting down, and if she does come down, we hope to be able to dispose of her." [5]

This day that Farragut ran past Vicksburg saw a change in the Confederate defense. General Earl Van Dorn succeeded General Lovell as commander of the department.

Next morning Davis left Memphis and headed southward to join Farragut. On July 1 the two fleets came together in an atmosphere of fog and smoke so dense they could not see each other. In clear weather and free of the Southerners' cotton-burning campaign this would not have been the case, for only a distance of little more than a mile separated them, and their masts would have been clearly visible to each other above the trees. In another of his gossipy letters to Foote at this time Lieutenant Phelps told of the meeting and of the great cheering that rose from the men. But he disclosed that officers were discouraged about taking Vicksburg without a land force. "It is presumed that the fleet will not linger here, but will run back to below the batteries very soon," he added. "One thousand Negroes are working hard upon a canal across the point here, one and a quarter miles long, which, if successful, will leave

Vicksburg some four or five miles from the river. . . . We are soon to go up the Yazoo to destroy the *Arkansas* and clear the river out." [6]

July days passed slowly. Sickness increased, intensified by the overflow of the river and the many dead animals in the swamps. Men apparently in good health at the close of a day's work died quickly during the night, victims of heat and malaria. Disease was an enemy that no weapons of war on either side could combat.

The bombardment continued. Meanwhile, Williams' men, bossing a great horde of Negro workmen assembled from surrounding counties, dug away at the canal, and all the time Farragut was becoming more and more disgusted and discouraged. He could not see that the Southerners were becoming at all disheartened, and newspaper stories tended to confirm his perception. One of the New York *Herald's* veteran reporters wrote from Vicksburg the first week in July: "Soon after the fleet anchored below the city they summoned Vicksburg three times to surrender, and three times the summons was rejected. Then they commenced shelling it, which has been kept up at intervals ever since. It is estimated that twenty thousand guns have been fired at the city and suburbs; yet only three soldiers and one woman have been killed, and two soldiers wounded. The damage sustained by buildings has not been more than one-twentieth part as great as might be supposed. Rev. C. K. Marshall, who has been an eyewitness of all the siege, says that ten thousand dollars would repair all the damages in that particular." [7]

Equally discouraging was the canal project. River engineers were standing by shaking their heads. They said it was doomed to failure, that the river was too deep in front of Vicksburg for it to follow a shallower course. They recalled that all the successful cutoffs made in the course of the stream had begun at a point where the main course impinged against the shore of some bend, whereas the upper end of this canal was located in an eddy. The foot or so of water that had trickled into the section of the ditch already dug tended to corroborate their opinion.

On July 10, Farragut wrote Welles: "It is not perhaps my province to take the liberty to say to the Department where my services may be most needed, but when I look at the state of affairs it impresses itself upon my mind that under existing circumstances the services of my squadron would be much more essential to the interests of the country on the coast than in this river." [8] The Mississippi was open at every point except Vicksburg, where it was a matter of taking a town, something that the Army ordinarily did by getting in the rear. No enemy rams or gunboats remained except the *Arkansas,* and that was up the Yazoo, "from where I do not think she will ever come forth," he opined. Therefore, why not leave Davis' fleet to seize Vicksburg and let him go to Mobile or Texas? This question would be answered by the *Arkansas.*

Two factors were bringing the ironclad out of the Yazoo. One was the alarming degree with which the water was falling, and the other was the desire to have her come out and fight rather than wait upstream until the Federals forced her to be burned.

The dropping level of the water was the more urgent of these. Isaac Brown, continuing the frantic pace with which he had operated since taking over command of the *Arkansas,* chose Lieutenant Charles W. Read, last heard from unloading wounded from a sinking ship at New Orleans, to determine the depth of the river and estimate how much longer the ironclad could safely remain at her location. The Yazoo, although narrow, had an excellent depth in some places, showing no bottom to a fifty-foot line. But it was a sluggish stream, and its water was exceedingly dark and brackish, contrasting sharply with the light yellow of the Mississippi. Mud and snags covered its bottom, and the stream was full of alligators, a colony that slept in the sun by day and fought and bellowed along the banks at night. Cranes screamed lonesomely above the trees, answered below by the angry hiss of the cottonmouth moccasin. Mosquitoes were a constant plague.

Read came back with a report that the *Arkansas* would have to move within a week. On this advice the vessel was taken twenty-two miles downstream to Liverpool Landing, where a huge raft blocked the channel, and it was there, above the flaming boats that marked the last of the River Defense Fleet, that she was seen by the two rams that had picked up the man in the skiff on the way up the Yazoo.

At Liverpool Landing, Brown continued his efforts to round up a crew. Gradually they came in—seamen, landsmen, firemen, soldiers, and boys—two hundred of them, a great many never having been on a ship before. They showed their excitement as they took their places on board the huge craft, all talking constantly of the day when she would try her might against the enemy. The *Arkansas* was a combination of the flat-bottomed boats of the West and the keel-built steamers designed for navigation in deeper waters. Her bow was sharp, and her stem tapered, permitting the waters to close readily behind her. She was one hundred and sixty-five feet long and drew eleven and a half feet of water. Most of her surface was covered with four-and-a-half-inch railroad iron, running horizontally, but only a thin coating of boiler iron lay over her quarter and stern. The wheel was within the shield, but the top of the pilothouse, two feet above the shield, was unfinished. She had two propellers, worked by separate engines, both new and built at Memphis. Her boilers were in the hold below the water line. Ten guns made up her armament—two eight-inch columbiads forward, two six-inch rifles astern, and two nine-inch Dahlgren shell guns, two six-inch rifled guns, and two thirty-two-pounder smoothbores in broadside. Brown referred to her as his "gun box."

A messenger reached Brown the last week in June, bringing a plea from Van Dorn, relayed through General Ruggles, for the ironclad to come out and sink the Union transports bringing troops to attack Vicksburg. As a prod, Van Dorn inserted in his message a thought that infuriated Brown: "It is better to die game and do some execution than to lie by and be burned up in the Yazoo." The naval officer immediately flung back: "I regret to find that by implication it is thought I would prefer burning the *Arkansas* in Yazoo River to hurling the vessel against the enemy. I have never required prompting in any duties that I have been called on to perform, and those who have been impatient spectators of my conduct here will not accuse me of having been idle. That I am not yet ready is because I could not perform impossibilities. The Montgomery fleet did not give me one man. They went from here paid off and with honorable discharges, though three months of their enlisted time had yet to run. This, too, when Montgomery knew the *Arkansas,* armed and with provisions and ammunition, was waiting for men. . . . Twenty-five men came today from Vicksburg, and I shall now soon have a crew. I trust we shall use our vessel creditably, and if the army will attack against the same odds as that which awaits me, the war will soon be over." [9]

On July 4, Brown took his ship up to Yazoo City on a trial run. As she floated she represented an outlay of seventy-six thousand, nine hundred and twenty dollars. She sat low in the water and was painted a dull brown to match the muddy surface of the river, and she was hard to see unless viewed against the green background of the vine-wrapped banks. After stopping overnight, he ran back the following day, expressing satisfaction with the performance of the vessel but alarmingly aware that she occasionally scraped bottom. He hurried at an even greater pace the final construction details, meanwhile dispatching three of his lieutenants to determine the problem involved in removing the raft. The man who had been in charge of placing it there said it could not be cleared away in a week, but Brown's aides came back with an estimate that they could open the channel in half an hour.

Brown on July 12 sent the mechanics ashore and replaced

them with his crew. The officers included would have been a tribute to any ship, for among them were men who already had distinguished themselves and, before the war was over, would bring even greater renown to their names. It was a lucky captain who could have under him such stalwarts as Henry Stevens, John Grimball, Arthur Wharton, Charles Read, George Gift, George City, and Dabney Scales. With these fighters at their posts, Brown slipped past the raft into deep water below Satartia Bar, five hours from the Mississippi. Anchoring, he gave his executive officer orders to begin training the men. It was the first training they had had.

At this period Farragut reminded Welles of the emergency that was slowly closing on him. "In ten days," he said in a telegram, "the river will be too low for the ships to go down. Shall they go down, or remain up the rest of the year?" [10] An answer would come a few days later: "Go down river at discretion. Not expected to remain up during the season." [11]

On the night of the 14th, two deserters who had slipped out of the Yazoo in a stolen skiff climbed the ladder of the first vessel they came to as they approached the Union fleet. It was the *Essex,* commanded by David Porter's brother, William. He took them into his cabin, and there they told him about a ram they continually referred to as the *Arkansas Traveler.* They related things that indicated Farragut was wrong in his estimate that the *Arkansas* would never come out of the Yazoo. They said she was at that very moment preparing to attack. Porter sent the men to Davis, and Davis directed them to Farragut. Soon a conference, with General Williams present, was called to talk about a reconnaissance up the river. No fear of the ironclad dominated or influenced the meeting. The two fleets were intact except for twelve mortar boats, which had left under David Porter for the James River on the 10th. The main purpose of the mission would be to look around. Three vessels were chosen for the assignment—the ironclad *Carondelet,* the ram *Queen of the West,* and the wooden gunboat *Tyler.*

Van Dorn at Vicksburg had much the same information as the deserters brought. This was because Lieutenant Read had been sent down by Brown to make a report, a mission that required the officer to ride horseback all night. Read returned with news from the general that there were thirty-seven Federal vessels in sight of Vicksburg, and that three miles from where he waited, Brown would reach the main channel. From there to Vicksburg he would have to run past sloops of war, gunboats, rams, and transports—all of the Union's two fleets except Porter's mortar boats tied up below the city. Read's intelligence was first-hand: he had actually stolen through vines and briars along the riverbank while at Vicksburg and had spied with a field glass.[12]

For days Van Dorn had been watching for the appearance of the ironclad. On July 14 he wired Jefferson Davis: "The *Arkansas* was to have been out this morning; have not heard yet why she has not made her appearance—look for her every moment." [13]

There was a reason for the ironclad's failure to appear as scheduled. After covering a third of the sixty miles from her starting point to where the Union fleet was anchored, it was discovered that faulty construction of the magazine had caused the powder on board to become dampened by steam from the engines. Brown ordered the vessel tied up at the bank of the river, at a clearing in the trees left by an old sawmill, and soon a crude drying process was under way. Every yard of canvas that could be spared was spread on shore, and over this, open to the sun's rays, the powder was scattered and frequently stirred. The plan worked. By nightfall the powder, dry enough to ignite, was returned to the magazine. But the *Arkansas* had been thrown hours behind schedule, and it was midnight before she reached Haynes' Bluff, a few miles from the Mississippi.

Brown allowed his men only three hours' sleep. It was still densely dark when they got under way again, and the vessel ran aground, causing more delay until it could be freed. He had hoped to reach the Mississippi by daylight, but this mishap upset his plans. The *Arkansas* chugged along, making six knots with the current. As the sky began to grow light in the east, he was able to see through the fog and smoke of burning cotton three enemy boats off the mouth of Old River, a lake formed by a cutoff. With his glass he was able to identify them: the ironclad gunboat *Carondelet* in the center, the ironclad ram *Queen of the West* on the starboard, and the gunboat *Tyler* on the portside. At six o'clock the *Carondelet* saw him, and a few minutes later the *Queen* ran past the gunboat, the men on board shouting, "The *Arkansas* is coming!," then proceeding on down the river.

The little fleet of Union vessels got under way at four o'clock that morning, after taking on board a number of sharpshooters from Williams' army. For all the ship commanders knew, it might have to run eighty miles upstream to the raft where the *Arkansas* last was seen. But they knew they would have no trouble spotting her, for it was common knowledge that her smokestack was seven feet in diameter, noticeably larger than those of other vessels.

As soon as he saw the enemy craft, Brown called his officers around him on the shield and addressed them in words they remembered: "Gentlemen, in seeking the combat as we now do, we must win or perish. Should I fall, whoever succeeds to the command will do so with the resolution to go through the enemy's fleet, or go to the bottom. Should they carry us by boarding, the *Arkansas* must be blown up. On no account must she fall into the hands of the enemy. Go to your guns!"

Lieutenant Gift, one of the officers assembled to hear Brown's words, described the scene that followed: "Many of the men had stripped off their shirts and were bare to the waist, with handkerchiefs bound round their heads, and some of the officers had removed their coats and stood in their undershirts. The decks had been thoroughly sanded to prevent slipping after the blood should become plentiful. Tourniquets were served out to division officers by the surgeons, with directions for use. The division tubs were filled with water to drink; fire buckets were in place; cutlasses and pistols strapped on; rifles loaded and bayonets fixed; spare breechings for the guns, and other implements were ready. The magazines and shell rooms forward and after were open, and the men inspected in their places." Executive Officer Henry Stevens, a deeply religious man, passed freely among the crew, directing and giving words of encouragement.

The *Arkansas* aimed for the *Carondelet*. Brown knew that the commander of the Union vessel was Henry Walke, a friend in the old navy and a messmate on a voyage around the world.

"When less than half a mile from us," Brown reported, "the *Carondelet* fired a wildly-aimed bow gun, backed around, and went from the *Arkansas* at a speed which at once perceptibly increased the space between us. The *Tyler* and ram followed this movement of the ironclad, and the stern guns of the *Carondelet* and *Tyler* were briskly served on us." [14]

The opening shot fired by the *Carondelet* came at 6:20 P.M., and was heard by the fleets gathered a few miles below on the Mississippi. The *Tyler* and the *Queen* joined in the firing, and soon there was an exchange from both sides.

On board the *Arkansas* an Irishman, curious to see what was happening, stuck his head out a broadside port. A ball that barely missed the ship decapitated him. Henry Stevens, happening to be nearby and fearing the effect of the corpse on the morale of the men, asked a sailor to help him throw the body overboard. The fellow cringed and turned away. "I can't," he said. "It's my brother." But Stevens got other help, and Walke took note of it, for in his report he recorded: ". . . One of his men was seen to be thrown overboard." [15]

The *Arkansas* was steered first to starboard and then to port, a flexible course that failed to confuse Union gunners. They found their mark, and they found Isaac Newton Brown, standing on the shield in plain view. One of their bullets caused a severe contusion on his head. A moment later a shot struck at his feet, penetrated the pilothouse and cut off a section of the wheel, mortally wounding Chief Pilot John Hodges and disabling the Yazoo River pilot, J. H. Shacklett. James L. Brady, a Missourian, took over in Hodges' place.

Brown moved near the hatchway, still in view. His marine glass fell at his feet, smashed by a bullet. And then a rifle ball struck him over the left temple, and he fell senseless down among the guns. His wounds were not as bad as they seemed, however. Before he could be taken to his cabin he regained consciousness, directed his helpers back to their posts, and climbed again to the shield.

Twice the *Arkansas'* flag was shot away. The first time it was raised by Dabney Scales amidst a rain of bullets. The second time Brown said for it to be left down.

Brown noticed the *Carondelet* was headed for shore, and he correctly assumed that her steering gear had been damaged. Her log later would reveal a major catastrophe: wheel ropes shot away, steam escape, exhaust, and cold-water pipes cut, and steam gauge shattered. "I gave the order 'hard aport and depress port guns,' " Brown related. "So near were we to the chase that this action of the helm brought us alongside, and our port broadside caused her to heel to port and then roll back so deeply as to take the water over her deck forward of the shield. Our crew, thinking her sinking, gave three hearty cheers. In swinging off we exposed our stern to the *Carondelet*'s broadside, and Read at the same time got a chance with his rifles. The *Carondelet* did not return the fire of our broadside and stern guns. Their ports were closed, no flag was flying, not a man or officer was in view, not a sound or shot was heard."

Brown stood in full view, within easy pistol range. This time he was the cat of the walk. He strolled to the after part of the shield and shouted across to his old friend, Walke. There was no answer. He knew there should have been, that not every man on board was disabled. Baffled, he ordered the *Arkansas* to move on. In his later report of this incident he dismissed Walke with a brief and simple statement: "We left him hanging onto the willows." [16]

Brown next turned his attention to the *Tyler.* The *Queen of the West* had already fled, and its action would bring serious charges against its commander, James M. Hunter, in the log of the *Tyler:* "Lieutenant Hunter . . . behaved in the most cowardly and dastardly manner, basely deserting us without making an attempt to bring his vessel in action." [17]

Brown hurried on after the fleeing *Tyler.* On reaching the Mississippi and seeing no other vessel in view, he took occasion to inspect his engine and fire rooms. There he found men suffering under a temperature of one hundred and twenty or more degrees. Crews were changed every fifteen minutes. But they persisted, for their minds were set on keeping the pressure at one hundred pounds, despite the holes that already were showing up in the smokestack.

On toward Vicksburg the chase continued. And soon, rounding a curve, Brown saw the test he faced. Just about the same time the Federals became conscious of his presence. In the U.S.S. *Benton's* log it was written: "At six-fifty Rebel ram *Arkansas* appeared, showing no colors." Ahead of her had come the *Tyler,* full speed on, engaged in a running fight.

The two Union fleets—Davis' and the part of Farragut's that had dashed past the Vicksburg batteries—lay ahead so close together they resembled a forest of masts and smokestacks. Included were rams, ironclads, gunboats, ordinary river steamers, and mortars—thirty-three of them. They had been lying there "like so many turtles on their backs," [18] and now they were all frantically preparing for attack. Because of Farragut's conviction that the *Arkansas* would never appear, they had been permitted to let their fires die down. Only one, the captured ram *General Bragg,* had up steam. The *Benton* was smoking furiously, but it did not have enough pressure to move. Along the right bank at their rear stretched a sea of tents as far as the eye could see.

Brown spoke to the Missourian Brady at the wheel: "Jim,

shave that line of men-of-war as close as you can, so that the rams will not have room to gather headway in coming out to strike us."

"As we neared the head of the line," Brown recorded, "our bow guns, trained on the *Hartford,* began this second fight of the morning, and within a few minutes, as the enemy was brought in range, every gun of the *Arkansas* was at work. It was calm, and the smoke settling over the combatants, our men at times directed their guns at the flashes of those of their opponents. As we advanced, the line of fire seemed to grow into a circle constantly closing. The shock of missiles striking our sides was literally continuous, and as we were now surrounded, without room for anything but pushing ahead, and shrapnel shot were coming on our shield deck, twelve pounds at a time, I went below to see how our Missouri backwoodsmen were handling their one-hundred-pounder columbiads. At this moment I had the most lively realization of having steamed into a real volcano, the *Arkansas* from its center firing rapidly to every point of the circumference, without the fear of hitting a friend or missing an enemy." [19]

The *Richmond* was the first vessel the ironclad passed. She was crippled by sickness, more than forty of her crew lying on deck, and these had to be removed before she could go into action.

Past the *Hartford, Iroquois, Oneida, Sciota,* and other famous ships of the Union Navy, all with a proud record in naval warfare, scurried the Confederate ironclad, in an action born of desperation in a setting of flood waters. From each she received a broadside, some of which took effect, others of which shattered or went awry. Back at them she fired, striking the *Hartford, Richmond, Iroquois,* and *Benton,* among others.

The *Sciota,* steam down, fired an eleven-inch gun loaded with a ten-second shell. This projectile struck the side of the *Arkansas,* glanced almost perpendicularly into the air, and exploded. Sharpshooters on the Union vessels opened with small arms against the ironclad's ports. One Southerner, in the act of sponging a gun, was seen to tumble out of the port, sponge and all, and enemy onlookers assumed he had been shot by a rifle ball.

The ram *Lancaster,* with barely enough pressure to move, edged out to stand in the way of the advancing ironclad. The entry in her log for the day began with defiance and ended with disaster: "Our anchor line was cut and we rounded to give her a little of our kind of warfare. When we were fully under way and about one hundred yards from her, a sixty-four-pound ball came through our bulwarks and eight feet of coal, cutting off three feet of our steam drum. Our head engineer, John Wybrant, was knocked down and badly scalded. Second Engineer John Goshorn, badly scalded, jumped overboard where he was shot in the water. George Boggs, assistant engineer, killed. Christopher Padlock, Company C, Sixty-third Illinois, missing. S. Casor and J. C. Alcorn, Sixty-third Illinois, wounded. John Dowell, cook, badly scalded. Died in a few minutes. Johnson, deck hand, scalded and leg hurt. Two died, names unknown, and perhaps others from scalding. Our pilot, Sylvester Doss, stuck to the wheel till he dropped from the platform. He being scalded inwardly, wounded in the left side, right shoulder broken and teeth all blown out. The *Lancaster* is disabled, having been shot all to pieces." [20]

A shell tore into the broken armor on the *Arkansas'* port side and exploded. Its fragments wiped out most of the crew at one of the bow guns, and wounded George Gift in the shoulder.

A charmed life saved Master's Mate John A. Wilson, commanding one of the *Arkansas'* broadside guns. Fragments of wood and iron nicked him in the arm and leg. A shell exploded in front of his gun port, killing his sponger and knocking flat the remainder of the crew. An eleven-inch solid shot tore through the ship's side above his gun, smashing in the bulkhead, killing two men and the powder boy, wounding three others, and cutting John's head and nose and knocking him senseless. This same shot went on across the deck, passed through the smokestack, killed eight of the gun crew Dabney Scales was commanding, and wounded three others. It finally struck the opposite bulkhead, broke in half, and fell on the deck, its damage done. Wilson was taken below, his wounds were dressed, and soon he was back at his gun.

The *Benton* finally got up enough steam to give chase. A Chicago *Times* correspondent was an eyewitness, and he wrote sarcastically of what he saw: "The small prodigy," he said of the *Arkansas,* "floated leisurely along, delivering her fire right and left among the astonished fogies, who were too much dumbfounded at her audacity to do much besides open their mouths and look, and finally rested under the protection of the friendly batteries. The *Benton* waked up then, and made a valorous rush at nothing, and got punctured for her pains. She might as well have rushed at the moon. She poked her nose around the corner, when there was nothing in the world to shoot at, and received the full fire of the batteries, and was glad enough to get back again, like a gander charging to protect his geese, after the danger is all past, and perchance running his nose into a hornet's nest." [21]

Commander Renshaw, below with what was left of Porter's mortar fleet—six mortar schooners and the ferryboat *Westfield* —was panicked by the happenings up the river. When he saw the *Arkansas* pushing through the mighty armadas of both Farragut and Davis, he acted in haste. One vessel that had gone aground, the *Sidney C. Jones,* was set afire; the others were rounded to and headed downstream.

It was ten minutes before nine when the *Arkansas* drew up at the Vicksburg wharf. Union officers would have difficulty explaining what she had done to them. "Her appearance was so sudden, and the steam of almost every vessel in the squadron was so low, or, in other words, so entirely unprepared were we," wrote Flag Officer Davis, "that she had an opportunity to pass without positive obstruction, though she was seriously injured by shot. The *Benton,* Lieutenant Commanding Phelps, got under way and followed her down to the point, but at her usual snail's pace, which renders anything like pursuit ludicrous." [22]

Waiting at the wharf to greet the *Arkansas* was an immense throng, and they cheered and shouted and whooped it up generally. A Chicago *Tribune* reporter described the scene: "Captain Brown, her commander, was standing on the deck, the blood running down his face. In response to the cheers of the crowd he removed his cap, disclosing a gap in his forehead, and said, 'Boys, I never was under fire before, but I am not so scared as I expected to be.' He afterwards stated in private conversation that, when he came in full view of the flotilla, he had no hope of ever seeing Vicksburg." [23]

None was more jubilant than Van Dorn. He had watched the engagement from the top of the courthouse in Vicksburg. In a report prepared as soon as the excitement died down he said that Brown "immortalized his single vessel, himself, and the heroes under his command by an achievement the most brilliant ever recorded in naval annals." [24]

As the *Arkansas* tied up, spectators pushed on board, but there they were stopped by a sight revolting even to the veteran warriors among them. The gun deck was a heap of mangled blood and flesh. Master's Mate Wilson, bandaged and groggy, looking at it, got a mental picture he afterward recorded: "Blood and brains bespattered everything, whilst arms, legs, and several headless trunks were strewn about. The citizens and soldiers of the town crowded eagerly aboard, but a passing look at the gun deck was sufficient to cause them to retreat hastily from the sickening spectacles within." And down below the wounded groaned and complained.

Brown looked up at the smokestack. It had sixty-eight perforations, and down in the engine room gauges showed that the steam had dropped to thirty pounds.

The *Arkansas'* captain lost no time in sending off a message of triumph to Secretary Mallory: "We engaged today from six to eight A.M. with the enemy's fleet above Vicksburg, consisting of four or more ironclad vessels, two heavy sloops of war, four gunboats, and seven or eight rams. We drove one ironclad vessel ashore, with colors down and disabled, blew up a ram, burned one vessel, and damaged several others. Our smokestack was so shot to pieces that we lost steam, and could not use our vessel as a ram. We were otherwise cut up, as we engaged at close quarters. Loss, ten killed, fifteen wounded, and others with slight wounds." And later: "We are much cut up, our pilot house smashed, and some ugly places through our armor." [25]

When the initial excitement of the morning had waned to some degree, Brown found time to get off a report to General Smith. He told of his encounter with the *Carondelet,* adding: "I wish it to be remembered that we whipped this vessel, made it run out of the fight and haul down colors, with two less guns than they had; and at the same time fought two rams, which were firing at us with great guns and small arms—this, too, with our miscellaneous crew, who had never, for the most part, been on board a ship or at big guns." [26]

Van Dorn in the meantime jubilantly wrote Jefferson Davis about the morning's activities, reporting that Brown had been wounded and the *Arkansas* had not been damaged except for a riddled smokestack. "Soon be repaired," he added, "and then, Ho! for New Orleans." [27]

Farragut, too, was writing. He penned a self-effacing message and got it off to Davis: "As the boy says, 'I told you so.' I blame myself for not going on board last night and begging you to send the ironclad vessels this morning. We were all caught unprepared for him, but we must go down and destroy him. I will get the squadron under way as soon as the steam is up, and run down in line—the ships inside in line with your ironclad vessels. We must go close to him and smash him in. It will be warm work, but we must do it; he must be destroyed. Porter can run down and anchor so as to fight the upper battery. We will go down in line of battle, and when past we will turn and come up again. Be sure to fire into the wharfboat. She is the place where they make their ordnance incendiary preparations." [28]

(*Above*) An artist's conception of the burning of the C.S.S. *Merri-mack* after she had been set on fire and abandoned by her crew in April, 1862. (*Below*) Bombardment of Island No. 10 in the Upper Mississippi was one of the fiercest of the war. Both gunboats and mortar boats participated in the attack.

(*Above*) Admiral David G. Farragut, a veteran officer in virtual retirement at the start of the war, left a Navy Department desk in New York to become one of the most colorful and distinguished naval officers in American history. (*Below*) His mortar flotilla commander, David D. Porter's fancy for gimmicks is portrayed in this artist's drawing of the trees he fastened as a disguise to the masts of the mortar boats used in bombarding the forts protecting New Orleans.

Mortars, such as this one on the deck of a schooner employed in the New Orleans campaign, dropped thousands of shells on Southern soil during the war.

This old wooden side-wheel steamer, the *Lexington*, was one of the first of the river gunboats fitted out during the war. It saw repeated action up and down the Mississippi and Tennessee rivers as the Union carried its war inland.

The C.S.S. *Alabama* (*below*), as Raphael Semmes (*left*), its commander, proudly launched her officially and started out on a cruise that took him to almost every part of the world except the Confederate States which he served.

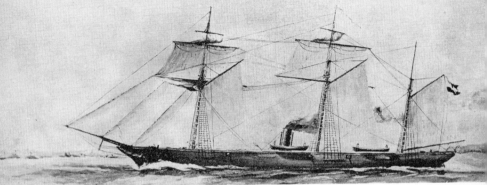

Blockade running became a flourishing business at one period of the war and was carried on by ships designed especially for the purpose. This rakish side-wheel steamer was captured by the Federals and converted into a blockader under the name of *Fort Donelson*.

In the C.S.S. *Florida,* a cruiser somewhat similar to the *Alabama,* John Newland Maffitt (*above*) formerly of the U.S. Navy, after twice running in and out of the blockade around the port of Mobile, Alabama, inflicted great losses on Union shipping. (*Below*) An artist has depicted the burning of one of his prizes, the *Jacob Bell.*

This small black leather satchel used by Captain Oscar B. Jolly, Union pilot, went through the entire Mississippi campaign. At present it is on display in the Museum of the Baltimore & Ohio Railroad at Baltimore, Maryland.

(*Above*) The U.S.S. *Hartford,* Admiral David Farragut's flagship, saw arduous service through the war. (*Below*) Transports carrying thousands of soldiers (*shown anchored in the background*) co-operated with warships in assaults on Southern ports as the North tightened its blockade.

At Vicksburg, in July, 1862, the *Arkansas* (*above*), under Isaac Newton Brown (*below*), defied an entire Union fleet, giving the Federal Navy one of its greatest scares of the war.

Admiral John A. Dahlgren, who succeeded Admiral Samuel Francis du Pont as head of the South Atlantic Blockading Squadron. President Lincoln leaned heavily on Dahlgren for advice.

U.S. Gunboat AROOSTOOK.

William M. C. Philbrick, carpenter's mate on the U.S.S. *Portsmouth,* often made sketches in his journal of the vessels anchored around him along the Lower Mississippi. (*Above*) The U.S. gunboat *Aroostook* as it appeared to him. (*Below*) The U.S. ironclad *Essex.*

The Battle of Port Hudson was one of the last of the Mississippi River campaign. Here are two artists' sketches of the dramatic scene of gunfire and burning ships that took place.

(*Above*) William (Dirty Bill) Porter, brother of David Dixon and one of the Union naval commanders engaged in the campaign to close the Mississippi. (*Right*) Henry Walke, one of the top Union naval officers.

Official U.S. Navy Photo

Library of Congress Photo

(*Above*) This print from a water color of the *Nashville* was made before she was captured by the Union and put to use against the Confederacy. (*Below*) An artist for the *Illustrated London News* made this drawing of the *New Ironsides* and two other ironclads as they fought the efforts of Southerners to break the blockade at Charleston, South Carolina, in 1863.

The Battle of Grand Gulf was another occasion in which the Union fleet ran past strong land batteries, delivering another blow that finally led to the closing of the Mississippi.

(*Right*) This sketch shows the crude design of some of the water mines, commonly referred to as torpedoes, planted in their harbors and rivers by the Confederates as they sought to offset the superior strength of the Union Navy.

No better example of Yankee ingenuity existed during the war than this device rigged up to cut trees below water to clear a channel. Men on the raft pulled the saw back and forth while the rig attached to the tree held it in position.

The capture of Fort Hindman at Arkansas Post, Arkansas, in January, '63, gave the Union a tremendous boost in morale. This artist's conception shows Federal troops charging in to take the huge fortification situated at the top of a cliff.

Confederate forts that held the steep riverbanks at Port Hudson, 1863.

An artist's conception of the Battle of New Orleans as the Confederate ram *Manassas* damages a Federal ship, April, 1862.

Admiral David Dixon Porter, commander of the mortar boats in the attack on New Orleans and later head of the fleet that closed the Mississippi River.

Porter's fleet ran past Vicksburg on more than one occasion. An artist captured this scene in April, 1863.

While the Federals were getting their plans in shape, the *Arkansas* was not to remain tied up in peace. During the morning and afternoon Union ships ran within range and fired at her. She answered them, occasionally with effect. One of these was the *Benton,* Davis' flagship. Farragut had crossed to her during the morning and was on board. He was "full of going down immediately to destroy the Rebel with his fleet—going off at once; couldn't wait a moment." The officers who conferred with him urged caution, and he finally settled for a run down the river to examine the new positions. The *Benton* got too close. A shot went through her shell room, wounding two men. Another struck her on the port quarter, knocked the cabin staterooms to pieces, came through the casemate covering of boiler iron, and killed a fireman. Her cutter and launch in tow astern were struck. After that she backed off and left the firing to the mortars, with Farragut still grumbling but consenting to wait until sundown.

Soon he sent out a terse general order to the fleet. Again, as in the run past the batteries on June 28, he ordered the vessels formed in two lines, with the ships on the inside next to the city and the gunboats on the outside. "They will keep their positions as far as practicable and have a good lookout for signals," he instructed, "but no one will do wrong who lays his vessel alongside of the enemy or tackles with the ram. The ram must be destroyed." [29] Davis consented to let Farragut take the *Sumter* from his fleet. Preparations were hurried but complete. Anchors were suspended from main yards and grapplings from the crossjack yards, ready to be dropped on the enemy.

Meanwhile crews on the Union vessels were kept busy putting up splinter nettings on the portside, the side that would be next to the city. Little tugs ran about carrying dispatches from the flagship to the various officers of the fleet. A council of war held on the *Hartford* confirmed Farragut's conclusion that the *Arkansas* had to be taken at all hazards.

At 12:40 P.M. the *Westfield* chugged up from below, towing three mortars. They were placed in position, the headmost being near the still smoldering wreck of the *Sidney Jones.* Shortly afterward they began firing, and were answered by the Vicksburg batteries, most of the shot falling short. Later in the afternoon the *Westfield* brought up two more.

A part of this time burial crews on both sides were kept busy. Brown had reported ten killed and fifteen wounded. The Federals lost twenty-seven men killed and wounded, including experienced engineers and pilots.

Heat throughout the day was suffocating. At 4:00 P.M. a violent thunderstorm broke, and for an hour rain poured in a welcome interlude that cleared and cooled the air.

General Signal 1218—"form order of sailing"—was given by Farragut at six-thirty. Ten minutes later the vessels were moving slowly. Captain Henry Bell of the Union fleet described the scene: "Getting dark, upper batteries very lively. In dark twilight saw the *Iroquois,* followed by a ship, turning the bend. All the batteries in full play, likewise the ram, her position being marked before dark, and her fire appearing low down on the water and pointed upstream. Darkness and smoke wrapped in all the vessels for a while till they began to emerge below. For a long interval the ram did not fire at all, and hopes sprang up that she had been rammed, but at the very close his fire opened again for one or two broadsides after our vessels had passed." [30]

The log of the *Hartford* gave this chronology of the attack: "At six P.M. the mortar boats opened fire on Vicksburg. At six-forty-five P.M. the fleet got under way and proceeded down the river. At seven-thirty beat to quarters for action. At seven-forty fired our bow gun. Steaming past the batteries at Vicksburg our port battery engaged with the enemy. At eight-twelve ceased firing. At eight-twenty came to below the city of Vicksburg." [31]

That in short was the story. Davis' fleet had remained above and maintained a crossfire. The *Brooklyn* and other boats below shelled from the opposite direction. In passing the batteries the column was headed by the *Iroquois* and *Oneida,* followed by the *Richmond,* the last of these with orders to run into the *Arkansas* with full force if she could be seen. Next came the *Wissahickon,* the *Sumter,* a vessel the Southerners had plated with railroad iron before they lost her to the Federals, the *Hartford,* and two gunboats. When they reached the point in the river just before coming in sight of the city, Rebels opened on them from the woods with muskets and artillery pieces. "Such a shower of missiles as came around us never was seen before," the journal of the *Richmond* noted. "We instantly sent a broadside of shrapnel into them; that was the last we heard from them." [32]

Vessels were allowed to drift with the current, some of them within thirty yards of shore. From them came broadside after broadside, and it was noted that the faster their fire the slower that from the batteries. But only one boat, the *Oneida,* saw the *Arkansas.* She was lying under the bank, her rust color providing almost complete concealment. "We must have missed her in the smoke," concluded the keeper of the *Richmond's* journal.

But the *Arkansas* did not entirely escape damage. "Unfit as we were for the offensive," related Brown, "I told Stevens to get under way and run out into the midst of the coming fleet. Before this order could be executed one vessel of the fleet sent a one-hundred-and-sixty-pound wrought-iron bolt through our armor and engine room, disabling the engine and killing, among others, Pilot William Gillmore, and knocking overboard the heroic Brady. . . . This single shot caused also a very serious leak, destroyed all the contents of the dispensary (fortunately our surgeon, Dr. Washington,[33] was just then away from his medicines), and, passing through the opposite bulwarks, lodged between the woodwork and the armor."

So close were the Union vessels at times that the gun crews on the *Arkansas* could hear the shells they fired crash through timbers of the enemy ships, followed by the groans of the wounded.

A little after 8:00 P.M. it was all over. But there still was no rest for the men on the *Arkansas*. Ahead of them was the necessity of sending ashore the second group of dead and wounded taken off the vessel that day.

At 9:00 P.M. Commander Bell arrived by small boat to talk with Farragut. Bell recorded the flag officer's mood: "He expressed deep mortification and vexation at his failure; said he had been dissuaded against his judgment by parties, naming them, from coming down in the morning and there had been unlooked-for delay in starting his fleet after signal was made. It is a terrible business and fraught with great danger. The ram must be attacked with resolution, of course, and be destroyed or she will destroy us. It would be an easy conquest but for the batteries which surround her on all sides." [34]

As the men in the fleet went to their hammocks that night, the reflection in the sky above Vicksburg was still glowing. It would not be there in the morning, for before dawn a heavy rain, driven by squalls of wind, began falling.

One of the first things Farragut did on the 16th was to send a report to Flag Officer Davis at the upper fleet: "We got down very well, except that it was just what I supposed from the first would be the case, that we started too late," he wrote. "It was so late when we got off the town that there was nothing to be seen of the ram. I looked with all the eyes in my head to no purpose. We could see nothing but the flash of the enemy's guns to fire at. It was remarkable that only five men were killed." [35] The *Winona* had been badly damaged and run ashore to keep her from sinking, he revealed, and the *Sumter* had received two shots that caused her to leak.

But Farragut's most urgent worry at the moment was coal, which he badly needed. "Do you not think you could bribe some of these river men to drift a coal barge down to me some dark night?" he asked Davis. "I would pay them liberally for the work if they will do it. I shall take another chance at the ram tonight, and I will continue to take chances or try to destroy her until my squadron is destroyed or she is. I see her now very plainly, but she must not have a chance to repair."

The ironclad could be seen steaming about the wharf at Vicksburg. In the late afternoon she ran across the river to the opposite bank and, turning around, chugged nonchalantly back. Van Dorn reported to Jefferson Davis during the day: "The *Arkansas* is the admiration of all, and her daring and heroic act has inspired all with the greatest enthusiasm. She is now being repaired and will soon be ready for orders." He also revealed that the reflection over Vicksburg the night before had come from a dwelling set on fire by a shell.[36]

A Marine named Oscar Smith, stationed on board the *Hartford,* was keeping a day-by-day record of events. Before going to his hammock the evening of the 16th he wrote in his diary: "The whole fleet was on the lookout for the ram last night and was very cautious. We kept watch at our guns. We can see the ram laying under the Vicksburg batteries getting up steam. We expected to go up today, but were disappointed. No fighting going on. I lay on deck part of the night at our guns. Nothing disturbed us during the night." [37]

Correspondence between the two Union fleets during the next twenty-four hours revealed a schism in the thinking of the flag officers. Farragut wrote Davis: "I find that we are peculiarly situated just now both in reference to the trust we have for the country and the great responsibility to which we would be held for any disastrous result from the escape of this ram and the evils attending such a misfortune. I can but think, as you have the ironclad boats, the country will expect you to cope with the ram better than my wooden vessels and will look to you for his destruction, but I desire to do my part and full share in this matter, and therefore have to propose that we make a combined attack upon him in Vicksburg, taking the fire of the batteries and looking only to the destruction of the ram, regardless of consequences to ourselves." He suggested that, if Davis would come down to Vicksburg before daylight, any day or hour of his choosing, the fleet from below would meet him there, and the two would battle both the forts and the *Arkansas*.

A stopgap reply to this message Davis returned by Farragut's courier next morning. An old friend of the Farragut family, he addressed his fellow flag officer as though he were a headstrong school boy: "You will not be surprised that having myself learned a lesson of patience at Fort Pillow, and witnessed its exercise at Columbus and Island No. 10, I should be unwilling to put in jeopardy all the great triumphs and interests which are placed in my keeping. I have watched eight rams for a month, and now find it no hard task to watch one. I think patience as great a virtue as boldness, and feel anxious, above all things, to save that portion of the Republic which lies adjacent to and dependent upon the Mississippi from an alarm which would interrupt its business, destroy its peace, and affect the public credit at home and abroad." [38] To this he added the cheering news that coal for Farragut, as well as a supply of cattle, had arrived from above in barges, but the barges were leaking badly. To try to float them past the batteries would only result in failure, he said, because they would be seen and captured. He suggested instead that both the fuel and the cattle be moved across the neck of land at night, a time that would not only provide concealment, but also relief from the oppressive heat.

Later in the day Davis dispatched a longer letter, justifying in greater detail his counsel of patience. He reminded Farragut that they had possession of the Mississippi River from its source to its mouth, with the exception of the short distance that separated the two fleets, that they had an efficient blockading squadron above and below, and that the military reinforcements necessary to capture and maintain possession of Vicksburg probably were on their way. He also pointed out that the *Arkansas* was harmless in her present position and would be more easily destroyed should she come out from under the batteries than while she lay under their protection. "I am as eager as yourself to put an end to this impudent rascal's existence," he added. "I have given a great deal of thought to it today. I have even laid down the plan of proceeding. We can not do anything until the *Essex* can get up steam, which will not be until tonight, if then, and we ought to have the *Sumter* above to do her ramming with effect." [39]

Similar advice was received by Farragut from closer at hand. His ship captains—De Camp, Alden, Renshaw, Bell, and others —heard him talk of running up to the *Arkansas* at night, and they cautioned against it, reminding that the Rebel vessel could not be seen, that the night would be dark, and the wind too fresh to work the ships in the current and narrow channel where they could not turn.

But Farragut could see no way to dispose of the ram except by attack. He was desperately short of coal and was growing short of ammunition, and he could see the *Arkansas* lying under the upper Vicksburg fort, with men "working like beavers on her." He suggested to Davis that "a few shells now and then would disturb the people at work on the ram very much."

Davis accepted the suggestion, and his mortars opened long-range fire on the ironclad. Every half hour or so the ram shifted to a new position. Farragut looked on jubilantly. "Do tell the captain that the shelling is magnificent," he wrote during the day. "They are falling all around him and I expect one to fall on board every moment." With his glasses he could see a long spar rigged across the deck of the Rebel vessel, and he assumed it was there for the purpose of getting out some heavy weight. The sight stimulated his impatience. "Now is the time to destroy him," he declared. "I wish to go at him tonight. He can not work his guns or steam, I think, and I can silence that fort in ten minutes and smash him in a few more."

In the late afternoon the batteries below Vicksburg opened on Farragut, throwing shells all the way across the river. The

Hartford, Brooklyn, and *Richmond,* main targets, called all hands to up anchor and dropped several hundred yards downstream.

It had been a strange day. During the morning all was quiet. The sun beat down mercilessly, burning all that stayed long under its rays. The men from the North suffered and mopped their faces, talking of the land they loved, and the Southerners made them all the more homesick by wafting across the water from the shade on shore an offering of band music. Then came the afternoon, and with it the bombardment from both directions.

Before going to bed that night Farragut steeled himself to the preparation of a departmental report. "It is with deep mortification," he wrote Secretary Welles, "that I announce to the Department that, notwithstanding my prediction to the contrary, the ironclad ram *Arkansas* has at length made her appearance and took us all by surprise. . . . It was a bold thing, and she was only saved by our feelings of security. She was very much injured and was only able to drift, or go at the slowest speed, say one knot, and with the current she got down to the forts of Vicksburg before any of us had steam up." [40]

In time this report brought an irate reply. "I need not say to you," Welles wrote, "that the escape of this vessel and the attending circumstances have been the cause of serious mortification to the Department and the country. It is an absolute necessity that the neglect or apparent neglect of the squadron on that occasion should be wiped out by the capture or destruction of the *Arkansas,* which I trust will have been effected before this reaches you." A similar message was addressed to Davis. But Welles' words were wasted, for they did not reach the addressees until after the campaign had ended.

No fires could be noticed on board the *Arkansas* the morning of the 18th. She lay snugly alongside the wharf boat, and wagons came and went from her sides frequently. During the morning Southerners began throwing up works on a hill a mile and a quarter from Farragut's fleet. Bell fired six rifle shots at them without effect. Davis' mortars continued to fire from the upper fleet.

Farragut on this day answered Davis' messages of caution. He admitted the impropriety of risking the advantages they had gained, but cited the risk of waiting and of being caught "in a position unable to move at pleasure either for want of room, steam or other cause." In waiting for the arrival of military reinforcements, he warned of the threat from suffering and sickness. As for the *Arkansas* being harmless in her present position, he advised that she would not remain that way as soon as she was repaired, and also that she could cause the Union ships a great expenditure of fuel. And the two fleets, he reminded, were waiting under different circumstances. Davis' was open to a downstream supply of stores from above, while his had to be brought upstream five hundred miles, past bluffs on which Southerners were waiting with loaded guns. "Hence the difference in our feelings," he concluded, "and I suppose it accounts in great measure for the difference in our instructions, for while yours advise the prudential course, mine advise exactly the opposite, 'that great ends are only to be attained by great risks,' etc." [41]

Later in the day, influenced by information brought by three men who came in from Vicksburg, he wrote Davis that the *Arkansas'* prow had been damaged, that the captain had been wounded over the eye and might lose it, and that the pilot and engineer had been killed. "Yesterday," he added, "they had to force men on board of her at the point of the bayonet. . . . Oh, if I had only known her position I could have destroyed her so easily, but I knew it was a failure as soon as I saw that we could not get off before we did. They say she will try to run the blockade down the river and go to Mobile. These men all say that is the confident talk on shore. Now is the time, while she is making her repairs, to destroy her." [42]

Farragut, the senior officer, was becoming more and more a problem to Davis. Only by the men around him was the veteran restrained "from taking his vessels up under these formidable batteries for the destruction of the one ram." [43]

The mortar and rifle fire was kept up through the 19th and on into the night. Crews on the *Arkansas* continued to work, but the shelling was fraying their nerves. Brown gave an indication of the effect with the observation: "I know of no more effective way of curing a man of the weakness of thinking that he is without the feeling of fear than for him, on a dark night, to watch two or three of these double-fused shells, all near each other, and seeming as though they would strike him between the eyes." [44]

Farragut continued to show impatience. He suggested sending William Porter against the Rebel ram in the *Essex,* a vessel fresh from the docks and with a new crew. "Let me hear from you as early as possible," he urged, "or I shall go in for the attack. The anxiety is too great to keep up." [45] Davis replied on the 29th: "I have come to the final determination, from which, indeed, I have hardly once deliberately departed, that it would be an inexcusable sacrifice of the greatest of the country to abandon the possession of the Upper Mississippi, and that this would be the unavoidable consequence of an attack, such as you propose." He mentioned his responsibility for the safety of General Curtis' army, that the Confederates were reported to be building boats which might give them control of the river from Vicksburg up, and that sickness was cutting into his personnel. He reported that one hundred of his one hundred and thirty mortar men were sick, that the sickness on some vessels was disabling from one to two to one in each four of their crewmen. Sometimes ten to fifteen died in one night, and General Williams did not have enough well men to take care of the sick ones. But he consented to send Farragut the *Essex,* reminding that he then would have "my largest ironclad boat and most powerful ironclad ram." [46]

July 20 was a Sunday, and the day was observed with divine services on board the Federal vessels: no fighting, just preparations for a new attack on the morrow. During the afternoon the crew of the *Hartford* gathered around the capstan, and the flag officer made a speech. "The Rebel ram lies at Vicksburg," he said at one point in his discourse. "She must be destroyed. To destroy her I want you to go to work with heart and hand. As soon as she is destroyed, we will go out of the river into salt water." [47]

During the day Farragut dispatched another report to Welles, explaining that his efforts were greatly handicapped by sickness. Williams' army, he said, had nearly a third of its members on the sick list, but this proportion was not nearly as bad as that of the Rebel army in the vicinity. "Refugees inform us," he reported, "that all the churches, meetinghouses, and barns are filled with sick, and they have no medicines. In shelling the town we blew up the apothecary's shop, which contained all the medicines they had in this vicinity." [48] And in closing he mentioned a worry that was constantly on his mind: the rate at which the Mississippi was falling.

Meanwhile Farragut got support for his idea of an immediate attack. It came from Alfred Ellet. The ram fleet commander, citing the "pernicious influence upon the confidence of our crews" caused by the presence of the ram, suggested that some risk should be incurred to insure her destruction. "I will myself command that boat that I shall select to run the *Arkansas* down, with a very small but carefully chosen crew," he offered.[49]

The 21st was one of the hottest days of the year. Added to the discomfort of heat was the monotony of guns roaring constantly in the upper fleet. Farragut, mopping and storming, needled Davis some more, asking in a message: "Do you think it necessary for us to go up and attack her, or will you drive her down to the lower forts?" Davis, consenting to an attack against his better judgment,[50] answered: "We shall either drive her down to you, destroy her, or force her to come up the river; in the latter case, we are ready for her." As soon as he received this message, Farragut arranged to be transported across the neck of land for a conference with Davis.

The meeting was held on board the *Benton*. Present was William Porter, and he consented readily to the suggestion that he attack the *Arkansas* with the *Essex*. Procedure was worked out: at four o'clock next morning the two fleets would open a bombardment, while the *Essex,* supported from above by the *Queen of the West,* would push in, strike the ironclad, and then fall behind the lower fleet. The *Sumter* would be held below in readiness to ram the Rebel vessel as soon as it was driven down. That afternoon Farragut directed five of his mortars to take position so they could shell the Rebel vessel with solid shot at 3:00 A.M.

Brown, moving about on the *Arkansas,* was distressed by the condition of his crew. He notified Van Dorn that some of his officers and all of the crew but twenty-eight were in the hospital. He was promised men from the Army next day.

Farragut got little sleep that night. At two o'clock next morning he informed Captain Bell of Davis' promise to drive the *Arkansas* down or destroy her, and directed him to await the signals.

Porter, dressed in a red jacket, duck trousers and a straw hat, moved on schedule, trailed by the *Queen of the West,* commanded by Alfred Ellet. As Porter passed the *Benton,* Flag Officer Davis hailed him and wished him success.

I now pushed on, according to my understanding of the program [he later reported], and precisely at half past four A.M. the enemy's upper batteries opened upon me, but I heard no response at this time from our fleets. I arrived at the ram, delivered my fire, and struck her; the blow glanced, and I went on the river bank with the bows of the ship, where I lay ten minutes, under three batteries of heavy guns. I backed off and loaded up. The enemy had drawn up three regiments of sharpshooters and several batteries of field pieces, ranging from six-pounders to twenty-four-pounders. I found it impossible, under the circumstances, to board the Rebel boat, though such was my original intention.

After I delivered my fire at but five feet from the ram, we distinctly heard the groans of her wounded, and saw her crew jumping overboard. She did not fire a gun after we had delivered ours, and I have since seen in the Rebel papers that they admit a loss of eighteen killed and thirty-five wounded. We knocked a very large hole in her side.

At this time I began to look for aid from the fleets, but without result.[51] I ordered the pilots to get the *Essex'* head upstream, with the intention of holding on until the lower fleet came up, and then make another attack on the ram. At this time I was under the guns of three batteries, one of which was not over one hundred feet off. A heavy ten-inch shot from the nearest battery struck my forward casemate, about five feet from the deck, but fortunately did not penetrate. A rifle seven-and-a-half-inch shot from the same battery struck the casemate about nine feet from the deck. It penetrated the iron, but did not get through, though so severe was the blow that it started a four-inch plank two inches and eighteen feet long on the inside. A conical shell struck the casemate on the port side as we were rounding to, penetrated the three-quarter-inch iron, and came half way through the wooden side. It exploded through, killing one man and slightly wounding three. A small piece grazed my head and another piece tore the legs off the first master's pantaloons.

I had now been under fire for upward of an hour, and thirty minutes of the time from eighty feet to one hundred yards of the enemy's heaviest batteries. I still looked for the arrival of the lower fleet, but saw nothing of it. I held on for a short time longer, but the enemy began to fire with such rapidity and we were so close that the flashes of his guns through my gun holes drove my men from the guns. At last, through the smoke, I saw the lower fleet nearly three miles off and still at anchor. Seeing no hope of relief or assistance, I now concluded to run the gantlet of the enemy's lower batteries and seek an anchorage below the fleet. I therefore reluctantly gave the order to 'put her head downstream'; but I was determined to be in no hurry. They had now plenty of time to prepare, and so rapid was their fire that for half an hour the hull of this ship was completely enveloped in the heavy jets of water thrown over her by the enemy's shot, shell, and rifle balls.[52]

Brown had on hand only enough men to fight two of his guns, but with the aid of the officers he was able to man all that could be brought to bear. The *Essex* and the *Arkansas* actually had collided, but without damage to either. "With a view perhaps to avoid our bow guns," Brown concluded, "the *Essex* made the mistake of running into us across the current instead of coming head-on with its force. At the moment of collision, when our guns were muzzle to muzzle, the *Arkansas'* broadside was exchanged for the bow guns of the assailant. One shot killed eight and wounded six of our men.[53] The *Essex* drifted clear of the *Arkansas* without again firing . . . and steamed to the fleet below." [54]

No mention was made by Brown or Porter of the *Queen of the West,* an extreme slight, it would appear from Ellet's report. He made it seem that his vessel had launched the attack alone. "I regret to say," he related, "that owing to a failure upon the part of the parties who were to cooperate with me in the attack, from some cause that is yet unexplained to me, I did not succeed, as I expected, in destroying the *Arkansas.* I did succeed, however, in striking her a very severe blow, and no doubt inflicted considerable injury upon her, but being unsupported by the *Essex* and *Sumter,* as I had been led to expect, and exposed alone to the united fire of all the upper batteries, I was obliged to draw off without accomplishing the full result anticipated."

He said the *Arkansas* occupied a very unfavorable position for his attack. "I could not reach her vulnerable side," he explained, "without rounding partly, and thus losing much headway. The consequence was that she failed to receive the effects of a full blow. In making my retreat, most unfortunately for me, our gunboats had retired, and I had the undivided attention of all the enemy's batteries and sharp-shooters that lined the river bank; the consequences were that the *Queen* was completely riddled with balls and very much damaged." [55]

Farragut also made no mention of Ellet. He had watched below, unable to see anything because of the bend in the river until the attackers reached the *Arkansas,* and he noted that forty-nine minutes passed from the time of the first shot until the *Essex* rounded to at his side. "I regret to say to you," he wrote Davis, "how much I was disappointed and chagrined at the result of Porter's fight this morning. It appears that in the first place he missed striking the ram by their skillful

management of her in loosing their shorefast, whereby Porter
slipped by her and ran ashore. He delivered his three bow
guns, but with what effect he does not know, but takes it for
granted that they went through the ram. This was all he was
able to do, and from this time he received the concentrated
fire of all the forts above and of the ram, which, although it
has not done him any very great injury for the moment, it has
started his casemates, and a few more shot of the same kind
would, in my opinion, destroy his protection." [56]

But Davis, in his report, gave special praise to Ellet, and
said the *Queen* struck the *Arkansas* with sufficient force to do
her some injury.[57] This was corroborated in the account of
the fight given by George Gift of the *Arkansas* in a letter
home. He told of the firing at the *Essex* as she approached.
"Her plan was to run into and shove us aground," he related,
"when her consort, the *Queen of the West,* was to follow and
butt a hole in us. . . . Brown determined to foil her tactics.
Slacking off the hawser, he went ahead on the starboard
screw, and thus our sharp prow was turned directly to her. A
collision would surely have cut him down and left us uninjured. . . . In an instant the enemy was alongside, and his
momentum was so great that he ran aground a short distance
astern of us. His only effort was to get away from us. He
backed hard on his engines and finally got off. . . . The
Queen of the West was now close to us. Brown adopted the
plan of turning his head to her also. She came into us going at
an enormous speed. . . . Her prow made a hole through
our side and caused the ship to career and roll heavily, but we
all knew in an instant no serious damage had been done. . . .
She ran into the bank astern of us, and got the contents of
the stern battery, but . . . was soon off into deep water." [58]

Van Dorn, witness to the entire affair, took some delight in
wiring Jefferson Davis: "An attempt made this morning by two
ironclad rams to sink the *Arkansas.* The failure so complete
that it was almost ridiculous. Several men were, however,
killed by a shot entering one of her ports. Canal will be a

failure. Nothing can be accomplished by the enemy unless they bring overwhelming numbers of troops. This must be anticipated." [59]

Porter's futile attack was the finale for Farragut. He now looked southward, his gaze directed to the falling water and increasing number of sick, as well as to a telegram from the Navy Department telling him to fall back on New Orleans. Williams already was loading his army on the transports, and most of his soldiers, especially those assigned to work on the canal, went gladly, for they recognized that water would not run uphill, and that was the impossible situation that developed as the level of the Mississippi continued to drop. The fever had almost decimated his army. Of three thousand, two hundred men, two thousand, four hundred were dead or in the hospital. Moreover, the Southerners now became more jubilant than ever. At 3:35 A.M. on the 23rd, firing was heard downriver, and at daylight the steamer *Ceres,* sent to return to their homes the Negroes who had been at work on the canal, reappeared, a dead Army captain on board, and reported she had been fired into by batteries on shore. Davis opened with his mortars at six o'clock and dropped shells on Vicksburg for two hours. The batteries in the city answered occasionally, and at 10:00 A.M. the *Arkansas* ran up the river out of sight. A conference on board the *Hartford* reached a definite conclusion: the big ships must go, leaving Davis behind with the upper fleet's boats of lighter draft. In the afternoon the *Arkansas* reappeared and slowly edged into her berth.

At 6:00 A.M. on the 24th the *Arkansas* could be seen lying against the bank in a cove, her head downstream, having shifted her berth during the night. On shore the Southerners were putting on a new burst of activity, planting guns and throwing up mounds of dirt. At 1:30 P.M. the *Hartford* began nosing slowly down the river. She was next to last in a line of ships that included the *Westfield, Sciota, Pinola, Iroquois, Oneida, Richmond,* and *Brooklyn.* Some of the vessels fired parting shots at Vicksburg before leaving.

Davis, higher up the river, prepared for a movement in the opposite direction. He was disappointed with developments. It had been his plan to blockade Vicksburg on both sides after Farragut left, but departure of the army under Williams put an end to this. Besides, Farragut took along two of Davis' ships, the *Essex* and the *Sumter,* leaving him the *Benton, Cincinnati, Louisville,* and *General Bragg,* and sickness was making a "sudden and terrible havoc" with his people. He took upon himself solely the responsibility of moving up to Helena, Arkansas, where he would be met by the army of General Curtis, driven back upon the Mississippi.

Farragut was leaving, but not in an aura of glory. One of his major critics, Ledyard Phelps, commander of the *Benton,* got off another long letter to Andrew Foote in which he said: "The whole thing was a fizzle. Every day we heard great things threatened only to realize fizzles. I fear that both S. P. Lee and Palmer had too much influence with Commander Farragut in the matter of the attacks on the *Arkansas,* but that does not excuse his 'great talk and little action.' I tell you, my old commander, I would rather have your little finger at the head than he who led the attack at New Orleans." [60]

Behind him, according to Van Dorn's account, Farragut was leaving a casualty list among the Southerners of twenty-two dead and wounded. Not a gun had been dismounted and only two temporarily disabled.[61]

Farragut pushed on to New Orleans. After arriving there on the 28th he wrote in a report to Secretary Welles: "I do not know whether the ironclad ram *Arkansas* will attempt to come down the river, but if she ever gets under the guns of one of my ships I hope to give a good account of her, but to attack her under the forts with the present amount of work before us would be madness." [62]

July ended in an unfriendly atmosphere for the invaders. The last night of the month was one they would not soon forget and that many would write about. Its hours were sleepless, for mosquitoes came in swarms. "We had to walk the decks to keep the mosquitoes from eating us alive," it was recorded in the journal of the U.S.S. *Richmond.*

Mosquitoes swarmed over the deck of the *Arkansas,* but they failed to stop the work that was going on there. Brown had gone to Grenada and, upon arrival, was taken ill. Henry Stevens, who succeeded him in command of the ironclad, sent him a telegram announcing that Van Dorn wanted the vessel moved downstream to aid General John C. Breckinridge in an attack on Baton Rouge. Brown wired back for the ship not to be moved until he returned.

But Stevens was under pressure from men of higher rank than Brown, and he had little choice in the matter. Van Dorn insisted. Stevens referred the decision to Commander Lynch, who instructed him to go to Breckinridge's aid.

Stevens hurried repairs as rapidly as possible. The *Arkansas'* main trouble was in her engines, damaged in the collision with the *Queen of the West* on July 22. Chief Engineer George City was still in the hospital, and his place had been taken by a volunteer from the Army, a man who was a willing worker, but who had never had experience with a screw vessel or short-stroke engine. This complicated matters, and it gave Stevens additional cause to worry.

At 2:00 A.M. August 3, Stevens ordered the lines of the *Arkansas* cast off, and she chugged away from the wharf, edged out into the channel, and headed southward. Her armor had been increased during her stay at Vicksburg. Her deck was now plated with iron, and more cotton had been compressed in her bulwarks. As she moved downstream her engines seemed to be working satisfactorily. Her crew was not complete, but it was ample. Word of her secret mission had reached the men in the hospitals, and some of them had ignored their injuries and hurried on board, their bandages much in evidence.

All that day she moved, making a good eight knots. It was hot, and the men stood on deck and talked about the ruins they could see along the riverbank on both sides. Grand Gulf was a heap of ashes, without a living thing in sight. Night came on again, and the ironclad still maintained her speed. But shortly before midnight a strange noise sounded from the engine room, and soon the engines were silent. The engineer sent word that the starboard engine had broken down and that the vessel would have to be tied up for repairs. Throughout the night they worked, and at eight o'clock next morning she started out again, twenty-two miles from Baton Rouge.

The fighting at Baton Rouge started the morning of the 5th, Breckinridge driving back the Federals and killing General Williams with a bullet through the heart.[63] The *Arkansas* at the time was only eight miles away, but her engines again were stilled. Once more Stevens had tied up at the bank and got his blacksmith forges in operation. The "wrist," or connecting rod, was broken, reported the engineer, and another would have to be forged.

Men worked frantically, and later in the day the engines were reported repaired but unreliable. She steamed around a bit, took on coal at a nearby plantation, and then the engines broke down again, more seriously than ever. Repairs on them were made during the night, and at nine-thirty the next morning four Union vessels, the *Essex, Cayuga, Katahdin,* and *Sumter,* were seen coming up the river. Stevens called his officers into conference: the decision was to attack.

"We had not steamed any distance when the port engine broke," Master's Mate Wilson wrote in his diary. "The ship was then headed for the shore, and in a few moments her starboard engine suddenly gave way and she drifted toward the enemy in a helpless condition, they opening fire upon us. Finally, however, she grounded near the river bank, stern downstream, and Lieutenant Read answered their fire with his stern rifles, but the enemy having halted, the fire of our guns was ineffective.

"The *Essex* continued to shell us at long range, but with no effect, her missiles falling short and out of range. Our engines were now beyond repair. In our present condition the ship was immovable and her guns could not be brought to bear upon the Federal fleet. Under the circumstances there was no alternative left Lieutenant Stevens but to destroy the *Arkansas* to prevent her falling into the hands of the enemy." [64]

Tears could be seen on his cheeks as he ordered the crew ashore. They went with small arms and ammunition and marched off toward the interior of the country. Behind on board, to aid Stevens in the destruction of the vessel, remained Read, Midshipmen Bacon, Scales, and Talbott, Gunner Travers, and Master's Mate Wilson. Engine machinery was broken up with axes and hand grenades, one of which exploded prematurely and burned Stevens' hands badly. Wardroom bedding was fired in several places. Cotton bales in the inside bulkheads between the guns were cut open and set afire. Magazines were opened, cartridges scattered about, and loaded shells placed on the gun deck between the guns. The guns were loaded and run out. Then the ironclad was abandoned, the men leaving her with nothing more than their side arms and the clothing on their backs.

The *Arkansas* was glorious even in death. She gradually drifted down toward the Union fleet, her guns discharging as the fire reached them. Puzzled by this turn of affairs, the *Essex* and her consorts turned downstream and gave her a wide berth. For an hour she floated, and then, a few minutes after noon, blew up with a terrific explosion.[65]

"It was beautiful," Stevens tearfully recalled, "to see her, when abandoned by commander and crew and dedicated to sacrifice, fighting the battle on her own hook." [66]

Only a short distance away at Pontchatoula, nearest railroad approach to Baton Rouge, was Isaac Brown. On receiving Stevens' telegram he had directed that he be taken to the railway station, and there he threw himself on the mail bags of the first passing train. For one hundred and thirty miles, until he reached Jackson, Mississippi, he did not move. There he applied for a special train to take him to Vicksburg, only to learn from the telegraph operator that the *Arkansas* already had moved downstream. He then turned his course in the direction of Baton Rouge.

What a career his ship had had! It lasted only twenty-three days, but as one observer put it: "It included so much action that there probably never was another vessel that averaged anything like as much fighting per day as did the *Arkansas*." [67]

Farragut, hearing that the ironclad had left the batteries at Vicksburg, hurried up from New Orleans, arriving at Baton Rouge on the 7th. "It is one of the happiest moments of my life that I am enabled to inform the Department of the destruction of the ram *Arkansas,* not because I held the ironclad in such terror, but because the community did," he soon wrote in an official dispatch. He followed this up with a gleeful letter home: "My delight would have been to smash her in *Hartford* style. . . . Although Bill Porter did not destroy her, he was the cause, and thought his shells did the work; for they would hardly have destroyed her unless he had made the attack. I insist that Porter is entitled to the credit of it. He said to his officers, 'That fellow keeps me uneasy and, after breakfast tomorrow, I will go up and destroy him.' And he did, to the best of his ability." [68]

Though jubilant over the destruction of the ironclad, Farragut went back downstream with no mercy in his heart for Southerners. When residents of Donaldsonville, Louisiana, fired on his ships, he burned hotels and wharf buildings in the town, as well as the dwelling of one Phillippe Landry, said to be a leader of guerrillas.[69] This happened just as he received notice that Congress had created the new rank of rear admiral and that he was to be its first recipient.

For sixty-seven days the Federals had remained in front of Vicksburg. During that time the efforts of two powerful fleets had been foiled, and a land force of three thousand, two hundred had been held at bay. It was estimated that from twenty thousand to twenty-five thousand shells were thrown at the city. Dead and wounded totaled in the dozens, destruction in the millions. And all of this had been offset largely by a combination of sickness and an ironclad that General Curtis said was "a terror to a divided flotilla." [70] The fleets parted, opening the Mississippi from Vicksburg to Port Hudson again to the Confederates and giving them new opportunity to build fortifications along the riverbanks.

The ironclad that Isaac Brown had built with such diligence was not only a memory; she was a live topic of conversation. During her last twenty-four hours Gustavus Fox paid her tribute in a letter to Admiral Du Pont: "Look at the course of the *Arkansas* out West. She passed down through both squadrons and killed more of our people than we lost in the capture of New Orleans." [71]

Ten days after the *Arkansas* disappeared from the waters of the Mississippi, Secretary Mallory prepared a letter to Commander Bulloch in England, announcing: "Intelligence has just reached me of the loss of the *Arkansas*. This is a severe blow and one which the late glorious career of this ship hardly enables me to bear with equanimity." [72] Then he prepared a report to the Confederate Congress. In it he told of the fate of the ironclad, and concluded: "Naval history records few deeds of greater heroism or higher professional ability than this achievement of the *Arkansas*." [73]

9

"He died quietly"

JUNE-AUGUST 1862

The James River, where it emptied into Chesapeake Bay, was a placid, brownish-yellow in the burning sunshine of the hot June day. The breezes of yesterday were gone, and in their wake a smothering stillness clamped down over land and water, sticky and stifling, keeping movement of man and beast to a minimum. Under the penetrating rays of the sun, even healthy, conditioned veterans in Federal uniform were beginning to mutter and curse. In an atmosphere of summer at its peak, they talked of the heat and the sun and the insects, enjoying in relaxed language their God-given privilege of griping, in which they found relief from the constant sight of wounded and sick hauled in for treatment at the crowded, dirty, riverbank camp in which they had their quarters.

Dominating this center was a line of wall tents, each with a label—"Office of Quartermaster's Department," "Telegraph Office," "Post Office," "Office of Land Transportation," "Harbor Master," and on down the miscellany of agencies needed to run a concentration of military forces. In one tent, under heavy guard, hovered the sweaty and miserable prisoners, brought in the day before. Along the bank, ordnance and forage barges were shoved in against one another, all with their noses toward land. A few big guns were scattered on shore, near piles of shot and shell, newly landed and baking in the relentless sun. The entire meadow, stretching out in a flatness peculiar to the area, was crowded with orderlies holding horses, dirty soldiers standing in groups, idlers, fatigue parties at work, sentries strolling back and forth, quartermaster's people, white and black, all busy, and a hundred army wagons loading with forage and biscuit boxes from the barges.

Such scenes as these were common to Union sailors on duty along the streams of eastern Virginia in the summer of '62. The big push was on. The *Merrimack* had been driven to destruction. The *Monitor* had learned it could not get to Richmond by water. And now the army of General McClellan was driving inland from the coast, dead set on getting there by land. Stand back Navy: your task is to bring supplies and take care of the sick and wounded.

From around a curve chugged the little gunboat *Yankee,* five small Rebel craft she had just captured in the Rappahannock stringing behind her. Avoiding the tugs and tenders flying back and forth, she drew up to the bank and dropped anchor near the camp. Soon the tiny schooner *Elizabeth* drifted alongside and began taking on stores. Nearby waited the *Wilson Small,* a boat of light draft fitted up as a hospital, ready to run up creeks and bring down the disabled. Beyond it lay the *Daniel Webster,* hospital transport de luxe, complete even to enamel slop jars.

A surgeon sat on the *Daniel Webster* writing a letter. His pencil moved slowly. He had no reason to hurry, for no patients were on board. "In sight are the abandoned Rebel quarters at Shipping Point, now used as hospitals by one of our divisions," he recorded. "A number of log huts finely built, but on low and filthy ground, surrounded by earthworks, which are rained on half the time and fiercely shone on the other half, and from which are exhaling deadly vapors all the time, a death place for scores of our men who are piled in there, covered with vermin, dying with their uniforms on and collars up—dying of fever."

June days passed slowly, most of them dripping with sticky heat. On a Sunday the *Ocean Queen,* hard aground where she had lain since the terrifying days of the *Merrimack,* was approached by two stern-wheel steamboats, one on each side. It was raining hard. A surgeon hurried out to investigate, his small boat making its way through the many vessels tied at the wharf. He found both of the newly arrived vessels loaded with sick and wounded from regiments that had been fighting the night before around Williamsburg. Sailors on board said these men had been sent during the night by ambulance to the shore of Wormley's Creek. Many more were still there, they added, lying on the ground in the rain, without food or attention. The surgeon objected. He could not take them on the *Queen.* He pointed out that she was a mere hulk, without beds, bedding, food, or attendants.

Crewmen on the stern-wheelers did some protesting, too. Some of these patients were very ill, they said, and some were dying. Many were in delirium, twenty-four hours without nourishment, racked by typhoid, wet from exposure, bruised by the motion of the ambulances over frightful corduroy roads through the swamps. The surgeon threw up his hands, stationed two ship's officers at the gangway with instructions to let no one come on board until he returned, and hurried ashore. He rounded up help, including a civilian doctor, and rushed back, to find that every patient who could walk had been permitted to come on board.

By noon of the next day conditions on the *Queen* had improved. The cabins and upper steerage had been divided into five wards for the bad cases, each having a surgeon, two ward masters, and four nurses. Assistant nurses, servants, convalescent soldiers, and contrabands stood by to aid. There were typhoid cases and they needed ventilation. Bulkheads were cut away and wind sails rigged to let in air. Over the rest of the ship, organized into squads of fifty each, lay the men assigned to the sixth ward—those with hernias, rheumatism, bronchitis, and the lame and exhausted.

Three days went by. A woman nurse on the *Ocean Queen* wrote about them later when things were quieter:

It seems a strange thing that the sight of such misery, such death in life, should have been accepted by us all so quietly as it was. We were simply eyes and hands for those three days. Great, strong men were dying about us; in nearly every ward someone was going. Yesterday one of the students called me to go with him and say whether I had taken the name of a dead man in the forward cabin the day he came in. He was a strong, handsome fellow, raving mad when brought in, and lying now, the day after, with pink cheeks and peaceful look. I had tried to get his name, and once he seemed to understand, and screeched out at the top of his voice, "John H. Miller," but whether it was his own name or that of some friend he wanted I do not know; we could not find out. All the record I had of him was from my diet list: "Miller—forward cabin, port side, number 119. Beef tea and punch."

Last night Doctor Ware came to me to know how much floor room we had. The immense saloon of the aft cabin was filled with mattresses so thickly placed that there was hardly stepping room between them, and as I swung my lantern along the rows of pale faces, it showed me another strong man dead. He opened his eyes when a nurse called "Henry" clearly in his ear, and gave her a chance to pour brandy down his throat; but all did no good; he died quietly while she was helping someone else, and my lantern showed him gone.

We are changed by all this contact with terror, else how could I deliberately turn my lantern on his face, and say to the doctor behind me, "Is that man dead?" and then stand coolly while he examined him, listened, and pronounced "dead." I could not have said quietly a year ago, "That will make one more bed, then, doctor." Sick men were waiting on deck, though, and every few feet of cabin floor were precious. So they took the dead man out, and put him to sleep in his coffin on deck. We had to climb over another soldier lying up there quiet as he, to get the blankets to keep the living warm.

It was a superhuman effort to feed men by the hundreds in the confined space on board ship, where cooking facilities were pitifully limited. For breakfast for every hundred, ten gallons of tea and fifteen loaves of bread in slices, buttered; for dinner, ten gallons of beef stew, made with vegetables, and fifteen loaves of bread. "After a battle, when men are brought in so rapidly that they have to be piled in almost without reference to their being human beings, and every one raving for drink first and then for nourishment," remembered one nurse, "it requires nerves to be able to attend to them properly."

At West Point, Virginia, a white flag waved from the roof of a small house. The day before a battery concealed behind the house had opened unexpectedly on vessels out in the river. A shell wounded an officer. Another tore a hole through the smokestack of a transport. But that was yesterday. Today thousands of Federal soldiers moved along the shore, with artillery and horses, and the battery was gone. A Blue column formed and stalked off toward some woods, bayonets glistening far away until they disappeared in the trees. The routine amid the anchored craft was quiet. Small boats hustled about, handing up fruit and ice for the sick bays.

A doctor moved among the patients on the U.S.S. *Wilson Small,* most of them dangerously ill cases, hauled in from the battle front by ambulance and wagon. He looked with satisfaction at a man with one leg amputated at the thigh. The day before when the patient had come in he had been staring wildly and muttering unintelligibly. Now he lifted his hand to the doctor and smiled. A nurse whispered that he had just awakened from a sound sleep and had said to her, "You saved my life for my wife, good woman." Next to him lay a corporal, also with a leg missing. Over and over this fellow muttered that he held no malice against the man who had shot him, but longed for the day when he could meet the wretch who had kicked him on the wounded leg before it was amputated.

The *Small* was properly named. She was so crowded that the well slept on the upper deck, rain or shine, leaving the lower decks to the sick and wounded. So little china was there on board that meat and potatoes were served out on slices of bread. The top of the stove also served as a table.

Not all news was good as the days slowly passed. The *Ocean Queen* slipped away to take some of the wounded to New York. There she was assigned to other duties, and soon in her place came the *S. R. Spaulding,* a large, seaworthy vessel fitted for hauling cavalry. Her stalls for horses were still intact, and about her was the strong and unmistakable odor of the stable. She needed complete interior reconstruction, as well as coal and water, and men were quickly assigned to the task.

A doctor rowed a small boat downstream toward the steamboat *Knickerbocker.* Beside him sat a sick man named Corcoran. The patient kept talking, whether the doctor listened or not. After the battle of Williamsburg he had felt sick, he related. An order to march had come and his captain—"God bless him in the name of me old country"—had commented, "Good Lord, Corcoran, you are not fit to march. Go into town and get into a hospital." Accordingly he had walked three miles, carrying his knapsack, and when he came to a hospital the surgeon on duty there told him he must have a note from his captain before he could be received. So on he went, until he came to a vehicle that looked like a milk wagon, crawled inside, and fell asleep. He was awakened when a man pulled him out by his feet, causing him to fall heavily on the ground. He begged the man—a Secessionist, he supposed—for some water. When the water was brought, the man said he would not have pulled him out of the wagon had he not wanted to use it. He had tried to walk away, Corcoran continued, and had fallen in a faint. When he came to, a Negro was standing over him, urging him to go to the hospital. But at the hospital, again he was refused admittance without a note. Corcoran remembered he had said: "For God's sake, doctor, do give me room to lie down here somewhere; it's not much room I'll take anyhow, and I can't go about any longer." That was three days back, and he had not tasted food since.

Corcoran talked, and the doctor rowed. For the talker it was the finale; he would die soon after reaching the *Knickerbocker.* A letter to his mother would be found in his pocket, and a nurse would gently stow it away until she could find time to write a note to accompany it.

Boats threaded up and down the little Virginia streams running into the James. Daily they made their rounds, picking up the wounded where they lay stranded on the banks, some helpless and in dying condition, with now and then a Confederate among them. Downstream they were transferred to larger boats, and there the activity around them was better organized. Cases of pillows, quilts, brandy, and bread were stacked on deck. Tea waited by the bucket. Two layers of blankets were spread, and over them rows of pillows a man's length apart. Patients were led or carried on board and laid side by side, as close as they could be packed. The conscious, crying for lemonade and ice, were given spoonfuls of brandy and water. As soon as possible they were fed.

One nurse penned a picture of the routine:

We are awakened in the dead of night by a sharp steam whistle, and soon after feel ourselves clawed by the little tugs on either side of our big ship—and at once the process of taking on hundreds of men, many of them crazed with fever, begins. There's the bringing of the stretchers up the side ladder between the two boats, and stopping at the head of it, where the names and home addresses of all who can speak are written down, and their knapsacks and little treasures numbered and stacked; then the placing of the stretcher on the platform, the row of anxious faces above and below decks, the lantern held over the hold, the word given to "Lower!" the slow moving ropes and pulleys, the arrival at the bottom, the turning down of anxious faces, the lifting out of the sick man, and the lifting him into his bed; and then the sudden change from cold, hunger, and friendlessness to positive comfort and satisfaction, winding up with his invariable verdict, if he can speak, "This is just like home!"

Another nurse heard with annoyance the screaming of a man suffering from rheumatism and cramp. She gave him mor-

phine, supposing it would not hurt him and assuming it would
be a mercy to those around him to stop the noise. Her diagnosis
was wrong: the morphine only made him rave that much
louder.

Each day was a madhouse of suffering accentuated by the
groans of the wounded and dying. And yet the women nurses
steeled themselves to the emergency and told themselves they
were glad to be able to take part. "We all know in our hearts
that it is thorough enjoyment to be down here," one of them
wrote. "It is life, in short, and we wouldn't be anywhere else
for anything in the world. I hope people will continue to sustain this great work. Hundreds of lives are being saved by it.
I have seen with my own eyes, in one week, fifty men who
must have died anywhere but here, and many more who probably would have done so. I speak of lives saved only; the
amount of suffering saved is incalculable."

The *S. R. Spaulding,* reconstructed, pushed up the muddy
Pamunkey River toward Richmond. McClellan's army was going that way, and the vessel must be ready to bring off the
wounded. It dropped anchor near a burned railroad bridge, in
the middle of a fleet of forage boats. Trees extended down to
the water's edge, all full-leafed and alive with summer. Through
openings in their branches the sailors could see great fields of
wheat, drinking up the sunshine in waves of gold. The Pamunkey winds constantly, turning back upon itself every half mile
or so. "It is startling to find, so far from the sea," wrote a doctor
stationed on board, "a river whose name we hardly knew two
weeks ago, where our anchor drops in three fathoms of water
and our great ship turns freely either way with the tide. Our
smokestacks are almost swept by the hanging branches as we
move, and great schooners are drawn up under the banks, tied
to the trees." An Army camp lay close at hand, and up the river
half a mile the "White House," a modern cottage built on the
site of the early home of Mrs. George Washington. Some of the
Spaulding's crew strolled toward it. They found it empty except
for some pieces of quaint furniture and some brass andirons.

A notice was posted on its door: "Northern soldiers who profess to reverence the name of Washington, forbear to desecrate the home of his early married life, the property of his wife, and now the home of his descendants." It bore the signature of Mrs. Washington's granddaughter, Mrs. Mary Custis Lee, and below it was an order from McClellan for the building to be protected.

For seven days guns roared in the direction of Richmond. Soon the wounded were coming into the camp near the burned bridge by every means of transportation. To accommodate them, straw, blankets, and supplies were moved from the ships. Five huge kettles were kept boiling, and doctors went ashore to work day and night. The weather was still hot. Two new wells were dug, but the water was unfit to drink, making it necessary to lug it by bucketfuls from the well at the "White House."

Gradually the patients were sorted out, some being moved on board ship. These were men who, in the opinion of a medical officer, would not be fit for duty within thirty days.

There was no rest. Doctors on the *Bay State* had been up all night with a new supply of patients when a captain arrived with the news that several hundred more were lying at the landing.

Such a scene as we entered and lived in for two days I trust never to see again [one of them wrote later]. Men in every condition of horror, shattered and shrieking, were being brought in on stretchers, borne by contrabands, who dumped them anywhere, banged the stretchers against pillars and posts, and walked over the men without compassion. There was no one to direct what wards or what beds they were to go into. The men had mostly been without food since Saturday, but there was nothing on board for them, and the cook was only engaged to cook for the ship, and not for the hospital. Imagine a boat like the *Bay State,* filled on every deck, every berth —and every square inch covered with wounded men—even the stairs and gangways and guards filled with those who are less badly wounded—and then imagine fifty well men, on every kind of errand, hurried and impatient, rushing to and fro over them, every touch bringing agony to the poor fellows—while stretcher after stretcher still comes along, hoping to find an empty place; and then imagine what it was to keep calm ourselves.

Wounded were brought up to the burned bridge by train, some of them entirely unattended, or at most with a detail of two soldiers to attend to two hundred or more patients. They were packed as closely as they could be stowed in freight cars, without beds, without straw, dead and wounded together, some with wounds festering and swarming with maggots. Many of the less seriously wounded were on the roofs of cars. A surgeon was told that not another foot of space could be found on a train for three patients he wanted to send away. "Then," said he, "these men must be laid across the others, for they have got to be cleared out of here by this train." The stench was horrible.

Nurses mused among themselves at the standard comment, heard over and over as the men were brought on board: "I guess that next fellow wants it more'n I do." Or: "Won't you just go to that man over there first, if you please, ma'am. I heard him kind o' groan just now. Must be pretty bad hurt, I guess. I ain't got anything, only a flesh wound."

June passed into July, and toward the end of the month the firing toward Richmond waned. But the noise at the riverside grew louder, for Union gunboats were coming to save McClellan's army. Negro contrabands, alarmed that the Federals were falling back, arrived in droves, bundles on their backs and frying pans hanging from their hips. The gay dresses and bright turbans of the women caused a sailor to comment that they looked like a load of tulips headed for a flower show. They stood on the bank and looked out toward the vessels, and now and then their voices drifted across the water in song:

"Go tell all de holy angels
"I done done all I ever can." [1]

10

Levi's red box

AUGUST 1862

Perhaps no one facet of the war puzzled the Southerners along the Carolina coast more than Captain Levi Hayden. A marine engineer unheard of until the war came along, he then somehow or other managed to wangle out of the Federal Government a contract to remove the various obstructions the Confederates were using to block their rivers and harbors.

On arriving in North Carolina from New York, Hayden went first to call on General Ambrose E. Burnside, commander of the army that had taken over the Roanoke Island area. He found the officer in a rude shanty, in the process of rising from a bed of cornstalks, with much yawning and stretching, apparently unaware that his chief of staff and secretary were roasting a pig over a campfire outside. Tall, bareheaded, bald, Burnside walked out and stood looking at the pig while he talked to the engineer. But all at once their conversation was interrupted by a visitor, a gray-haired old man who stumped toward them with the aid of a gnarled cane. Walking beside him, and much more active and alert than he, was an aged woman with a basket of wood chips on her arm. They were there, they said, because the soldiers had robbed them of all their edibles, including a pig. Their complaint seemed to shake Burnside. He spoke to them with the kindness of a father and sent them away satisfied they would be amply reimbursed for their loss. Not once in their presence did he glance toward the animal his aides were browning over the fire in front of his cabin, even though it was sizzling and steaming and giving off a mouth-watering aroma.

With this amusing introduction to his contracted job, Levi Hayden went to work. Soon he was clearing the streams of old wrecks, using snatch blocks and a galvanic battery that set off powder charges and blew canal boats and similar craft to tiny bits.[1] As he worked, he came across more and more evidence of the ingenuity of the Southerners. Out of the waters were lifted infernal machines and other devious devices designed to blow to smithereens all enemies, including himself.

As a part of his routine, one day he came brazenly into the village of Little Washington, much to the surprise of its inhabitants who had spent hours throwing up a formidable barricade to keep out Levi and all other foes who approached by water. But this barrier caused the marine engineer no problem at all. Three charges of his torpedoes, set off twenty minutes apart, tore it into fragments.

One day he visited the battleground where armies had fought in the campaign to take New Bern. The trees and bushes had been cut up by shot and shell, and here and there were stains of blood, as well as blood-stained garments strewn over a wide area. The rifle pits had been well planned for defense, except that they were so close to water they came within range of the gunboats.

Hayden was pleased to find the natives friendly, but they were badly in need of clothing, the women without shoes. They were glad to sell him eggs and chickens, for the war had paralyzed their trade. Men in canoes brought him fish, supplied him with wood for his vessel, and one Mr. Willis let him take the boards from a pigpen to protect the boiler of his little steamboat from the weather. Southern lunches of corn cake and tea were frequently set before him.

Another day he ran up to Carolina City, where he was greeted by Union General Nathaniel P. Banks. Excitement stirred the town. The Stars and Stripes waved from its houses and martial music of the North sounded along its streets, a sharp contrast to what was happening over at nearby Fort Macon where the Stars and Bars could be seen flapping in the breeze above the serenading notes of "Dixie." In the midst of a round of sightseeing, firing sounded downstream, and soon up to the wharf at the fort came the blockade runner *Albatross,* ending a successful run.

Sometimes as he went about blowing up sunken vessels, delegations of natives, including women, gathered to watch. For each he put on a show. Dramatically running out hundreds of yards of wire well up on the bank, he would fasten it to the little red box containing the battery, jump behind a tree, yell at the top of his voice as a warning, "Look out!" and then set off the charge. The question most often asked was how he could make fire in the water. He answered by patting the little red box and pointing to the wire stretching from shore.

But it was firewater and not fire in the water that almost spelled his undoing. This happened on a fine, joyous day, just after he had completed the destruction of a huge dredge. The weather was hot, and during the morning he was serenaded by a small bird that sat in the trees and whistled a shrill, measured note that seemed to him to sound like "picken, picken, picken," with a rest of two or three seconds between each note and then a silence of fully half a minute. This went on for several hours, and it seemed to him quite ludicrous, because there were hawks and owls aplenty in the neighborhood, and it was a mystery why they did not dispose of the whistler. But it all fitted in with the unusual life Levi was living, more recently given a touch of the aesthetic by the fragrant magnolia blossoms his men daily placed around his cabin.

In the midst of this peaceful atmosphere two distinguished natives called upon him, one professing to be a doctor, the other, a more portly individual, identifying himself as Judge Manino. After a little friendly conversation, they adjourned to the Widow Campbell's grocery for a spot of liquid refreshment. As Levi drank what he instantly recognized as bad whiskey, he became aware of an unusual number of loiterers around him, all dressed in butternut homespun. He glanced at his visitors, but got no reassurance, for they obviously were enjoying themselves. Hayden suspected a trap, so he raised his glass with one hand and patted a Navy revolver under his coat with the other. Just as his fingers were sliding toward the trigger, in walked Corporal Herd of his demolition crew, followed by several fellow workers, all armed with rifles.

Herd must have known what Levi's tricky companions had in mind, for he immediately proceeded to effect a deft rescue. From under his coat came the little red box, and from his mouth a lecture that should have gone into the records.

In this box, an item of great scientific achievement, existed a sort of enchantment, he alleged. It could demolish wrecks. It could create explosions under water. It was so valuable a device that the gentleman at his elbow partaking of convivial drink with new-found friends slept with it under his pillow. It was all that, and it was more: it could be vicious. It was capable of broadcasting a circuit of fire two miles in radius. Think of it! From this tiny container, he said, holding it aloft, could come hell on earth.

With this nerve-tingling benediction, he tucked the box under his coat and walked away. Levi emptied his glass and followed.

"Thus was frustrated," it was written in the Hayden journal, "what I afterwards learned was a nice plot to get me quarters at Libby Prison." [2]

11

"A terrible blow to our naval prestige"

AUGUST 1862

No developments of the war so jolted the morale of the Union blockade as did the devastating activities of the *Nashville*. She was an elusive vessel. Into Beaufort, North Carolina, from England she came, by way of Bermuda, a one-hundred-thousand-dollar Confederate Government investment in the art of evading the stranglehold the Federals were trying to tighten around Southern ports. Included in her cargo were tons of cannon, powder, lead, and iron, and thousands of yards of flannel. Her successful run brought strong reprimands from the high command at Washington, followed by definite steps to bottle her up in Beaufort Harbor. But catching her was like dropping a cup over a grasshopper. Despite all the North's attempts to trap her, she escaped. "It is a Bull Run to the Navy," wrote Gustavus Fox.

One evening between seven and eight o'clock, before the moon had climbed into the sky, Federal blockaders stared into the intense darkness along two of three channels leading into the harbor. One of these they more or less ignored because a pilot said it was not deep enough for the *Nashville* to get through, but that was the very route she chose, running close to shore to take advantage of the deep shadows. The U.S.S. *Cambridge* meanwhile innocently patrolled the channel along which the *Nashville* was expected to come, and the *Gemsbok,* a sailing bark, lay at anchor at the mouth of the third, the one along which the ship had originally entered.

Lieutenant J. N. Miller, commander of the *Cambridge,* admitted he might have known she was about to flee. He had stared at her through his glass the day before and noticed that the afterpart of her hurricane deck had been taken off, which changed her appearance, but he thought nothing more about it.

The following night was calm, and soft air blew from the southwest at a temperature of fifty-six degrees. Darkness was not long settled when sailors on the *Gemsbok* noticed against the light of Fort Macon at Beaufort that the runner was moving, and they fired a gun and threw up a rocket as a signal to the other blockaders. Then the *Gemsbok* began frantic action. Twenty times she fired in a northeasterly direction, at a distance of a mile and a quarter, but the *Nashville* kept going, her lights mysteriously flashing on and off.

Such a blow to Louis Goldsborough, the North Atlantic Blockading Squadron chief, and to others! She escaped at the very time General Burnside was organizing for a land attack. It was to be launched against Beaufort with the co-operation of the Navy, and one of its primary objectives was the capture of Fort Macon and the vessel lying beneath its guns. When Burnside finally attained his goal, the fort was still there to take, but the runner had left a week earlier, headed for Charleston where she would be sold to the shipping firm of John Fraser & Company and renamed the *Thomas L. Wragg.*

Reports flew back and forth: she was at Beaufort, she was not at Beaufort. And then came the confirmed truth. Goldsborough was greatly distressed. He wired Fox: "Alas! Alas!

The *Nashville* has escaped. It is terrible." And again: "I am excessively annoyed at the escape of the *Nashville,* and well know the cry it will occasion, and the intense vexation it will cause the Department." [1] It was in answer to these telegrams that Fox came back with his "Bull Run" comment, adding: "It is a terrible blow to our naval prestige, and will place us all very nearly in the position we were before our victories." [2] Throughout the North there was an uproar of protest, and petitions calling for removal of Gideon Welles were circulated. [3]

Scarcely had the furor over the *Nashville's* escape disappeared from the newspapers before she was back in the headlines again. In little more than a month Secretary Welles received a clipping from a paper that quoted an officer as saying this vessel had run the blockade and entered the harbor of Wilmington, North Carolina, with sixty thousand stand of arms and forty tons of powder, had unloaded that cargo, and six days later had run out with her hold bulging with cotton. [4]

Welles sent a query to Goldsborough, and the North Atlantic Blockading Squadron's chieftain replied that he knew nothing about it and, furthermore, didn't believe it. But the story finally became official, and the details again were embarrassing. The U.S.S. *Jamestown,* one of the blockading ships off Wilmington, was forced by a wind of gale proportions to haul off New Inlet into deeper water. Next day, on her way back, she discovered a large steamer and five smaller vessels, all flying the Confederate flag, near the batteries on shore. Her commander, Charles Green, tried to draw them away from land, but they refused to move, and then it was discovered that the big ship was aground.

Night was drawing near, and Green, realizing it was getting too late to do much about the grounded ship, sent up rockets to attract the attention of Federal blockaders on the other side of New Inlet. This failing, he dispatched a boat across in the dark. Next morning the *Monticello* appeared, but by this time it was too late: through his glass Green could see the large steamer had managed to get into port.

A few hours later two deserters from nearby Fort Caswell

identified the vessel and said she had sailed in under English colors, after lying aground twenty-eight hours.[5] Other reports stated that she had hoisted the United States flag and, thus disguised, had gone through the blockade. Welles was furious. He wrote Goldsborough: "The Department is surprised not only at the insufficiency or mismanagement of the blockading force off Wilmington when the Rebel steamer *Nashville* ran into and out of that port, but also at the neglect of the commanding officers to report those circumstances promptly." [6]

Almost simultaneously with this flaunting of the blockade came another blow—the recapture of the *Emily St. Pierre*, a full-rigged ship of about one thousand tons, bound for Charleston from Calcutta, India, with a cargo of two thousand, one hundred and seventy-three bales of gunny cloth. This was the vessel that a year earlier had created a sensation by drifting up to the Liverpool docks with the Palmetto flag of South Carolina waving from her helm. When she was captured, she still had the word "Liverpool" lettered on her stern.

The Union was given ample warning that she would head for some Southern port. Even while taking on cargo at Calcutta the consul wired that she was "loading here with gunnies," and Goldsborough learned that just fifteen days before sailing she had a Confederate flag flying. Thus alerted, the blockaders took her easily and sent her northward to Philadelphia for adjudication. Twelve men and three officers—Acting Master Josiah Stone, First Assistant Engineer John S. Smith, and Acting Master's Mate Philip Hornsby—were sent along as a prize crew. With them went the commander of the *Emily*, a Scotsman named Wilson, and the steward and cook, the latter two directed to keep on with their duties as though the ship had not changed hands.

Some thirty miles off Cape Hatteras, Wilson came on deck in pleasant mood, spoke of the nice wind that had been blowing during the night, and otherwise displayed an attitude of friendliness. Stone returned his cordial greetings, having the mistaken notion that he was speaking to a paroled man.

Fifteen minutes or so later the captured commander asked Stone to go in the cabin and show him the ship's position on the chart. Stone obliged, and as he bent over the chart Wilson grabbed him by the collar, drew a belaying pin from hiding, and threatened his life. At the same time the cook and steward sprang out of a stateroom with revolvers in their hands. The three officers of the captured vessel were quickly overpowered and gagged. Six of the prize crew, asleep in the forecastle, were locked in without knowing what was happening.

When he heard of the incident, Goldsborough raved. But there were other embarrassments in store. The North Carolina coast in the vicinity of Wilmington became a hotbed of runner activity. At a quarter after four one hazy morning a steamer was seen running in at full speed. She was slate-colored and hard to follow in the growing light. Two blockaders, the *Cambridge* and the *Stars and Stripes,* went after her, firing rapidly and striking her several times, but she kept on to within half a mile of the fort at Federal Point, and there was run ashore. Soon her crew was striking for the beach in small boats, and the vessels on her trail followed until they got close enough to see the name *Modern Greece* across her stern. Meantime the Confederates on land opened such a hot fire that the blockaders had to withdraw. At a distance they watched the Southerners haul in her cargo of rifled cannon, arms, equipment, clothing, and spirits. In her hold was a thousand tons of powder, and this accounted for an odd development that the *Cambridge*'s commander told of in his report: "A curious circumstance connected with this affair was the fact that after several of our shot had struck the steamer the fort fired several shot at her. We were unable to account for this maneuver at the time, but I have since learned that the officers at the fort fired at the steamer solid shot to admit water into her and thus prevent our shells from exploding the large quantity of powder in her hold, and also to insure her sinking in case we should try to tow her off the beach." [7]

Blockade running at Wilmington went on so regularly that

it was a maddening subject to the Union officers concerned. On one occasion the consul at Nassau gave notice that a steamer named *Giraffe* had just arrived from Liverpool and was said to be destined to run the blockade to some Southern port. He described her as a long, low vessel, painted a light lead color, with two masts and two pipes, her topsail schooner-rigged, her masts and pipes very raking and wide apart. He said she was a fast side-wheeler, and had come up the harbor at clipper speed. A few days after, it was reported officially that she was at Wilmington. It was known from the consul at Liverpool that she had important dispatches and documents on board.

From the consul at Cardiff, Wales, arrived notice that the bark *Hero* was loading there with coal, but that she would stop at Cork, Ireland, to take on thirty tons of gunpowder. "Her clearance from this port," he added, "will show nothing but coal for Nassau, and therefore may deceive some of our ships that may overhaul her. But she is a Trojan horse, with munitions of war, if not armed men, inside." [8]

In another development that upset Welles, the *Gladiator*, an early runner, stole out of Liverpool. Six days after her departure, entry was filed for her to load for Bermuda, official publication following a day later. The first notice of her cargo—six hundred and seventy-five thousand cartridges, two million, nine hundred and forty thousand percussion caps, one hundred and six thousand, six hundred pounds of gunpowder, eleven thousand five hundred and seventy rifles, nine thousand eight hundred and forty muskets, eighteen brass cannon, six steel rifled cannon, eighty-six tons of saltpeter, plus swords and pistols—was given eight days after she had gone. By that time, the Union consul noted, she was probably one thousand miles away.

Farragut, himself on blockade duty down in Pensacola Bay, gave Fox an explanation of how the runners got in and out of port. "It is impossible to prevent these fast steamers from running the blockade on very dark nights," he wrote. "You are lying still, and the vessel is upon you going twelve or fourteen knots, and before you can get your men to aim a gun she is past you. If you hit her, it is all up with her, but the chance of hitting is small under such circumstances." [9]

But not all incidents along the miles of blockaded coast went in favor of the Southerners. Some days as many as four runners were captured, and one day the *Bermuda*, the ship that in September '61 had stolen into Savannah with a million-dollar cargo, fell into the hands of the blockaders. She had on board seven rifled fieldpieces, carriages and all, a number of heavier rifled cannon, more than forty thousand pounds of powder in barrels, a large quantity of cartridges and shells, and a complete set of signals on how to run the blockade off Charleston. These signals Gideon Welles ordered relayed to every vessel on the station. They were explicit, some reading:

"A blue light with a white light above it will signify: The chances are bad for getting in Maffitt's Channel; try Ship Channel tomorrow night at high water.

"A blue light with a white light to the south of it will signify: The chances are bad for your getting in here at present.

"A blue light with a white light to the north of it will signify: Try Pumpkin Hill Channel tomorrow night at high water.

"Two red lights, one above the other, will signify: Steer in west by north." [10]

This system of lights, developed into a code used generally along the Southern coast, was the salvation of the runners, especially after the Confederates darkened all lighthouses to make navigation more difficult for the Northern invaders. In the beginning, the lights of the blockaders themselves were used by the runners as a guide, but when the Federal Navy Department discovered this and ordered all vessels blacked out at night, substitutes had to be used. A runner, usually drawing much less water than the craft guarding against its entrance, would run in close to shore and flash a light on the land side, where it could not be seen by the Federals. Two lights would answer from the darkness on shore. The incoming vessel would steer until these lights were in line with each other and then would run directly into port, knowing it had a clear route.

The *Albert* was captured one morning. A large part of her cargo was made up of boxes of knitting needles and assorted merchandise, but hidden underneath were other boxes filled with muskets.

The U.S. bark *Braziliera*, off the coast of Georgia, caught the schooner *Defiance* on her way in from Nassau, and on board recognized some old offenders. The captain of the prize boasted of having been captured twice within six weeks, and announced as defiantly as the name of his vessel that when he got clear he would try again, possibly with the result that the captain of the *Braziliera* instead of himself might be captured next time.

He was held under close guard while his captors commented with amazement on the variety of his cargo: three hundred sacks of salt, ten barrels of kerosene oil, sundry boxes of matches, one hundred and forty boxes of soap, one hundred and eight cheeses, one box of spoons, two thousand pounds of cascarilla bark, thirty kegs of sal soda, thirty kegs of soda ash, one hundred cases of gin, forty boxes of tin, one case of gutta-percha raincoats, sundry cases of envelopes and writing paper, one chronometer, one sextant, one octant, one spyglass, two small revolvers, nineteen pieces of calico, four packages of pins, sixteen pairs of ladies' gaiters, and a few nautical instruments.[11]

Each capture was evidence that the blockade was gradually tightening. No longer did Liverpool newspapers carry such advertisements as: "A first-class steamship will be dispatched from Liverpool to Charleston on or about the 15th July next. A monthly service will be established. Goods and passengers for New Orleans, Mobile, and Savannah can be forwarded by this line, Charleston having direct railway communication with all the Southern and Western cities." [12]

The tightening blockade was due in part to the alertness of the American consuls abroad. Their messages came regularly and were widely distributed among the blockaders:

"The bark *Mary* . . . is clearing today. She will attempt to run the blockade. Her cargo consists of coal, iron, hardware, bales of clothing, blankets, shoes, spades, etc." [13]

"The *Minho*, two hundred and fifty-three tons, was bought by an intimate friend of James Bulloch, was hastily laden with a cargo of clothing, hardware, and heavy cases, contents unknown. She is to ply between the Southern states and Nassau, Bermuda and Havana." [14]

"The *Sophia*, four hundred and fifty-three tons, is loading. She has taken on board some nine hundred kegs of saltpeter, a number of large heavy cases, contents unknown, a large quantity of quarter-inch wire, a large quantity of iron in bars, hoops and heavy plates, and six railway turntables."

Through captures on the blockade, tons of valuable supplies were coming into Federal hands. On board the schooner *Mary Stewart* when taken were one hundred and fifty-eight sacks of Liverpool salt, one hundred and fifty sacks of Bahama salt, one case of paper, one box of soap, one barrel of mackerel, ten kegs of soda, six barrels of salt, four barrels of alum, two barrels of castor oil, and one box of tea. Another schooner, the *Will-o'-the-Wisp*, had kegs of gunpowder in fish barrels and bags, percussion caps, thick shoes, and large cases marked clothing. The *Lodona* was filled with brandy, wines, tea, coffee, salt, clothing, boots, drugs, matches, figs, raisins, whiskey, starch, soap, tin plates, soda, dry goods, paint, and quinine.

But, despite captures, blockade running increased at a rapid rate. In a five-month period in late '61 and early '62 only fifteen thousand stand of arms reached the Confederacy. But the number rose to nearly fifty thousand during the four warmest months following. One capture in nine had been the rate in the opening year of the war; '62 saw it change to one in seven.

Losses failed to deter investors. The *Harriet Pinckney* brazenly loaded at an English port. Arms from Hamburg, Germany, were transferred from another ship, men working all night, and the next morning she took on gunpowder. She also had on board twenty-four thousand rifles and eighteen cannon, with carriages. Her owner was cocky: in a trial run she had done eighteen knots, and if captured, why should he worry? He could lose two steamers out of three and make a profit, he said.

Secretary Welles was notified that a fleet of steamers was fitting out in England to run the blockade, and he warned that they must be looked for daily. These vessels would be difficult to see, for they were built especially for the business of blockade running. They were long, low, rakish craft, lead-colored, with short masts and convex forecastle deck, designed to go through instead of over rough seas. Some of their names soon would appear in the records: *Wild Rover, Stormy Petrel, Chameleon, Whisper, Banshee, Owl,* and *Night Hawk.*

Welles was employing every device that came to his attention to stop the runners. When he learned that they used anthracite coal because it burned without smoke and strengthened their chances of getting into port without being seen, he banned all shipments of this fuel to foreign ports.[15]

Suddenly the North awakened to the fact that the runners were resorting to a new trick to offset the information on their movements supplied by the consuls. Not all vessels were risked against the blockade. Some of them were sent instead to Nassau, Bermuda, Havana, and other intermediary points, and there cargoes were transferred to smaller craft and sneaked into points along the Southern coast at night. If discovered, they ran in as close to shore as possible, beached, and then tried to unload before the blockaders could overtake them.

Nassau at this period of the war was the busiest of intermediary points. Vessels were constantly coming and going. Some were in from England and Scotland, waiting to transfer their cargoes for the final run to the Southern coast. The consul there named sixteen in one report.[16] The *Eliza Bonsall* arrived with five hundred tons of coal, eight hundred bags of saltpeter, twenty cases of nitric acid, and forty-three large casks said to contain soda crystals, as well as other supplies taken from the *Sophia* en route. The steamers *Leopard* and *Minho* sailed for Charleston with full and valuable cargoes of munitions and powder. Behind them came the *Columbia.* She had lain at the wharf for a week, in full view of the Union consulate, openly taking on heavy ordnance, munitions of war, and large bales marked "C.S.A." The *Kate,* an annoying runner, left for Charleston with a complete and powerful steam engine to be installed on board a ram building there.

Samuel du Pont who, as head of the South Atlantic Blockading Squadron, came in for his share of criticism whenever any of the runners got through, cited the transshipment of cargoes as evidence that the blockade was effective. He called this to the attention of Gustavus Fox in a message that ended: "The *Isabel* and *Nashville,* with local pilots of extraordinary skill, fogs and accident, and steam, have eluded us—but how many have been kept out? Steam has quadrupled the advantage to those who run the blockade, over those who cover the ports." [17]

Working against the blockade was the boredom forced upon the men stationed out along the coast in the ships on guard duty. Except for the excitement that came their way when a runner was sighted, one day was like another. Carpenter's Mate Philbrick, still keeping up his diary, although life had little spark to it these days following the New Orleans campaign, faithfully recorded:

August 11—Our men are getting very uneasy for the want of a run on shore. Some have been near a year shipped, and have had no liberty. Rather tough for men who call themselves free.

August 16—At last there is some chance of the men getting on shore. The old doctor has come to the wise conclusion that the health of the men demands it. Two hundred men in a ship of one thousand tons, and getting liberty only once in a year. Think of it, you who live on shore, and then no wonder a sailor runs wild when he gets on shore.

August 24—An important event occurred. We were visited by a lady nurse of the Army Hospital. It has been so long since we have seen one. She was quite a novelty and caused much excitement.

The strain of long months cooped up on board ship applied to Confederates as well as Federals, but situations varied according to the leniency of the men in command. Some officers realized what their crew members were going through and were sympathetic, allowing special privileges whenever possible. One of these was George W. Gift, first lieutenant of the C.S.S. *Chattahoochee,* outfitting at a Florida port. But at times even he found his tolerance exhausted and patience growing thin. Such was the case the Sunday morning he mustered all hands and discovered missing a conscript he had given permission to remain on shore the night before for a visit from his young wife. The lieutenant pocketed his lists, landed in angry mood, and went out on foot in search of the derelict crewman. He found him, camped beneath a live oak tree, seated with his bride at breakfast on the ground beside an open fire. As Gift approached unnoticed, he heard the sailor say, "Sugar, give me a tater." She answered: "Honey, I ain't got narry nuther." Suddenly the anger went out of George Gift, and he turned and stole away, choking to keep from laughing aloud. "The scene reminded me of two buzzards playing pigeon," he wrote his sweetheart later that day.[18]

But the greatest strain on the morale of the blockaders was the curtailment of their liquor ration by act of Congress.[19] In place of it each sailor was given five cents extra in pay per day. With the first day of September the new rule became effective. It had been brought about by abuse, both on the part of servicemen and sutlers who went along to supply them with the little needs which were not Navy issue. The first protest against these private merchants concerned the quality of the product they sold—"two dollars a bottle and more for most wretched stuff worth perhaps ten cents." [20] And then it was pointed out that such valiant men-of-war as the U.S.S. *Massachusetts* could be cited by the soldiers as "liquor dealers under protection of the Government." [21] So the ban went into effect, and there was an immediate howl. On board the U.S.S. *Portsmouth* the Stars and Stripes were found at half-mast. One seaman observed that sailors, whom he considered should have received credit for striking "the only real terror to Rebeldom," were rewarded instead by being deprived of their "eighty-four drops of bourbon twice a day." Into the diary of Carpenter's Mate Philbrick went this entry: "Yesterday sent all the whiskey that was in the ship on shore, except what is necessary for sickness. While conveying it to the shore, some of the men got quite happy. It put one in mind of Town Meeting at home." It took quite some time for adjustment to the new regulation. When the Thirteenth Connecticut Regiment came along on the steamer *Laurel Hill*, the crew of the *Portsmouth* cheered and struck up *The Star-Spangled Banner*. Resenting the salute to the rival branch of service, their captain threatened to take away their grog, a standard punishment of long standing, and got back a laugh in his face and a reminder that inflicting this penalty no longer was within his power.

Another development at this period that was a deterrent to the effectiveness of the blockade was the departure from Wilmington on board the steamer *Kate* of a man who would become one of the most successful blockade runners in the business. He was John Wilkinson. Virginia-born and forty-one years old, his war career to date had not been worthy of note. He had been among the officers captured in an open boat following the destruction of the *Louisiana* at Forts Jackson and St. Philip. After months in a Massachusetts prison he was exchanged, and soon afterward the Confederate Government chose him as one of its runners. He was ordered to go to England, buy a ship, load it, and bring it in to some Southern port. No assignment could have been more fitting. Both he and his father, a naval veteran from the War of 1812 and later commander of the famous old frigate *United States*, had conducted coastal surveys, and also in his background was a period of service under the indomitable Farragut. Wilkinson was dedicated to his new task, so much so that he never took off his clothes at night.

As the summer waned, the North Atlantic Blockading Squadron command changed. Charles Wilkes, the problem officer who had almost brought England and France into the war by seizing the *Trent* with Confederate Commissioners James Mason and

John Slidell on board, had been given such éclat by the incident that Welles found himself in the embarrassing position of having to dispose of him in some way that would meet with public approval. This problem finally was solved by assigning Wilkes to direct the James River Flotilla, but complications arose when he refused to report to Goldsborough. Finally, to get out of this dilemma, the Department made his command independent, an action that angered Goldsborough to the point of asking to be relieved. "To this I had no objection," Welles wrote in his diary, "for he was proving himself inefficient—had done nothing effective since the frigates were sunk by the *Merrimack*, nor of himself much before." [22]

Thus Welles took advantage of an opportunity to shelve an officer whose operations had become increasingly embarrassing to the department. And Goldsborough in turn maintained his independence, although, it would seem, quite foolishly, for Wilkes soon was out of his way entirely. In a matter of weeks the man who had come so near changing the complexion of the war was shipped off to the West Indies to watch for Confederate cruisers, as commander of a squadron made up of the steamers *Wachusett, Dacotah, Cimarron, Sonoma, Tioga, Octorara,* and *Santiago de Cuba.*

Goldsborough's resignation was a blow to the runners. Into his place stepped Acting Rear Admiral Samuel Phillips Lee, member of the distinguished Virginia family of that name and a distant cousin of General Robert E. Lee. Fifty years old at the time he took over the North Atlantic Blockading Squadron, he had commanded the sloop of war *Oneida* in the battle of New Orleans and had compiled a service record that made him stand out as one of the Union's most efficient officers. He was serious-minded, usually solemn, although occasionally he would unbend and laugh at a joke. A pipe was in his mouth most of his waking hours, and sometimes for periods after midnight the glow of the Virginia tobacco he smoked could be seen as he silently paced the bridge. He was an alert disciplinarian. Nothing seemed to escape his eyes, and there were subordinates who would swear he never slept.[23] But his diligence paid off, for in time he would amass a record amount of prize money. One of the first changes he made in the blockade was to institute a double system—a row of ships inshore and another offshore, the latter to seize runners that managed to elude the former.

The ship that first induced Lee to make this change in the blockade system was the runner *Kate*, the same vessel that earlier had brought the entire steam engine for the ram building at Charleston. Here was one of the most elusive vessels in the business. She made so many successful runs the total became a variable figure in later years, given sometimes as forty and again as sixty. But regardless of the number of times she got in and out of port, her captain, Thomas J. Lockwood, a ship officer as sly as a fox, made a fortune at her helm.

The *Kate* was a side-wheeler, with two masts and an upper cabin. As the *Carolina*, before the war she had operated on the line between Charleston and Palatka, Florida. Her speed was not great—seven or eight knots—but her draft was light; she had a walking-beam engine and carried no booms or yards. It took the Federals a long time to learn the system she used on occasion to get through the blockade—innocently loitering among their ships by day, a United States flag as a disguise, and by night stealing away to her destination. Such was her success that she was referred to as a "regular packet—sailing on moons." She arrived so frequently the New York *Times,* accepting fate, philosophically suggested: "Let us console ourselves, like Mr. Disraeli, by allowing them to 'increase our respect for the energy of human nature.' " [24]

But Samuel Phillips Lee was not consoled by quotations from Disraeli. "The Department will be extremely mortified to hear," he wrote, "that the *Kate* has run the blockade off Wilmington, out by New Inlet, with a load of cotton, an article now so valuable that a single cargo will purchase a large quantity of arms."

An investigation followed the *Kate*'s run that brought Lee's attention to her. It revealed that she had slipped past three blockaders. Lee found they remained at anchor five miles off the inlet, two miles apart, day and night. This seemed to him to be the answer to the escape, and he directed that henceforth they should draw closer at night and form two cordons. If the runner got past those in the first, they were to signal the second with rockets so it could close in and form a trap. "Every officer on the blockade loses reputation by the escapes," he reminded. "The senior officer and every commanding officer should feel and act as though his command was subject to censure for every failure to keep the blockade as close as the weather will allow." [25]

The *Kate* on her next trip into Wilmington got through the blockade all right, but found less of a welcome at the dock. On her previous visit she had brought yellow fever germs, and the disease had spread into an epidemic. Inhabitants fled the town. The telegraph office was closed, after the operators became ill. Panic spread, and crews working on two ironclad gunboats, building there for river defense, walked off the job. It was while she lay in port on this latter trip that the blockaders decided to use a different method to destroy her. They would go in by small boat and set her on fire. The idea originated with Lieutenant F. M. Bunce of the U.S.S. *Penobscot*. It was referred to the senior officer, Commander G. H. Scott, who wrote back that he would "like to see the miserable craft destroyed," that it would be a glorious affair for those engaged and redound to the credit of the Navy generally.[26] The effort was made, on two separate occasions, but it failed. "The surf ran so high that after nearly losing the boats in the breakers the attempt was abandoned," reported Bunce.[27]

As weeks and months slipped past, there was evidence on all sides that the Confederates, aided by their friends abroad, were in the blockade-running business to stay. The consul at Liverpool reported that they were making "formidable preparations to get supplies into Southern ports, citing that they were buying fast side-wheel steamers of light draft, covered with steel plates instead of iron, especially for the purpose of conveying cargoes from Bermuda and Nassau. A few days later he passed along the information that within the last week they had bought the *Iona, Pearl, Thistle, Antonia, Eagle, Havelock, Princess Royal, Nicolai I, Northumbria, Douglass, Perley, Britainnia, Wave Queen,* and *Justitia.*

It was even suggested to the Confederate Government that it was more or less faced with going into the blockade-running business more heavily itself. Private enterprise, it was pointed out, would bring in light cargoes that brought them the best profit, ignoring such heavy items as steel, iron, copper, zinc, ordnance, munitions, chemicals, and engines. And any investment in ships for such purpose, it was explained, would be quickly covered by the immense profits current: salt worth six dollars and fifty cents a ton at Nassau brought seventeen hundred dollars at Richmond, while the price of coffee had jumped from two hundred and forty-nine dollars per ton to five thousand, five hundred dollars.[28]

There was no effort to conceal the fact that the Confederates were quite successful in flaunting the blockade. In the midst of this activity, the South's famous expert in hydrography, Matthew Fontaine Maury, the "pathfinder of the seas," then on duty in England, wrote the London *Times*: "I have heard since leaving the South a great deal said about our want of arms, about the half-starved and worse clad soldiers of the South. There is no lack of food among us. As for arms, we have taken enough from the enemy to equip all the force that we require; and then as to clothing it is enough for me to say that the custom house receipts at Charleston for the month of July, 1862, were greater than they have been for the corresponding month of any year of the last ten; and this revenue was derived chiefly from duties on clothing and munitions of war, notwithstanding the famous blockade." [29]

★ *12*

"Another mortifying acknowledgment"

SEPTEMBER 1862

A combination of circumstances, miraculously occurring at the same time, was responsible for the outcome at Mobile, Alabama, September 4. So said Commander George Henry Preble, the naval officer who paid for it by getting ousted from the United States Navy—without trial, court of inquiry, or hearing until ten years after the incident. Explanations were many and varied, but David Farragut diagnosed it succinctly: "Damn bad shooting."

There was no want of vigilance, it was agreed. But from a blockade standpoint, Mobile was about as wide open as it had been at any time since the war started. Preble had taken over August 30. He was an able commander, prudent, careful, descended from a distinguished Maine family of soldiers and seafarers. For twenty-seven years he had been in the service, compiling an outstanding record, one of his achievements being the successful command of the *Katahdin* at the battle of New Orleans. But his newest assignment would not add to his laurels.

256

To begin with, the blockading squadron off Mobile was reduced to three vessels: the flagship *Oneida*, a sloop armed with nine guns, and the wooden gunboats *Winona* and *Cayuga*, all built at the beginning of the war. Three others assigned to the station, the *Pinola, Kanawha,* and *Kennebec,* had been sent away for repairs or coal, and the steam frigate *Susquehanna* was on her way to Pensacola to go into dry dock.

On the afternoon of September 3, Preble awakened suddenly to the fact that the entrances to Mississippi Sound had been left unguarded, and he quickly sent the *Cayuga* cruising northward and westward to look around. She had barely disappeared before the chief engineer reported that one of the *Oneida*'s boilers was leaking badly. Preble told him to haul the fires under it, to hurry repairs, and to keep full pressure of steam in the remaining boiler.

September 4 dawned clear. Welles on this date took occasion to write in his diary: "Something energetic must be done in regard to the suggested privateers which, with the connivance of British authorities, are being sent out to deprecate on our commerce." [1]

Soon after daylight a square-rigged sailing vessel was observed by Preble's lookout to the southward, and the *Winona* was sent in pursuit. The engineer meanwhile was busily engaged in repairing the leaky boiler of the *Oneida,* and by noon he was able to report the work progressing satisfactorily.

Preble remained at ease. He got a signal from the *Winona* that the vessel she was pursuing was friendly. At 2:00 P.M. another sail was sighted, and this the *Winona* boarded with similar results.

At three-forty-five the engineer completed the repairs, and the fire under the port boiler was rekindled. Preble at the moment was staring toward the southwest: ten minutes earlier the lookout had reported a sail in that direction. Through his glass he could see that the *Winona* was standing toward him, apparently unaware of this latest visitor, so he fired a howitzer to attract her attention and made signal: "Speak the strange sail and bring the commander-in-chief intelligence, if any; if none, return to your station."

The *Winona* immediately stood off in the direction of the strange sail. She proved to be the friendly schooner *Rachel Seamen,* newly in from Texas, and things returned to normal again. Smoke was pouring out of the funnel of the *Oneida* and the steam on her repaired boiler was gradually building up.

At five-five the masthead lookout yelled from aloft that still another stranger could be seen on the horizon, one that appeared to be the *Susquehanna,* bearing about southeast. Preble, realizing that the work on this vessel could scarcely have been completed in five days, assumed it was the *Connecticut,* known to be at Pensacola undergoing repairs and momentarily expected. He could see black smoke pouring from her in great volume, and he signaled the *Winona* to "chase at discretion."

Despite his assumption, Preble kept a careful lookout. Soon he could see that the strange steamer was standing for him, with her three masts in a line, and that she had square yards forward, although hull down. At five-fifteen a slight yaw in her course revealed that she was barkentine-rigged. At this he became convinced she was an English gunboat feeling out the blockade. He signaled accordingly to the *Winona.*

At 5:30 P.M., believing he had steam under both boilers and that it would look more vigilant to the English man-of-war to be under way and at quarters when he met him, Preble gave chase. The stranger appeared to be about six or seven miles away. By 5:45 the *Oneida* had furled awnings and was at general quarters.

Preble steered toward the port bow of the oncoming vessel. She was headed directly toward him. Soon she raised an English red ensign. Already she had put up a short coach whip or night pennant.

By this time Preble could see that she carried quarter and waist boats, had a broadside of guns with tampions out, hammock nettings and air ports fore and aft, and every appearance of an English dispatch gunboat. His estimate might have been different had the *Connecticut* arrived with the mail from Pensacola, for among the dispatches she carried was a message advising him that the Confederates had received delivery of two new British-built vessels, the *Oreto* and the *No. 290,* and that they were sailing the seas and preying on Union commerce.[2]

As he neared the stranger, Preble put his helm to starboard in order not to pass her, and then came round northward and westward so as to lie abeam of her, or at best a little across or on her port bow. Within one hundred yards he hailed, but there was no answer. He next directed a shot from the rifled forecastle pivot to be thrown across her bow. Acting Master Francis M. Green, standing at the gun, complied. This shot was followed by a second and a third, in rapid succession, all fired by Green. They seemed to make no impression.

Now alarmed, Preble ordered the fire directly at the stranger, and the whole starboard broadside was discharged. Men jumped to the eleven-inch pivot gun. A heavy sea was on, and the *Oneida* rolled so much and with such a rapid motion that they had difficulty in aiming. But they got off a shot. It was just over the stranger's rail, between her fore and main masts, a dud that fell in the water without exploding. The deck timepiece showed and the captain's clerk recorded that the first warning shot had been fired at 6:00 P.M., and the order for the direct fire had come three minutes later.[3]

Several times Preble signaled for the ship to go ahead faster. Seeing that she did not, he walked into the steerage and inquired what was the matter. One of the engineers told him the *Oneida* was doing all she could with the steam she had.

At 6:05 the stranger hauled down her colors and pennant, but there was no slackening of her speed. She raced on, with shots from the *Winona* and a little later from the *Rachel Seamen* falling around her. Preble gave orders for the firing to continue. A thick curtain of smoke developed, at times completely shutting off the view of the gunners. Now and then it was so bad they could judge the fleeing ship's position only by the black fumes coming from her funnel.

At 6:10 the stranger attempted to put on speed by loosing the fore-topsail and fore-topgallant sail, but a shell exploding over the deck brought the men down from aloft before they had got the sheets fairly home. On two occasions it was thought the newcomer was aiming her guns. The boatswain even shouted that he was training his forward pivot gun. But no fire resulted from the newcomer.

Several men could be seen on the deck of the stranger at the start of the action. These rapidly disappeared, and at the last there were only three or four—the man at the wheel, one forward, and one or two passing along the deck.

At 6:27, in three fathoms of water and with dusk rapidly closing in, the chase ended. Across the shoal, without striking, and up into the main ship channel toward Mobile went the stranger, at the last barely distinguishable. She had drawn ahead so fast that the Union gunners, in a period of less than fifteen minutes, increased their elevation from four hundred to fifteen hundred yards. Preble several times sent his clerk, J. Frank Dalton, to the engine room to inquire about the speed. The answer remained the same: not enough steam.

Although Preble was unaware of it, one of the men seen on the deck of the newcomer to the very last was an old acquaintance. He was John Newland Maffitt, Irishman born at sea, the officer who at the start of the war had refused to surrender his ship to the Southerners, and the same man who the preceding January had slipped the *Cecile* through the blockade off Charleston and headed to sea as a runner. The feat just accomplished, getting into Mobile, was one of his greatest, and it was done at a time when he was so ill from yellow fever that he had to be helped on deck.

Thus into a Southern port had come the first cruiser built abroad for the Confederacy. The preceding winter months had seen her take shape in the yards of Fawcett, Preston & Company, shipbuilders at Liverpool. She was watched closely by the Union consul there, and as early as February 3 he warned: "She is now taking in her coal, and appearances indicate that

she will leave here the latter part of this week without her armament. The probability is she will run into some small port and
take it and ammunition on board. This of itself is somewhat
suspicious. They pretend she is built for the Italian Government,
but the Italian consul here knows nothing about it. There is
much secrecy about her, and I have been unable to get anything
definite about her, but my impressions are strong that she is intended for the Southern Confederacy. She has one funnel, three
masts, bark-rigged, eight portholes for guns on each side, and
is to carry sixteen guns." [4]

But delay set in, the result of several causes. Three weeks
later the consul sent word: "The *Oreto* has not sailed; it is understood she will ship her crew for Malta or Gibraltar. Her guns
will be smuggled on in some way. There is no doubt that she
is intended as a privateer." [5] The next day he wrote that he had
positive evidence she was intended for the Southern Confederacy, that she had taken on board seventy barrels of pork and
beef, sixty sacks of navy bread, and six barrels of cabin bread,
with other provisions, and that her guns would be shipped at
some other port in England.[6]

More weeks passed, with the consul constantly watching the
Oreto. During this period the Confederate agent, James D.
Bulloch, arrived and looked her over carefully to satisfy himself that not a single article contraband of war had been shipped.
He also secretly proceeded with plans for her to leave Liverpool
on March 22, about a month later than the sailing date originally scheduled.[7] He himself, under orders dated the past November 30, was to have commanded her, but other matters detained him in England, so he made arrangements for Captain
James Alexander Duguid, an English certificated master mariner, to take the helm temporarily. Articles were signed for a
voyage from Liverpool to Palermo, and thence, if required, to
the Mediterranean or West Indies and return, the voyage not
to exceed six months. Actually she was to go to the Bahamas.
Behind, on the steamship *Bahama,* would come her guns and
other equipment, as well as instructions on how to install them.

The day before she left, Bulloch wrote a letter to be conveyed to John Maffitt by Master John Low: "It has been with much difficulty, and only by the most cautious management, that she has escaped seizure or indefinite detention here. . . . I hope it may fall to your lot to command her, for I know of no officer whose tact and management could so well overcome the difficulties of equipping her or who could make better use of her when in cruising order." He also reported that he would send out four seven-inch rifled guns for her. Longingly he added that another ship would be ready in about two months and that he would take her to sea himself, "although I perceive many difficulties looming in the future." [8]

When the *Oreto* finally left port the consul was not watching. But four days later he missed her and quickly got off a report that she had departed the preceding Saturday afternoon. "The pilot who took her out," he announced, "says she will not return, but go direct to Bermuda. That may be true or not. Captain Bulloch and the officers referred to in my Dispatch No. 38 were not on board." [9]

On May 2, Charles Jackson, a businessman living at Nassau, sent a message to New York that a steamer had arrived there and was supposed to be intended as a Rebel privateer. This message was relayed to Gustavus Fox, who identified the vessel as "no doubt the *Oreto*." He passed the information on to Commander D. B. Ridgely, of the *Santiago de Cuba,* tied up at New York and scheduled to leave soon for Nassau.

Maffitt was not on hand when Low arrived with the *Oreto* the last of April, so she was moved to an anchorage about six miles from town, where there was deeper water and less likelihood of her creating suspicion. At eleven o'clock the night of May 4, Low knocked at the door of a hotel room in Nassau and was admitted by Maffitt, newly arrived. They talked in subdued tones, and Low delivered the letter from Bulloch.

The *Oreto*'s period of waiting was of short duration. One June day the *Bahama* quietly steamed into port. Maffitt would have gone to sea at once, but there was no coal in Nassau, a circumstance that threatened to be serious. Nearby lay the H.B.M.S. *Bull Dog.* Her commander, Captain Henry F. McKillop, seized the *Oreto* as a lawful prize under the Queen's neutrality proclamation, but next day she was released by advice of the Queen's Attorney. The *Bull Dog* left and in came the British steamer *Greyhound,* whose captain, Henry D. Hickley, also seized the vessel, relinquishing her a few hours later. The following day a former boatswain of the *Oreto* made declaration that she was a Confederate gunboat, and Hickley this time filed adjudication proceedings in Admiralty Court.

There was another threat from this delay. About July 20, yellow fever appeared in Nassau. Most cases were fatal. Maffitt, trained in nursing from his long experience on ships without doctors, was kept constantly busy at the hotel.[10]

By July the Union Navy was hard on the trail of the *Oreto.* The *R. R. Cuyler,* preparing to leave New York for Key West, was ordered to stop at Nassau to investigate reports that this English-built ship had been fitted for war purposes. A week later another vessel, the steam sloop *Adirondack,* was given similar instructions. Secretary Welles, who issued them, revealed he had other worries. He announced that the "notorious" Raphael Semmes, little heard of since he had abandoned the *Sumter* at Gibraltar during the spring, was reported to have arrived at Nassau about the same time as the *Oreto,* and to have with him a portion of his crew.[11]

In the meantime matters rocked along. Maffitt wrote Secretary Mallory on August 1 that the case of the *Oreto* would be decided the following day and that it was believed she would be liberated. His difficulties, he revealed, had been great. Twelve men-of-war lay around him, all on the lookout. Seamen, firemen, and engineers were hard to get. In a bonded warehouse were stacked boxes he dared not open because he had no invoice to tell him what was in them, and because he feared they might contain war items which would convict his ship. As a consequence, he planned to go to sea and there fit out the vessel, without knowing what had been put on board.

When the *Oreto*'s case was called, the Admiralty Court was crowded with witnesses and spectators. But in half an hour the judge raised his gavel and dismissed the case on grounds of insufficient evidence.

Formalities occupied the morning of the next day, amid rumors that Union agents were determined to seize the *Oreto* and run her back to England for a new trial. The verdict was recorded, papers were made out for any Confederate port, and Maffitt's stepson, J. Laurens Read, was listed as captain. At 11:00 A.M., with eleven deck hands and five firemen and coal heavers—"all that money and cunning could obtain" [12]—she steamed out of the harbor to the outer anchorage, and at 4:00 P.M. Maffitt went on board. With him was Lieutenant J. M. Stribling, one of Semmes' mainstays on the *Sumter*, especially loaned to Maffitt. He had come in on the *Bahama* and was canceling a trip home to join his young bride. Other officers included Acting Lieutenant Otey Bradford, Acting Master Richard S. Floyd, Midshipman George D. Bryan, Clerk E. Vogel, and Engineers John Spidell, W. W. Scott, Charles W. Quinn, and John Seeley. The entire crew totaled only twenty-two.

Next day a visiting ship appeared and ran all around the *Oreto*. It was the *R. R. Cuyler,* stopping at Nassau to investigate, as ordered by Welles. But she was not allowed to stay. The H.B.M.S. *Petrel,* captained by Maffitt's friend, George W. Watson, ran out and ordered her either to come in the harbor or go outside the marine limits.

That night the *Petrel* came back and passed a hawser to Maffitt. This was owing to the thoughtfulness of Watson, who knew that his friend had not enough men on board to weigh anchor. A little after midnight the *Oreto* dropped quietly down under the shadow of the land until off the west end of the island, and then steamed to the southward. An hour later she fell in with the schooner *Prince Albert*. The hail that came out of the dark from that vessel was given by Lieutenant Stribling. She was bringing arms and equipment, and was taken in tow.

At three the following afternoon, nearly two miles from Green Cay, a small desert island about sixty miles from Nassau, the two vessels anchored. "Now commenced," Maffitt reported, "one of the most physically exhausting jobs ever undertaken by naval officers. All hands undressed to the buff, and with the few men we had commenced taking in six and seven-and-a-quarter-inch guns, powder, circles, shell and shot, etc. An August sun in the tropics is no small matter to work in." On the 15th several cases of fever appeared among the crew. That day the wardroom steward died and was buried on the island. "At first I thought it but ordinary cases, originating from hard work and exposure to the sun," wrote Maffitt, "but in twenty hours the unpalatable fact was impressed upon me that yellow fever was added to our annoyances. Having no physician on board, that duty devolved upon me, and nearly my whole time, day and night, was devoted to the sick." [13] One sailor was making notes on this new emergency: "We had scarcely men enough on board to handle the ship; the circle of the pivot gun did not fit; Yankee cruisers all about; disease on board, and no help on hand but the indomitable energy of our captain, who, in addition to his many duties, was nursing the sick." [14]

By the night of the 16th, despite the sickness, all armament and stores were on board. Next morning the *Oreto,* now newly christened the *Florida,* a name that would strike terror to Union shipping, unfurled a Confederate flag to the cheers of her crew, parted company with the *Prince Albert,* and stood to the southward and westward. She was under great handicap and was not to go far. On opening the boxes from the bonded warehouse, it was found that not a single bed, quoin, sight, rammer, or sponge for the guns had been sent. Moreover, the fever was on the increase and Maffitt's activity as a nurse was constant. He turned toward Cuba.

At eleven-thirty the night of August 18 the lights of a Federal cruiser loomed in front of the *Florida.* Veering and running in close to the reef, Maffitt escaped without being seen. In less than two hours he entered the harbor of Cardenas. He had on watch a single fireman who was completely exhausted; only four other men were able to move. After daylight he continued into the inner harbor, informed the authorities of his helpless condition, and was given permission to remain as long as necessary.

By the following day the fever had almost complete possession of the vessel. Only four men—three deck hands and the lone fireman—were on duty. Maffitt watched each case with particular care. Through necessity, the quarter-deck was turned into a hospital. Two of the ablest men, one of them Stribling, were sent off to Havana in quest of more manpower and a doctor.

On August 22, Maffitt recorded in his journal: "My duties as physician have prostrated me considerably; do not feel well At two P.M. was taken with a slight chill, which I fancied originated from getting wet in a thunder squall. Took a foot bath and felt better for a time. At four, while giving medicine to the sick, was seized with a heavy chill, pain in the back and loins, dimness of vision, and disposition to vomit. The painful conviction was forced upon me that I was boarded by this horrible tropical epidemic." He called before him Acting Master Floyd and, realizing that fever affected the brain, gave him as quickly as possible complete instructions regarding the sick and the vessel. A few minutes later, just after he had stepped from a tub of warm water mixed with mustard, he was gripped by a fierce fever.

As if anticipating the illness, Maffitt only a few hours before had written James Bulloch a letter asking for rammers, sponges, and other missing items. He told of the sickness, of his difficulties in sailing, and that his experience as a coast surveyor had been of great advantage. His crew was green, he said, Stribling being the only member with nautical knowledge.

For a week, until the 29th, Maffitt was out of his head. When he regained his senses, largely through the ministrations of a physician who had come on board from the Spanish gunboat *Guadalquivir*,[15] he was informed that Laurens Read, who had cared for him several nights, was the latest to be attacked by fever. Next day his stepson died. "This blow came like the raven wings of fate, darkening my very soul and nearly producing a relapse," Maffitt wrote in his journal. A sympathizing seaman recorded: "Poor Laurens! He died at sundown, and just after him four seamen and the third assistant engineer." [16]

The dead were buried, the bills paid, and the *Florida,* her crew reduced to skeletal proportions, prepared to leave. The Union consul had been watching and dispatched a swift craft to notify the Federal ships lying outside the harbor. That night when the Spanish mail boat from Havana left, it was chased and fired at by these vessels until it ran, still unrecognized, into the harbor at Matanzas. This was the golden opportunity for the Confederate vessel to escape, and she raised anchor and slipped out along the coast unmolested, taking advantage of the cover provided by a severe thunder and rain storm.[17] Maffitt had had some trouble with the captain of the port in getting permission to leave, even though giving assurance he would interfere with no vessel until after he had left Havana. This official did not feel authorized to act, so he wired Havana for instructions. He got back a brief telegraph: "Let her sail: the word of a Southern gentleman must be taken." [18]

Next morning the *Florida* entered the harbor of Havana and drew up before a large assembly on the quay. There she met with disappointment. The season of sickness had warned seamen away from the port, so few additional crewmen could be obtained. But among those who consented to come on board was a pilot from Mobile named Smith. Conferring with the prostrated Maffitt, he informed him that only one man-of-war guarded the entrance to the harbor at Mobile.

Maffitt was desperate, and he knew his only hope lay in getting to some Southern port. So he stole out of the harbor that night and, running close to shore, managed to get away unnoticed.

His disappearance brought a quick reaction. When the Union consul learned that the *Florida* was gone, he immediately sent word to Washington, and the blockade stiffened. All along the Eastern coast, ships on duty posted extra lookouts at night to watch for the incoming vessel. Among those called on in the emergency was Captain Guert Gansevoort and the *Adirondack*. One morning she ran into an uncharted current off Port Royal, South Carolina, struck a reef, and was lost, although stores and materials on board were saved.

At three o'clock the afternoon of September 4 the *Florida* drew in sight of Fort Morgan at Mobile and kept running. Maffitt, still dangerously feverish, had been lifted on deck. There, sitting on the quarter rail, he stared at three blockaders some distance off the bar. Sight of them deterred him not in the least. At his direction combustibles were arranged in ten locations on the ship: they would be fired if necessary to keep the vessel out of the hands of the enemy.[19]

"At four-fifty P.M.," he recorded, "the cannonading commenced upon our helpless craft, for we could not return their shots for want of men and proper provision for our guns. The *Oneida* . . . made an effort to cut us off, but I sheered toward him, and feeling he would be run down he backed, giving me a momentary advantage. As I ranged ahead of him he poured out a whole broadside that swept away hammocks and some running rigging. . . . Hauled down the English flag, and as soon as the signal halliards could be rerove, ran up the Bars and Stars." [20]

Two shells struck the *Florida* and failed to explode, but others were more damaging. All the standing riffing except three shrouds was shot away. The hull was peppered.

Maffitt ordered the topsail and topgallant sails loosed. The crew climbed to carry out his wishes, and as they did so the Union ships sent a new burst of shrapnel at them, wounding several. Maffitt then directed everyone below but the officers and two men at the wheel.

The *Florida* approached the bar. Just before she reached it a nine-inch shell entered her port beam only a few inches above the water line, passed through her coal bunker, grazed the boiler, and entered the berth deck, there decapitating one of the ablest men on board, James Duncan, captain of the main-top, and wounding four others. The ship continued. At dusk she drew in under the guns of Fort Morgan, a stark symbol of what gunfire could do. Her fore-topmast and fore-gaff were shot away, boats cut to pieces, hammock nettings on one side swept off, main rigging set adrift. She also had been badly hulled, but as one staunch Confederate proudly recorded: "The poor little crippled craft limped like a wounded stag into the friendly port." [21]

Colonel William L. Powell of the Army was there to greet her, and he yelled to Maffitt that he had performed "one of the most dashing feats of the war." [22] Crews of the C.S.S. *Morgan* and the C.S.S. *Gaines,* anchored nearby, cheered loudly. Maffitt's courage and determination had paid off.

The Federal vessels in pursuit stopped just out of gun range. There they listened to the cheering and then turned about and steamed away, the *Winona* reversing her course in only twelve feet of water. As Preble looked back into the dusk hiding the Rebel ship, he paced to and fro frantically. Finally he shouted to all within hearing: "Is there no way we can go in and catch that fellow?" No one answered. Thirty minutes had passed since the first shot.[23]

But Maffitt's troubles were not yet ended. Four days later his young lieutenant, John Stribling, came down with fever. His mind wandered, and he refused to take medicine except from Maffitt's hands. For four days this went on, with the ship captain administering to the younger officer at a time when he himself was so ill he could barely stand. At 6:30 P.M. on the 12th, as dusk was settling over Mobile Bay and bringing into sharper focus the lights of the city, the warrior whose young bride waited at home breathed his last.

A few days later Maffitt sat writing a letter to his daughter. His cabin seemed a flower garden, and scattered about him were "frills, cakes and delicacies," all brought by admirers from shore. He wrote: "It was awful. The little craft is riddled, riddled. Such a run was never before heard of." He suddenly grew faint and laid down his pen. But later he picked it up and continued: "I ran in here under such a fire of shot and shell as has never been encountered in the war. . . . I never dreamed of such a time as we have had—and to have saved the vessel, under contending circumstances, is quite a satisfaction." [24]

What was to Maffitt "quite a satisfaction" caused much embarrassment in Union circles. From his flagship in Pensacola harbor Farragut was forced to send off a report that recalled the escape of the *Arkansas:* "I regret to be compelled to make another mortifying acknowledgment of apparent neglect, viz., the running of the blockade at Mobile by a ten-gun gunboat, supposed to be the Laird's gunboat, Captain Bulloch." [25]

Welles reacted quickly. After a hurried visit to the President, he wrote Preble: "I received from him prompt directions to announce to you your dismissal from the service. You will from this date cease to be regarded as an officer of the Navy of the United States." Then he recorded in his diary: "Am vexed and disturbed by tidings from the squadron off Mobile. Preble, by sheer pusillanimous neglect, feebleness, and indecision, let the pirate steamer *Oreto* run the blockade. She came right up and passed, flying English colors. Instead of checking her advance or sinking her, he fired all round, made a noise, and is said to have hurt none of her English crew. This case must be investigated and an example made." [26] He also notified Farragut that the Department "regretted" that Preble was not immediately removed from his command, adding that printed copies of a general order to be read on the quarter-deck of each vessel would be sent soon.

Before receiving Welles' letter, Preble read in the newspapers a report of his dismissal. Shocked, he forwarded a long commentary to Farragut, citing his twenty-seven-year record of honorable service and reminding: "The poorest boy or man in the service has for his petty offenses the privilege of a summary court-martial and a hearing." [27] He also had a ready answer for the flag officer's opinion that he should have fired one shot

across the Confederate's bows and the next directly at him:
"Had I not been almost convinced he was an English man-of-
war I would undoubtedly have done so, but the deception was
perfect, and his 'unparalleled audacity' in standing directly
and bodily for us helped the deception. I did not wish to break
our neutrality or be wanting in courtesy with a friendly nation." [28]

He afterward cited, on a basis of Rebel accounts, that the
Florida had one man killed and two wounded out of a crew of
thirteen, mostly sick. "Allowing her to have had twenty or thirty
for a crew," he observed, "this is a greater comparative per-
centage of casualties than happened to this squadron in passing
the Mississippi forts, and greater also than it was each time the
batteries at Vicksburg were successfully run." [29]

But the North was in no mood to listen to George Henry
Preble, at the moment disgraced. It had been embarrassed by
a disease-ridden ship, commanded by a man whose hat always
looked too small for his head. This fellow had ignored his own
illness to stand on deck at a time when shrapnel was flying so
fast he would not permit the few men in his crew who could
still stand to share the danger beside him. John Newland Maffitt
had written his name in history, and ahead were months in
which he would add greater luster to it. Meanwhile another
threat was at hand: definite reports came to confirm Gideon
Welles' warning that Raphael Semmes, the old scourge of Yankee shipping channels, was loose again.

★ *13*

A blazing comet in the sky

SEPTEMBER-DECEMBER 1862

The sleek, greyhound ship taking shape in the stocks of the Laird Brothers in Birkenhead, England, was shrouded in mystery. Plainly, she was no ordinary craft built for peaceful purposes in the trade lanes of the world. There were too many unusual features about her. Her hatchways, for one thing, were too small. But this was only the beginning: her sides were fitted with shot racks, her magazines were copper-lined and large for the size of the vessel, and certain bolts in her deck suggested locations for gun platforms. These features the builders brushed off by circulating word she was intended for the Spanish Government, to be used in the war then going on in Mexico. On the other hand, there were factors about her that hinted she might be intended as a blockade runner rather than a warrior. The huge coal bins, the condenser system to supply drinking water on extended cruises, and the long lower masts, designed to carry an immense spread of lower canvas so she could lay close to the wind, told that she was built for speed rather than for battle.

Only the number *290* was used to identify this mysterious

craft, but that was easily explained, for she was the 290th vessel to be built in the Laird yards. However, she was of much concern to Thomas H. Dudley, Federal consul at Liverpool—he had heard the Confederates already were calling her the *Alabama.*

Her construction had started the preceding fall. Day after day, as carpenters and other craftsmen labored, Dudley walked past her and studied her dimensions. In time he was able to give a fairly complete description: screw steamer of one thousand fifty tons, built of wood, two hundred feet long, bark-rigged, with two engines, gilt carvings, and the motto, *"Aides-toi et Dieu t'aidera."*

Through the winter, work on her continued. It was rumored that when finished she would represent an investment of two hundred and fifty-five thousand dollars.

By spring she was almost ready for sea, and James D. Bulloch, the Confederacy's trustworthy agent abroad, made plans to sail in her. Toward the end of April, J. R. Hamilton arrived from Richmond and reported as first lieutenant of the new vessel. Then came a dispatch from Secretary Mallory, announcing that it was thought advisable to order Raphael Semmes, then in Nassau, to return to England and take command of her.

Mallory's message made sense. Semmes, the most successful foe of Union commercial shipping, had been biding his time since laying up the *Sumter* at Gibraltar in April. No ship captain was more feared, or capable of causing greater resentment. Even as he waited in idleness, his enemies were denouncing him. One of these, T. Augustus Craven, commander of the U.S.S. *Tuscarora,* a vessel at the moment held in the Mediterranean to watch the *Sumter,* referred to him in official correspondence as a "pirate captain" and "a deeply-dyed traitor to our country, a man who had violated his oath of fidelity to the laws and Constitution of the United States, a man whose chief boast is that he had plundered, robbed, and destroyed the unarmed merchant vessels of our country." [1]

Semmes arrived at Nassau from London June 15. There in the hands of John Maffitt was an order dated May 2, assigning him to command the *Alabama*. While in England he had cast longing eyes at the vessel, and he promptly wrote Mallory that he would return by the first voyage. He added: "The *Alabama* will be a fine ship, quite normal to encounter any of the enemy's sloops of the class of the *Dacotah, Iroquois, Tuscarora,* etc.; and I shall feel much more independent in her upon the high seas than I did in the little *Sumter*. I think well of your suggestion of the East Indies as a cruising ground, and hope to be in the track of the enemy's commerce in those seas as early as October or November next, when I shall doubtless be able to make other 'burnt offerings' upon the altar of our country's liberties." [2]

Semmes' presence at Nassau, quickly reported to Washington, was confusing to the Federal high command. Gideon Welles quickly connected him with the *Florida,* spreading the word that he had arrived almost simultaneously with that ship and that he had with him a portion of the crew from the *Sumter*.[3]

Standing by at Liverpool, superintending the preparations of the *290* for sea, was an officer the Confederacy had employed solely for that purpose. He was Captain Matthew J. Butcher, an efficient man dedicated to his business. He held a Board of Trade certificate, and he had served as first officer on a Cunard steamship, so there was nothing about him or his record to create suspicion or give grounds for indictment.

During the middle of June, Consul Dudley sent an official warning that "the gunboat building for the Confederates by Messrs. Laird will soon be completed." He said she already had been tested and found satisfactory, and that she would be ready for her armament in about ten days or two weeks. The description he gave of her included such minor details as the fact that her powder cases or cans were two hundred in number, made of copper, with patent screws on top that cost two pounds apiece. "No pains or expense have been spared in her construction, and when finished will be a superior boat of her class; indeed, they say there will be no better afloat," he added.[4]

Ten days later he forwarded another message: "This vessel is ready for sea, and if not prevented will sail before the end of next week. Captain Bulloch will command her. She will enter upon the business as a privateer at once and not attempt to run into a Southern port. It is said that her armament will consist of eleven guns, all of heavy caliber." [5]

All efforts of the consul to get the customs surveyor at Liverpool to intervene met with failure. Investigation failed to reveal any violation of the Foreign Enlistment Act, the only act that came anywhere near covering the circumstances. There was no evidence that the Lairds were either arming a ship for a foreign power or assisting in the enlistment of British nationals. While a current report that the *290* was being built for a foreign government was not denied, neither guns nor gun carriages could be found on her to prove she was intended for war purposes.

On July 21 the consul appeared at the custom house at Liverpool. With him were a solicitor and several witnesses, and in his hand he carried certain depositions relative to other Confederate privateers and blockade runners, such as the *Oreto, Sumter,* and *Annie Childs.* Waving these, he demanded the arrest of the *290.*

Again he was reminded that there was no violation of the law, that the Lairds were building the ship as a commercial transaction, and that all that could be proved against them was admissible in English law, international law, and American law. The customs collector was as vehement as the consul was insistent. He said over and over that the surveyor of customs stationed at the Lairds' yard would make an arrest the moment he found some violation on which to base an indictment.

For the next four or five days more depositions were presented, but none that proved the *290* was either arming or enlisting. The consul's repeated requests that the ship be seized were ignored.

On July 26, in the midst of these proceedings, Bulloch received information from a private source that it would not be safe to leave the ship in Liverpool for another forty-eight hours.[6] Upon receiving it, he went immediately to the office of the Laird brothers and told them he would like to have a thorough, all-day trial of the ship on the outside. He next went to Captain Butcher and informed him confidentially that the ship would not return. Butcher at once began ordering extra coal and supplies on board.

The *290* came out of dock on July 28. Gone from her stern was the board on which her number had been painted. In its place, newly lettered, was the name she was officially christened —*Enrica.*

Among the men moving about her decks was a young Georgian, C. R. Yonge, serving as acting assistant paymaster. Bulloch had taken him into his confidence and had given him a specific task to perform. When the vessel was fairly at sea, Yonge was to mix freely with the warrant and petty officers, show interest in their comfort and welfare, and endeavor to excite their interest in the approaching cruise of the ship. He was to talk to them of the Southern states and how they were fighting against great odds only for what every Englishman enjoyed—liberty. No set speeches, just hints to the leading men which might be commented upon on the berth deck. "Seamen are very impressionable, and can be easily influenced by a little tact and management," Bulloch advised.[7]

That night the *Enrica* anchored off Seacombe. There was no stealth. The Lairds were on board, and so were a number of guests, including both ladies and gentlemen, but these would soon leave her. Next morning at nine o'clock she leisurely got under way, followed hours later by the steam tug *Hercules* as a tender. In the trials that day it was found her average speed was twelve and eight-tenths knots.

As the night of July 30 approached, the *Enrica* came to anchor in Moelfra Bay. But there were reasons why she could not stay. Bulloch and others knew that the *Tuscarora,* commanded by T. Augustus Craven, had come into Southampton for repairs from Gibraltar where she had been watching the *Sumter,* and now was watching the *Enrica.* So at two-thirty the morning of the 31st Butcher got the ship in motion and moved out of the bay under steam alone. Eight o'clock next morning found her off the Calf of Man, the sky clearing and wind dropping. By one in the afternoon the breeze was so light she again had to rely on her engines. At six o'clock that night they halted off Giant's Causeway, a fishing boat was hailed, and Bulloch was taken ashore in a pouring rain, leaving Butcher to go on alone.

Bulloch spent that night at the nearest hotel on shore. The rain continued to pour and the wind "swirled and snifted" about the building in fitful squalls while the foreign agent for the Confederacy sat comfortably in the dining room sipping a toddy of the best Coleraine malt. "But my heart," he recorded, "was with the little ship buffeting her way around that rugged north coast of Ireland." [8]

While Bulloch sipped and the *Enrica* ran away from England at a speed of thirteen and a half knots, the consul at Liverpool was choking with frustration. On the 30th he had reported to customs that the ship from the Laird Brothers' yard had left port the day before, ostensibly on her trials, while the tug *Hercules* was at that very moment at Woodside Landing with arms and gun carriages to be transported to her. In answer to the consul's plea that "this flagrant violation of neutrality" be prevented, the surveyor of customs reported that the *Enrica* had left the dock the evening of the 28th, that he had visited the *Hercules* as she lay at Woodside and had found on board no guns, ammunition, or anything else of a suspicious character.

The *Enrica* headed directly for the Azores, carrying a thirty-day supply of coal, enough to take her all the way across the Atlantic. She arrived at the island of Terceira, a Portuguese possession, August 10. On board were men who would help her make history, men who, of their own choice, had signed up with her. One of these was Philip D. Haywood, just back from a China voyage.[9] He had examined her while she was still in dock and had observed that she was bark-rigged, with unusually long lower masts, indicative of speed, and that her engines took up a good deal of room on board. His curiosity was so stimulated that he promptly volunteered to go along on her first voyage.

On August 8, two days before the *Enrica* reached the Azores, Semmes arrived in London from Nassau. Consul Dudley kept a close watch on him, and three days later reported: "They are shipping fifty additional men for the gunboat, and are to take them out on a tug tomorrow night. I think she is in some creek or bay on the north coast of Ireland." [10]

More men quietly gathered around Semmes. One of these was John McIntosh Kell, a twenty-year veteran of the old navy who had accompanied every expedition of a warlike nature fitted out by the United States during that period. He had served both afloat and ashore during the Mexican War, had been with Perry in Japan, and had taken part in the Paraguayan expedition. Some were celebrities—Acting Master I. D. Bulloch, brother of James D., Midshipman E. A. Maffitt, son of John Newland, and First Lieutenant B. K. Howell of the Marine Corps, brother-in-law of President Jefferson Davis. Second Lieutenant R. F. Armstrong and Chief Engineer Miles J. Freeman had both served on the *Sumter*. Third Lieutenant J. D. Wilson of Florida, like Armstrong, had resigned from Annapolis at the start of the war. Fourth Lieutenant Arthur Sinclair, Jr., of Virginia was the son and grandson of captains in the U. S. Navy. Surgeon F. L. Galt of Virginia was signing up after long years in the old service.

Semmes and these men, with others including James Bulloch, on August 13 went quietly on board the *Bahama,* standing by under command of Captain E. L. Tessier of Charleston. Here was a vessel that already had run the blockade with valuable cargoes several times. She was another rakish craft, a new screw steamer with much gilt and filigree work about her bows and stern. Everything about her implied speed. That night, while Liverpool slept and Consul Dudley fretted, she slipped away, got clear of the coast, and struck out for the Azores.

On August 18, mild cheering could have been heard on board the *Enrica,* tied up at Praya, on the east end of the island of Terceira. That day the *Agrippina* arrived from London, bringing six guns, ammunition, coal, and stores. Two days later the *Bahama* appeared. "As we approached the port," Semmes wrote in his journal, "we looked with eager eyes for the *Alabama* and her consort, the *Agrippina,* which had been dispatched to her from London with her armament. Greatly to our satisfaction we soon discovered the spars and then the hulls of both vessels lying snugly in the bay, and apparently in contact, indicating the transshipment of the battery, etc." [11]

But Semmes was not satisfied with their rendezvous. The harbor was open to the east, and the wind was blowing from the northeast and driving in a considerable swell, causing the vessels to lie uneasily alongside one another. He gave orders for the others to follow him and led the way to the Bay of Angra, where they anchored at four in the afternoon. There was no delay. The *Bahama* was immediately hauled alongside the *Enrica,* and crews began transferring guns and other equipment.

Semmes proudly pointed out the features of the *Enrica.* He explained to the men on board that in fifteen minutes her propeller could be hoisted by steam and she could go through every evolution under sail without any impediment; in less time, her propeller could be lowered, sails furled, yards braced within two points of a head wind, and she was a perfect steamer. Under favorable circumstances she could make fifteen knots. He followed this up with a little speech in which he told the men they were released from the contract they had entered into in Liverpool and were free to go their individual ways. He spoke of the war, explained the objects of the cruise he contemplated, cited the prize money and other inducements, and invited them to sign up with him. Half of them agreed. He suspected that those who held back were waiting for better terms, and he recorded in his journal: "There are, perhaps, some sea lawyers among them influencing their determination." [12]

Before dark Semmes moved his baggage on board and prepared to spend the first night on his new vessel, a mysterious and elusive craft that, like the *Sumter,* would emblazon his name across the horizons of history. But his sleep was not untroubled. Before bedtime, local authorities warned him that West Angra was not a port of entry and that he must move to East Angra.

Next morning Semmes looked out on a world little resorted to by commerce. Every square foot of the island seemed under elaborate cultivation, the little fields divided by hedgerows of what appeared to be sugar cane. Dotted about were white one-story houses, the number giving evidence of a sizable population. But he was afforded no time for sightseeing. The disturbing factor of the evening before was soon renewed in the form of a letter repeating the warning that he must move to East Angra. Complying, he steered his little fleet out to sea and, when far enough from shore, his crewmen again busied themselves with the transfer of gun carriages and coal.

In late afternoon he raised anchor, and this time steamed into the harbor of East Angra. As they came in, they were hailed vociferously in what they took to be either Portuguese or bad English, and someone fired a shot at them. The *Bahama,* reacting nervously, pulled away and stood by cautiously throughout the night.

Semmes was undisturbed. He dropped anchor at 8:30 P.M. and went to bed. Near midnight the watch aroused him with the announcement that a man-of-war schooner was firing at them. He drowsily brushed off the news, commenting that someone might be firing at him, but no one dared fire into him. With that he went back to sleep, and next morning learned that all the disturbance had come from a mail steamer in the harbor using up a few blasts to notify her passengers to come back on board.

August 22 was fairly quiet until evening. Much of the day was spent in coaling, and at one period customs officers and the English consul arrived for a visit. As darkness settled, a disturbance suddenly erupted on the *Agrippina*. For a time it threatened to be serious, but belaying pins finally quieted a drunken crew riotously engaged in a general fight.

Rain that started late on the 22nd kept up through the 23rd. The coaling continued until 9:00 P.M. A fine supply of fresh provisions and fruit, including apples, pears, plums, and melons, also was put on board.

At noon of the 24th, a Sunday, the *Enrica* and *Bahama* steamed out to sea. Four or five miles from Angra, Semmes fired the starboard bow gun, hauled down the English flag, and hoisted his own ensign, saluting it with a rendition of *Dixie* from the small band on board. The *Bahama*'s crew cheered and blasted away with a howitzer, and the *Enrica*'s men returned the cheer with hearty good will, after which they assembled on the quarter-deck to hear the words of the captain.

Whether he realized it or not, Semmes at the moment was at the peak of his career. He was middle-aged, of medium height, possessed of a fine presence set off by a pair of "wonderfully appointed" mustaches. Facing his crew, he spoke as if he were commanding an English man-of-war. Citing the glory won by British seamen and their hatred of oppression, he next described the horrors of the war waged by the North against the Confederacy, concluding with an announcement that the *Enrica* henceforth would be known as the *Alabama* and that all his listeners were invited to ship with him on the cruise she now was about to take.

Eighty men finally signed up with him, some after he had increased the wages he had planned to offer. "The modern sailor," he observed in reporting this development in his journal, "has greatly changed in character, as he now stickles for pay like a sharper, and seems to have lost his former love of adventure and recklessness." [13]

Much of the afternoon was taken up with clerical work, preparing allotments to be sent the sailors' wives, sending small drafts for them to Liverpool, and paying their advance wages. About midnight the *Bahama* steamed away for Liverpool, taking as passengers James Bulloch, Butcher, and the sailors who refused to sign up. Bulloch wrote the Confederate commissioner, James H. Mason, about the departure: "I stepped over the *Alabama*'s side with feelings very much akin to those which oppress a man when he leaves his home behind him. The heavens were brilliant with stars, a blazing comet illuminated the sky to the northwest, the lanterns of the *Alabama* gleamed brightly as she rose and fell to the sea; the signs were all favorably ominous, and, banishing every sentiment but hope, I predicted a glorious cruise for the dashing little craft and her gallant commander." [14]

Pertinent comment went into this letter to the commissioner. "The *Tuscarora*," reported Bulloch, "has been in the British Channel for more than two months waiting to intercept the *Alabama* when she attempted to move. Means were adopted to mislead Captain Craven, who, I must say, has proved himself a very credulous officer, as well as a very rude man. He went prying about in the harbors and bays of the Irish and English coast long after the *Alabama* was fairly off, until he was flatly refused permission to coal at Belfast and was compelled to go to Cadiz for fuel. If Captain Craven continues to be curious in reference to the *Alabama*'s movements, he will, I think, very soon be gratified by frequent announcements of her locality." [15]

Semmes wound up the day his ship was commissioned with this entry in his journal: "I turned into an uneasy bed, absolutely worn out, and to make me still more uncomfortable, it began to blow a moderate gale of wind, and the ship rolled and tumbled at a great rate during the entire night."

At last the *Alabama*, the ship that would sail the seas for the Confederacy but never enter a Southern port, was on her way. For twelve days she proceeded, through storm and sunshine, until September 5, when she burned her first prize. The 5th was a cloudy day, with a light wind from the eastward. A brig sighted soon after daylight outsailed Semmes, but soon afterward he sighted a vessel lying to, with her fore-topsail to the mast. When he got close he saw she was the *Ocmulgee* of Edgartown, Massachusetts, her crew stripping blubber from a huge whale moored alongside. When her captain, Abraham Osborn, came on board the *Alabama* with his papers, he was found to be "a genuine specimen of a Yankee." [16] There was politeness but no mercy in Semmes' voice as he informed his captive of the fate awaiting his ship. He then took from her a quantity of rigging, her supplies of beef, pork, and small stores, and thirty-seven prisoners. After daylight on the 6th, at an hour when no reflection would be cast to warn other whalers in the area, she was burned.

At 11:00 A.M. on the 7th, a fine, clear day, Semmes mustered his crew for the first time and had the articles of war read aloud. That afternoon he put his prisoners ashore on the island of Flores, and then set out after a schooner that appeared to be running inland. A mile from her he hoisted English colors, but she failed to respond, so he fired the lee bow gun. When she still paid no attention and endeavored to pass, he fired a shot athwart her bow. With a third shot, between her fore and main masts, she hoisted the American colors and came to. She was the *Starlight,* on her way home to Boston from Fayal. If Osborn had impressed Semmes, the captain of this second ship, a man in his late twenties, did so to greater degree. "The master was the cleverest specimen of a Yankee skipper I have met," Semmes wrote.

For the next week the *Alabama* averaged a victim a day. On the morning of the 8th Semmes put his prisoners ashore on Flores, exchanged pleasantries with the governor of the island, and that afternoon gave chase to a bark, coming up with it at sunset. She was a whaler, the *Ocean Rover,* many months out of Massachusetts and loaded with eleven hundred barrels of sperm oil. Semmes forced her about, but allowed her captain and crew to pull for shore in six whaleboats. He watched them for a time as they moved slowly away in the moonlight, then went to his cabin and wrote in his journal: "This was a novel night procession."

That night, as the *Alabama* lay to with her prizes close at hand and silhouetted in the moonlight, a large bark suddenly appeared. The chase lasted throughout the night. At daylight Semmes hoisted the English flag. When it brought no response, he fired a blank cartridge, followed by a shot astern of the fleeing vessel, then about two miles away. This brought her to, with the United States flag at her peak. A boat was sent to take possession of her. Her papers showed her to be the *Alert,* sixteen days out of New London, Connecticut, and bound for the Indian Ocean. From her Semmes obtained underclothing for his crew, tobacco, and other items.

The 9th and 10th were days of conflagration. At 9:00 A.M. of the 9th, the *Starlight* was burned; at 11:00 the *Ocean Rover;* and at 4:00 P.M. the *Alert.* Semmes next chased a schooner, coming up with the *Weather Gauge* of Provincetown, Massachusetts, six weeks out. Still later he pursued a bark and overhauled her at 3:00 in the morning, finding her to be the *Overman* from Bangkok. At 10:00 A.M. on the 10th the *Weather Gauge* was burned.

From one of his prizes he took off a supply of cabbages and turnips, "very necessary antiscorbutics for the crew, as they have been now some seventy days on salt diet," and from another he got soap, tobacco, and three hundred and forty barrels of oil. One whaling schooner, the *Courser* of Provincetown, was used as a target for gun practice, which Semmes found "pretty fair for green hands for the first time."

Late September was beset with gales, and for ten days Semmes saw not a sail. He kept his crew busy calking the ship and exercising, mainly at the battery and with small arms. On October 3 two prizes came into his bag, the *Brilliant* and *Emily Furman,* and he concentrated his prisoners on one and burned the other. Four days later he captured the brigantine *Dunkirk* from New York, loaded with grain for Lisbon, and found on board a number of Portuguese Bibles and religious tracts, with a notice saying: "When in port, please keep conspicuously on the cabin table for all comers to read, but be very careful not to take any ashore, as the laws do not allow it." But these directions had been scratched through by pen, and Semmes observed: "It thus appears that the Yankee ships are engaged in smuggling prohibited religious literature, along with their cargoes, into the countries they visit."

October brought more gales. Semmes waited until they died down, and then, as November approached, headed across a track of sea seldom crossed by a sail, aiming for the route followed by vessels from Capes Horn and Good Hope on their way to New York.

He wrote dutifully in his journal. One day he recorded: "We are to be embarrassed with two females. . . . Poor women! They are suffering for the sins of their wicked countrymen who are waging this murderous war upon us." A few hours later he added: "My menage has become quite home-like with the presence of women and the merry voices of children." He forged on day after day, stopping first one vessel and then another, all the while maintaining strong control over his crew, most of them toughs from the streets of Liverpool. "Our ship begins to look quite like a ship of war, with her battery in fine order, her decks clean, freshly painted outside, masts scraped, etc., and the crew well disciplined. Thus far I have never seen a better disposed or more orderly crew. They have come very kindly into the traces." [17]

One November day, off the north end of Martinique, he found the bark *Agrippina* awaiting him with a cargo of coal which he took on board. It was needed, even though most of his captures to date had been made under sail. In this respect the *Alabama* held one advantage over the *Sumter,* which could give chase only with steam.

As the weeks passed newspaper accounts added steadily to

the mystery that had begun to develop around Semmes and his fabulous *Alabama*. Members of the crew were described as "very dainty gentlemen," taking nothing but the best from the vessels they captured. Of Semmes they reported: "He sports a huge mustache, the ends of which are waxed in a manner to throw that of Victor Emanuel entirely in the shade, and it is evident that it occupies much of his time and attention. His steward waxes it every day carefully, and so prominent is it that the sailors of the *Alabama* term him 'Old Beeswax.' His whole appearance is that of a corsair, and the transformation appears to be complete from Commander Raphael Semmes, United States Navy, to a combination of Lafitte, Kidd and Gibbs." [18]

Reports of his successes became routine, and officials at Washington and the Union navy yards sought vainly for some way to stop him. The New York *Times* stated frankly: "It is not worth while to conceal the fact that a whole fleet of steamers are after the *Alabama*." [19]

Gideon Welles was furious. "The ravages by the roving steamer *290,* alias *Alabama,* are enormous," he confided in his diary. "England should be held accountable for these outrages. The vessel was built in England and has never been in the ports of any other nation. British authorities were warned of her true character repeatedly before she left." [20]

Semmes in the meantime was going steadily ahead, living on the best to be taken from his victims and rapidly amassing money from them, at the same time keeping records of his captures by the papers he took from them and by their chronometers, piled up in his cabin in a prize collection. He remained constantly alert, cautious, and active. Some nights he was aroused from his cot four or five times by reports of approaching vessels. When his own ship needed repair, he drifted up to some faraway island and whiled away his time during the hours the crew labored, making entries in his journal, such as: "Strolled on the island toward sunset, with the gannets for companions, the surf for music, and the heavy sand for a promenade."

Semmes had one goal: to destroy the maritime commerce of the United States. And as the weeks passed it looked as though he might reach that goal.

Lively times up the Yazoo

SEPTEMBER-DECEMBER 1862

The weather cooled, as the calendar moved toward October. Down along the Mississippi the news that came to Union sailors confined aboard ships pushing up the river was not good. It told of disasters befalling Federal armies in the field, and finally that McClellan had been driven back from Richmond. Influenced by these tidings, Lieutenant Francis A. Roe, commanding the U.S.S. *Katahdin* since July and still entering almost daily recordings in his diary, put down thoughts that would still be very much alive a century later: "The condition of the country is critical in the last degree. The hour looks dark and portentious. But the struggle of liberty, of civilization, of human progress, was ever a hopeful one in darker hours of the world's history than it is now. For myself, I feel that this struggle is one in behalf of humanity, of all mankind, and of all nations." [1]

Since Roe wrote as a naval officer, there must have been a note of triumph mixed with his thoughts, for the Army again had failed, while the Navy continued relentlessly to hack away at the South's life line. It was easy to describe the heroism of men on land, charging on foot or horse, but what excitement could be worked up over a gunboat, supported by powerful weapons, beating up crooked Southern streams, with little in front of them except women and children and a few home guards who had such a fear of these vessels that they ran at the first sight of them? Such circumstances stifled proper eulogy of the Navy, but the credit was due. A war is fought to be won, and while the Army reaped the praise, the Navy kept persistently at the job of defeating an enemy that had little in the way of guns or ships with which to fight back.

Even now the Union Navy was starting a new offensive. Heretofore the numerous armored craft had centered their attention along the coast and up the Mississippi and its major tributaries. By the fall of '62 the war had developed to the point that it called for a big push inland, up the many smaller waterways where the dreaded gunboats could spread terror and destruction to the more isolated areas, the bread-producing areas still vital to the Confederate armies. This would mean in effect carrying the war "into the heart of the country." [2]

The campaign quickly developed. One morning two steamers, the *Kensington* and *Rachel Seamen,* ran into Sabine Pass, Texas, to knock out a Confederate battery. They found anchored there the friendly mortar schooner *Henry Janes,* and they solicited her aid in forcing the Rebels to evacuate their stronghold. When crewmen pushed into the town of Sabine, a deputation of three residents met them and announced that the mayor and half the population had in recent weeks been wiped out by yellow fever.

The Federals were relentless. Acting Master Frederick Crocker pushed on upstream in the *Kensington* and successfully levied on the little community of Charleston a contribution of sweet potatoes and beef. Preparing to return, he was informed that Southerners in numbers were waiting below to attack him. To safeguard his ship he gathered up a dozen inhabitants, posted them around his helmsman, and made his way down the river unmolested. Later he notified Farragut that he had destroyed all the navigation along the way, "besides teaching the people a lesson they will not soon forget." He added that "the importance of Sabine Pass to the Rebels appears to have been entirely underrated by us, the quantity of goods of all kinds and munitions of war that has been run in here has been enormous, and large quantities of cotton have been exported." [3]

In another successful raid, steamers and transports made their way up the St. John's River in Florida, landed troops, and prepared for combined operations against a battery situated on a high bluff. The Rebels opened a vicious fire, dropping shells so close to the ships that water was thrown on their decks, and the vessels fell back. Next morning the attack was renewed, but without response. The Southerners, it was learned, had departed, leaving behind guns, munitions, provisions, camp equipage, and a Confederate flag that one officer reported "shows the excessive panic they must have experienced so soon as the army commenced moving in their rear." [4] Searchers found beds warm and fires burning in homes in the area, but all occupants had disappeared.

The journey up the St. John's was continued cautiously. The stream was so narrow it was feared the Southerners might block the return by felling trees across the channel. Between two hundred and three hundred small boats were destroyed, and in this the Federals were satisfied. They could tell by the undisturbed leaves of plants growing in the water that no large vessels had gone up in flight. At Magnolia Springs, a public spa, a brief stop was made to post a copy of Lincoln's Emancipation Proclamation.

As they drew up to the little town of Palatka, two lone citizens standing at the landing were brought on board the *Cimarron* and questioned by Commander Maxwell Woodhull. One of them identified himself as former Governor William D. Moseley, the other as a resident named Blood, a strong Unionist who reported that the Southerners had threatened to make him "ornament a pine tree." Men up and down the river, they said, had fled to the bushes in panic, hurried along by a persistent rumor that every white man would either be executed or sent to a Northern prison. Presently about fifty armed horsemen were seen approaching from beyond the town. Whatever their objective, a few shells aimed in their direction caused them to turn about and disappear into the swamps. A little later Woodhull was asked to meet a deputation of women who had assembled on the wharf. They explained they had come to beg that the community be spared, that they had no control over the horsemen who had just fled. "I told them that their pretense of having no influence with the men just now I did not believe, as it was a well-known fact that this war had been mainly kept alive by the violence and the influence the women brought to bear on their fathers, husbands, and sons," Woodhull reported.[5] But he granted their request, and the vessels departed without further shelling.

While the river war developed, the United States Congress put its house in order by taking the command of the Western Flotilla away from the Army and assigning it to the Navy, thus ending a system that Andrew Foote had said made it so that "every brigadier could interfere" with him. Shortly afterward Charles Henry Davis, who had had sole command of the river fleet since Farragut's departure for the Gulf, was called back to Washington to serve as chief of the Bureau of Navigation. David Porter was named to the post thus vacated, a logical choice in view of his role in developing the war along the Mississippi.

Promptly taking charge, Porter brought into play an innovation in ships that had much to do with the Union's success in pushing inland by way of shallow streams. They were the so-called "tinclads," designed especially for the work they had to do. Hastily bought at Cincinnati and other points and converted from peaceful use, they were light-draft stern-wheelers covered with an inch and a quarter of boiler iron to make them bulletproof. But they had virtually no protection against heavier projectiles. They drew only about three and a half feet of water and mounted ten guns. Soon they were making a record for themselves, and bringing new names into official correspondence—*Forest Rose, Brilliant, Rattler, Romeo, Juliet, Marmora, Signal,* and others. Twenty-five in all were acquired, and five were quickly put into service, the others within a month.

A few days after Porter arrived at Cairo, the quartermaster gave a party, mainly to provide Army and Navy officers an opportunity to become acquainted with one another. As the group was preparing to sit down to dinner, a small travel-worn man in mufti was ushered in and introduced as General U. S. Grant. Without formality, he asked to speak with Porter alone.

Out of hearing of the others, Grant asked bluntly, "When can you move with your gunboats?"

"Within twenty-four hours," Porter replied.

"Very well, then," said Grant. "I will leave you now and write at once to Sherman to have thirty thousand infantry and artillery ready to start for Vicksburg the moment you get to Memphis. I will return to Holly Springs tonight and will start with a large force for Grenada as soon as possible. I will draw Pemberton, with the larger part of his army, out of Vicksburg, and in his absence you and Sherman will be able to take it." [6]

Without stopping to eat, Grant rode away. His visit was evidence that the Union was still fuming over Farragut's failure to take Vicksburg with ships. Now an effort would be made to carry it from the rear, either by way of the Yazoo or the Big Black, which ran in behind the city. The urgency Grant displayed resulted from awareness that any offensive would have to be executed before winter rains made the roads impassable.

Acting promptly, Porter assigned the task of opening the Yazoo to Henry Walke, so helpful to Foote in running past the forts at Island No. 10. Walke was informed that Union General John A. McClernand would be ready to move in about two weeks and "we must have the place clear for him to land his troops."

But first there was delay because of a seasonal drop in the water level in the rivers. Porter fretted over this setback, over a shortage of personnel due to sickness, and over failure of officials at Washington to send him either men or supplies. He also was much put out by the Army leadership paired with him in the joint operation. "I find it pretty hard work to comply with all the requests of Army officers," he wrote Walke. "There are so many generals acting independently of each other that the whole American Navy could not comply with their demands. I find also that the Army officers are not at all acquainted with the rise and fall of the water; they are getting up expeditions at improper times, making us expend a deal of coal, and nothing comes of it. . . ." [7]

But at last the water reached a safe level for the gunboats, and Grant notified Porter that General Sherman would move from Memphis toward Holly Springs, Mississippi, and that he himself would start action three days later. There was no mention of McClernand.

Grant advanced on Vicksburg, moving southward down the Mississippi Central Railroad from Grand Junction, Tennessee, directly on the Confederate lines behind the Tallahatchie River. In three weeks his first echelons had possession of Holly Springs. And then matters took a turn. Rebels appeared unexpectedly on his flank, forcing his army to retreat in confusion and drawing it away from its supplies. This eased the pressure on Pemberton so that he could better defend Vicksburg. Sherman had been delayed and was still at Memphis. Walke meanwhile was sending his boats up the Yazoo. A Negro from Yazoo City informed him the Confederates had no rams or gunboats up the river, but that they did have a heavy timber barricade and a fort twenty-three miles from the mouth.

Through reconnaissance, Walke found his chief problem the water mines that the Southerners had planted in liberal numbers along the river. These mines, commonly referred to as "torpedoes" or "infernal machines," were of crude design. When lifted from the water, usually in pairs, they were found to be ordinary demijohns filled with powder and so arranged as to be set off by a pull on a connecting wire attached to friction primers and fastened to objects on shore, or by a galvanic battery controlled by Confederates concealed along the banks.[8]

One day two of the tinclads, the *Marmora* and *Signal,* ran up the Yazoo some twenty miles and rounded to on sighting several suspicious objects floating on the river. Someone on board the *Marmora* fired a rifle shot at one of them when within fifty feet of it, and the result, far from anticipated, sent everyone's heart into his mouth. A tremendous explosion shook the boat from stem to stern and threw water over a wide area. Shortly afterward there was another explosion near the *Signal.* Neither caused damage.

Respect for these Confederate weapons immediately soared. "Carefully avoided contact with others, for they were infernal machines," it was recorded in the *Marmora*'s log.[9]

But the men on the ships learned that by acting carefully the objects could be safely lifted from the water and deactivated. So at eleven-thirty the next morning the *Marmora* and *Signal* were sent back up the Yazoo, supported this time by the ironclads *Cairo* and *Pittsburg* and the ram *Queen of the West.* They were under direction of Lieutenant Commander Thomas O. Selfridge, descendant of a seafaring family, ambitious, willing, an officer of high forehead and well-brushed sideburns, who had served a useful but not particularly outstanding role in the war. Fame had touched him lightly on one occasion: earlier he had served temporarily in command of the *Monitor.*[10] But it never tapped him seriously again. Assistant to the executive officer on board the *Cumberland,* he had commanded the forward division of guns on that ship when she was sunk by the *Merrimack.* From a practical standpoint, he was too impulsive to get along well with the men around him, and they were prone to criticize him. In this attitude they were supported by at least a modicum of reason, for success was never a dominant part of his career. Once, while experimenting with the crude submarine

Alligator on a trial trip from the Washington Navy Yard, he had barely escaped disaster for himself and the entire crew.

In the move up the Yazoo, the tinclads *Marmora* and *Signal* took the lead, followed in order by the *Queen of the West, Cairo,* and *Pittsburg.* Along the way enemy sharpshooters frequently fired at them from trees on shore, causing interruption and delay while shells were thrown back at them.

Around ten o'clock the *Marmora,* commanded by Lieutenant Robert Getty, overhauled a skiff carrying a white man and a Negro. The former identified himself as Jonathan Williams of Vicksburg, overseer on a plantation along the river, and the latter called himself Jonathan Blake, a servant. The Negro said Williams knew the exact location of the mines placed in the Yazoo and, when questioned, the white man reluctantly admitted having such knowledge. His admission stimulated no sympathy. They were both placed in irons and booked for a fare of bread and water.

At 11:10 A.M. the *Marmora,* coursing steadily up the stream, came in sight of the mines and stopped. Selfridge on the *Cairo* yelled to ask why the other vessel had halted, and Getty shouted back, "Here is where the torpedoes are!" The *Cairo* immediately began shelling the right bank and soon it sent out a boat's crew to secure the nearest of the explosives. Walter E. H. Fentress, commanding a detail of sharpshooters on the *Marmora,* recorded the sequence of developments at this point:

The *Marmora* being about one hundred yards in advance, her engines were stopped and the fleet closed up to "close order." The steamer *Cairo* came nearly abreast of us, and hailed the *Marmora* to "go ahead," which order was obeyed, and we moved ahead very slowly. Soon we discovered an object ahead, resembling a small buoy, and I requested Captain Getty to allow me to examine it. As I approached it, I found a boat from the *Cairo* on the same errand, and I pushed forward to reach a line that I saw on the bank. As soon as I could I severed the line with my sword, and a large object immediately arose in the middle of the river. Pulling to it by the line, I soon discovered it to be some "infernal machine," and upon closer examination I found a wire running from it to the shore, and was ordered from the *Cairo* to cut it, which I did, and towed the torpedo to the *Marmora*. As I was engaged in breaking it to pieces, I heard an explosion from the *Cairo,* and on looking up I saw her anchor thrown up several feet in the air. In an instant she commenced to settle, and was run to the bank and a hawser got out; but shortly she slid off the bank and disappeared below the water.[11]

Selfridge had his own account. He reported that the *Marmora* was partially hidden by a bend in the river, that he heard musketry fire coming from her, saw her backing up, and immediately supposed she was attacked from shore. "I hastened up to her support," he related, "when I found the firing was from the *Marmora* at an object—a block of wood—floating in the water. . . . They fished it up and found it to be a portion of a torpedo which had exploded the day before. In the meanwhile, the head of the *Cairo* having got in toward the shore, I backed out to straighten upstream, and ordered the *Marmora* to go ahead slow. I had made but half a dozen revolutions of the wheel and gone ahead perhaps half a length, the *Marmora* a little ahead, leading, when two sudden explosions in quick succession occurred, one close to my port quarter, the other apparently under my port bow." [12]

In a matter of minutes the first Federal ship to be sunk by a water mine was down in six fathoms of water, only the top of her masts showing above the surface.[13] In time these, too, were submerged, the *Lioness* coming upstream and hitching to them and pulling them over, so that no trace of the vessel would be left for the Confederates.[14] The only items saved were a few hammocks and bags that floated off.

The *Cairo* was one of the ironclads built in St. Louis by contract with James B. Eads, the expert on Western rivers. She was one hundred and seventy-five feet long and of six hundred tons displacement. From a foot above the water line her sides were inclined at an angle of thirty-five degrees and her bow and stern at forty-five degrees. Iron plating covered the bow and sides abreast her boilers, as well as the pilothouse forward and paddle wheel astern. She carried six thirty-two-pounders, three rifles, three eight-inch guns, and a thirty-pounder Parrott rifle. Her loss brought her commander much ridicule. As one officer sarcastically recorded: "On December 12 Lieutenant-Commander Selfridge of the *Cairo* found two torpedoes and removed them by placing his vessel over them." [15]

Selfridge himself later wrote: "As a young officer in command of a large ironclad, the *Cairo,* I had been so unfortunate, by pushing perhaps a little farther to the front than prudence dictated, to lose my ship by the explosion of a torpedo in the Yazoo River." [16] Porter, in this instance, was the most tolerant. He reported to Welles, without heat, that "the *Cairo* incautiously proceeded too far ahead," [17] and that "my own opinion is that due caution was not observed." He added, in violation of complete accuracy: "These torpedoes have proved so harmless heretofore (not one exploding out of the many hundreds that have been planted by the Rebels) that officers have not felt that respect for them to which they are entitled." After investigation of the incident, he wrote in a departmental report: "I can see in it nothing more than one of the accidents of war arising from a zealous disposition on the part of the commanding officer to perform his duty." [18] And then he turned the heat in another direction: "Captain Walke went up and made a reconnaissance and afterwards sent up an expedition agreeable to my orders, but he did not calculate how smart the Rebels would be who, in the meantime, put down some hundreds of torpedoes." [19]

Thus Selfridge, unlike George Henry Preble, escaped disgrace. Upon reporting the loss to Porter, he said, "I suppose you will want to hold a court."

"Court?" replied Porter. "I have no time to hold courts. I can't blame any officer who puts his ship close to the enemy. Is there any other vessel you would like to have?"

Selfridge answered that he knew of only one at the time without a commander.

"Very well," said Porter, "you shall have her." And turning

to his fleet captain he directed: "Make out Captain Selfridge's orders to command the *Conestoga*." [20]

Following this conversation, Porter reported to Welles his disposition of Selfridge: "I have put him in command of the *Conestoga,* trusting that he may be more fortunate hereafter, this being the second time during the war his vessel has gone down under him." [21]

Through Selfridge the Federals had learned their lesson. Henceforth a wary eye would be kept for the Confederates' floating weapons. When Porter a few days later gave Lieutenant Commander William Gwin of the U.S.S. *Benton* directions to proceed up the Yazoo with an expedition to secure a landing place for Sherman's troops, he issued explicit instructions regarding these explosives: "The river is full of torpedoes. . . . You will have plenty of rowboats to go ahead of the light steamers, provided with drags and searches of all kinds. Some boats must pass along close in to the banks and, with boat hooks, scrape the banks deeply near the water's edge, to see that no wires are concealed; this must be done thoroughly, for there is the danger. Others must spread themselves across the river and drag the bottom. Whenever a buoy or floating object is seen, it must be approached cautiously, and a long running bowline thrown over it; the bow will then haul the torpedo on shore and make it fast. No one must be allowed to handle these torpedoes or break them up until we know more about them." [22]

Two days later, when Walke ordered Lieutenant Commander John G. Walker of the *Baron de Kalb* to assist Gwin, he was given similar instructions. Strictest care was urged. "Avoid the channel as much as possible," Walke advised, "and if there is any apparent danger relinquish the project and return to the squadron immediately, until better means can be obtained to scour the shores and drag out the torpedoes." [23] That day, Acting Master's Mate Robert Hamilton was shot through the head and killed while dragging the channel in an open boat, and plantation houses in the immediate area were burned in retaliation.

After three busy days of mine removal, concerted action came on December 27, somewhat altered from Sherman's standpoint because of the commencement of heavy rains, fulfilling fears that the Army had delayed too long.[24] Chickasaw Bayou was to be the line of attack, and the first effort would be aimed at making a lodgment on the hills at its head. But progress would be difficult for the land troops, owing to felled timbers of large size behind which numerous Rebel sharpshooters were hidden. The ultimate drive would be on the hills behind Vicksburg, provided an opening could be found in the abatis the Southerners had thrown up in all directions.

Porter, by this time, had changed his opinion of army officers, and had become a great admirer of Sherman. "The military movements have been masterly," he wrote Welles, "and I regret to hear that a change of leaders is about to take place." [25] According to his way of thinking, there had been perfect accord between the Army and Navy, and, unless the enemy received large reinforcements, he was convinced "Vicksburg will be ours with small loss." Three good landings had been found for the troops, and now there were some twenty-five thousand within a short distance of the city. He believed the expedition up the Yazoo had been a complete surprise to the Confederates, that they had been expecting General McClernand and, when their spies informed them he was making no move to raise men, they assumed no action was planned.

But Porter's assumption that the Confederates were surprised was not borne out by their defense along the Yazoo. How many waited on the hills behind Vicksburg was not known, but two thousand of them, it was estimated, lay in rifle pits along both sides of the river, ready to snipe at the squadron and to blaze away at crews sent to remove the water mines. They were in a mood to contest every inch of ground, and from the overhanging banks they could fire on the vessels with immunity. To counteract this sort of defense, two squadrons of Sherman's troops were landed and moved upstream to the mouth of Chickasaw Creek, and there they enfiladed Blake's levee, known to be one of the main points behind which the Rebels controlled their explosives. Navy vessels meanwhile advanced up the river to Drumgould's Bluff and concentrated on a series of forts and batteries behind the site where the *Cairo* had gone down. The object was to keep reinforcements from being sent to Vicksburg by way of Mill Dale Road.

By three o'clock that afternoon the vessels were within three-quarters of a mile of the batteries. At that hour Lieutenant Commander Gwin pushed to the front in the *Benton*. In this officer the Union had a patriot who was brave to the point of rashness. He had been in the Navy from age fifteen, and only three weeks had passed since he had observed his thirtieth birthday. His behavior on numerous occasions demonstrated that he loved a fight, and it was this characteristic that rescued him from monotonous blockade duty on the Atlantic Coast the previous fall and moved him to command of the little gunboat *Tyler*. In the latter vessel he set a record for activity. At Forts Henry and Donelson he was in the front of battle, and at Shiloh he helped rescue Grant's army from a fierce attack by the Confederates. But his greatest distinction had come the previous July 15, when he took his vessel up the Yazoo with the *Carondelet* and *Queen of the West* in search of the *Arkansas*. It was his craft that battled the ironclad and led it downstream into the waiting Federal fleet. His promotion to lieutenant commander occurred the following day. He served briefly on the ill-fated *Mound City* following her boiler explosion, and then he was transferred to the ironclad *Benton*, largest and most powerful of the river fleet. This last assignment would mean his end, for he had an old-fashioned idea that the place for the captain of such a warship was outside the armor.

For an hour and thirty-five minutes on this December afternoon up the Yazoo, not far from where only a few months past he had battled the *Arkansas,* Gwin bore the brunt of the fight, drawing the fire of eight heavy guns and, in so doing, exceeding his orders, for Porter, knowing that the forts would be taken only by a landing party and a strong one at that, had instructed him merely to make a feint.[26]

The wind was blowing with gale proportions, so hard as to check the current and make the ironclads unmanageable. The *Benton,* always a difficult ship to steer, had a tendency to turn broadside to the wind and she finally had to be tied to the bank. There, in a stationary position, the Confederates found her range and poured their fire in her direction, nearly every shot hitting. "They struck her almost every time they fired," Porter later reported. "It will be well not to mention this, as the Rebels will hear of it and find out the vulnerability of our vessels." [27]

Near the close of the action Gwin fell, a rifle shot tearing off part of his breast and carrying away the muscle of his right arm. Ten men in all were either dead or wounded. That night Porter, who had come down to the Yazoo to be closer to the scene of action, sent a message back to Cairo: "We have had stirring times today, engaging the Yazoo batteries and taking up the torpedoes. The old war horse, *Benton,* has been much cut up, and the gallant, noble Gwin, I fear, mortally wounded." [28]

The rains continued steadily, wetting the men, soaking the countryside, flooding the swamps, and softening the roads. On the 28th, Sherman came within skirmishing distance of the enemy defending Vicksburg. This day he made a feint on the forts and fired across on Mill Dale Road to block reinforcements. Headed off by innumerable bayous, he was finding the ground almost impassable. But by the 29th, he was ready for the assault, and it began early in the morning. In several hours of fierce fighting, one division succeeded in getting into the Confederate lines on the hills, and then was forced to fall back because another division was late in coming to its support.

That night the men of both armies lay in a cold, heavy rain. Early in the evening Sherman visited Porter on his flagship and sat down for a conference about the exact condition of affairs. The conversation was not light. His army that day had met fierce resistance from Georgia, Louisiana, Mississippi, Tennessee, and Texas troops, at the peak of the fighting losing an estimated fifteen hundred men in ten minutes.[29] He knew the Confederates were bringing in reinforcements from Grenada and Jackson—thirty thousand it was thought. His part of the overall campaign had gone according to schedule, but no message had been received from Grant, who was supposed to push on to Canton with fifty thousand men and to come in from that direction for the main assault.

Next day the skies cleared, and Sherman went out and examined the various positions. It was his conclusion the Federals could not break the Confederate center without becoming too crippled to act vigorously afterward.[30] He decided instead to take the batteries at Drumgould's Bluff by assault, thus gaining control of a substantial portion of the Yazoo and putting himself in position to await contact from Grant. At the moment he was losing faith and looking for help from some other source.[31]

He relayed his new plans to Porter: in a night move ten thousand troops would be brought up and secretly landed while gunboats shelled the forts, and then, at a signal, the assault by land would begin. In the meantime he would attack the lines behind Vicksburg and hold the Confederates there in check to prevent reinforcements from being sent to the Bluff.

Porter, also feeling somewhat desperate, was more than willing to help. "I am preparing one of the rams to clear the torpedoes out of the channel," he promptly replied to Sherman. "I propose to send her ahead and explode them; if we lose her, it does not matter much." He promised to be ready by the following night. In making the advance, steamers that made the least noise would be selected. They would carry the lowest steam they could get along with, their boilers would be protected with bales of hay, and canvas or boards would be used to hide their fires. No lights were to be shown, not even lighted cigars. The sides of the vessels next to the enemy were to be camouflaged with bushes and with mud "taken from the banks and mixed with water about the consistency of whitewash."

No white spot would be permitted to show. Whistles would be unrigged, and bells, which could be heard a long way on the river, would be either rung lightly or not at all. These were dodges that Porter had tried at one time or another and found successful.

On the 31st, General Order No. 25 was issued to the squadron. The vessels were to go into action a little above Chickasaw Bayou at 3:30 A.M. They would proceed up to the fort and shell it until rockets were sent up from a point down the river. This would be the signal that the troops had been landed and were ready to start the assault. Only battle lanterns were to be lighted.

The day was one of busy planning. Just after dark two divisions were loaded on the transports, gunboats were all in position, and up to midnight everything appeared favorable. At that hour Sherman left Porter's flagship and went to his camp. All officers were at their posts and ready to act at the first sound of cannonading in the direction of Drumgould's Bluff.

But nature, as in the case of the rains, again sided with the Confederates. Porter sent a report to Sherman early next morning: "We could do nothing on account of the fog last night, until too late to make a safe movement of the transports. It was also twenty minutes of five when the ironclads got to Chickasaw Bayou, when they would have been (but for the fog) at their station, under fire, at half past three A.M. 'Man proposes, God disposes.' It is all right. What next? The moon does not set tomorrow until twenty-five minutes past five; that makes the landing a daylight affair, which is, in my opinion, too hazardous to try." [32]

The report about the moon, coupled with a rain that poured in torrents during the afternoon, convinced Sherman it was time to stack arms. General McClernand, who outranked him, had come in during the day and agreed with this conclusion. So the Union forces were ordered back from Vicksburg, and the descent of the river began.

"Of course I was sadly disappointed," Sherman reported to

the War Department, "as it was the only remaining chance of our securing lodgment on the ridge between the Yazoo and Big Black Rivers from which to operate against Vicksburg and the railroad east, as also to secure the navigation of the Yazoo River; but I am forced to admit the admiral's judgment was well founded and that even in case of success the assault on the batteries of Drumgould's Bluff would have been attended with a fearful sacrifice of life." [33]

The squadron came back down the Yazoo and crossed over and turned up the Mississippi to Milliken's Bend, five miles above Vicksburg, and there Sherman's army went into camp. Porter directed his fleet with an air of triumph; it had done all that was expected of it. And while Sherman's men lay entrenched, it would stand by in protection, covering with its guns a semicircle of eight miles. Soon he was writing to the veteran Admiral Foote, now at his desk as chief of the Bureau of Equipment and Recruiting in Washington, a cheerful letter in which he reported: "We have had lively times up the Yazoo. Imagine the Yazoo becoming the theater of war! We waded through sixteen miles of torpedoes to get at the forts (seven in number), but when we got that far the fire on the boats from the riflemen in pits dug for miles along the river and from the batteries became very annoying, and that gallant fellow Gwin thought he could check them, which he did until he was knocked over with the most fearful wound I ever saw."

As Porter wrote, Gwin lay dying in the flag officer's cabin. His death that very day would bring no victory and serve no purpose other than to help impress the Federals with the obvious fact that they had to find another way to take Vicksburg.

Another ironclad for Davy Jones

DECEMBER 1862

The violent storm that seemed to side with the South in up-
setting Sherman's plans at Vicksburg was not confined to Mississippi, nor were its adverse effects restricted to the Army. It
also spelled trouble for one of the Union's major ships—the
Monitor. And the lull in the weather that caused Federal forces
along the Yazoo to prepare for an attack at Drumgould's Bluff
and then abandon the idea was equally deceptive to those responsible for the ironclad, influencing them to start her out on a
wintry voyage from which she never returned.

It was a startling blow, this loss of a mighty ship, and it gave
the Union a "sick turn," as Gustavus Fox put it.[1] Unexpected,
it came at a time when the North was having no success with its
land forces. Lee had blocked Burnside at Fredericksburg, the
Southerners had upset the Grant-Sherman drive to take Vicksburg, and now the ironclad that had brought so much hope to
the Government at Washington was at the bottom of the sea,
an iron coffin for a part of her faithful crew.

But the *Monitor*'s fate might have been foreseen. There was ample warning, particularly from Lieutenant Samuel Dana Greene, the second officer ever to command her. Asked for his opinion back in March, he told Gideon Welles that he did not consider her a seagoing vessel. On the trip down from New York, he admitted, she had pitched very little and with no strain whatever. "But," he added, "she has not the steam power to go against a head wind or sea, and I think it very doubtful if she should go from here to Delaware Bay." [2] And then rumors spread that the Confederacy was preparing to break the blockade at Wilmington. So authentic and credible did they seem— some were from consular sources abroad—that the Union considered the emergency grave enough to ignore Greene's advice and take the gamble.

During most of the period since her battle with the *Merrimack,* the *Monitor* had been standing by at Newport News, looking up the James River for the appearance of a new ironclad, the *Virginia No. 2,* that the Southerners were said to be building at Richmond. The only break in this monotonous rountine came in the fall when the Ericsson dream ship was taken up the Potomac to the Washington Navy Yard for repairs. A month and a half she stayed there, lightening her draft, receiving new fans, and undergoing improvements to her machinery, the last on the advice of Admiral Lee, who said she had been so long under steam that she was "very liable to derangement." [3]

At the Union capital the ironclad was an object of such curiosity that she was kept under heavy guard. In early November, after her hull had been scraped and painted, a reception was held on board, and President Lincoln climbed to her deck to say a few words of praise before stepping back to allow the "beardless" Dana Greene to give a first-hand account of her action in battle. A few days later she was opened to public visit, and a long line of people, including women in bounteous skirts, squeezed through her crowded quarters and stared at her revolving turret.

While at Washington she was in charge of a new commander,

Captain John Pine Bankhead, son of a distinguished South Carolina soldier. Forty-one years old, he had been in the Navy more than half his life. The Department considered him an experienced, level-headed naval officer. At the battle of Port Royal he had commanded the *Pembina* and had fought her as though unaware that the shells he was firing were falling on his native state.

The *Monitor*'s stay at the capital was not delayed unduly, for the threat at Wilmington became a growing problem, and she was scheduled for a part in efforts to solve it. This trouble spot had been worrying the Union high command for months. In May, Louis Goldsborough, then head of the North Atlantic Blockading Squadron, wrote Fox: "I can and will take the forts at Wilmington as soon as I can avail myself of the services of the *Monitor* and the other vessels now engaged hereabouts, provided the Department says the word. The job would afford me very great pleasure." [4] But nothing was done about it, even though there was evidence enough that runners were going in and out of that port pretty much at will.

In December it was reported beyond doubt that the Confederates would attempt to break the blockade. Added to this was information, brought by a carpenter who arrived from the Wilmington shipyards, that two ironclad gunboats were being built there and would be ready by January. Welles was stirred to action. Only a few weeks earlier Fox had suggested that it would be a "grand stroke" to tow the *Monitor* and *Passaic*, first two ironclads built by the North, down to North Carolina in good weather "and clean out Wilmington and its railroad connections." He had a notion that the forts along the Cape Fear River would fall, once the town was captured. [5]

Orders to move the two ironclads were given December 24 to Commander Stephen Decatur Trenchard of the supply ship *Rhode Island* and Commander James F. Armstrong of the *State of Georgia*. Trenchard was to tow the *Monitor* and Armstrong the *Passaic*. Time of departure from Newport News was left to their own judgment: "Avail yourself of the first favorable weather for making the passage." [6] They were to head for Beaufort.

It was hoped the journey could be started the following afternoon, but by that time the storm had broken and departure was delayed. For four days rain fell, whipped by a high wind. But by the 29th, a Monday, the skies had cleared, a light wind was blowing from the southwest, and there was every evidence that the gods of weather had settled their differences and were ready for a period of calm. At 2:30 P.M. the four vessels steamed away. There was no excitement, no fanfare such as had marked the Hatteras and Port Royal expeditions. The war was now a serious proposition, and naval craft with jobs to do no longer waited on ceremony.

Veteran Pilot John H. Bean steered the *Rhode Island,* with the *Monitor* in tow, out of Hampton Roads. By six o'clock they had passed Cape Henry. The course was south-southwest, and the water was smooth. Everything was working well. Darkness settled beneath a glittering of stars, and there was great confidence that the good weather would continue. No one was particularly concerned. The journey ahead was no longer than the distance from New York to Hampton Roads.

But at five o'clock next morning the *Monitor*'s crew felt a swell from the southward and noticed a slight increase of wind from the southwest. She was making about five knots. The sea was becoming rough, breaking over the pilothouse and striking the base of the turret. And still there was no alarm.

Throughout the day the weather varied, changing from clear skies to occasional squalls of wind and rain. There was less swell in the afternoon, and bilge pumps were able to keep ahead of the water coming on board through various openings.

On the *Rhode Island* things were even more peaceful. Trenchard made note in his journal: "The *Monitor* is making good headway in the good weather and is turning easily. Our speed averages five to six miles an hour. At one o'clock in the afternoon we sighted Cape Hatteras light, bearing west by southeast fourteen miles distant. . . . The steamer *State of*

Georgia, with the *Passaic* in tow, was in sight some six or eight miles to the north and east of us, and the steamer *Cahanta* was this side of her with a troop ship in tow." [7]

By 7:00 P.M. the wind had hauled more to the southward. It grew stronger and caused the sea to rise, and water coming into the *Monitor* was of noticeably greater volume. The navigator estimated they were fifteen miles south of Cape Hatteras, which would put them in an area off Diamond Shoals, famous for occasionally stirring up the angriest seas on the American coast. The ironclad by this stage was beginning to yaw and tow badly, and it was increasingly obvious that more water was washing on board. To combat this threat, two Worthington pumps of modern invention, adjuncts to the bilge pumps, were put to work, and the centrifugal pump was readied for operation if needed. Together they could force out a minimum of two thousand gallons per minute.

Within the next hour the sea rose rapidly, completely submerging the pilothouse and at times entering the turret and the blower pipes. The *Monitor* plunged wildly. "The sea rolled over us as if our vessel were a rock in the ocean, and men who stood abaft on the *Rhode Island* have told me that we were thought several times to have gone down," related a survivor. "It seemed that for minutes we were out of sight as the heavy seas entirely submerged the vessel." [8]

Each time she rose to the swell the flat undersurface of her projecting armor came down with great force, making a noise like a clap of thunder and causing considerable shock to the vessel. It was a growing cause of worry. The base of the turret had been well calked before leaving port, but leaks were appearing in increasing numbers as the sea beat against the ironclad. Water also was coming in through the sightholes of the pilothouse and through the hawsehole.

Commander Trenchard, realizing an emergency, signaled the *Rhode Island* to stop, hoping the *Monitor* would ride easier out of tow. But, instead, she fell off into the trough of the sea, rolling badly and taking on as much water as ever. The engineer reported that the bilge and Worthington pumps were losing the battle, and that the centrifugal pump would have to be called into action.

The sea continued to rise. By 10:30 P.M., with seven inches of the sea swirling around the engine-room floor despite the madly working pumps, and with the water continuing to gain in volume, Bankhead gave the distress signal, hoisting a red lantern to the top of the turret. It was immediately answered by the *Rhode Island*.

Gradually the *Monitor* was brought close to the steamer. Then Bankhead shouted through his trumpet that the water was gaining on him rapidly and asked that boats be sent to take off his crew. A launch and a cutter were lowered from the *Rhode Island*.

While waiting for the boats to get within reach, Bankhead noticed that the heavy stream cable used in towing rendered the ironclad unmanageable while hanging slack to her bow. Since the engines had to be kept going to work the pumps, he ordered the cable cut. James Fenwick, quarter gunner, reached the bow and tried to obey, but was swept overboard. Boatswain's Mate John Stocking took his place and, with a few swift blows of an ax, cut the rope. At that moment a giant wave lashed the ship and away he went, shouting a single, haunting word as he disappeared into the darkness: "Farewell."

Before the boats arrived, the *Monitor* rolled down under the lee of the *Rhode Island,* almost touching her. By this time the ashpits were more than half full of water, allowing little air to reach the fires, and the blowers used for producing a current of air to the flames were throwing great gushes of water.

Out of the darkness, guided by much yelling back and forth, the two boats finally appeared. Bankhead shouted to Dana Greene to get as many men into them as they could safely carry. It was a dangerous operation. A heavy sea was breaking over the deck, and several members of the crew were washed overboard before they could get footing in the boats. Ropes were thrown on board the *Monitor* from the *Rhode Island*. It was wasted effort. Reported Trenchard: "So reluctant did the crew appear to leave their vessel that they did not take advantage of this opportunity to save themselves." [9]

During the rescue, the two vessels touched slightly, nearly crushing the launch. This panicked Trenchard, for he realized the sharp bow and sides of the ironclad might stove in his ship. Without a moment's thought of abandoning his task, he ordered the *Rhode Island* to steam a short distance ahead.

Finally the boats were loaded, and they struggled through the heavy sea toward the *Rhode Island,* drifting so rapidly that in time she would be a mile away. Only the cutter would return; the launch had been too badly damaged for further use.

During the cutter's absence the *Monitor's* engineer sent word to Bankhead that the engines and pumps had ceased to work, that the water had put out the fires, and that there was no steam pressure. In a futile gesture, a bailing party was organized, "not so much with any hope of diminishing the water, but more as an occupation for the men," explained the commander. "It was like bailing out the ocean," one of those who took part reported.[10] Buckets starting out from below fairly well filled arrived at the hatchway at the top of the turret with only a few drops in them.

With the engines stopped, the *Monitor* could no longer be kept head to sea, and she fell off into the trough and rolled so heavily Bankhead knew the boats would be unable to approach her. In a desperate hope, he ordered the anchor to be lowered, and this brought the vessel up and swung her around head to wind.

There were still twenty-five or thirty men on board. The vessel was filling rapidly, so rapidly the deck was on a level with the water. Bankhead ordered the remaining men to leave the turret and be ready to get into the boats when they returned. A third assistant engineer, Samuel A. Lewis, lay below in the wardroom, too ill to get out of his bunk, and he curled there with eyes glued on the water coming nearer and nearer his bedding. A seaman passed. "Is there any hope?" asked the prostrate sailor. Compassion influenced the answer, made in the knowledge that here lay stretched a man who was near his end: "As long as there is life there is always hope." [11]

The cabin cook, an African Negro whose white eyes rolled in the darkness, blended a rather gruesome humor with his terror: "Don't be skeered, gen'men!" he yelled hoarsely from the berth deck. "Only de debble can pick yo' bones. Ain't no shark go' find his way into dis here iron coffin." [12]

Francis B. Butts, one of seven men signed on the *Monitor* while she was undergoing repairs at Washington, stood in the turret passing buckets from the lower hatchway to the top. Thinking of his coat, received from home shortly before leaving Newport News, he rolled it up with his boots, drew the tampion from a gun, and shoved them inside. A black cat, pet of all on board, sat on the other gun. Butts stuffed her inside, too.

"As I raised my last bucket to the upper hatchway," he related, "no one was there to take it. I scrambled up the ladder and found that we below had been deserted." He shouted to those still underneath on the berth deck: "Come up—the officers have left the ship and a boat's alongside!"

Butts felt for the ladder from the top of the turret. In his confusion he failed to locate it, but his fingers touched a loose line, and he fastened it to a stanchion and let himself down on deck. A man was floating to leeward, calling in vain for help. Another jumped down from the turret and was swept away by a breaking wave.

"The moment I struck the deck," Butts remembered, "the sea broke over and swept me as I had seen it sweep my shipmates. I grasped one of the smokestack braces and, hand over hand, ascended to keep my head above water, and it required all my strength to keep the sea from tearing me away."

Soon the cutter could be heard coming back, approaching cautiously. Several men were washed overboard, one of them fortunate enough to be hauled out of the water before he drowned. Bankhead himself got hold of the painter of the boat and held on to it while he directed his men to jump. Those already seated in the cutter were pushing with oars to keep it from crashing against the side of the ironclad.

Several men were still in the turret. Bankhead knew they were there, and he shouted repeatedly for them to come out. His words were wasted. "They were either stupefied by fear or fearful of being washed overboard in the attempt to reach the boats," he concluded.

Quartermaster Richard Najier was still at his post at the *Monitor*'s wheel. Bankhead shouted for him to get into the boats. "No, sir," he yelled back, "not till you go!"

The last men who would come out now appeared. Bankhead watched all but two of them safely transfer, and then, feeling that he had done everything within his power to save vessel and crew, jumped across himself, helped by the two remaining sailors, Najier and Butts. Then they leaped.

Alongside the *Rhode Island,* the boats unloaded their passengers. "We found that getting on board the *Rhode Island* was a harder task than getting from the *Monitor,*" Butts recalled. "We were carried by the sea from stem to stern, for to make fast would have been fatal, and the boat bounded against the ship's sides; sometimes it was below the wheel, and then, on the summit of a huge wave, far above the decks; then the two boats would crash together, and once while our surgeon was holding onto the rail, he lost his fingers by a collision which swamped the other boat. Lines were thrown to us from the deck of the *Rhode Island,* which were of no assistance, for not one of us would climb a small rope, and, besides, the men who threw them would immediately let go their holds in their excitement to throw another—which I found to be the case when I kept hauling in rope instead of climbing and concluded . . . that the end was cut off."

Butts finally caught a rope that held. In panic he pulled himself up in the dark, to within a foot or two of the *Rhode Island*'s rail—it seemed to him. But his strength failed, and he could haul himself no further. A few feet away from him was Acting Ensign Norman Atwater, hanging to the cathead. Their hands grew weak with pain; they yelled in vain for help. All about them was darkness and desperation and confusion. Atwater got a foothold, slipped, caught again, and then, muttering, "Oh, God!," he dropped into the water and disappeared. Butts continued to yell, but the wind shrieked above his voice. The sea rolled, and the rope in his hands jerked. He fell, expecting to drop into the sea, but, instead, he landed in the boat, and from a surprised seaman came words he would never forget: "Where the hell did he come from?"

Two trips had been made by the cutter and now, commanded by Acting Master's Mate D. Rodney Browne, it started back in a last desperate effort to rescue the remainder of the *Monitor*'s crew. Browne was hailed and directed to lie on his oars, or drop astern and be towed up until the *Rhode Island* could steam nearer the *Monitor,* but he misunderstood and continued on the return trip. Seven men were with him. The darkness swallowed them, and the waves roared and shut off all communication.

The red light on the turret of the ironclad was still visible to those on the *Rhode Island*. They watched it bob and roll, and then for a moment it steadied before it slid out of sight.

It was 1:30 A.M.[13]

Trenchard shouted in vain to Browne. The roar of the sea was his only answer. But he would not leave. Throughout the hours of blackness he attempted to keep his ship as near as possible to the spot where the *Monitor* was last seen. At intervals night signals were burned. Daylight came, but it revealed nothing but the angry seas of Diamond Shoals, an estimated twenty miles from Cape Hatteras. Soundings at 7:00 A.M. showed thirty-five fathoms of water.

At 9:45 the crew of the *Monitor* was mustered. There were forty-seven officers and men.[14] Sixteen were missing.[15]

It was four days later, on January 3, before reports of the loss of the *Monitor* reached Washington. But there was good news with the bad. That day a leaky schooner was towed into Beaufort. She was the *A. Colby,* and on board were Rodney Browne and the crew of the missing cutter. They had been picked up fifty miles east of Cape Hatteras on the morning of December 31.

The news gave Gideon Welles occasion to set the record straight. He wrote in his diary on this date: "The fate of this vessel affects me in other respects. She is a primary representative of a class identified with my administration of the Navy. Her novel construction and qualities I adopted and she was built amidst obloquy and ridicule. Such a change in the character of a fighting vessel few naval men, or any Secretary under their influence, would have taken the responsibility of adopting. But Admiral Smith and finally all the Board which I appointed seconded my views, and were willing, Davis somewhat reluctantly, to recommend the experiment if I would assume the risk and responsibility. Her success with the *Merrimack* directly after she went into commission relieved me of odium and anxiety, and men who were prepared to ridicule were left to admire." [16]

On January 5, the day Commander Bankhead arrived in Washington to give an oral account, the Secretary made this record in the diary: "The loss of the *Monitor* and the report of Admiral Lee and others of the draft of water at the inlet is unfavorable for a naval attack on the battery at Cape Fear, and the Army object to move on Wilmington except in conjunction with the Navy. It is best, therefore, to push on to Charleston and strengthen Du Pont." [17]

One other matter remained before the *Monitor* would be fully disposed of. A petition dated January 3 came into Welles' hands. It was signed by twenty men who identified themselves as "all who now remain of the original crew of the U.S.S. *Monitor.*" In consideration of this distinction, they asked their discharge from the Navy and that they might be "privileged to serve our country in whatever capacity may seem best." The Secretary read it and added his endorsement: "Give them two weeks' leave, with twenty per cent of all they may have due them. At the expiration they may return to the receiving ships nearest their residence." [18]

A white flag means truce

JANUARY 1863

Appearance of Raphael Semmes and his *Alabama* in the waters off Galveston, Texas, would have been evidence enough that the Federals on duty there were in for trouble. But disturbances in that vicinity already had been sufficient proof that there was still a lot of fight left in the Southerners. The year had started off badly for the Union at that port. Late in '62 Confederate General John Bankhead Magruder took over command of the Department of Texas. He came to his new post with stars in his eyes, resolved to regain the Texas harbors and to occupy in force the valley of the Rio Grande.

The Union's grip on Galveston had been established by Farragut in October. At that time four vessels, the *Westfield, Clifton, Harriet Lane,* and *Owasco,* sailed in—the Confederates charged they were flying flags of truce—and set up a patrol. Later, three companies from the 42nd Massachusetts Volunteers, under Colonel Isaac S. Burrell, arrived to occupy the wharves, and still later, in came the steamer *Sachem,* badly in need of repairs, escorted by the schooner *Corypheus.*

Burrell's troops—two hundred and sixty in all—were quartered in buildings along the wharves, under protection of the fleet's guns. In addition, barricades were thrown up, both indoors and out, and a part of the planking on the wharf was removed. Burrell felt secure. He had entrenching tools for five hundred men, a thirty-day commissary supply, three months' medical supplies, and about twenty-five thousand rounds of ammunition.

By day the Federals kept a careful watch on the town. Pickets were posted at the corners of the main streets, patrols moved regularly through the city, and up in the cupola of the Hendley Building a lookout stared over the entire community and suburbs. But at night the pickets were drawn in closer to the main body of troops, where they would be less likely to become victims of pot shots in the dark.

This precautionary withdrawal at the close of day was not without reason. Parties of Rebel cavalry came into town almost every night. They generally rode along the beach, concealed by a range of sand hills, and on reaching the suburbs, separated into parties of two or three and scattered about the streets, spying and seeking information. Before daylight they rendezvoused at Schmidt's Garden, a favorite loitering spot, and then rode out the same way they had come.

On December 30, some refugees came to the wharf and reported a rumor in town that an attack would be made on the Massachusetts soldiers that night. Burrell was no alarmist, although he did throw up a new barricade of planks, timber, and barrels of plaster found in a warehouse. True enough, about 11:00 P.M. a party of Rebel cavalry dashed upon the pickets and drove them farther in, but then withdrew.

The next day was quiet, despite Magruder's presence in the neighborhood. His plan of attack was in its final stage. He had had no trouble getting volunteers to assist him with his plan for driving out the invading Northerners. Captain A. R. Wier, commander of a fort on the Sabine, offered the services of his soldiers to man a steamboat. Others were equally willing.

Magruder had started out by making the rounds, staying a day or two in Houston and then moving on to Virginia Point, and finally to the mainland, opposite Galveston Island. There he gathered around him a party of eighty men and stole across the bay one night to determine the situation inside the city of Galveston. He found that the forts abandoned by the Confederates when the town was given up were of no use to him because they were open in the rear and within range of the enemy ships from that direction.

But one discovery was highly encouraging. Among the Confederates lurking around Galveston he found an old California steamboat captain, Leon Smith, an acquaintance from his army days in the West. Smith was an artist in steamboat management, and Magruder promptly added him to his staff, assigning to him the task of rounding up all the steamers available along the bayous emptying into Galveston Bay. Among the most important of these were two packets, the *Bayou City* and the *Neptune,* the latter requiring such overhauling that it was necessary to work the crews night and day.[1]

When the steamers were ready, Magruder ordered Captain Wier and his artillerists, as well as a company of cavalry, to board the *Bayou City*. Volunteers, called for from Sibley's Brigade, were sent to the *Neptune,* among them a company of infantry under Lieutenant L. C. Harby, lately captain in the U. S. Revenue Service, now acting as artillery. Most of the men were armed with Enfield rifles brought from Richmond and with double-barreled shotguns. The *Bayou City* was armed with a thirty-two-pounder rifled gun, and the *Neptune* with two howitzers. Bulwarks of cotton were built up on their decks. The *Neptune* was so well protected in this manner that a newspaper correspondent reported "she had much the appearance when she left Houston of a well-loaded cotton boat taking her cargo down to Galveston for shipment." [2] They were ordered to Half-moon Shoals, fifteen miles from Galveston, and there they dropped anchor to await the signal from shore to go into action.

Magruder knew that the Union fleet consisted of the *Harriet*

Lane, armed with four heavy guns and two twenty-four-pounder howitzers; the ferryboat *Westfield,* flagship of Commodore W. B. Renshaw, a large side-wheeler mounting eight heavy guns; the *Owasco,* a two-masted screw steamer similarly armed; the ferryboat *Clifton,* with eight guns; the *Sachem,* a screw steamer with four heavy guns; two large barks, two armed transports, and an armed schooner. The Confederates had six siege pieces, fourteen fieldpieces, some rifled, and an eight-inch Dahlgren mounted on a railway flatcar.

The plans for attack were readied. On a siding sat the Dahlgren, waiting to be hauled by rail to within a few hundred yards of the *Harriet Lane,* nearest of the ships. A large quantity of cotton in bales was hauled in to be used as a breastwork for this gun in case the fight was not ended before morning. Three of the heaviest of the siege pieces had to be transported nine miles, the others seven, over the most difficult roads. A signal system for rapid communication between the gunboats and the troops on shore was arranged. The attack was to be launched at midnight, and the signal was to be the fire of the land batteries. The charge on land would be against three different wharves. In this it would be necessary for the men to advance by wading through water past the point where the planks had been removed and then to climb up by means of fifty scaling ladders.

After nightfall on December 31, refugees begged entrance to the Union picket lines and, once inside, talked freely. They said an attack was imminent. But the early evening hours were just like any others. Along the wharves sounded the usual noises of soldier life, with here and there a raucous laugh or burst of song. Out in the harbor the Union vessels were dark shadows in the moonlight. The *Harriet Lane* lay in a narrow channel near the shore. Abreast of the town farther to the east were the *Sachem* and *Corypheus.* Down the bay a mile out, the *Clifton* and *Owasco* were anchored, and two miles away the *Westfield.* They were all dark and silent. And from the city itself there was no sound of hostility. Dogs barked monotonously, the echoes of their yapping fading lonesomely across the water. As usual the business section of town had gone to bed before midnight, and lamps that shone from the windows of private homes were beacons of domesticity. Midnight passed and not the faintest symbol of alarm was noticeable. But at one-thirty the watch on the *Clifton* trained night glasses toward the distant moonlit waters of the bay. Out there they spotted two or three steamers, obscure but distinguishable in the darkness, which they assumed to be Rebel. Lookouts on the *Westfield* saw the same thing. Soon afterward pickets on shore reported enemy artillery taking position in the market place a quarter of a mile away. Captain George Sherive, from one of the Massachusetts companies who went out to investigate, confirmed the report. Burrell roused his men from bed and placed them behind the barricades. Then he flashed an alarm toward the gunboats. The *Harriet Lane,* nearest shore, picked it up, and soon it was transmitting the warning to the more distant vessels: "Enemy on shore." The *Westfield* made a signal, too, but it was not clear, at least not to Lieutenant Commander Henry Wilson, watching from the *Owasco.* But apparently the *Clifton* deciphered it correctly, for it raised anchor, got under way, and stood toward the *Westfield.*[3]

The early morning hours ticked by, and the moon sank toward the horizon. At 3:00 A.M., a cannon blast sounded out of the darkness on shore. It was fired by General Magruder himself, inside the city, from a gun pointing toward the center of three wharves under attack.

Immediately an outburst of musketry and cannon fire followed, as the other Confederates swung into action. The attack was centered initially on the warehouses in which it was supposed the Federal soldiers were sleeping. Soon the fighters in gray were wading into the water beneath the wharves, the scaling ladders on their backs. To their great disappointment the ladders were too short and this part of the assault collapsed completely.

At Halfmoon Shoals the *Bayou City* and the *Neptune* heard

the signal and got under way. The river steamer *John F. Carr* was there, too, and it followed along. Magruder's California friend, Leon Smith, stared ahead impatiently from the deck of the *Bayou City*. A reporter from the Houston *Telegraph* was on board, and he heard Smith shout: "Let's get back to Galveston with all the steam we can crack on! We must get there as quick as we can!" [4] Men below were feeding the fires with resin.

The moon had disappeared and daylight was approaching before the Rebel vessels neared the enemy. On shore Magruder stepped up his attack, the Confederates firing from the protection of buildings. They had managed to get two pieces of artillery up to the second story of a warehouse, and these were blasting away at the nearest wharf. Out in the water only yards away the schooner *Corypheus,* men flat on her deck, trained her guns in protection of the Federals behind the barricades. The *Owasco* and *Sachem* were farther out, also firing in defense of the wharves, but the *Harriet Lane* and other vessels were looking toward the approaching Confederate fleet.

The *Bayou City,* in the lead, steered toward the *Harriet Lane*. Captain Wier aimed the *Bayou's* thirty-two-pounder rifled gun. The first shot went wild, but the second struck behind the *Lane*'s wheel and made a hole big enough for a man to crawl through. There was loud shouting among the Confederates, and one of them, remembering the date, called to Wier: "Give us another New Year's present like that!" The captain, thrilling to the moment, shouted back, "Here it is!" and pulled the lanyard of the gun. A deafening explosion followed as the weapon flew to pieces, killing Wier and several others.[5]

The *Harriet Lane* ran into the *Bayou City,* carrying away her wheel guard, passed her, and gave her a broadside that did little damage. The *Neptune,* coming up, headed for the Federal ship and was so damaged in the collision that she veered off and sank in eight feet of water. By this time the *Bayou City* had straightened out. Her engines roared as she ran hard against the *Harriet Lane*. With a loud crash, her prow went into the

Union vessel, locking them together, and immediately over the side came the Confederates, led by Leon Smith.

Volleys of musketry and pistol fire rang through the rigging. Commander Jonathan F. Wainwright ran out on deck, gun in hand. Behind him came his executive officer, Lieutenant Commander Edward Lea. They both were shot down, Wainwright killed by Smith and Lea mortally wounded, and in a matter of seconds the *Harriet Lane* was in possession of the Confederates.

The *Owasco,* seeing the *Harriet Lane* in trouble, tried to bring her guns to bear in support, but was prevented by the narrowness of the channel in which she lay and by the intense fire of musketry from shore. The *Westfield,* meanwhile, had got herself in trouble. When the approach of the Rebel vessels was first discovered, she got under way. Soon she ran aground on Pelican Island, and there she waited helplessly, sending signals for assistance. The *Clifton* responded, but was unable to get her free.

After capturing the *Harriet Lane,* Smith quickly took command of the situation. He hoisted a flag of truce, and soon a boat bearing it was on its way across to the *Clifton.* There it was received by Lieutenant Commander Richard L. Law, who, upon considering the demand for surrender, asked a waiting period of three hours in which to consult the fleet commander, W. B. Renshaw of the *Westfield.* This was granted, and a boat took him across for a conference.

The Confederates waited. They apparently had no suspicion of what was taking place over on the *Westfield,* but they should have had, for matters were not proceeding along the anticipated pattern. Renshaw was adamant, insisting that they refuse to accede to the Southerners' proposition. He directed Law to get all the vessels out of port as soon as possible. As for his own stranded ship, he would blow her up and then go on board the transports *Saxon* or *M. A. Boardman.*

Law's movements also were suspicious. On his return from the *Westfield* he was rowed close to the schooner *Corypheus,* standing with her guns silent since she had seen the flags of truce set, and when near enough he called up in a low tone to Acting Master A. T. Spear: "Spike your guns, burn your vessel, and take to boats for Bolivar Channel." Later these instructions were followed by another order: "Wait until the flags of truce are hauled down; then make sail and escape."

As the three-hour period drew to a close Colonel Thomas Green, one of Magruder's favorite officers, and Captain Henry Lubbock of the *Bayou City* went across in an open boat to close the negotiations, a flag of truce waving above them. They had gone only a short distance toward the *Westfield* when a loud explosion sounded, and the Union vessel seemed to disintegrate in a great cloud of water, smoke, and debris. When the smoke cleared away, not a living thing could be seen. Some parts of the ship were still visible, among them her guns aft, which were double shotted and run out and which sounded off at intervals, like the dying gasps of a warrior. The Federals who looked on were stunned: they knew she had just been supplied by the *Tennessee* with a large stock of provisions and clothing.[6]

Seeing the vessel disappear in front of them, the two officers changed their course and headed for the *Clifton*. This they boarded, and shortly afterward she got under way and steamed toward the bar. Soon she was met by a boat from the *Westfield*. It brought shocking tidings: the explosion, preceded by pouring turpentine over the forward magazine and over the part of the ship that had gone aground, had been premature and had killed Renshaw, his executive officer Lieutenant C. W. Zimmerman, Engineer W. R. Greene, and others.[7]

"When the first period of truce expired," Magruder reported, "the enemy's ships under our guns, regardless of the white flag still flying at their mastheads, gradually crept off. As soon as this was seen I sent a swift express on horseback to direct the guns to open fire on them. This was done with so much effect that one of them was reported to have sunk near the bar, and the *Owasco* was seriously damaged." [8]

Leon Smith noticed the Union ships creeping toward the bar. Jumping on board the *Carr,* he hurried after them, but reached

Bolivar Channel too late to head them off. However, he found there and captured the barks *Cavalle* and *Elias Pike,* loaded with coal, as well as a schooner.

Galveston once more was completely in possession of the Confederates, for the Massachusetts troops under Colonel Burrell, seeing the fleet scattered, surrendered without further fight. The crew of the *Harriet Lane* was ordered ashore. As the men descended the ladder, some of them were recognized as survivors from the *Congress* and *Cumberland,* the two mighty vessels that a famous ironclad had destroyed in Hampton Roads the preceding March 8. "It's hard to be 'Merrimacked' a second time," one of them was heard to say as he took his place in the boat that would convey him toward land.

Wounded from the ships were taken to a hospital on shore. In the process Magruder was met by one of his most distinguished and scientific staff officers, Major A. M. Lea, formerly of the United States Army. The latter seemed stunned. "I've just found my son Edward on board the *Harriet Lane* mortally wounded," he announced, his voice trembling.[9] Edward had died in his arms.

The Confederates counted their losses as twenty-six killed and one hundred and seventeen wounded, in addition to the sunken *Neptune* from which the guns were removed. Their captures included the *Harriet Lane,* the two coal barks, a schooner, between three and four hundred prisoners, fifteen guns, and a large quantity of stores, coal, and other material.

January 2 was a quiet day at Galveston. In the afternoon Captain Wainwright and Lieutenant Lea were buried with Masonic and military honors in the same grave while a silent throng looked on. The burial service was performed by Major Lea, grieved by loss of a son who had gone into battle as his enemy. Just the day before, Farragut had written an order directing the son to take command of the mortar boats at New Orleans, but he had been killed before it was delivered.[10]

Once more this Texas port was open to shipping, but with trickery afoot. From the custom house and from the mastheads of ships U. S. flags waved, placed there by Confederate hands in the hope that Union vessels would be fooled into entering. And further, a line of buoys established to guide vessels into the harbor was displaced and so arranged as to run aground those without friendly intent.[11]

The fleeing Union ships steamed for New Orleans to report to Farragut. Behind them at Galveston, Magruder got off a report to Richmond in which he stated: "The *Owasco,* the *Clifton,* and the *Sachem* escaped under a flag of truce, so that the harbor of Galveston was entered under a flag of truce and left by the same flagrant violation of military propriety." [12]

Farragut was highly critical in his evaluation of what had happened at Galveston. "It is difficult to conceive a more pusillanimous surrender of a vessel to an enemy already in our power than occurred in the case of the *Harriet Lane.*" [13] Because of the speed and armament of this ship, he feared what would happen if she got to sea as a cruiser.[14]

Welles was greatly upset when the news reached him. "The rumor of the capture of the *Harriet Lane* with the little garrison at Galveston is confirmed," he wrote in his diary. "I am grieved and depressed, not so much for the loss of the *Harriet Lane* as from a conviction that there has been want of good management. It is about three months since we took Galveston, and yet a garrison of only three hundred men was there when the Rebel army approached the place. Someone is blamable for this neglect." [15]

Fox frankly admitted his embarrassment over the incident in a letter to Du Pont. "We were defeated at Galveston," he wrote, "by two gunboats which only mounted one sixty-eight-pounder, which burst at the third fire, and the whole attacking force were soldiers. It was the most disgraceful affair that has occurred to the Navy during its whole history, without a single redeeming feature, and to complete our disgrace and complications the senior officer left the fort with three gunboats and ran for New Orleans." [16]

The *Clifton* reached New Orleans at ten o'clock the night

of January 3, followed a few hours later by the *Owasco* and *Sachem.* All were damaged. The *Owasco's* smokestack was down. The *Sachem* had lost a propeller. They confirmed the discouraging news that had preceded them.

Farragut dined that afternoon with Commodore Henry H. Bell, and while they ate they discussed the crisis at Galveston. "I am ready for any service," said Bell. "Then go down," directed the flag officer, "and reestablish the blockade as soon as you can." [17]

Bell started out in the *Brooklyn,* in company with the *Sciota,* on the 5th, somewhat delayed by the necessity of getting back on board about sixty of his men who "were on shore on a debauch." On the 6th he met the *Cambria,* standing off in a distrustful mood, for a boat sent ashore had not returned. For twenty-four hours it had been awaiting its return.

Bell anchored off Galveston Bar at 11:00 A.M. on the 7th. Back of the town he could see what he took to be the *Harriet Lane,* two barks, two schooners, and two bay steamers. Men were throwing up an earthwork at the northeast end of the island, tents were plainly visible, and troops could be seen marching up the beach. Next day the *Cayuga, Sciota,* and *New London* arrived.

On the 9th a boat flying a white flag came out from town bearing a letter from General Magruder, who wanted to know whether the truce was still in effect. Bell answered the next day by shelling the shore.

At four o'clock on the afternoon of the 11th, Bell called the commanders of the *New London, Clifton, Sciota,* and *Cayuga* on board the *Brooklyn* for a conference. Should they attack? Bell outlined the problem succinctly: only one pilot, a narrow, intricate channel, with no landmarks to guide them, and, on the outer shoals, only buoys, which they did not understand. All of the officers were willing to go in, but they admitted their fears of what might happen if the ships grounded. The final decision was recorded in Bell's journal: "It is with a bitter and lasting pang of grief I give it up, as the blockade of the port with the

Harriet Lane ready for sea is a difficult task for so small a fleet as is in the Gulf. There will be censure, inconsiderate censure, but I can't help it. I can't overcome the difficulty of shoal water and a crooked, narrow channel without pilots, or small draft vessels to assist such as ground." [18]

A short time before the ship commanders went into conference the *Hatteras,* newly arrived from New Orleans, was sent in chase of a sail to the southeast-by-east. At sunset she was still in sight, about twelve miles to the south, but visibility soon faded. At seven-fifteen flashes of guns could be seen in her direction, and soon came the echo of heavy weapons—heavier than any carried by the *Hatteras.*[19] The firing lasted perhaps a quarter of an hour and was judged to be about sixteen miles off.[20] The *Brooklyn, Sciota,* and *Cayuga* set out to investigate, carrying all the steam they could get up. Throughout the night they searched, but by seven-thirty next morning they had seen nothing. The Galveston light was sixty-two miles north, three degrees east.

At 11:00 A.M. they came upon two masts standing out of the water, perfectly erect except for the rake in them, with a United States naval pennant flying "playfully and unconscious" from the main truck. No ensign was visible, but the hurricane deck was adrift, and officers were able to identify it as that of the *Hatteras* by a scar put there by the head guys of the *Brooklyn* when the two vessels had swung afoul of each other at New Orleans on January 3.

At noon three boats adrift from the wreck, all empty and two tied together, were picked up. The *Brooklyn* anchored off Galveston at 3:00 P.M., and up her ladder climbed Acting Master Leander H. Partridge and five other survivors of the *Hatteras.*

Partridge could tell only part of the story. They had given chase to the strange sail and finally had come close enough to see she was a bark-rigged steamer with a high mainmast. She stood away slowly from land, and this had caused them to signal in the late afternoon: "Suspicious sail." The *Hatteras'* captain, Homer C. Blake, suspected her identity. "I continued the chase and rapidly gained upon the suspicious vessel," he reported. "Knowing the slow rate of speed of the *Hatteras,* I at once suspected that deception was being practiced, and hence ordered the ship to be cleared for action with everything in readiness for a determined attack and a vigorous defense. When within about four miles of the vessel, I observed that she had ceased to steam and was lying broadside on, awaiting us. It was nearly seven o'clock and quite dark, but notwithstanding the obscurity of the night I felt assured from the general character of the vessel and her maneuvering that I should soon encounter the rebel steamer *Alabama.*" [21]

Finally he got close enough to hail.

A strange voice answered: "Her Majesty's steamer *Petrel.*" [22]

"I don't understand you!" Blake yelled back.

"I don't understand you!" replied the stranger.

"I'll send a boat on board of you!" shouted Blake.

"What ship are you?" asked the stranger.

"The U.S.S. *Hatteras!*" [23]

Shocking words came back over the water: "We are the C.S.S. *Alabama!*" [24]

Immediately afterward the stranger could be heard directing his lieutenant to fire.

Partridge and the five other survivors had in the meantime been ordered to board the stranger. They had barely shoved off when the firing started, the *Alabama* opening with the aftergun first and following it with the second and third broadside guns. The *Hatteras* responded, and both vessels moved ahead, leaving Partridge and his companions behind. The two ships closed, at times within twenty-five yards of each other, and the men in the open boat heard pistol shots, followed by cheering. They listened only briefly, and then swung their craft around and pulled for land.

It would be a long time before the Federals learned of the crafty way in which they had been handled by Raphael Semmes. Northern newspapers found on one of his captures during November informed Semmes that General Banks was planning an expedition into Texas. There would be twenty thousand men involved, according to this information, and he assumed a large number of transports would be needed to convoy them. Moreover, because of shallow water on the bar at Galveston, they would have to anchor outside. So he headed for the Gulf of Mexico, not knowing that Banks had taken another direction and landed at New Orleans.

Semmes intended as he approached Galveston either to spy on the shipping at a distance, without being seen himself, or to anchor just out of sight until the moon had risen and then to attack. At ten-thirty on the morning of his arrival he wrote in his journal: "This is as serene and lovely a May as one often sees, and we hope it is Providence smiling upon our approach to Galveston. There is now every prospect of my obtaining a good position from which to run in tonight." [25]

But the lookout at the masthead was careless and permitted the *Alabama* to get close enough to be seen. When the *Hatteras* set out in pursuit, Semmes kept sail on as a decoy and enticed the chasing vessel away from the fleet before giving battle. The action ended when Blake signaled he was in a sinking condition. Semmes dispatched boats to take off the crew, just managing to complete the rescue before the ship went down.

When Blake came on board he handed Semmes his sword.

"We're glad to have you on board the *Alabama,*" Semmes said to him. "We'll try to make your stay as comfortable as possible." [26]

Semmes knew he had had the advantage of the *Hatteras,* and in his journal he wrote to soothe his conscience: "A great disparity in weight of metal in our favor, but we equalized this, to a considerable extent, by the fair fight which we showed the enemy in approaching him so very near as to render his smaller guns almost as efficient as larger ones."

Two men had been killed and three wounded on the *Hatteras,* while two on the *Alabama* had received slight wounds. An hour or so after the battle, someone mentioned to Semmes that the boat with Partridge and the others had escaped. "As the sea was smooth and the wind blowing gently toward the shore, distant about nineteen miles," he wrote, "this boat probably reached the shore in safety in five or six hours. The night was clear and starlit, and it had no difficulty in shaping its course. But for these circumstances I should have turned back to look for it, hopeless as this task might have proved in the dark." [27]

While Semmes steamed away in victory, Farragut sat on the *Hartford* at New Orleans and wrote a letter home. "Misfortunes seldom come singly," he observed. "This squadron, as Sam Barron used to say, 'is eating its dirt now.' " [28] And a little later: "Our disaster at Galveston has thrown us back and done more injury to the Navy than all the events of the war." [29]

Arkansas Post (Fort Hindman)

JANUARY 1863

Fort Hindman at Arkansas Post, county seat of Arkansas County, sat high on the east bank of the Arkansas River. Key to Little Rock, the state capital, and to a rich farming area, Hindman was recognized as one of the strongest bastions the Southerners had ever built. Even so, there seemed to be no particular reason why the Union should suddenly decide to knock it out in early January '63, sending an entire army variously estimated at from thirty to fifty thousand men, in fifty transports, guarded by a fleet of warships, many crooked miles up two different streams.

General Grant, with his mind centered on the capture of Vicksburg, said it was a "wild-goose chase." [1] And Confederate General Theophilus H. Holmes, commanding the Trans-Mississippi Department, said: "It never occurred to me . . . that such an overpowering command would be devoted to an end so trivial." [2] These comments put General McClernand and Admiral David Porter, leaders respectively of the Army and

Navy forces that took part in the assault, on the defensive. The former said it was done to build up the nation's morale, and the latter, recalling Sherman's failure up the Yazoo, simply reported: "We thought it wrong to lose time, so we pitched into Arkansas." [3]

Considered in any way, however, it was embarrassing that such a large army as Sherman took up the Yazoo had advanced on Vicksburg and done nothing at all. Even if an assault on the fort at this time was not a worthy procedure, sooner or later it would have become advisable. Besides, no defense of the action at Arkansas Post was necessary, for it was a complete Union success. As a result, the Northerners took their largest bag of prisoners since the capture of Island No. 10, and the Confederates were forced to burn all the vessels they had on the Arkansas River. But not all the undertaking was harmonious, for it developed into the type of joint operation that raised jealousies, again bringing charges from naval sources that the amphibious fighters were not receiving their share of the credit.

The idea for the expedition appears to have originated with McClernand, although some sources give Sherman the credit. McClernand recorded that he first suggested the importance of the move to General Willis A. Gorman on December 30, while they were on their way down the Mississippi.[4] At any rate, it was McClernand who proposed to Porter on January 4 that they cooperate in the attack. The Admiral consented, taking immediate steps to get his fleet ready, and one of the first things he did was to remind his sailors of the way to judge explosion of shells by length of fuse—one-second, five hundred yards; two-second, nine hundred and thirty yards; three-second, one thousand, three hundred and thirty yards; four-second, sixteen hundred yards, and five-second, one thousand, nine hundred yards.

A refugee picked up in a starving condition in a boat on the river was brought into camp just before they were ready to start, and, after being fed, was ready to talk. He said the force at Arkansas Post consisted of eleven regiments, two companies of cavalry, and two batteries of artillery. The river above the fort, he added, was barricaded by rows of piles arranged in triangles and secured with hog chains.⁵

On the day the refugee arrived, Porter issued General Order No. 30: "Lieutenant-Commander Watson Smith will go ahead in the *Rattler,* sounding with two leads, and when he comes to shoal water (less than nine feet) he will hoist the cornet. If he can get through with that depth of water he will hoist the blue jack. The *Romeo, Juliet,* and *Forest Rose* will follow the *Rattler,* sounding with two leads, their guns trained forward and the fuses cut to one second. The *Marmora* will go ahead of this ship, sounding, and the guns similarly prepared. . . . The *Louisville, Baron de Kalb,* and *Cincinnati* will come after this vessel. The *Signal* will cover the 20th transport, and the *Lexington* will bring up the rear. . . ."⁶ In addition to these vessels, the armada included the ram *Monarch,* gunboats *Black Hawk* and *Tyler,* the tinclad *Glide,* and the tug *Ivy.*

One by one the transports swung out from Milliken's Bend and steamed up the Mississippi. Some of them were pulling the gunboats, for coal was scarce and with only wood for fuel the larger vessels could not make their way against the current. At the mouth of the White River, a few miles past the mouth of the Arkansas, they turned to the left. But the route followed was a dodge, for twelve miles up that stream they swung to the left again, through Smith's Cutoff, and headed for the Arkansas. Shrapnel fuses were cut at one second, and guns were trained forward and pointed at the top of the banks, in anticipation of guerrilla attacks.

On the night of January 9 the squadron tied up three miles below Arkansas Post, fifty miles from the mouth of the river. Slowly the troops filed from the transports, three regiments onto the west bank, to move upstream and prevent the Confederates from escaping by crossing the river, and the other onto the east bank, from which they would start at dawn on a wide circuit to get in behind the fort. Swamps were prevalent, and the soldiers would have to move with care.

Reconnaissance forces stood in the dark and stared at Fort

Hindman, perched high atop a hill on a horseshoe curve of the river. It was a square fort, the front not more than twenty yards from the bank. Reports said it had been built with the best engineering skill. On the side facing the river were three casemates. Approaches on the opposite side were defended by a line of trenches a mile long, beginning at the fort and ending in an impassable swamp. Around the fort and above the reach of floods spread the historic little village of Arkansas Post, founded by the French in 1685 and nourished by a country rich in cattle, corn, and cotton. Its twinkling lights gave it an air of peace in the darkness of this January night, but the scouts now staring at it knew it was a trouble spot for the North. Only a few days had passed since some of the Southerners on duty there had captured the Union transport *Blue Wing* and escaped with both the vessel and its cargo of valuable military stores.

The Confederates at the fort were prepared to fight. They knew the Federals had arrived, for their pickets had seen the Union boats turn into the cutoff. There were three brigades, one of them under command of Colonel J. W. Dunnington, an officer who had seen duty with both the Army and Navy during the war. Some of the men gathered around him were from the crew of a gunboat on which he recently had served. This was the *Pontchartrain,* formerly the side-wheel river steamer *Lizzie Simmons,* tied up now at Little Rock and waiting to be burned if the fort fell. Spread out in trenches and in fieldworks scattered through the swamps and forest was an army of about three thousand under General Thomas J. Churchill, whose Arkansas Mounted Rifles had been one of the first regiments to rise to the aid of the Confederacy.[7]

Throughout the night three companies of Confederate cavalry kept watch on the Federals. At nine o'clock next morning, a cloudy and chilly day, some of the gunboats moved up the river and opened fire on the fort. Churchill, having but one battery of fieldpieces, decided against returning the fire, relying upon the guns in the fort. But these were having trouble. Owing to some defect in the powder available for their use, they were scarcely able to throw shells beyond the trenches.

By early afternoon the first of the Union land forces began to arrive on the scene, and there was sporadic fighting around the trenches. At one point Churchill saw that he was being flanked by cavalry and artillery and, for safety purposes, fell back to an inner line of entrenchments under cover of the guns of the forts. There he repulsed every attack thrown at his lines. When the Federals occupied some cabins in his old encampment, he sent out a regiment to drive them away, and this mission was accomplished, resulting in the capture of a number of prisoners.

In the late afternoon McClernand came riding down to the riverbank to tell Porter he was ready for the main attack. This was not exactly true, and Porter knew it, for a large number of Sherman's troops were still slogging through swamps and bayous in an effort to reach the scene. But he immediately ordered his ironclads to shell the fort. Firing commenced with ten-second fuse, shells bursting at a distance of twenty-seven hundred yards.

The *Black Hawk* and *Rattler* ran up and shelled the Confederates in the rifle pits on the lower side of the fort, driving them out and enabling the Federals to take possession of the woods at that point. Then the *De Kalb* pushed up, followed by the *Ivy,* with Porter on board, the *Cincinnati,* and the *Louisville.* As darkness came on, the *Rattler* was ordered to break through the obstructions in the river. It made the attempt but got jammed among the logs and was riddled with shot from the fort, just fifty yards away. She finally managed to back out, and off she went downstream.

For nearly two hours, until well after dark, the attack continued, and then the vessels withdrew—in a crippled condition, the Confederates thought. Smoke was so thick at the time neither side could see. The *Louisville* had eleven dead and wounded, the *De Kalb* seventeen.

During the night, Churchill received a telegraphic dispatch from General Holmes, the department commander. It ordered him "to hold out until help arrived or until all were dead." [8] Churchill passed this stark communication along to brigade commanders with instructions to "see it carried out in spirit and letter." [9] At dawn he spread his forces to meet what he anticipated would be a desperate conflict. During the hours of darkness a few Confederates had stolen into the lines, and after daylight a whole regiment of one hundred and ninety men came dashing in, amid heavy Union fire on the flanks.

It was nearly noon before the Union troops were in position, and at 1:00 P.M. Porter's ironclads moved up and began shelling. In three hours every gun the Southerners had, except a small six-pounder Parrott facing the land side, had been silenced and many of their artillery horses slaughtered. But the attack by the Union soldiers who had spent hours slogging through the mud to get at the rear was less successful.

"On the right they were repulsed twice in attempting to storm our works," reported Churchill, "and on the left were driven back with great slaughter in no less than eight different charges. To defend this entire line of rifle pits I had but one battery of small fieldpieces . . . contending with some fifty pieces in front."

The end, which came suddenly, was not expected by Churchill. "The fort had now been silenced about an hour," he recorded. "Most of the fieldpieces had been disabled; still the fire raged furiously along the entire line, and that gallant band of Texans and Arkansans, having nothing to rely upon now save their muskets and bayonets, still disdained to yield to the overpowering foe of about fifty thousand men, who were pressing upon them from almost every direction. Just at this moment, to my great surprise, several white flags were displayed in the Twenty-fourth Regiment Texas Dismounted Cavalry, First Brigade, and before they could be suppressed the enemy took advantage of them, crowded upon my lines, and not being prevented by the brigade commander from crossing, as was his duty, I was forced to the humiliating necessity of surrendering the balance of my command." [10]

Churchill had hoped to keep his forces intact until night, and then, if reinforcements did not arrive, to cut his way out. But in surrendering he had his reasons for feeling proud, although his estimate took no account of the troops in the fort: "In no battle of the war has the disparity of forces been so unequal. The enemy's force was fully fifty thousand, when ours did not exceed three thousand, and yet for two days did we signally repulse and hold in check that immense body of the enemy. My loss will not exceed sixty killed and seventy-five or eighty wounded. The loss of the enemy was from fifteen hundred to two thousand killed and wounded." [11]

The surrender was quickly executed, Dunnington capitulating to Porter and Churchill to McClernand. An hour or so later, as Marines walked guard and sailors were busy taking prisoners to the gunboats, a Union adjutant galloped madly up to the fort and, jumping from his horse, shouted above all the attendant noises: "Get out! Everybody clear the fort! General Smith is coming to take possession! Clear out at once!"

Porter, standing on a rise, saw a cavalcade of horsemen approaching, A. J. "Whiskey" Smith at its head. The audacity of the adjutant riled him, and he shouted down: "Who are you, undertaking to give orders here? We've whipped the Rebels out of this place, and if you don't take care we'll run you out also." His words brought no reply from the excited aide.

Up dashed the cavalcade, and the adjutant rushed to Smith. "Here, General," he reported, "is a man who says he isn't going out of this fort for you or anybody else, and that he'll whip us out if we don't take care."

The officer roared: "Will he, by God! Let me see him! Bring the fellow here!"

Porter, wearing a blouse with small shoulder straps indicating his rank, stepped forward. "Here I am, sir, the admiral commanding this squadron," he announced.

Smith, surprised, dropped his hand, and Porter momentarily imagined he was reaching for his pistol. But there was to be no further shooting. Instead the hand brought out a bottle, and with a flourish the general said, "By God, Admiral, I'm glad to see you. Let's take a drink."

As if this little moment of libation were symbolic, the smoke of battle had scarcely cleared before the Army and Navy were in heated controversy over which deserved the greater credit for capturing Fort Hindman.

"The importance of this victory," said an official Navy Department report, "can not be estimated. It happened at a moment when the Union arms were unsuccessful on three or four battlefields, and when Jeff Davis has in his hands a large proportion of Union officers, who were not being treated very well. It rejoiced the hearts of all Union men in the North to have one victory that was complete, and the Navy might well feel proud of the share that belonged to them.

"As usual, the reporters gave garbled accounts of the affair, and tried to claim for their particular friends in the army more credit than they were entitled to.

"A mean effort was made to make it appear that the Navy only played a secondary part in this affair, but it deceived no one, and the Arkansas Post is credited to the Navy by those who love truth and justice." [12]

It would take a long time for Porter, never one to display modesty in claiming credit, to drop the argument. He was so biased that his reports failed even to include McClernand's troops in close action. "We used up the Post of Arkansas fort today in three hours, dismounting every gun in the fort, eleven in all, and such destruction of men, horses, and guns you never saw," he wrote Fleet Captain A. M. Pennock, commanding the naval station at Cairo. "This has been a naval fight, although the Army attacked with long range, but did not assault." [13]

He was even more upset by the fact that the Army had beaten him in getting a report of the battle back to Washington. "I sent a fast boat off immediately with a telegram," he informed Welles, "but the Army boat beat her. If you did not receive my communication so soon, you will find it more reliable than the one received at the War Department, which states that the Navy cooperated, when in fact it forced the fort to surrender, and then cut off the retreat of the Rebels, who were driven back on the Army. I find that Army officers are not willing to give the Navy credit (even in very small matters) they are entitled to, but you will find that I do not fail in my reports to give my officers and men the credit they justly deserve, even at the risk of hurting the sensibilities of the Army." [14]

Only one other interest compared with Porter's concern over getting proper credit for the Navy. That was a little item of preparation he had ordered the ships to attend to before going into action. A great hand for gimmicks and dodges, he had ordered the pilothouses and casemates of each vessel to be coated with tallow. "The *Cincinnati* was struck eight times on her pilothouse with nine-inch shells, which glanced off like peas against glass," he announced to Welles. "I am perfectly convinced that a coating of tallow on ironclad gunboats is a perfect protection against shot if fired at an angle." [15]

But even as he growled in defense of the Navy, Porter turned back down the Arkansas with his eyes on Vicksburg. "I am sorry I could not present the nation with Vicksburg on New Year's," he wrote A. D. Bache, superintendent of the Coast Survey. "Had the soldiers shown true grit, we would have gone in on the 30th of December; but they are greenhorns, and it will take a large ledger to book all they do not know. We will present you Vicksburg next New Year; it is only eleven months off." [16]

The *"piratical"* Maffitt

JANUARY 1863

The Federal campaign of 1863 began with an archenemy
threatening dangerously from one of the southernmost trouble
spots—Mobile. There lay John Newland Maffitt with his cruiser
Florida, poised and waiting for the opportune moment to escape. In September, when he had dashed into the port through a
hail of shot and shell, everyone from Gideon Welles on down
realized he would stay only long enough to repair his well-
riddled ship before doing his best to get to the high seas and
strike at Union shipping again. The problem was how to stop
him.

Welles took prompt action. In place of the deposed George
Henry Preble he assigned one of his new commodores, Robert
Bradley Hitchcock, a fifty-nine-year-old veteran from Connecticut who had spent two-thirds of his life in the Navy. Down to
Mobile, also, he sent more ships—the *R. R. Cuyler, Pembina,
Aroostook,* and *Pinola,* all screw steamers—bringing the total
fleet to seven large ships, plus several smaller vessels. Of these
the *Cuyler* was the fastest and most powerful, able to reach a
maximum speed of nearly fifteen knots.

By November, reports of Maffitt's activities caused the Union to issue a memorandum to the commanding officers of all blockading vessels. "There is good reason," it stated, "to believe that the Rebel steamer *Oreto,* which ran this blockade some time since, is ready (or preparing) to attempt to run out. No effort should be spared to prevent this vessel from getting to sea." Only two ships, the *Cuyler* and the *Oneida,* were considered able to compete with the Confederate in speed, and they were ordered to pursue her "until she is either sunk, captured, or lost sight of." [1]

Maffitt in the meantime was impatient to get away. "Our tarry has far exceeded my expectations, and all hands are very restive," he wrote in his journal.[2] A part of the delay was caused by the quarantine of his ship after her arrival in port. During this period no work could be done on her, which delayed completion of repairs until December. Then she was held up by weather, the season developing unusually pleasant and devoid of the storms that Maffitt was waiting for to screen his vessel during the escape.

While Maffitt fretted over being tied to port, the Federals were kept on their toes by repeated rumors that the *Florida* already had gone to sea. Welles was taken in by them and, when it was reported that another "piratical steamer" besides the *Alabama* was in the West Indies, he immediately advised that it might be Maffitt's ship.[3] A New York newspaper added more fuel to the rumor by announcing that a blockade runner had recently escaped from Mobile. This was promptly denied by Commodore James S. Palmer, commanding the West Gulf Blockading Squadron, who assured that all the vessels bottled up in the port were still there.

During December the *Oneida* was damaged in a collision with the storeship *Supply,* and her commander, Thornton Alexander Jenkins, a Virginian of long naval experience who had remained with the Union, took her off to Pensacola for repairs. Her absence was noted by the Confederates, but the weather still was unsuitable for Maffitt to attempt flight.

This delay did not meet with the approval of Confederate authorities at Richmond. They could not understand why one of their two important cruisers should remain idle in port so long, and finally they took action. Standing by without a ship was Lieutenant Joseph Nicholson Barney, an officer who had taken part in the fighting on the James in the time of the *Merrimack*. They decided to put him back in action, and on December 30 he was ordered to relieve Maffitt. But this change was not to take effect at that time. In command of the fleet at Mobile was Franklin Buchanan, now recovered from his wound of the preceding spring, and, by coincidence, Jefferson Davis was there on a visit. Buchanan complained to the President that, in replacing Maffitt, the Navy Department had acted without consulting him, the commanding and responsible officer concerned. Davis sympathized, and a telegram annulling the action was soon on its way. Maffitt observed bitterly in his journal: "My services (unrequited as they have been) surely entitled me to a slight consideration and call for information. The commanding officer was indirectly hit over my shoulders, and Mr. Mallory, with characteristic littleness of mind, has permitted surreptitious naval gossip to operate, without the least magnanimity of soul or manliness of purpose." [4]

It was a narrow squeak for Maffitt, but he in no way let the rebuff interfere with his activities. Shortly afterward he received a message from Buchanan advising him to paint his ship lead color. The admiral added that, if paint were lacking, the color could be approximated by using lampblack in whitewash. "A friend from Havana sent me word that a vessel of that color can not be seen well at night—he has tried it," Buchanan added. Maffitt got his crew busy, and coated the *Florida* so thoroughly that one of the men wrote she was "white-washed all over." [5]

Maffitt was finding plenty of time these days to write in his journal, and such colorful prose as this rolled from his pen:

In the winter season N.E. gales, as a rule, are prevalent. They last several days with a misty sky, and heavy sea upon the bar, both favorable to the *Florida*'s safe exit, and 'tis to the interest of the Confederacy that we get out intact, as my orders are to assail their commerce only, that the mercantile part of the Northern community, who so earnestly sustain the war by liberal contributions, may not fatten on its progress, but feel all its misfortunes. As the *Alabama* and *Florida* are the only two cruisers we have just now, it would be a perfect absurdity to tilt against their more than three hundred, for the Federals would gladly sacrifice fifty armed ships to extinguish the two Confederates.

When a man-of-war is sacrificed 'tis a national calamity, not in-individually felt, but when merchant ships are destroyed on the high seas individuality suffers, and the shoe then pinches in the right direction. All the merchants of New York and Boston who have by their splendid traders become princes in wealth and puffy with patriotic zeal for the subjugation of the South, will soon cry with a loud voice, peace, peace; we are becoming ruined and the country damned!

I doubt not but that there will be much criticism and condemnation among the restless spirits of the service, who are always finding fault, yet most faulty themselves. 'Tis a curse in military as well as naval life that gossiping is carried to such reprehensible extremes, and as a general rule it belongs to weak-minded, shallow-pated persons, living in glass houses, but always throwing stones.[6]

The evening of January 10 was chosen by Maffitt for an attempt to head for the high seas. Next day he wrote his daughter about the experience: "I made an effort, darling Florie, to get out last night, but the clouds all left, and the enemy (thirteen in all) were so plainly in sight that I knew I could not pass without having sixty guns fired at me—and we would no doubt be lost. So I must abide a better time, though exceedingly disappointed. . . ."[7]

Jenkins returned with the *Oneida* on January 12, and there found orders to report as fleet captain at New Orleans. He gave up his ship and went on board the *Susquehanna* to await transportation to his new post, thus placing himself in an advantageous spot to observe what was about to happen.

On the 13th the wind commenced hauling to the southward, and gradually increased to gale proportions, with rain. A heavy sea set in, rocking the ships so violently that additional precautions had to be taken to secure the guns to the deck. The atmosphere became thick and hazy, blocking out objects to landward. Maffitt made a reconnaissance down to the bar, and on the return grounded. Two other ships came to his assistance, but before he was freed, coal, guns, and other items had to be taken out of the *Florida*.

Maffitt waited until the following night, in the meantime getting his ship once more in order. After nightfall he attempted the run. Again he failed. Circumstances were not right; in addition, an enemy vessel appeared in his path, and he turned back.[8]

At dawn on the 15th the storm was still raging, but the low range of the barometer indicated a change. It came between 9:00 and 10:00 A.M., when the wind veered to westward and finally to west-northwest. That afternoon the clouds and mist lifted, bringing into view the Confederate cruiser as she lay just eastward of Fort Morgan, full bark-rigged, apparently ready for sea.

The *R. R. Cuyler* was the first to flash the signal that she had been seen. When notified by the officer of the deck, Commodore Hitchcock stared at the ship with his glasses and concluded that Maffitt would try to escape that night. A general signal was made to the entire squadron to keep up full steam. Then the *Pembina* was ordered to within easy hailing distance and told to instruct the *Cuyler* and *Pinola* to reduce their distances from the *Susquehanna* by half. This would draw the blockaders into an arc around the main entrance and place them so close together that it was presumed no vessel could pass between any two without being seen.

The sea increased during the afternoon, and night came on in a boisterous, howling fury. Jenkins and Hitchcock on the *Susquehanna* remained up until after midnight, anxiously expecting to hear of the approach of the *Florida*. Finally, Jenkins took off his coat and shoes and lay down, leaving Hitchcock laboring over reports and clerical work.

About 3:00 A.M. Jenkins was awakened by an orderly tapping on the cabin door and calling to Hitchcock that the *Pembina* had signaled that a vessel was running out. He hurriedly slipped on coat and shoes and rushed up on deck. There he found Hitchcock staring through glasses toward the position the *Pembina* had occupied at dark.

"Yes, there's the signal," he heard Hitchcock say.

Immediately afterward lights were run up on board the *Susquehanna,* repeating Signal No. 2, white and red: "Vessel running out of this pass."

While Jenkins stood there near Hitchcock, he was able to make out the dim, dark outline of a vessel, his attention directed to it by a red lantern swinging back and forth in the gale. Then a more urgent alarm, special Signal No. 3, white and green, was seen in another direction, and he heard somebody say that it came from the *Cuyler.*

More lights went up on the *Susquehanna*—a single directive: "Chase."

Maffitt had decided to wait until after midnight on the advice of his pilot, who said it was too dark to attempt to run earlier in the evening, and it was obvious he was right, for no object could be distinguished at twenty yards. During the intervening hours the captain had stretched out in his cabin to rest and finally fell asleep. At 2:00 A.M. he was called. He went on deck and found the storm had abated somewhat, although the sea was still foaming and lapping noisily. But the stars were out, and a light mist had settled over the surface of the water, offering the very cover he had been awaiting.

"Got under way—the wind puffy from W.N.W.," Maffitt's journal records. "Double reefs were taken in our topsails and balanced reefs in the fore and main trysails. The topsails I caused to be mastheaded, and the gaskets replaced by split rope-yarns which would give way when the sheets were hauled upon and the sail set without sending the top-men aloft. Everything was secured for bad weather, a double watch set, and the crew piped down. At 2:20 all hands were called, steam was up, and we were heading for the bar."

The *Florida* got clear of the bar, passed the *Pembina* and then another vessel. The pitching sea drowned out the noise of her propeller, and she scurried through the mists like a dream ship out of a fairy tale. She stole past the *Cuyler,* with Maffitt and his crew virtually holding their breaths in suspense. But three hundred yards farther along a fireman in her engine room, finding no coke handy, threw on several shovelfuls of coal. It was the wrong time to use such fuel. Coal dust caught fire, flames shot up through her funnels, and the night that had been quiet except for the fury of the sea suddenly became alive with the stir of a fleet aroused to action. Drums beat, lights flashed, and there was general commotion as sailors rushed to slip cables.

The *Cuyler*'s captain, George Emmons, had gone to bed, thinking the time past for Maffitt to make an attempt to escape. He came on deck, partly dressed, and gave orders for the *Cuyler,* her steam gauge at twenty-three pounds, to go in chase.[9] The signals from her deck had been flashed in proper code, although not without some delay: the gunner's mate had had trouble lighting the lights in the damp, windy weather and had burned his hand severely.

Maffitt's activities during the next fifteen hours were summarized in his official report: "We were not discovered until in the midst of them; an animated chase that lasted all day then commenced. The *Florida,* under a heavy press of canvas and steam, made fourteen and a half knots an hour, and distanced all her pursuers except two in a few hours, and that night, by changing the course, the two that held their way with us were eluded." [10]

To the surprise of Hitchcock in particular, the *Oneida,* one of the fastest ships in the fleet, was not among Maffitt's pursuers. Her log recorded that the signal from the flagship was seen and the crew alerted, but, after no vessel running out could be detected, she quieted down and remained at anchor. There she rocked at dawn.

It was the *Pembina* that joined the *Cuyler* in the chase.

She ranged ahead of us very fast [reported the *Pembina's* commander, William G. Temple] and crossed our bows, standing about
S.S.E. while we were standing E.S.E. She soon (within fifteen or
twenty minutes) burned the signal for "sail outside of me to the
southward," and seeing no other of our vessels in chase, we answered it, changed our course accordingly, and continued the pursuit, guided solely by the light at the *Cuyler's* peak, as the strange
vessel was no longer seen. We were running from that time until
7:00 A.M. at our greatest possible speed. The foresail and jib were
set. The wind was W.S.W., so that the square sail would not stand,
and indeed it was too strong a gale to set either this or the fore
gaff-topsail. The vessel was carrying a turn and a half of weather
helm, and therefore the mainsail could not be set. The sea was so
heavy that the propeller was constantly thrown entirely out of the
water, and raced to an alarming degree; but still by careful and
skillful attention the engineer was able to keep up to an average of
eighty-three revolutions per minute and sometimes even eighty-six,
having been ordered to run as fast as he dared, with anything like
safety to the engine. We were making ten knots an hour. By half
past five, however, the *Cuyler* had drawn ahead so far that we had
lost sight of her and her light. Still we kept on after her, and some
twenty minutes later she hoisted (apparently) the whole five lights
composing her night numbers, which we could again catch sight of
at times. Soon these also dipped below the horizon, and we ran on,
waiting for daylight, to see if we could hope to be of any service by
continuing the chase. . . . When it was full day, it became evident
that we were rapidly dropping astern. The *Cuyler* I judged to be about
eight miles ahead of us, as I could just see the tops of her smokestacks. . . . The chase I judged to be about twelve miles ahead of
us, as I could only see her with the glass, and then only her upper
spars. Both vessels were crowding on more sail.[11]

Maffitt was on his way. Behind him Federal ship commanders wrote doleful reports. "From fancying myself near
promotion in the morning," Emmons of the *Cuyler* recorded, "I
gradually dwindled down to a court of inquiry at dark, when I
lost sight of the enemy." [12] Hitchcock was more resigned to his
fate: "I do not expect to get out of the scrape any better than
Preble; still it does not trouble me very much. I think it hard to
have been kept here for a year in this ship, but if I can get home
and out of the service it will be enough for me." [13] "It now be-

comes my duty to report the running out of the *Oreto* from Mobile," began Farragut. ". . . Had Captain Hazard, in the *Oneida,* obeyed his orders and chased also there would have been but little doubt of her capture; as it is, I fear for the result." [14]

The "result" Farragut feared began to take shape in short order. On the 17th, Maffitt was off the coast of Mexico; on the 18th, he was standing toward Cuba.[15] At 2:00 P.M. the 19th he bore down on a sail. "Called all hands to quarters," it was recorded in the ship's log, "and when about five hundred yards astern rounded up under his quarter and fired a shot across his bow. He immediately heaved to and hauled down his colors. . . ."

The prize was the brig *Estelle* of New York, on her first trip and bound from Cuba to Boston with a cargo of honey, sugar, and molasses, valued at a hundred and thirty thousand dollars.

When John Brown, master of the *Estelle,* went on board the *Florida,* he was received by Maffitt with great courtesy. Inviting him into his cabin, Maffitt said: "I regret that it is necessary to burn your vessel. The consequences of this unnatural war often fall most heavily upon those who disapprove of it. I trust your vessel is owned by abolitionists." [16] After receiving such treatment, Brown wrote a Northern newspaper: "Generosity and courtesy on the part of enemies should not pass unheeded by, as the rigors of a sad and unnatural war may be somewhat mitigated by politeness and manly forbearance. I would add that Captain Maffitt returned our personal effects, but retained the chronometer and charts." [17]

At 8:00 P.M. on January 20, Maffitt ran into the harbor of Havana, Cuba, looking both for coal and clothing, for his men were running short of wearing apparel. New port rules specified that no incoming ship could unload passengers after sundown, or before she had been visited by the health officer, but Maffitt, unaware of these restrictions, landed with his first lieutenant and went to the home of the Confederate agent, Charles J. Helm. Next day both he and the agent visited the captain of the port, and, after such apologies as were thought "honorable and dignified" for the breaches of two rules, all was forgiven. "The excitement in Havana on our arrival was intense," Maffitt wrote. "Crowds were on the wharf, and a very strong Southern feeling was exhibited." [18] The Havana correspondent of the New York *Herald* was on hand, and soon he was preparing an article about the *Florida*'s arrival: "It appears that the pirate Maffitt came out of the port of Mobile with as much impudence as he entered it." [19] He noted that the ship was formerly black, "but has since been painted white, though the paint is wearing away gradually, imparting a dirty effect."

This reporter had a high opinion both of the *Florida* and her captain.

From reliable information [he wrote] I am enabled to state, or, rather, I am convinced, that this vessel will sail for the East Indies in a few days. Our government had better look out for her advent in these waters. Captain Maffitt is no ordinary character. He is vigorous, energetic, bold, quick and dashing, and the sooner he is caught and hung the better it will be for the interests of our commercial community. He is decidedly popular here, and you can scarcely imagine the anxiety evinced to get a glance at him. He was at the Dominico this morning in citizens' clothes, and was the observed of everyone. Nobody, unless informed, would have imagined the small, black-eyed, poetic-looking gentleman, with his romantic appearance, to be a second Semmes, probably in time to be a more celebrated and more dangerous pirate. He was alone, taking a cup of coffee, seemingly unconscious of having any more serious occupation on hand. As soon as he perceived that his presence attracted attention, he blushed like a girl, paid his bill and decamped.

During the day, Maffitt took on a full supply of coal, enough to last his vessel nine days. At sunset she was ready for sea again, but her crafty captain waited until dawn before sailing. That day he burned two vessels, the brig *Windward,* bound for Portland with a cargo of sugar, and the *Corris Ann,* carrying barrel staves from Philadelphia to Matanzas. Into Havana at 6:30 that night sailed Commander Wilkes in the *Wachusett,* missing Maffitt by only a few hours.

On the morning of the 23rd, Maffitt's engineer in charge reported to him that the coal they had taken on board at Havana would not make steam, that it would not hold a steady head of more than five pounds. Investigation revealed that enough of the supply taken on before leaving Mobile remained to run the vessel three days. Maffitt steered for Nassau, arriving at 2:00 A.M. the 26th. But he waited until dawn to run in, immediately putting his crew to work tossing the condemned coal overboard and taking on a new supply. While his men shoveled, he went to breakfast with the family of J. B. Lafitte, chief agent for Henry Adderly and Company, a subsidiary of the Charleston firm of Fraser, Trenholm and Company, shippers for the Confederate Government, and with Louis Heyliger, Confederate purchasing agent in the Bahamas. Returning on board later in the day, he sat down to prepare a report to Mallory, one of the few he sent at this period. "Shall sail in two hours for the coast of New England," he wrote.[20]

Maffitt also at this time made a notation in his journal: "On shore the demonstration was most friendly and congratulatory. Nassau is decidedly a Confederate stronghold. . . . Among the commanders I met Lieutenant Wilkinson, of the Navy, who commanded the *Giraffe,* and was about making his second trip." He noticed more than a dozen vessels, some with full cargoes, waiting to run for the South.

But troubles other than faulty coal lay ahead for the cruiser. "When I last wrote you," Maffitt next reported to Mallory, "I was on the eve of starting for the coast of New England. When I proceeded as far as Cape Hatteras a violent gale of wind overtook the vessel and handled her very severely. I was compelled to cross the Gulf Stream to get out of it, and by this time my coal was so reduced that I was necessitated, reluctantly, to relinquish my dash on the New England coast and bear up to one of the West Indian islands to supply the vessel with coal." [21]

Maffitt kept to Southern waters, sailing leisurely, watching for sails, and steering no farther from land than he could safely go with a nine-day supply of coal. At the first opportunity he put his crew to work repainting the ship. There were some singers on board. "Of a night," recorded one of the sailors, "the forecastle rings with . . . song in almost every note and pitch of the gamut." [22]

February came and with it two of the Union's mightiest ships, the *R. R. Cuyler* and the *Pembina,* still hard on the trail of the *Florida.* Had Maffitt known of the search being made for him, he no doubt would have smugly noted in his journal that he had furthered the cause of the Confederacy by weakening the blockade. And that was what he had done, for when Charles Wilkes learned that the pursuing steamers were in his neighborhood in the West Indies he immediately added them to his fleet, for a time taking them away from Farragut and Mobile.

On the morning of the 12th a large sail was noticed off the *Florida*'s port beam. Maffitt started in chase and at four o'clock that afternoon caught up with the *Jacob Bell* of New York, considered to be one of the most splendid vessels in the China trade. She was bound homeward with a choice cargo of tea, camphor, chowchow, and other items valued at more than two million dollars.

Receiving word that there were women on board the prize and that the captain's wife was on the eve of confinement, Maffitt sent his physician to investigate and to convey them safely to the *Florida.* "The ladies came, and with tons of baggage," Maffitt noted. "I surrendered the cabin. The party consisted of Mrs. Frisbee (captain's wife), Mrs. Williams, whose husband is a custom-house officer at Swatow, China, a lad, Louis Frisbee, and another. . . . Mrs. Frisbee was a very quiet, kind-hearted lady; Mrs. Williams, I fancy, something of a tartar. She and Captain Frisbee were not on terms." [23] For five days they occupied the cabin, and then they were transferred to a Danish brig bound for St. Thomas. "If they speak unkindly," Maffitt wrote in farewell, "such a thing as gratitude is a stranger to their abolition hearts."

Maffitt arrived at Barbados Island. "What a contrast to the

last time I visited this place in the *Macedonian* frigate in 1841," he observed nostalgically. "Then the Stars and Stripes floated over my head and the Union seemed as firm as the Rock of Ages. Abolitionism was considered treasonable, and the North and the South were as one, for nullification had died a natural death and harmony guided the national associations. Now, the Confederate flag, till this day a total stranger to Barbados, floated from our gaff, and the *Florida* became the first herald of nationality the inhabitants had realized." [24]

While there he dined with Governor James Walker and found him quite a pleasant gentleman, though much troubled with a nervous disease. Visitors crowded the decks of the *Florida*. The gallantry of the Southern troops was the theme of their conversation, and Generals Lee and Jackson received high professional compliments. McClellan was regarded as an able General, but too fond of the spade. Maffitt was affected by the enthusiasm and friendship of these people. "Did the host to a late hour," he wrote in his journal, "and was not benefitted thereby, for my piloting was not perfect, and I fouled one of the merchant ships, parting our starboard main braces and lifting our second cutter from the fall hooks." [25]

A few days later he ran alongside the Boston ship *Star of Peace* and found her loaded with saltpeter and cow and goat skins. After she had been set afire, he drew off and ordered his crew to exercise the guns upon her. That night, twenty miles away, he looked back on the burning vessel and was influenced to write: "A more beautiful panorama was never witnessed on the ocean. The flames were so high and so brilliant that the focal rays illumined our sails, and the ship did not appear more than five miles distant." [26]

The *Aldebaran* from New York went into his bag, with a cargo of flour, provisions, and clocks. Next came the Boston bark *Lapwing,* bound to Batavia with provisions, lumber, furniture, and coal. Two days later he captured the *M. J. Colcord,* with such an assorted cargo that Maffitt noted: "Living like lords on Yankee plunder." More variety, including tobacco, came with the *Commonwealth* of New York and the bark *Henrietta* of Baltimore. The merchant ship *Oneida,* newly from China with a cargo of tea, boosted his prize total by close to one million dollars.

In May the brig *Clarence,* taking a cargo of coffee from Rio de Janeiro to Baltimore, was captured. Before she could be burned, Lieutenant Charles Read, the Mississippian whose services Maffitt personally had solicited, came forward with a proposition that he put in writing: "I propose to take the brig which we have just captured, and with a crew of twenty men to proceed to Hampton Roads and cut out a gunboat or steamer of the enemy."

Maffitt's estimation of Read had increased steadily during the months the young officer had been with him. Just twenty-three years old, he had joined the crew November 4, and due notation was made at the time, of his "reputation for gunnery, coolness, and determination at the battle of New Orleans." [27] Added to this were the reports about the part he had played on the *Arkansas.* He had come aboard the *Florida* after a few weeks of chafing for action at Port Hudson, and he was impatient to do his part for the Confederacy. Early in December Maffitt noticed that their delay in getting away from Mobile so affected Read that he "suffers particularly in this and has become somewhat bilious; every passing squall is to him a fine night for going out, even though it be of fifty minutes duration only." [28]

Maffitt decided to let Read try his wings with the *Clarence.* It was a decision he would never regret. A few weeks later the Northern press was screaming in headlines over the success along the New England Coast of one Charles William Read and referring to him as the John Paul Jones of the Confederacy.

Those stubborn Southerners!

JANUARY 1863

A tense atmosphere set in around Charleston late in January, and might have been accepted as a definite indication something was about to happen. This uneasiness was most noticeable in the Federals themselves. Farragut, had he been on hand, could have given warning of it, for in his opinion the Galveston affair "has emboldened our enemies to undertake anything." [1] Firing at night had become more frequent, much of it unexplained, and vessels remained at quarters, constantly on the lookout. Often they set off on a chase of some craft seen or heard making its way through the darkness, only to come up with a troopship or some other friendly boat bent on a justifiable errand. As for the Southerners, they kept secret what they were doing and what they had in mind.

That the defenders of Charleston had been busy was a well-known fact. "For twelve long months," the South Atlantic Blockading Squadron chief, Samuel Francis du Pont, wrote Gustavus Fox, "it has been the remark of our blockading officers that the industry of these Rebels in their harbor defenses is beyond all praise. It has been ceaseless day and night." [2] Reports leaking out of the city of Charleston said that two ironclad boats were under construction there, and that John L. Porter, the engineer who had helped build the *Merrimack,* was on hand to assist with them.

Du Pont was never fooled about the task involved in blockading Charleston. He knew its capture would not come easily. This conviction he passed on in a letter to Fox: "Do not go it half cocked about Charleston—it is a bigger job than Port Royal. . . ." [3] In answer the Navy Undersecretary sent a challenge: "If we can take Charleston, Savannah, Wilmington, Mobile and the *290,* the Navy on the ocean and coast has finished its hard work. . . . We have added a story to our Navy Department building and erected a fine flag staff thereon and shall not raise the American flag upon it until Charleston falls." [4] Du Pont, an unassuming man, must have noted mentally that one government structure in Washington would be pennantless for some time to come.

The siege of Charleston had been under way for months, so long that residents of the city were accepting their confinement with grim humor. This was exemplified by a set of glistening silver coffin handles that the commander of one of the blockading vessels, John Pine Bankhead, fastened conspicuously to the dark walnut panels over his cabin transom. They had come from a former sweetheart in Charleston, along with a message that the coffin to which they belonged was waiting for him in the city. [5]

By late summer Du Pont had managed to assemble a fleet of nineteen steamers and seven sailing vessels. He stationed them in a circle around the entrance to the harbor and worked out an elaborate set of signals for their use in daylight, at night, or in time of fog. Some of the ships, like the *Powhatan,* had seen service from the start of the war. But despite this strong guard and all the efforts that Du Pont exerted to tighten it, runners still sneaked out of the port on occasion, causing such typical reports as the following: "Near 10:00 o'clock Acting Master

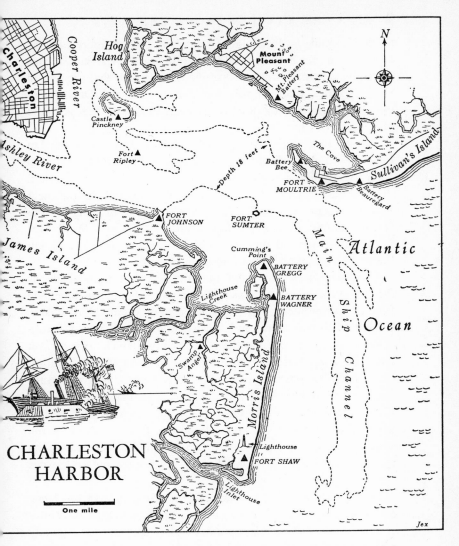

CHARLESTON
HARBOR

One mile

Rogers saw a steam propeller passing outward close along the
beach, moving silently and swiftly. He immediately fired a
rocket and burned a blue light—the signals agreed upon—and
the *Bienville* at once slipped her cable, alarmed the rest of
the fleet, and gave chase, but was unable to see anything of
the escaping vessel. . . . Though the steamer passed within

three hundred yards of him, yet when the land behind was higher than the hull he could see nothing of her, and it was only when she passed a low opening in the beach that she was in sight at all. I refer to this particularly that the Department may be apprised of one of the great difficulties of the blockade of this port of Charleston." [6]

At one time during the fall of '62 it looked as though Du Pont would get help from an officer of high rank. Admiral John A. Dahlgren, chief of the Bureau of Ordnance, asked that he be permitted to command an ironclad in the fleet trying to capture Charleston and thus raise his flag in the South Atlantic Blockading Squadron. But Gideon Welles refused on the ground that it would be "inconsistent," since Du Pont was a full grade below Dahlgren in rank.[7]

The uneasiness that crept into the Charleston blockade as the new year advanced was difficult to explain. The blockade fleet at the moment was no smaller than usual. Nonetheless, the tenseness was there, and some justification of it was recognized in an incident along the nearby Stono River. This stream had been maintained by Du Pont as a base for further military operations, but pressure of the blockade had made it necessary for him to reduce his force to two light-draft vessels, the *Isaac Smith* and the *Commodore McDonough,* both formerly used as ferry and freight boats. Each day for weeks one or the other of these ran up the river on reconnaissance, surveying the shore with glasses to make sure the Southerners were not fortifying.

On the afternoon of January 30 it was the turn of the *Isaac Smith* to carry out this daily chore, and she chugged off under command of Acting Lieutenant Francis S. Conover. Shortly after 4:00 P.M. she passed Legareville and anchored opposite Tom Grimball's plantation, about four and a half miles above Stono Inlet. The signal quartermaster and one or two officers were at the masthead, staring over the countryside, but nothing suspicious could be seen. For nearly half an hour she lay there, and then suddenly, from a thick clump of trees on James

Island six hundred yards away, a battery of three twenty-four-pounder rifled guns opened on her. Conover immediately gave orders to get under way and clear for action, and in less than two minutes the *Isaac Smith*'s guns were replying. But suddenly she was in a cross fire, as batteries on John's Island, on the other side of the river, opened with a terrific cannonade.

Conover started downstream. The odds were against him. For more than a mile, because of a bend in the river, his ship was the victim of a raking fire from between twenty and thirty guns, to which he could reply only with an occasional shot from the pivot gun.

"As soon as our broadside could be brought to bear," Conover reported, "we opened upon the enemy with shell and grape, at from two hundred to four hundred yards distance. At one time I had hopes of getting by without any very serious loss, but a shot in our steam chimney effectually stopped the engine, and with no wind, little tide, and boats riddled with shot, we were left entirely at the mercy of the enemy." [8]

Conover came out of the fracas with a light contusion caused by a rifle ball's striking his forehead. "Had it not been for the wounded men, with whom the berth deck was covered," he reported, "I might have blown up or sunk the ship, letting the crew take their chance of getting on shore by swimming, but under the circumstances I had no alternative left me. We had eight men killed and seventeen wounded."

The *Commodore McDonough,* hearing the firing, ran up past Legareville to investigate. When she came in sight of the *Isaac Smith,* lying aground a quarter of a mile above the bend in the river, a white flag could be seen waving from her mast and two of her boats heading for shore loaded with officers and men. The *McDonough,* running up toward her, suddenly was caught in the cross fire, and only by repeated backing and filling managed to escape.

After proceeding downstream a safe distance, the *Mc-Donough* turned about and opened an exchange with the batteries, keeping it up until darkness obliterated the range. Then she threw a few shells into Legareville, "in the hope of setting fire to the place," [9] after which she withdrew for the night.

But much was to happen a few miles away before another dawn bared the coast, for the Southerners had other tricks in mind. Over in Charleston harbor, at 11:00 P.M., a few hours after the guns on the Stono River became silent, the lookout on the *Flag,* one of the blockaders, saw a boat inshore pulling in the direction of another blockader, the *Mercedita.* There was nothing particularly alarming about the tiny craft, and yet the *Flag* went to quarters and remained at quarters until it passed out of sight, still pulling toward the *Mercedita.* Then the *Flag*'s captain, J. H. Strong, remembering directions to pay no attention to boats inshore since they would be friendly, piped down. But he remained alert. Every officer in the fleet knew that two of its biggest ships, the *Powhatan* and *Canandaigua,* were away at Port Royal coaling.

The weather was pleasant, the sea smooth, but a thick haze lay over the harbor, the kind of fog that Du Pont had said over and over made the task of keeping out clever runners impossible. Next in line among the blockaders, the *Keystone State,* Captain William E. Le Roy, lay quietly at anchor, but with a tenseness on board that belied her calm appearance. Six of her fires were spread in good order and the other six banked. She was ready to move at short notice.

Had Le Roy known what was on its way, perhaps all twelve fires would have been blazing. At 11:15 P.M. two ironclad rams steamed away from the wharf at Charleston and headed for the main ship channel. They were the *Chicora* and *Palmetto State,* pride of every Southerner, for they had been built by the Confederate Government through co-operative effort that stretched over months, the hull of one of them having been laid behind the Charleston post office. Five hundred or more tons of iron had gone into each. Much of their cost was covered through fund-raising efforts of ladies in the city.

The *Palmetto State,* in the lead, bore the flag of sixty-year-old Duncan Nathaniel Ingraham, native of Charleston and one of the first officers from the old navy to resign and take up arms for the Confederacy. Behind, in the other vessel, was an officer who in just forty-five minutes would begin celebrating his fiftieth birthday. He was John Randolph Tucker, member of an early and distinguished Virginia family, who had fought along the James River for his native state even before she seceded.

These vessels steamed slowly down to the bar, awaiting high water, and at the right moment crossed with a foot and a half to spare. Everyone was keyed to a high pitch of excitement. For days they had worked to keep their ships in condition, expecting action at any moment. "Tonight we had steam, and it looked like we were going to do something," wrote Second Assistant Engineer James H. Tomb of the *Chicora*. "As we steamed down the harbor we knew it was an engagement outside, and from constant talk felt the sooner it came the better. The intention is to ram the first ship we come to." [10]

At 3:00 A.M., even before the Confederate vessels got past the bar, the *Mercedita* had a scare. History does not reveal whether the little craft the *Flag* had seen inshore belonged to this particular vessel, but at that hour the *Mercedita* heard a noise, slipped cable, and ran toward it, overhauling a steamer running for the channel by mistake. Back at her anchorage her captain, H. S. Stellwagen, lay down. It was then 4:00 A.M. On deck, his executive officer, Lieutenant Commander Trevett Abbot, was still stirring about, giving orders.

An hour or so later other blockaders thought they saw an object moving in the direction of the *Mercedita,* but they were not sure. Stellwagen, still lying down, heard someone shout: "She has black smoke! Watch, man the guns, spring the rattle, call all hands to quarters!" [11]

Acting Master Thomas J. Dwyer came to Stellwagen's cabin door. "A steamboat is close aboard," he called.

The captain by that time was getting into his pea jacket, and he ran out, following Dwyer, and jumped to the poop ladder. From there he saw smoke and a low boat, apparently a tug, although he thought it might be a little propeller that had come in to join the squadron. She was coming directly toward them, so he called out: "Train your guns right on him and be ready to fire as soon as I order!"

Next he hailed: "Steamer ahoy! What steamer is that? Drop your anchor or you will be into us!"

All he heard in answer was "Halloo!" There was more to the reply, but the other words were indistinct. Stellwagen could not determine whether this was intentional or because the words were spoken inside the mail armor of the other vessel.

But soon he heard someone shout: "This is the Confederate States steam ram——!"

Without waiting for the rest of the sentence, he called out: "Fire! Fire!"

He was wasting his breath, for no gun could be trained on the oncoming vessel: she was too low in the water. Within seconds that seemed hours it struck the *Mercedita* just abaft her aftermost thirty-two-pounder gun, at the same time firing a heavy rifle, the shell diagonally penetrating the starboard side, passing through her Normandy condenser, the steam drum of the port boiler, and exploding against the portside of the ship, blowing a hole in it four or five feet in diameter.

Stellwagen's head rang with the reports that were brought to him during the next few minutes: "Shot through both boilers. . . . Fires put out by steam and water. . . . Gunner and one man killed. . . . Number of men fatally scalded. . . . Water over fire-room floor. . . . Vessel sinking fast. . . . The ram has cut us through at and below water line on one side, and the shell has burst on the other about at the water's edge."

After the low vessel struck, she swung around under the *Mercedita*'s starboard counter, her prow, bearing the name *Palmetto Star,* touching. From on board of her someone hailed, "Surrender, or I'll sink you!" After a pause, another call: "Do you surrender?"

Stellwagen answered: "I can make no resistance. My boiler is destroyed."

"Then do you surrender?"

"Yes."

Several times the voice on the ramp called for a boat to be sent. Finally one was lowered, and Trevett Abbot prepared to step into it.

"What shall I say?" he asked of Stellwagen.

"See what they demand," he was told, "and then describe the condition we are in."

On board the ram, Abbot was met by two men who introduced themselves as Lieutenants Parker and Shryock. The former led the way to the cabin and there presented him to Captain Ingraham, whose name the Union officer did not retain.[12]

"I have come in the name of Captain Stellwagen to give up the U.S.S. *Mercedita*," Abbot announced. "She is in a sinking and perfectly defenseless condition." [13]

A conference among the Confederates followed, after which Captain Ingraham returned to Abbot. "We have decided to parole your officers and crew," he said, "provided you will pledge me your sacred word of honor that neither you nor any of the officers and crew of the *Mercedita* will again take up arms against the Confederate States during the war, unless you are legally and regularly exchanged as prisoners of war."

Abbot gave his pledge and was permitted to return to the *Mercedita*. As he was rowed back over the water, he could tell from the lights of approaching ships that the alarm over the harbor was by this time general. But it was easy to see that the nature of the emergency was not understood. Most of the Union vessels within hearing distance had been fooled, thinking the disturbance no more than the routine outbursts which came whenever a runner was discovered trying to get in or out of the harbor. As an example, Lieutenant Commander P. G. Watmough of the U.S.S. *Memphis* reported: "At about 5:00 A.M. the flash of a single gun on the bearing of the *Mercedita* was seen and the report heard. We also imagined we saw an object moving in that direction, but were not sure. In the course of twenty minutes a gun on the bearing of the *Keystone State* was heard, followed, after a very short interval, by quick and rapid firing, and as an object was very distinctly seen moving in that direction, we inferred that both the *Keystone State* and *Mercedita* were in pursuit of some steamer that had passed out." [14]

The fight continued as dawn neared. After Abbot left her side the *Palmetto State* steamed away, and soon her guns were roaring again. Somewhere out there in the fading darkness she found the *Chicora,* standing off and blasting away at the *Keystone State.* Her ram was unused, because the chief engineer and chief pilot had a notion she lacked sufficient power to back out after it tore into the enemy ship. But Second Assistant Engineer James H. Tomb, who had seen service on the *McRae* in the battle of New Orleans, did not agree. "There was no reason why we should not have rammed and every reason why we should have done so," he said in his report. "The blow we should have struck, while sufficient to sink the enemy, would not have passed beyond the incline of the heavy cast-iron prow or ram on our bow. We could not hope to catch them once we were sighted, and, unless disabled with our guns, would get away from us." [15]

The two Confederate vessels combined their attack now in an effort to bring about their foe's finish. The executive officer of the *Keystone State,* Lieutenant Commander Thomas H. Eastman, in a matter of hours was writing his wife about what happened to his ship:

I slipped on my clothes, went up, and sent the crew to quarters and saw a small vessel approaching us. I, in the meantime, gave an order to slip our cable, which was done. The vessel came nearly alongside and I hailed him to stop or I would fire. He said "Halloa!" I fired into him seven guns, one after the other, hitting him at the distance of fifty yards, without hurting him. He fired into us without more words and tried to ram us, but we evaded him. His shot set us on fire and we had to run before the wind to put it out. As he kept firing on us, we were very busy. After ten minutes we put the fire out and in ten minutes more were on fire again, this time alongside of our shell room, and it kept us hard at work with water for twenty minutes. Dark all the time, so we could see his smoke and feel his shell. After our fire was subdued we got ready, manned both sides, and ran for him to run him down or sink us. All this time we were working our guns and part of the time fighting a second iron-clad. Just as we got within three hundred yards, going at the rate of twelve miles, he put a shot through both our boilers and blew us up. Then we were done. The ship fell over on her side; she had four large holes in her bottom; we could not move any more, and one-fourth of our strong crew were killed or wounded.[16]

But the Confederates told a different story. According to an eyewitness on the *Chicora* "this vessel [the *Keystone State*] was fired both fore and aft, and volumes of smoke were observed to issue from every aperture. As we neared her, she hauled down her flag and made a signal of surrender, but still kept under way with her starboard wheel, and changing her direction. This was just after daybreak. We succeeded in catching this vessel, but having surrendered, and the captain supposing her boilers struck and the escaping steam preventing the engineers from going into the engine room to stop her, ordered us not to fire." [17]

Commander Tucker of the *Chicora* was convinced that the Federal ship had surrendered when he saw men waving their arms from her deck as if they were in distress. "I at once gave the order to cease firing upon her," he reported, "and directed Lieutenant Bier, first lieutenant of the *Chicora,* to man a boat and take charge of the prize; if possible, to save her; if that was not possible, to rescue her crew. While the boat was in the act of being manned I discovered that she was endeavoring to make her escape by working her starboard wheel, the other being disabled, her colors being down. I at once started in pursuit and renewed the engagement. Owing to her superior steaming qualities she soon widened the distance to some two hundred yards. She then hoisted her flag and commenced firing her rifled guns, her commander, by this faithless act, placing himself beyond the pale of civilized and honorable warfare." [18]

Apparently the Confederate officer, in making this report, was unaware, according to Federal records, that the U.S.S.

Memphis had pushed to the scene, passed a hawser to the *Keystone State* while the fighting continued around her, and had managed to tow her away. There were two feet of water in the stricken ship at the time, and Le Roy had thought he was sinking. He was so sure of it that boats were ordered ready, and the signal book and some small arms were thrown overboard. He claimed that the Confederates continued to fire at him after his flag was lowered and, for that reason, he rehoisted it and resumed firing from the afterbattery.

The Confederate vessels turned their attention to other Union ships. The *Augusta,* reaching the scene, was shot at and struck several times in the hull. The *Housatonic,* tardily running toward the excitement, exchanged a few shots, but stayed far enough away to avoid damage. Commander James Madison Frailey of the U.S.S. *Quaker City,* thinking from the beginning that the firing was aimed at some Southerner trying to get through the blockade, ran brazenly up to within three to four hundred yards and drew a shell that passed harmlessly above him. "I immediately returned her fire with the Parrott gun on the forecastle," he reported, "the shell from which passed over her. A second shell was then fired at us by the strange sail, which entered this vessel amidships about seven feet above the water line, cutting away a portion of the guard beam and a guard brace, and then on its course through the ship's side exploding in the engine room, carrying away there the starboard entablature brace, air-pump dome, and air-pump guide rod, and making sad havoc with the bulkheads." [19]

A running fight developed as daylight spread. "We next engaged two schooners, one brig, and one bark-rigged propeller," reported Tucker of the *Chicora,* "but not having the requisite speed were unable to bring them to close quarters. We pursued them six or seven miles seaward. During the latter part of the combat I was engaged at long range with a bark-rigged steam sloop-of-war, but in spite of all our efforts was unable to bring her to close quarters, owing to her superior steaming qualities." [20]

By 7:30 in the morning the battle was ended. With the enemy ships seven miles or more clear of the bar, standing to the southward and eastward, the Confederate rams ran back toward the city and by 8:30 were anchored in four fathoms of water off Beach Channel. The fog had cleared, bringing the ironclads clearly into view so that the townspeople could see they had not been damaged. What they had done would be ranked with two other Confederate successes: the *Merrimack* and the *Arkansas*.

But the cheering that rang through the streets of Charleston that morning was not such as would mark an unqualified victory. Soon the people were asking questions. Where were the victims? Had they been sunk? Or were they still off the bar waiting to be towed into port? The *Chicora* and *Palmetto State* ran back out toward the entrance to the harbor and looked around. Not a Union vessel was to be seen. At the moment the victims they were looking for were on their way to Port Royal. Even before the fighting ended the *Mercedita* had been repaired to the point at which she could get a little steam on, and off she went, Abbot's pledge to Ingraham notwithstanding.[21] The *Keystone State,* after the *Memphis* took her in tow, headed away from Charleston and never once stopped before she got to Port Royal.[22] Men were dead on both ships, and others would die. A fourth of the *Keystone State*'s crew of one hundred and fifty-eight were either wounded or awaiting burial.

Without waiting to learn what had become of the Union fleet, General Beauregard, commander at Charleston, wired Richmond: "Last night the Confederate gunboats *Chicora* and *Palmetto State,* under Commodore Ingraham, sank (outside) the steamer *Mercedita.* Captain Tucker set fire to one vessel, which struck her flag, and thinks he sank another. Our loss and damage, none. Enemy's whole fleet was dispersed north and south. I am going to proclaim blockade of Charleston raised." [23]

During the afternoon the General arranged for a steamer to

take foreign consuls on duty at Charleston out into the harbor to see for themselves that no blockade existed. Both the French and Spanish representatives went along. Already the British consul, in the *Petrel,* had been ɔut five miles beyond the usual anchorage of the blockaders and returned to report that he could see nothing, even with glasses. Just before dark four blockaders reappeared, but remained far out. That night the consuls held a meeting and unanimously agreed that the blockade of the port had been legally raised.[24] Beauregard and Ingraham already had made such a claim by formal proclamation.[25]

Next evening the usual number of blockaders were in sight, all keeping steam up ready to run. They were evidence that, if the blockade at Charleston actually had been broken, the Union ships assigned to duty there were not yet ready to admit it. As one officer observed: "It seems evident that people are determined to see things through the spectacles that suit themselves." [26] And foreign nations, aware of armed vessels waiting off Charleston bar to nab any craft that tried to run into port illegitimately, were forced to concede that the blockade still existed.

So the South's mighty effort of January 31, 1863, went for naught. "The upshot of the engagement," wrote Engineer Tomb of the *Chicora,* "was a grand bit of glory, but not a prize or ship destroyed, and when we passed back over the bar and back to Charleston we all felt disappointed at the night's work. We did not accomplish as much as our sister ship, the *Palmetto State.* They say we raised the blockade, but we all felt we would have rather raised hell and sunk the ships." [27]

Lieutenant Commander Thomas McKean Buchanan, twenty-five-year-old Naval Academy graduate and a persevering man, stood in front of the pilothouse on the upper deck of the *Calhoun* and stared with his spyglass at a line of obstructions in the Bayou Teche, deep in Louisiana's Berwick Bay country. He called aloud what he saw: the wreck of a bridge, a little steamboat, a flatboat load of bricks, big logs that looked like live oak. Acting Third Assistant Engineer George W. Baird, standing at his side, verified his statement.

Suddenly rifle fire rang out from a series of pits along the shore.

"Oh, God!" cried Buchanan, and his glass flew over his shoulder as he tried to raise his hands to his head.

"He fell like an ox," Baird wrote in his diary, "and as he fell I saw a blood spot the size of a half dollar in front of his right ear and from it the blood began to flow. So quick was it all that the spot was visible to me before the blood came." [28]

The still form at George Baird's feet represented one of the costly payments the North would have to make for the destruction of the Confederate ironclad gunboat *J. A. Cotton*. McKean Buchanan, descended from a seafaring grandfather and an actor father of the same name, was looked upon as one of the Union's most gallant officers. Graduated from the Academy in 1855, he had been made a lieutenant in 1860, and only recently had received his promotion to lieutenant commander. His death would be attributed to impulsiveness—pushing too rapidly into battle and paying too little attention to the marksmanship of Rebels in rifle pits lining the banks of the Bayou Teche.

This action in which he fell was characteristic of January '63. As the month faded, Southern resistance at widely separated points proved beyond doubt that the Confederacy was still in business and that the days ahead would not be marked by inactivity. Undoubtedly influenced by desperation, the opposition was chiefly against occupied or blockaded points, and in almost all instances the Union suffered the major damage. But the odds were against the South, for the North, its strength now better organized and clearly in evidence, was definitely closing in.

The fighting along the Bayou Teche was initiated by Union forces mainly to get rid of the *J. A. Cotton,* then threatening the safety of Union camps at Brashear City. General

N. P. Banks, succeeding Butler in command of the Louisiana Department, arrived at New Orleans in December, and it was not long before he let it be known he wanted the *Cotton* eliminated. The assignment went to a little fleet of four gunboats under Buchanan and to troops under General Godfrey Weitzel.

The expedition was stepped up when it was reported that the Confederates were meditating an attack in the Berwick Bay area. It was said they were strengthening the armament of the *Cotton,* both in caliber and number. Realizing this vessel would be a large element of the Southerners' offensive, Buchanan decided to anticipate them.

At Brashear City he gathered together his little armada— the *Estrella, Calhoun, Kinsman,*[29] and *Diana*—all hastily built and of light draft, supported by the Eighth Vermont, Sixteenth and Seventy-fifth New York, Twelfth Connecticut, Sixth Michigan, and Twenty-first Indiana Regiments, the First Louisiana Cavalry, and the Fourth and Sixth Massachusetts and the First Maine Batteries. The vessels pulled out at three o'clock one morning, and the first thing they did was to ferry Weitzel's cavalry and artillery to the west bank of the bayou. This was completed before noon, after which they took on board the infantry, headed up the Bayou Teche, and came to a halt at Pattersonville. When line of battle had been formed, Buchanan went off on foot on reconnaissance. On his return and report, Weitzel advanced his entire force to Lynch's Point and bivouacked it under cover of the gunboats.

At seven next morning the *Diana* crossed the Eighth Vermont Regiment over to the east bank of the bayou to cover the gunboats. Weitzel's line on the west bank was moved up to attack the *Cotton,* plainly in view beyond the barrier of bricks and logs near Cornay's Bridge.

Resistance by the Southerners, led by Brigadier General Alfred Mouton, was concentrated chiefly in a series of rifle pits opened along the banks. These were manned by Louisiana troops, supported by the Second Louisiana Cavalry and guns from Faries' Battery. This time they were desperate, for they were meeting in Weitzel's men a force that had routed them at Georgia Landing less than three months ago.

The general fight began at 8:00 A.M., when the gunboats pushed up within range of the Confederate guns. Out of the rifle pits came a hot, peppering fire that Commander George Wiggin of the *Kinsman,* in the lead, answered by ordering his men to lie down on deck and to use small arms. During the exchange his brother, Alexander S. Wiggin, the boat's executive officer, was wounded in the shoulder.

A reporter from the Houston *Tri-Weekly Telegraph* was on hand. "Owing to the superior range of their guns," he recorded, "the batteries of the *Cotton* did not at first reply to their salutations; but as they neared the obstructions the deep thunder of our heavy guns trembled on the wind, and we knew that the game had ceased to be altogether on one side. For hours the roar of artillery was almost incessant, and the high wind which had been prevailing seemed frightened into silence." [30]

The *Cotton* struck the *Kinsman* five times. More trouble lay ahead for the Union vessel. While she maneuvered near the obstructions in an effort to get out of range of the rifle pits, a mine exploded under her stern, unshipping her rudder, and she backed off down the bayou. Buchanan, on board the *Calhoun*, third in line, saw what had happened and shouted to Lieutenant Commander A. P. Cooke, ahead in the *Estrella,* to push on up to the obstructions. Cooke shouted back, "The rifle pits line the shore!" Regardless of what he intended to imply, his vessel began dropping back. Buchanan next yelled: "Then move out of the way and I will go!" A moment later he was killed.

"I was right at his side," Baird wrote in his diary. "He was directly between me and the pits, and had that ball missed him it would have hit me in the neck, for I was a little taller than he was. Quartermaster Lewis was struck in the leg and Perkins in the back, and as I stepped back behind the pilot-house for protection, both Lewis and Perkins tumbled out on deck and lay down behind the little deck house; the pilot ran aft and escaped. I observed the ship had run her bow ashore on the side where the rifle pits were."

At this moment occurred an act of heroism later recognized by a Congressional Medal of Honor. Behind on the *Diana,* it was observed that the Confederates were readying boats to board the *Calhoun,* and a call was made for a volunteer to carry a message on foot to the Eighth Vermont about five hundred yards distant on the west side of the bayou. First Sergeant S. E. Howard, a sharpshooter on board, answered the call. "Run, for God's sake," H. F. Dutton, his company captain, told him, "and tell Colonel Thomas that if he doesn't take those rifle pits in five minutes the *Calhoun* is lost. She is hard aground, Buchanan is killed, the men are driven from the guns, and the enemy are preparing to board her."

Howard, throwing off all equipment, was put on shore by small boat, and there he ran for his life, drawing a heavy fire from the Southerners the moment he scrambled up the bank. Unhurt, he delivered his message. It brought the Eighth Vermont, until then unaware of the emergency, swooping down on the rifle pits. The Southerners were so busy trying to capture the *Calhoun* that they had ignored their flank and rear and, before they knew it, the regiment of Federals was on them.[31]

Meanwhile the *Cotton* was withstanding the fire of the combined land and sea forces. She stood it for some time, but then, especially hard hit by the attack from sharpshooters on shore, she commenced slowly retreating. It was about this time that the Southerners lost one of their best fighters—Lieutenant Henry K. Stevens, an officer who had distinguished himself repeatedly, including service on the ill-fated *Arkansas.* "He fell," wrote the *Tri-Weekly Telegraph* reporter, "fighting like a hero, brave as a lion, and calm and immovable as the very statue of silence."

Immediately afterward the *Cotton*'s captain, Edward W. Fuller, was shot through both arms. But he remained at his post, blood dripping from his clothing, until his vessel was moored in line with the troops on land. Then he turned over the command to Lieutenant E. T. King, who removed the dead and wounded, then headed the boat once more back toward the scene of action. But the peak of battle had passed. Slowly the firing died down, until there was only slight skirmishing between the land forces, and this kept up for the remainder of the day.

Next morning before daybreak a reflection welled up in the dark skies above the stream, and soon word arrived that the *Cotton* was on fire. "The *Cotton,* which had become the pet and pride of our community, the *Cotton,* which had come to be regarded as personal property among us," wrote the *Telegraph*'s correspondent, "is no more. . . . She now lies a gloomy wreck upon the water, though lost and abandoned, defiant in her loneliness, and still, as she was when afloat, a barrier to the advance of her foe."

It was left to this reporter to write the epitaph of the battle of Bayou Teche: "The enemy have retreated to Berwick Bay. What are their intentions for the future in regard to this, the fairest portion of our State? The red blaze of incendiarism, the smoldering ruins which mark their backward march, would seem to indicate that they are about to abandon this section and seek to leave cruel remembrances of their fanatical hate behind them. Among the houses destroyed on this side of the bayou we notice those of Colonel P. C. Bethel, Mr. A. A. Fuselier, and Mr. Numa Cornay."

★ 20

The ship that went to sea in pieces

FEBRUARY 1863

Ignoring setbacks that occasionally crept in between victories, the Union Navy remained dedicated to a task and pursued its course relentlessly, taking the Confederacy apart piece by piece. While Vicksburg remained the major objective along the Mississippi, of particular annoyance to the South Atlantic Blockading Squadron was a side-wheel merchant steamer with two masts, a powerful craft propelled by an engine that had an eighty-six-inch cylinder and an eight-foot stroke. This was the C.S.S. *Nashville,* lying at the moment in the Big Ogeechee River south of Savannah, Georgia, and awaiting an opportunity to run out to sea again. She was armed with two twelve-pounder brass cannon, and the Federals knew that once she got in the open she could be as dangerous as the *Alabama* or *Florida.* That was the principal reason they had kept her bottled up for months, assigning ironclads and other men-of-war to the task of guarding her.

The *Nashville* was winding up an active career. Had it not

been feared she was too closely watched, she might have conveyed Confederate Commissioners Mason and Slidell to Europe. Missing this distinction, she next brought fame to herself
by sinking the *Harvey Birch* while en route to England, where
she became the first man-of-war to fly the Confederate flag in
English waters. Then she added new laurels by escaping from
foreign port by duping the *Tuscarora,* a Union ship standing
by just for the purpose of making her a prize. Returning to
the South in February '62, she was sold to a private mercantile
concern, and soon she was running in valuable cargoes from
Nassau. This continued until July, when she made her last
voyage to bring in badly needed arms and ammunition, winding up at Savannah. Thereafter she was blockaded, biding her
time in the narrow, crooked Ogeechee, sixteen miles south of
the mouth of the Savannah River.

Her last voyage had been a heartbreaker, and she had barely
managed to scurry back into port. Du Pont wrote Fox about
it: "We hear . . . that the *Nashville* threw over all her cargo
in the chase—worth a million—burned all her bulkheads,
sawed all their beams and got up the pork to keep up the
fires." If squalls had not concealed her path, he added, she
would have been taken.[1]

It was after her return from Europe that the Federal Government took up a continuous watch. The Confederates schemed
to get her out. Under their various wiles she changed from the
cruiser *Nashville* to the runner *Thomas L. Wragg,* a transformation that in no way altered her future. For months she
lay with a valuable cargo of cotton on board, hoping to get it
to England. Then she disappeared, and when she was seen
again she had unloaded the cotton, undergone further alterations, and assumed the new name of *Rattlesnake.*

The Federals wanted her out of the way, but the one obstacle
that kept them from storming up the Ogeechee and destroying
her was Fort McAllister, above which she usually lay. This
fortification, a formidable casemated earthwork with bomb-
proofs, named for the owner of the plantation on which it was

built, was thrown up by the Confederates in '61. It was an important work, guarding Savannah's backdoor and denying the use of the Ogeechee to Union vessels. Situated on Genesis Point, it was surrounded by a wide area of marshy land, punctuated here and there by columns of smoke rising either from rice mills or from Confederate camps.

In January, Captain J. F. Green of the U.S.S. *Canandaigua* wrote Du Pont that "no reliable information has reached me in regard to the manner or means the Rebels design employing to rescue the *Nashville,* but I think it probable if an attempt is made it will be at the next high tides with an ironclad steamer of light draft through the Romerly Marshes." He recommended obstruction of this passage by sinking an old hulk loaded with stones.

Remembering the Stone Fleet, the assortment of old rock-filled ships uselessly scuttled in river entrances of the South, Du Pont took action of a different nature. At nine o'clock one night two boats filled for reconnaissance left the *Montauk* and pulled upstream, their oars muffled with sheepskin. Ten men armed with revolvers, rifles, and cutlasses were in each. "Up we continued," one of the participants reported, "half the crew rowing, the other half with arms in their hands, until we reached a line of obstructions that diagonally crossed the river, and effectually closed it, with the channel passage through it skillfully concealed. A third of a mile beyond was the fort, its side toward us dark in the shadow, and the sentry pacing the parapet. Here we remained a while, listening and watching, but nothing broke the stillness of the night, and we returned, removing the range stakes along the banks as we came across them, and before midnight we reached the ship." [2] Early next morning a squadron of five vessels went up to shell the fort. Heading them was the U.S.S. *Montauk* and J. L. Worden. Du Pont wanted particularly to test the ironclad's power of resistance against Fort McAllister, planning, if it was strong enough, to send her against the defenses of Charleston.

They ran up to within fifteen hundred yards of the fort, to a point where they could see the masts of the *Nashville* protruding above the trees which covered a wooded neck of land. For more than four hours the firing continued, and then the attackers withdrew, their subsequent reports convincing Du Pont that McAllister was another fort that could be taken only with the co-operation of troops. The *Montauk* meanwhile had stood up well. Her armor was dented, but there was no serious damage.

Five days elapsed before they were ready for a second attack. During this period more ammunition and supplies were brought in and numerous contrabands questioned. The Confederates, it was plain to see, were equally busy. A little tug was going about constantly, putting down mines and assisting the *Nashville,* which lay once more just above the fort. The Union sailors could see her from the mastheads of the gunboats, and they knew that she was still piling on cotton, hoping in some manner to get past them in the dark.

"It was her greediness for cotton that proved her downfall," opined Bradley S. Osbon, reporter for the New York *Herald,* who had been permitted to ship on board the *Montauk.*[3] This veteran correspondent was observing every little happening. "On the 29th," he recorded, "a little bird lingered about our decks all day, very tame and friendly, and the sailors thought it a good omen. In the evening we heard a heavy gun go off from the works, and concluded that the enemy had mounted and was trying a new gun. Later we discovered a bright light near where we had anchored. On the next day the Confederates burned off the rice and brush fields back of the fort, doubtless expecting a land attack." [4]

When the second attack was launched on February 1 the Union vessels were able to move much closer to the fort because a contraband had revealed the location of the mines placed by the Confederates, and crews had worked at night removing them. After a light predawn breakfast the squadron chugged upstream. Osbon was busy making notes on the experience:

There is always something peculiar to the sensation a man has going into battle aboard ship. He has usually known of the impending engagement for hours, even days ahead. The situation has been discussed from every conceivable point of view. Every possibility, even that of defeat, has been considered, and, if possible, certain letters have been written home. Then at last it is the moment of starting. A sharp order is given, and the anchor chains click in the windlass. The crew bustles—a rapid walking goes on about the decks. A bell in the engine room jingles, the vessel moves. There begins a rushing sound of water along her sides. All these are accustomed sounds and movements, but there is always a different note and a special significance in them than when the ship is going into battle. Even the lamps below burn with a peculiar glare. A glass of water has a different taste. One finds that he is nervously impatient. Why doesn't the first gun go off and begin it all? Then, suddenly, the enemy opens—a shot strikes the vessel, or tears through the rigging. Why don't we fire? Why in hell don't we fire? Click! goes a gunlock—snap! goes a primer, and there is a tremendous report which shakes the vessel and wakes it to new and sudden life. There is no more hesitation, no more nervousness, no more cold sweat. One suddenly becomes a fierce, eager creature with the energy of a demon. The engagment has begun.[5]

At 7:45 the *Montauk* opened with a fifteen-inch gun. A short while later Osbon was down on one knee writing a note when a shell struck the pilothouse and loosened some of the plate bolts. One of them struck him on the shoulder, another displaced a kneecap, and still another broke two of his ribs. These developments he faithfully recorded.

For four hours and forty minutes a terrific cannonade continued, the Southerners blasting away so effectively at the *Montauk* it was struck forty-eight times. Colonel R. H. Anderson, commanding the Confederates along the Ogeechee, said of the engagement in his report: "I think that the brave and heroic garrison of Fort McAllister have, after a most severe and trying fight, demonstrated to the world that victory does not, as a matter of course, always perch itself on the flag of an ironclad when opposed even to an ordinary earthwork manned by stout and gallant hearts." [6]

After this second trial, the Union vessels settled down into a blockading fleet, watching across the marshes by day and by night to see if the *Nashville* was moving. Weeks passed. At eight minutes after four the afternoon of February 27, while the crew was at dinner, the *Nashville* was reported in sight.[7] It was cloudy and rainy, and a light breeze was blowing from the southeast. The U.S.S. *Seneca,* after changing signals with the *Montauk,* steamed upstream on reconnaissance and returned with the important news that the Confederate ship had gone aground in that part of the river known as Seven-Mile Reach.

From the ships the Northerners studied the *Nashville* closely with glasses. A wisp of smoke and steam rose in a thin cloud from her funnel. Men moved busily about her decks, at the mastheads, and in the rigging, and the Federals knew that every effort was being made to lighten her. Dawn would tell the story.

All hands on the *Montauk* were called at four o'clock next morning. After a hasty breakfast of coffee and crackers, they started upstream.

"There was a haze on the river," reported Osbon, "and we steamed slowly to avoid new obstructions. At 7:05 we let go anchor about twelve hundred yards below the fort, and about the same distance from the *Nashville,* lying across the bend. There indeed she lay, hard and fast aground, the hasty unloading and the sturdy labors of the little tug, which had been going on through the night, having failed to relieve her. She was a fair mark and knew that she was doomed, and when we sent toward her an envoy of death in the form of a screaming eleven-inch shell, those who had not already deserted her fled hastily, leaving her to her fate." [8]

The fort opened on the *Montauk,* but its fire was returned only by the other vessels of the squadron. The shells that struck McAllister caused no serious worry to the Southerners, merely damaging the quarters of the Emmett Rifles and plowing up the parade ground.

At twenty-two minutes after seven [Osbon continued] we landed a fifteen-inch shell close to the *Nashville,* and five and one-half minutes later we sent another—it was our fifth shot—smashing into her hull, just between the foremast and paddlebox. Almost immediately followed the explosion. Acting Master Pierre Geraud was working both guns finely, considering that from his position in the turret below only the masts and smokestack of the vessel could be seen. We were proud to show the enemy that we had a gunner, too. Smoke settled about us, and after the eighth shot we ceased firing to let the air clear. Presently a breath of wind swept the drift aside, and we saw to our great joy a dense column of smoke rising from the forward deck of the stranded vessel. Our exploding shell had set her on fire. A few minutes more, and flames were distinctly visible, forcing their way up, gradually creeping aft until they had reached nearly to the base of the smokestack.[9]

Worden chronicled her end in this manner: "At 9:20 A.M. a large pivot gun mounted abaft her foremast exploded from the heat; at 9:40 her smoke chimney went by the board, and at 9:55 her magazine exploded with terrific violence, shattering her in smoking ruins. Nothing remains of her." [10]

After the explosion the *Montauk* withdrew out of range of the fort. She moved, while Southerners in the fort looked on with bated breath, amazed at the manner in which she "apparently passed and repassed with impunity over the spot where the torpedoes were sunk." [11] But she was not to escape with just the few dents inflicted by the guns of the fort. Engineer Stephens gave this report from the engine room: "At 9:35 a violent, sudden, and seemingly double explosion took place. I instantly called the men from the starboard side to prevent their being scalded, expecting a gush of steam, supposing from the locality of the sound that a shot had penetrated or some part of the starboard boiler had given way. While looking at the boiler to see the effect, the dust, debris, and smoke came down from the angle formed by the deck and smoke pipe on starboard side, causing the impression for a moment that a shell had penetrated and exploded there. While intently watching for the effect to develop itself from the starboard boiler, the man stationed in port passage with lantern as lookout reported that the port boiler was burst underneath. Took a view in the port passage, saw the water cascading, judged the cause to be the castiron outboard to blow off." [12]

As Stephens searched in vain for the cause of the trouble, the answer was sent down to him from the pilothouse: the *Montauk* had struck one of the mines the Confederates had been seen so busily planting. Her pilot, a tough-looking little Georgian named Murphy, admitted the fault was partly his. He had seen a rag floating on the water, and although his subconscious had warned him he should steer clear of it, he had ignored that "second sense" and had gone into it bow first.

But now he made amends for what he had done. He beached the stricken vessel, on level keel and without list, in such a manner that the mud of the Ogeechee blocked the inflow of water through the hole in her bottom until it could be repaired.

Back up the river a column of smoke still rose from the shattered hulk of the *Nashville*. The cruiser that had caused so much anguish to the North was at last obliterated, and no one could be happier over it than Du Pont. "That vessel, the *Nashville*," he wrote, "seemed an idea in the public mind; for, although I have had her blocked up for eight months, the press, with its usual accuracy, has had her running the blockade about every three weeks. Still, had she got out as a privateer and joined the *290* and *Oreto*, I always felt it would have been a serious matter, and altogether different from carrying out a load of cotton. At this particular moment, too, I feel extremely gratified at being rid of her." [13]

During the hours the crew of the *Montauk* worked to repair the damage done by the mine, those on deck cast their eyes repeatedly toward the surface of the Big Ogeechee. There they could see quantities of loose and scorched cotton sticking to fragments of the wrecked vessel, slowly drifting by. The sight made a deep impression on one of the onlookers. "As these silent witnesses of the havoc drifted past us," he wrote, "they seemed to show a determination that, if we would not allow the *Nashville* to go to sea as a whole, she was going to run the blockade in pieces." [14]

The black terror

FEBRUARY-MARCH 1863

From Vicksburg down to Port Hudson, a matter of a few miles as the crow flies, the Mississippi bends and turns and twists in an assortment of tortuous gyrations. It was a stretch of river that formed a sort of funnel through which the Southerners were busily shuttling valuable supplies from the rich granaries of Arkansas, Louisiana, and Texas.

In this snakelike stretch lay a life line, an index of Southern courage, that kept the pulse of the Confederacy beating. Once stifled, it would be an easier matter for the North to bring the South to its knees with the fight starved out of it.

Technically, the problem of blocking up this part of the river was David Porter's, for Porter commanded the region of the upper Mississippi. But no matter: Farragut might be blockading down in the Gulf, somewhere off New Orleans, and yet he would feel the burden, too. People in the North still looked upon Farragut as the man who would close the Mississippi.

Occasional developments during February brought encouragement to Northern strategists. Before dawn one chilly morning the youthful Charles R. Ellet, with Porter's blessing, ran the batteries at Vicksburg in the ram *Queen of the West,* taking her through almost without damage. En route he slowed up long enough to attack the C.S.S. *City of Vicksburg,* lying at a wharf under the protection of numerous guns. The *Queen* had been stacked with cotton bales to protect her crew from Confederate bullets, and these very bales were the element that prevented a complete success. Just as Ellet, after his first strike, was backing off to gather speed for another thrust, the cotton burst into flame, and for a brief period more attention was given to fighting fire than to fighting Rebels.

The venture was executed under orders that were specific to the point of being ridiculous. Porter, the believer in gimmicks, thought of everything. Fires must be banked to prevent smoke, lights extinguished, and the vessel kept close to the right shore. On the way Ellet was to think of the fate of the *Harriet Lane* and, on arriving, shout the name of the unlucky craft into the ears of the Confederates. And one final note: "Don't be surprised to see the *Indianola* below. Don't mistake her for a Rebel; she looks something like the *Chillicothe.*" [1]

In addition to the burden of all these instructions, Ellet was late getting started. A broken steampipe held him up the first night, and the following night he delayed an hour or more to adjust his steering apparatus. Before he could get started the sun was rising, thus depriving him of the advantage of darkness. The Confederates, on first sighting the *Queen,* opened a heavy fire, striking her three times in quick succession.

When he was preparing to ram the *City of Vicksburg,* Ellet found the current of the river against him. Just as he was about to strike, the stern of his boat swung around in such a manner that all her momentum was lost. But he fired incendiary projectiles into the enemy vessel, setting her afire, just as the return shells set aflame the cotton stacked for protection on the *Queen's* deck. Smoke rolled into the engine room, suffocating the men there, so Ellet veered off, his crew busily fighting fire.

For once the Southerners were taken by surprise. Despite

all the guns placed at high points along the Mississippi, Ellet made his way to the mouth of the Red River, his boat carrying evidence that twelve shells had found their mark, and there he pounced upon three vessels loaded with pork, sugar, molasses, and military supplies. They were burned. A few days later the torch was applied to cotton and other items farther up the Red. Next he ran six miles along the Atchafalaya. On his way back a party of overseers and civilians fired into him from behind a levee, striking Master James D. Thompson in the knee, and then fled in the darkness. Ellet anchored, and the next morning burned all the buildings on the three nearest plantations.

That same day, fifty miles from the mouth of the Red River, Ellet captured a transport, the *Era No. 5,* laden with four hundred and fifty bushels of corn. Hearing of three large vessels lying with steam down at Gordon's Landing thirty miles above, he hurried on, followed by his tender, the *De Soto.* On rounding a bend, he suddenly ran hard aground under the death-dealing muzzles of a four-gun battery. Nearly every shot struck, and soon steam was pouring up from below. Crew members scurried like rats, some of them in a boat that safely reached the tender. The remainder, Ellet included, floated downstream on cotton bales. Behind them they left the *Queen* waiting for the Confederates to take over. She could not be destroyed because the wounded Thompson was still on board. The fleeing men looked back ruefully, knowing that the best ram in the fleet had passed into the hands of the enemy with no damage other than a burst steampipe.

On board the *Queen* during her brilliant but short career up the Red River had been Finley Anderson, reporter for the New York *Herald.* The adventure was to be a test of "my own personal courage . . . just to see what kind of stuff I am made of." [2] He got more of a test than he expected, for he was among the captives who fell in the bag of the Southerners. They threw him into "an iron dungeon" in Texas for ten days and then moved him elsewhere for eleven months of prison life.

After fleeing from the *Queen,* Ellet boarded the *De Soto.* A dense fog set in, and soon the vessel ran into the bank and lost her rudder. She was allowed to drift. Fifteen miles below she came upon the *Era No. 5.* Ellet burned the *De Soto* and pushed on in the *Era,* throwing off corn to lighten her as he moved slowly through the fog. The Mississippi was reached at dawn and, shortly afterward, opposite Ellis Cliffs, the *Era,* drawing less than two feet of water, grounded, her wheels making several revolutions after she struck. This aroused Ellet's suspicions: one after another, three vessels had gone aground. His regular pilot, Scott Long, was ill and had been unable to come along, and in his place was Thomas W. Garvey. "The disloyal sentiments openly expressed by Mr. Garvey a few hours previous to the occurrence," reported Ellet, "rendered it necessary for me to place him under arrest, and forced upon me the unwilling conviction that the loss of the *Queen* was due to the deliberate treachery of her pilot." [3]

At the time of the *Queen's* capture help was already on its way. Two days after she ran past the batteries at Vicksburg, Porter sent the *Indianola* to her support. One factor that moved him to dispatch aid was a report from spies that the Confederates had at their service the ram C.S.S. *William H. Webb,* an old towboat armed and cotton-clad and now capable of doing fifteen to twenty knots, making her one of the fastest vessels afloat. The *Indianola,* captained by Lieutenant Commander George Brown, a twenty-eight-year-old Indianan still looking for glory in his military career, was one of a group of new ironsides, embracing many features not included in the original nine—a grotesque affair constructed at Cincinnati at a cost of nearly two hundred thousand dollars. Her deck was flat and barely above water. Forward was an armored casemate in which were mounted two eleven-inch smoothbores. Amidships rose tall twin stacks, with a towerlike pilothouse between them and the forward casemate. In addition to paddle wheels, she had twin screws, each worked by a separate engine. But her maximum speed was only six knots.

On the night of February 13, with a barge on each side loaded with seven thousand barrels of coal, she chugged downstream. Brown, like Ellet, had received instructions from Porter before leaving: "The object in sending you is to protect the ram *Queen of the West* and the *De Soto* against the *Webb,* the enemy's ram; she will not attack you both. . . . Go to Jeff. Davis' plantation and his brother Joe's and load up said steamer with all the cotton you can find and the best single male Negroes." [4]

Although Brown chose darkness for his run, the Southerners had learned he was coming and were primed. A terrific fire was opened from the batteries. In a period of eighteen minutes, at the peak of the bombardment at Vicksburg and Warrenton, nineteen shots were fired at the Union vessel, but she went through unscathed, displaying two red lights to let other Federals know her identity. Porter was delighted over her success, and quickly wired Welles: "This gives us entire control of the Mississippi, except at Vicksburg and Port Hudson, and cuts off all the supplies and troops from Texas." [5]

The morning of the 16th the *Indianola,* a little below Natchez, met the *Era No. 5* chugging upstream. After a conference in which Brown suggested that he might be able to ascend the Red River and destroy the battery at Gordon's Landing that had stopped the *Queen,* the *Era* turned about and led the way back down the river. That afternoon they got a brief glimpse of the *Webb* and fired a couple of shots at her as she rounded a bend below them, but she fled out of danger, making the most of her superior speed. Brown, given confidence by the sight of her in flight, wired Porter that he had no doubt the Rebels would use her in an attack, but that he felt prepared to meet both the *Queen* and the *Webb.*

Brown reached the mouth of the Red River on the 17th and learned that the *Queen* had indeed been repaired and was ready for service. He was told also that the *Webb* and four cotton-clad boats, with boarding parties on board, were fitting out to attack the *Indianola.* Having no pilot to guide him up the Red River, the *Indianola*'s captain decided against such a venture and, on the 21st, remembering Porter's instructions to protect his vessel with cotton, he steamed upstream. By the next afternoon he had procured as much cotton as he needed, but he decided to continue upstream, still towing the coal barges. The morning of the 24th he approached Grand Gulf, at the mouth of the Big Black. This once flourishing village of a thousand inhabitants was now desolate and nearly deserted, reduced to a mass of ashes by the angry Farragut the preceding summer when some of its residents persisted in throwing shells at his transports.

It was noon before the *Indianola* passed Grand Gulf and chugged on, its four engines laboring against the current and making no more than two or three knots. Four hours later, after she had passed out of sight, a little squadron flying the Confederate flag steamed into view from below, making twice the speed of the *Indianola*. In the lead was the *Queen of the West,* once more in fighting condition. Repairs, following her capture, had been pushed day and night, the latter by the light of wood fires along the shore. The accompanying vessels were the *Webb* and the river boats *Dr. Beatty* and *Grand Era,* the latter two protected with cotton bales behind which waited sharpshooters and boarding parties. The plan was to overtake the Union boat after dark.

Steadily they pushed on along the winding course of the stream. Major J. L. Brent, commander of the Confederate flotilla, gave this description of their approach: "The moon was partially obscured by a veil of white clouds, and gave and permitted just sufficient light for us to see where to strike with our rams, and just sufficient obscurity to render uncertain the aim of the formidable artillery of the enemy. We first discovered him when about one thousand yards distant, hugging the eastern bank of the Mississippi, with his head quartering across and down the river. Not an indication of life was given as we dashed on toward him—no light, no perceptible motion of his machinery was discernible. We had also obscured every light, and only the fires of the *Era* could be seen, two miles back, where she was towing the *Beatty*." [6]

Their pursuit was not unknown to Brown. Since noon of the preceding day, the trail of smoke emerging from the Confederate vessels had been of concern to the men on the *Indianola,* and half the members of each watch were kept constantly on deck.[7] Brown wrote Porter about the manner in which they overtook him: "At about 9:30 P.M. . . . the night being very dark, four boats were discovered in chase of us. I immediately cleared for action, and as soon as all preparations were completed, I turned and stood down the river to meet them. At this time the leading vessel was about three miles below, the others following in close order. The *Queen* was the first to strike us, which she did after passing through the coal barge lashed to our port side, doing us no serious damage. Next came the *William H. Webb.* I stood for her at full speed; both vessels came together bows on, with a tremendous crash, which knocked down nearly every one on board of both vessels, doing no damage to us, while the *Webb's* bow was cut in at least eight feet. . . . At this time the engagement became general, and at very close quarters. . . ." [8]

For an hour and twenty-seven minutes the battle raged, with the two rams repeatedly striking the *Indianola* and the cottonclad gunboats standing off while the sharpshooters on board delivered their fire. H. M. Mixer, acting assistant surgeon on the Union boat, kept his eye on Brown during the fight. The construction of the *Indianola*'s pilothouse was such that in the night her pilots could see nothing, so that management of the vessel devolved on her captain. "To accomplish this," Mixer reported, "he exposed himself everywhere. He stood upon the hurricane deck, swept by volleys of musketry, grape, and canister shot, looking out for the rams, giving orders to his pilots, and with his revolver firing upon the pilots of the enemy. He stood on his knees on the grating on the main deck to see that the engineer correctly understood the orders from the pilots. He went to the casemate repeatedly and ordered the fire to be reserved until the rams were close upon us and then fire low. He aimed and discharged one of her guns himself, but the working of our guns was of necessity left largely to his subordinate officers." [9]

The seventh blow received by the *Indianola* came from the *Webb*. "Through and through, crushing and dashing aside her iron plates," reported Brent, "the sharp bow of the *Webb* penetrated as if it were going to pass entirely through the ship." [10] The starboard rudder box was so badly damaged that water poured in in large volumes. Brown kept her in a deep part of the stream until the floor was covered with two and a half feet of water, and then he started the screw engines and ran her nose on shore on the Louisiana side of the river. It was 11:07 P.M.

Immediately after the surrender, the *Webb* and *Dr. Beatty* took the *Indianola* in tow and pulled her across the river where she sank in ten feet of water opposite the head of Palmyra Island, near the plantation of Joseph Davis, brother of Confederate President Jefferson Davis. The work of raising her started next morning.

That day the *Queen of the West* steamed up to Warrenton after salvage equipment. While it lay in communication with the town, attention suddenly was diverted upriver, toward an object floating down with the current, a huge gunboat that in the glare along the river looked like a black terror. Smoke poured from its stacks. With the aid of glasses, guns could be seen protruding from its armor. It had the lines of a huge *Monitor*.

Men on the *Queen* drew conclusions immediately. Here was a new fighting machine from the North, a monster sent down by the Federals to offset the resistance the Southerners were putting up along the Mississippi, to drive away the little squadron that had captured the *Indianola,* and to salvage or destroy that vessel before the Confederates could make use of her. The fastenings of the *Queen* were hastily cut, and off downstream she went to spread the alarm, while gunners at Warrenton loaded their pieces and prepared to blaze away at the "black terror" when it came along.

The *Queen* moved in great haste. When, miles below, she drew up beside the wreck of the *Indianola,* no formalities were involved in the delivery of her message: a huge monster of a gunboat was on its way to drive off the Confederates. In the face of what was accepted as overwhelming power, only one recourse was left. On the sunken ship fire soon lapped at the woodwork that protruded above water, her guns were put mouth to mouth and exploded, and in a matter of minutes she was an abandoned craft, only her wine and liquor stores salvaged.[11] Confederates fled toward the Red River, there soon to suffer embarrassment too profound to attempt explanation.

For the "black terror," this thing that the *Queen* had raced madly to give warning about, was another of David Porter's gimmicks. From upriver he had listened to firing from the direction of the *Indianola* and the other vessels sent below. He wanted to help them, but since his flotilla even now seemed too small for the task it faced, he was reluctant to send more boats after those he had already committed. In this emergency he turned to his gimmicks. Crews were set to work building a dummy *Monitor.*

An old flat-bottomed barge was found, and log rafts were attached to it to increase its length to three hundred feet. Bulwarks were raised, a large casemate of logs was constructed up forward, and Quaker guns were set in its ports. A pilot-house and two huge paddle-wheel houses were attached. Two smokestacks made of pork barrels piled one upon another rose above its deck, each with a big pot of burning tar and oakum at its base. Every disguise was employed. Two boats swung from realistic-looking davits. Then the whole thing was covered with a coat of tar. And as a final touch someone fastened a sign to its bow: "Deluded people, cave in."

In the middle of the night it started on its lonesome trip down the Mississippi. Soon Confederate gunners at Vicksburg were blazing away at it, but it drifted on, undaunted, to head into the west bank below the city. There a group of Union soldiers pushed it back out into the current. Later it went aground again, and once more was shoved free. From then on it drifted on a true course on its mission, throwing such alarm into the Confederates that the *Indianola* was destroyed long before the "black terror" rounded the last curve above Joe Davis' plantation.

When the editor of the Vicksburg *Whig* heard of the *Indianola*'s destruction, he was furious. "Who is to blame for this piece of folly?" he asked through his newspaper columns. "This precipitancy? It would really seem we had no use for gunboats on the Mississippi, as a coal barge is magnified into a monster, and our authorities immediately order a boat— that would have been worth a small army to us—to be blown up." [12]

So Porter's gimmicks put an end to the supremacy of the Mississippi which the Confederates had maintained briefly between Vicksburg and Port Hudson.

Blood, brains, and bodies

MARCH 1863

On the morning of March 15th the U.S.S. *Richmond* was horrible to look upon. Her decks were splattered with arms, legs, and other pieces of flesh that lay in a nauseating mass along the trails of shells that had found their marks. Throughout the night sailors still able to do so were kept busy taking care of the wounded, righting things in general, and preparing to dispose of the still forms that lay in a row. Some of the victims would be greatly missed, for the Confederate shells had paid no attention to rank.

"At 10:00 A.M. all hands were called to bury the dead," stated an official report. "The coffins were placed in the port gangway when the funeral services were read by a chaplain who was on board as guest. The coffins were then placed in the boats and taken ashore and interred. An oak board was placed at the head of each grave, with the inscription painted on it with the name and place of birth, age and date of death. An escort of Marines, commanded by a corporal, fired

393

three rounds over their graves. The funeral party then returned to the ship." [1]

With this simple entry in her journal, the *Richmond* concluded an account of her part in the action along the Mississippi at Port Hudson the night of March 14. It was a story that would add more laurels to the record of David Farragut. For his ship and her escort, alone out of the fleet that tried to get past the Confederate batteries at that point, had succeeded.

In this offensive Farragut was answering the demand of the public. When, despite his success with the dummy *Monitor,* Porter's efforts to block the flow of Confederate supplies from the Red River failed, Farragut stepped into the act, leaving the Gulf and heading up the Mississippi. It was another desperate move by the Federals to tighten the grip on Vicksburg.

Port Hudson was the gateway through which passed, in war as in peace, the great outpouring of cotton and cattle from Texas. Across the river these commodities came by boat out of the mouth of the Red. As at Vicksburg, the Mississippi at that point made a sharp turn. On its left, or eastern, bank were bluffs fifty to a hundred feet high, whereas the opposite bank was a low, flat peninsula, within the bend of the stream. Under the bluffs the current was strong and sweeping; across the river the water was shallow and filled with eddies. Even under favorable circumstances it was difficult to navigate ships in either direction.

What to do about the formidable works the Confederates occupied at Port Hudson had bothered the Federals for months. Reconnaissance parties that moved so close they could distinguish the color of the clothes worn by their enemies reported the defenses stronger than Forts Jackson and St. Philip and more capable of resisting passage of a fleet than those at Vicksburg.

Farragut ignored these warnings. At Baton Rouge on the morning of March 13 he sat in consultation with General Banks, a leader backed up by seventeen thousand infantry,

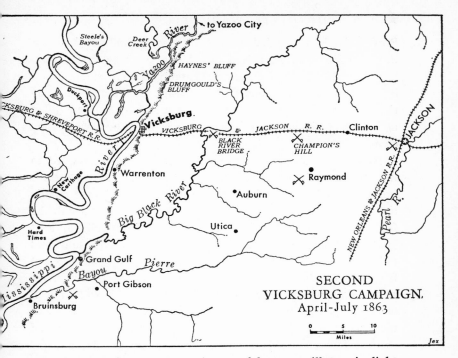

SECOND
VICKSBURG CAMPAIGN,
April-July 1863

0   5   10
Miles

Map labels: to Yazoo City, Steele's Bayou, Deer Creek, Yazoo River, HAYNES' BLUFF, DRUMGOULD'S BLUFF, VICKSBURG & SHREVEPORT R.R., Duckport, Vicksburg, VICKSBURG, JACKSON R. R., Clinton, JACKSON, BLACK RIVER BRIDGE, CHAMPION'S HILL, New Carthage, Warrenton, Raymond, Auburn, NEW ORLEANS & JACKSON R.R., Pearl R., Hard Times, Utica, Mississippi, Grand Gulf, Bayou Pierre, Port Gibson, Bruinsburg, Jex

one Negro regiment, one regiment of heavy artillery, six light batteries, one twenty-pounder battery, and ten troops of cavalry.[2] Plans were dovetailed. Running the batteries at Port Hudson would establish contact between the land and naval forces at Vicksburg, prevent the construction of new batteries, cut off supplies from the Red River area, and open the way for destruction of Confederate steamers still resisting. Banks, for his part, consented to move against Port Hudson immediately, making a diversion in the Navy's favor, and to attack the place if practicable. With this assurance, Farragut went out to inspect the squadron he had assembled.

Three sloops of war, the *Hartford, Richmond,* and *Monongahela,* were at hand. Fastened to these on the portside, to increase their speed, were three gunboats. The side-wheel steamer *Mississippi,* also available, was to make the attempt unassisted.

That afternoon the fleet got under way and moved up to near

Profit Island, a wooded area a little over halfway between Baton Rouge and Port Hudson. Along the way crews were kept busy preparing for action. Hammocks were stacked into bulwarks around the poop and forecastle. Decks and gun carriages were whitewashed. Sand and water buckets were filled and put in their customary places. It was 8:00 P.M. when they came to anchor.

At five o'clock next morning the advance was continued to the head of the island, where the *Essex* and several mortar boats were lying ready for the attack. The weather was cloudy and a heavy mist hung over the river. At 10:00 A.M., with the fog clearing so they could see the yellow clay cliffs at Port Hudson, Farragut called his commanders around him and talked over such problems as the resistance they could expect from the Confederate batteries and the nature of five river steamers they could see ahead. Two of these, it was known, were cotton-clad rams, and one was the *Queen of the West,* the vessel Ellet's pilot had cleverly brought into the hands of the Confederates. When the conference ended, the mortars commenced firing, to get the range. They found the distance too great, so they moved up half a mile nearer.

Each commander was given permission to arrange his ship according to his own ideas. On the *Hartford,* Farragut had a trumpet fixed from the mizzentop to the wheel, so the pilot could take his position aloft where he could see over the fog banks along the river and call directions below to the steersman. The pilot in this case was Thomas R. Carrell, a man in whom Farragut placed great faith, for the two had been together in the run past Vicksburg a few months back.

At two o'clock that afternoon the mortars opened a slow bombardment at long range, finally throwing shells within the lower part of the Confederate breastworks. Cheers from the batteries along shore greeted each explosion. At one period the gunboat *Sachem* ran up close to draw the fire of the Confederates, but they remained silent, hiding their positions.

At 5:00 P.M. Banks sent word he was at Barnes' Crossroads,

his troops occupying the road to Ross Landing, on the flank and rear of the Rebel batteries, and ready to move.[3] Farragut replied that he planned to be past Port Hudson by midnight.

At dusk signal lights on the flagship ordered the other vessels into position. Slowly they moved. Night came on, dark and still. Nine o'clock passed. An hour later a little tug moved about leaving word for the ships to draw closer together. As soon as he saw they were at their proper stations, Farragut moved ahead.

A noncombatant stood on the bridge of the *Richmond*. He was Thomas Scott Bacon, a civilian minister from Alexandria, Louisiana, a guest of the ship's officers, all intimate friends. He was much impressed with what he saw that night: "Even I, with all the eagerness of curiosity then, and the awe of such suspense and probable nearness to death, have now no recollection of how slowly moved the minutes of that hour or hour and a half of silence and darkness in which we crept up to the batteries. It was the understanding on our ship that Farragut's wish and hope was to push on without returning the enemy's fire, if possible; and with this in view to steer close into that bank of the river so that they could not depress their guns enough to do much damage. The intense darkness and the strong current, as well as our ignorance of what devices they might have in store, made it necessary to use prompt discretion in varying from this as occasion might demand." [4]

For a stretch of three miles along the river the Federal ships would be running past the guns on shore—first, Albert Rust's two field batteries at Troth's Landing; next, a twenty-pounder Parrott gun; then the heavy guns of Paul de Gournay's battalion and the First Tennessee Artillery; and finally, a battery served by four companies of the First Alabama Regiment. Sharpshooters lay in lines along the bluffs.

On toward the lights of Port Hudson the ships moved, the *Hartford,* in the lead, churning the waters; at her side the gunboat *Albatross,* chugging with all the horsepower in her engines. Next came the *Richmond*.

Progress was slow, for the night was so black they could not see one another. The vessels, no lights showing, moved through the darkness like phantoms, only the roar of their exhausts marking their progress. If the Confederates anticipated their approach, there was no evidence of it.

"I think we took them by surprise somewhat," Farragut reported, "as they did not open fire upon us until we were abreast of a large light placed on the opposite side to guide their fire. There the lookout threw up rockets and a battery soon opened upon us, at about 11:20 P.M." [5]

The firing became general. Smoke drifted in clouds across the dark water, lightened only by the flashes of guns and the blaze of bonfires along the opposite shore. In the background the mortars hammered away with thunderous roar. Of the noise one eyewitness wrote: "On the bluff we had some fifty guns, ranging from twenty-four to one-hundred-and-eighty-pounders. The noise was simply terrific. My home was about twenty miles from Port Hudson, and my people said the reverberation was so great it seemed that the glass would be shaken out of the windows." [6]

The *Hartford* moved up in good style, stopping occasionally when the smoke hampered visibility. Batteries on shore fired at her, and she answered with her broadside, blazing away whenever a fresh battery opened.

As she neared the point above Port Hudson, the current from around the bend caught her on the bow and threw her around, almost on shore. The *Albatross'* engines were quickly thrown in reverse, and they slowly swung the larger vessel about and started her upriver. Ahead, the upper Confederate batteries opened, answered by the two guns on the *Hartford's* poop, a nine-inch and a thirty-pounder Parrott rifle.

Farragut stood on the poop deck and watched the advance. Hours were ticking away. Near him were the fleet captain, Thornton A. Jenkins; clerk, Edward A. Palmer; E. C. Gabaudan, Farragut's secretary; and the flag officer's son, Loyall Farragut.

"I soon saw a vessel on fire and apparently grounded,"

Farragut related in his report, "and I feared she was one of ours. I saw her drifting along the river with her guns going off and the shells exploding from the heat. We now arrived at the conclusion that one or more of the vessels had met with disaster and the rest had dropped down the river again. The firing ceased about this time (2:00 A.M.), and near 4:00 A.M. the burning vessel blew up with a great explosion."

Finally the *Hartford,* with the *Albatross,* made her way around the curve and out of danger. Four holes in the flagship's hull told of the large shells that had struck her.

But the fate of the other vessels behind was far different. The *Richmond* was taking a pounding. Her captain, James Alden, stood on the bridge. At his side was the executive officer, Lieutenant Commander A. Boyd Cummings, a thirty-three-year-old Philadelphian winding up his sixteenth year in the Navy. Thomas Scott Bacon, the minister, was there, too. He heard Cummings call through his trumpet in a strong, steady voice: "You will fire the whole starboard battery, one gun at a time, from the bow gun aft. Don't fire too fast. Aim carefully at the flashes of the enemy's guns. Fire!"

Bacon drank in each development: "Already for some minutes splinters and ravelings of sails and ropes were falling around us in quite a shower. . . . The thunder of cannon from the river banks was loud. The *Hartford*'s broadside was very much nearer and more startling. But the crash and roar of the *Richmond*'s own guns under our feet, with every timber of the strong ship quivering with discharge and making her stagger like a drunken man, was more than on land to be in the midst of 'battle's magnificently stern array' and action. To see the earnestness of devotion to duty, suppressing all thoughts of fear, was a great instance of the power of discipline and of the habitual sense of duty."

Suddenly a cannon shot took off Cummings' left leg below the knee, throwing him to the deck. His words were urgent but unexcited: "Quick, boys, pick me up. Put a tourniquet on my leg. Send my letters to my wife. Tell her I fell in doing my duty." Below, as the surgeons worked over him, he said, "If there are others worse hurt, attend to them first."

He glanced at the cot next to his. Recognizing the man lying on it, he said, "Nolan, are you here, too?" Then he looked around. His mind seemed to wander as he asked about different officers. Suddenly a shell struck with terrific explosion, followed by a loud hissing.

"What is that?" he asked.

Someone brought the answer: "The steam pipes have been hit in the vicinity of the safety valves. Our pressure has dropped to nine pounds. We're turning back."

Cummings squirmed. "I would rather lose the other leg than go back. Can nothing be done? There is a south wind. Where are the sails?"

No one answered. The *Richmond* already had been struck sixteen times, and a mine exploding under her stern had blown in the cabin windows. Three men were dead, twelve wounded. Cummings would die in four days.

The *Richmond*'s journal graphically describes the experience through which she had passed: "We opened on the batteries with grape, canister, shrapnel, shell, and everything we had. The Rebel sharpshooters opened on us, but they were soon silenced. The engagement now became terrible. The Rebels' guns raked us as we came up to the point. The lower batteries were all silenced as we passed, but misfortune now befell us; as we were turning the point almost past the upper batteries we received a shot in our boilers, and almost at the same time the *Genesee* [her gunboat] got a shot in her machinery and a fire broke out in her, and another shot went through our steam drum. Our steam was all gone; our steam all escaped and put the fires out; we could not steam up against the current with one boiler. Torpedoes were exploding all around us, throwing water as high as the tops. We were, for a few minutes, at the Rebels' mercy; their shell were causing great havoc on our decks; the groans of the wounded and the shrieks of the dying were awful. The decks were covered with blood. We got afire in the starboard bulwarks, which was soon put out. We found we could not go up; we turned her head downstream. We still kept up a steady fire as we came down in crippled condition." [7]

The *Mississippi* was the burning vessel that Farragut had seen. Under command of her veteran captain, Melancton Smith, she pushed on up to the last and most formidable batteries, and members of her crew were congratulating themselves upon success, when she grounded and heeled over to port. The engine was reversed and the port guns were run in to try and bring her on an even keel, but without success. For thirty-five minutes her engines tried to back her off, during which time the steam pressure was nearly doubled. At that point the pilot announced that it would be impossible to get her free.

Smith prepared to abandon ship. He ordered the port battery spiked, and the pivot gun thrown overboard, but the fire from shore was too hot for the latter to be done. Before the wounded and the crew were crammed into three small boats, the only ones available, small arms were tossed into the water, the engine damaged, and the vessel set afire in the forward storeroom. As the flames began to spread, a shot struck, opening a hole that let in water and put out the fire. She was then set ablaze in four different places between decks.

Smith and his first lieutenant, George Dewey, were the last to leave. Dewey wrote of their experience: "The fire we had started in the wardroom broke through the skylight in a great burst of flame, illuminating the whole after part of the ship. It must have revealed our boat clearly . . . and it was a signal to those on the bluffs along the banks to break into that Rebel yell which I then heard in full chorus of victory for the first and only time in my life. It was not pleasant to the ear. . . . I remember thinking: 'How they must hate us!' . . . Captain Smith had on his sword, and also buckled to his belt a pair of fine revolvers. He still had a cigar in his mouth, and was as calm as ever. But suddenly he unbuckled his belt and threw both sword and revolvers overboard. 'Why did you do that?' I asked. He was a man of few words. 'I'm not going to surrender them to any Rebel,' he said." [8]

The *Mississippi* would burn for hours, and just before dawn would blow up below Profit Island. When a final check was made, sixty-four of the men who had lined her decks were found missing, twenty-five of them believed killed.

The *Monongahela* also grounded and was exposed to a severe fire for thirty minutes. About midnight the bridge was shot from under her commander, Captain J. P. McKinstry, and he was thrown to the deck and seriously bruised. The same shell killed three men. A few minutes later, the little gunboat *Kineo,* struggling valiantly, managed to get the larger ship free, but shortly afterward the crankpin of the *Kineo*'s forward engine became overheated, and that was the end. With both vessels unmanageable, they drifted downstream. The Confederates pounded away at them in their helpless condition, killing six and wounding twenty-one of their crewmen.

The next five days were busy ones for Farragut. On the morning after the run past Port Hudson, he dropped down almost within range of the batteries at that point and tried to communicate with the remainder of his squadron across the peninsula, but no signals could be seen from the mastheads. Before proceeding up the river to the mouth of the Red, he fired three guns as a signal to Banks of his safe passage. On the 16th he exercised his crew at target practice, and on the 17th he ran up to Natchez, anchored for the night, and tore down the telegraph wires leading to Port Hudson. The night of the 18th he anchored below Grand Gulf, running past next morning through a barrage of gunfire, losing two men killed and six wounded. Late that afternoon he anchored below Warrenton, Mississippi.

Next day, after moving near Vicksburg, he sent Grant an announcement of his arrival: "Having learned that the enemy had the Red River trade open to Vicksburg and Port Hudson and that two of the gunboats of the upper fleet had been captured, I determined to pass up and, if possible, recapture the boats and stop the Red River trade, and this I can do most effectually if I can obtain from Rear-Admiral Porter or yourself coal for my vessels. . . . I shall be most happy to avail myself of the earliest moment to have a consultation with yourself and Rear-Admiral Porter as to the assistance I can render you at this place; and, if none, then I will return to the mouth of the Red River and carry out my original designs." [9] A somewhat similar message was dispatched to Porter.

Porter quickly replied: "I would not attempt to run the batteries at Vicksburg if I were you; it won't pay, and you can be of no service up here at this moment. Your services at Red River will be a godsend; it is worth to us the loss of the Mississippi at this moment and the severest blow that could be struck at the South. They obtain all their supplies and ammunition in that way." [10]

Porter's reply was written at a time when he had a reason to be despondent. He had just returned from an expedition from which he had gained more impressively than ever before a knowledge of the tricky terrain and the desperate fighting being waged by the outnumbered Southerners. This offensive had resulted from an effort to take Vicksburg in the rear, by making a wide circuit through contiguous streams in a new version of the attempt up the Yazoo that had failed for Porter and Sherman a few weeks back.

Grant had an idea of getting to Vicksburg by a back route. This led through Yazoo Pass, a channel that had been closed for many years. Just one pilot could be found who had ever traveled it, but it was his opinion that a passage could be made. Vessels were sent to cut the levee and let the waters of the Mississippi rush through and clear out the pass.

"The difficulties attending the opening of the Yazoo Pass," it was recorded, "could not be described; they were far greater than anticipated, and it was found necessary to send in a party of six thousand soldiers to aid in cutting away the trees and removing the logs that had accumulated years gone by. A good deal of time was lost in this operation, though the soldiers and sailors worked as never men worked before, and the discipline and spirit of the Mississippi Squadron could not be better manifested than in witnessing the efforts put forth by the gallant fellows of the fleet to overcome obstacles that were deemed by some to be insurmountable." [11]

In two weeks nine vessels had been moved into the pass. They found navigation difficult. The current ran like a millrace down a course that was only wide enough for one boat at a time. Soon the Southerners learned what was happening, and they gathered in guerrilla bands and sniped at the crewmen. Six thousand additional soldiers were added to the expedition, causing further delay. But fair progress was made until the advance reached Fort Pemberton, and there it was blocked, for the Confederates took advantage of the delay to fortify. At one point the Federals found a steamer scuttled in the channel to block their path. It was the *Star of the West,* the ship that had tried to reprovision Fort Sumter in January 1861.[12]

After the failure of the Yazoo Pass expedition, Porter determined to try moving up Steele's Bayou and Deer Creek to Rolling Fork, then passing along Rolling Fork to the Sunflower River and thence to the Yazoo, thus enabling troops to skirt the forts at Drumgould's and Haynes' bluffs. Guided by information from a contraband, he made a reconnaissance. It led up Steele's Bayou, a stream that in low stages was little more than a ditch. For thirty miles to Black Bayou he moved, running through five fathoms of water, and there his progress seemed to be blocked until he discovered that by removing some trees his vessels could be forced around the bends, but with hardly a foot to spare.[13]

On March 14, Porter started on the expedition, taking the *Louisville, Cincinnati, Carondelet, Mound City, Pittsburg,* four mortars, and four tugs. Sherman in the meantime was to follow with a co-operating body of troops, marching a much shorter route by land, with the intention of meeting the vessels somewhere along Rolling Fork.

At Black Bayou, a four-mile trough leading into Deer

Creek, the difficult work began. There the water was dark, and the trees of much denser growth, a mass of foliage that met overhead. For twenty-four hours crews labored to clear the way, pulling up or pushing over giant cypresses two feet in diameter and cutting branches at random. Decks of the vessels as they pushed along became covered with broken limbs, a growing annoyance, but this was partly offset by the beauties of the landscape. The bottom land along their route was covered with wild eglantine, briars, and grape vines, and with spreading trees hung heavily with Spanish moss.

Once clear of the bayou, ahead of them lay thirty-two miles of Deer Creek, a channel they found much narrower than expected and filled with small willows. They expected progress to become easier as they advanced. Watching them from the banks were large groups of Negroes and an occasional white inhabitant. Soon, smoke blanketed the countryside, for one of the whites, an agent of the Confederate Government, had ordered destruction of the great stores of cotton intended for shipment abroad.

"Finding that our presence was discovered," Porter informed Welles, "I pushed on the vessels as fast as the obstacles would permit, not making more than half a mile an hour. We were passing through a beautiful country filled with livestock of all kinds, and containing large granaries of corn belonging to the Confederate Government. The people were more than surprised at the presence of such an expedition, having supposed themselves far removed from the horrors of war. . . ." [14]

Within seven miles of Rolling Fork, Porter learned that Negroes, muskets held at their backs, were felling trees in his path. "The labor of clearing out these obstructions," he recorded, "was very great, but there is nothing that can not be overcome by perseverance. . . . The sailors worked night and day, without eating or sleeping, until the labor was accomplished." [15] Three miles from Rolling Fork smoke was seen in the direction of the Yazoo, and he was informed that the Confederates were landing troops to dispute his passage. He immediately sent two boat howitzers and three hundred men to hold the stream until he could cover it with his guns.

Throughout the night and the following day crews worked to clear the obstructions. At sunset they laid down their tools, just eight hundred yards from the end of the troublesome creek, to get a few hours of sleep. Work was resumed at dawn, but progress was slow. The lithe trees defied the utmost efforts of man. Some had to be pulled up, others cut off under water— all required tedious labor. Added to this was the disturbance of occasional gunfire from the wooded recesses along the banks, plus the disheartening news that the enemy was cutting down trees in their rear.

Porter had received a letter from Sherman informing him of the difficulties the soldiers were encountering. In the face of all these discouragements and amid a chorus of rifle fire from sharpshooters lying along the banks, he unshipped his rudders and allowed the vessels to drift backward. Soon he met the Eighth Missouri and parts of other regiments of Federal troops sent by Sherman, but these were not enough to make him turn back. Artillery barked at his men along the way, and occasionally this was answered. At last he met Sherman.

"We might now have retraced our steps," Porter wrote Welles, "but we were all worn out. The officers and men had for six days and nights been constantly at work, or sleeping at the guns." [16]

By the 24th they were back where they had started. "Still raining hard this morning," recorded the journal of the *Cincinnati*. "Sherman's soldiers in bad plight . . . presenting a ludicrous appearance, covered with cotton, adhering to their beards, hair and clothes from planks of a cotton gin upon which they had slept the night. . . . The Rebels follow and shoot at us. The Negroes, too, are following . . . and they form a motley group, of all ages and sexes, the lame, the halt, and the blind, as well as the stalwart and active. They are in all kinds of vehicles that can be conceived of, and on horses, mules, and afoot, in high glee—'goin' to freedom, sure,' they say. Their antics and expressions are most amusing. Some shout to the animals they are driving, 'Go 'long, dar, old fool hoss, don't know nothin'; you's gwine to freedom, too.' " [17]

So ended another attempt to take Vicksburg. Porter had covered one hundred and forty miles of crooked streams with Southerners hounding him at every turn. His guns were so low and the woods so far back that he could fight them off only with mortars. He had lost a third assistant engineer, killed by a rifle shot, and had had two men severely wounded.

"There is but one thing now to be done," Porter advised Welles, "and that is to start an army of one hundred and fifty thousand men from Memphis, via Grenada, and let them go supplied with everything required to take Vicksburg. Let all minor considerations give way to this and Vicksburg will be ours. Had General Grant not turned back when on the way to Grenada he would have been in Vicksburg before this." [18]

★ *23*

The Navy opens a door

APRIL 1863

Failure to get to Vicksburg by way of the Yazoo forced the Union to turn finally to the slow process of siege. It was officially recorded in the office of Secretary Welles that "neither the Army nor Navy were disheartened by these disappointments, but were rather incited to further exertions." The invaders knew they were weakening the Confederacy with every advance and, at the same time, were gaining resources themselves. But a change of strategy was necessary. The drive had been from the north, from the region of the Yazoo; now it would come from the south, from the direction of Grand Gulf. Grant's army would have to be moved across the Mississippi at some point and a base established from which it could operate while tightening the siege.

During the period this new strategy was taking effect, movements of the Navy were keyed to those of the Army. In the meantime Farragut was busy. Arriving below Vicksburg with the *Hartford* and the *Albatross* while Porter was still up Deer Creek, he sent a message across the neck of land in the bend of the river at that point. It was addressed to General Alfred W. Ellet, head of the Marine Brigade, and it asked him to come on board the flagship for a conference. Ellet walked the entire distance of eleven miles. What Farragut wanted, he learned, was for Ellet to send down two rams and an ironclad to aid in the blockade of the Red River.

"Is it to the benefit of the country and of the cause to have them below Vicksburg?" asked Ellet.

"Certainly," replied Farragut.[1]

"Then you shall have the rams tonight," promised the General.

Ellet left Farragut at 2:00 P.M. and hurried back. On arriving at the upper squadron, he found Porter had returned from the Steele's Bayou expedition, but for some reason Ellet failed to inform his superior of the conference he had just left.

The two rams chosen to go below, the *Lancaster* and the *Switzerland,* were placed under command of Colonel Charles R. Ellet and his cousin, Lieutenant Colonel John A. Ellet. They were to start in the night, but there were unexpected delays and it was nearly dawn before they passed Vicksburg. This put them at a disadvantage, for the Southerners had found out what was happening and were waiting. Signal lights flashing from battery to battery on shore revealed their alertness.

The rams steamed into a fusillade. First came the *Lancaster,* and the Confederate guns showered her with missiles, one of them finding its mark and sinking her. "She was struck in the stern post," it was officially recorded, "and the shot passed fore and aft, opening the vessel as if she was a watermelon, showing her weakness and unfitness for the service." [2] The second ram managed to get past with only a shot through the boiler.[3]

After the attempt to send rams to him, Farragut lost no time in dropping down to the mouth of the Red River, and there he received a long letter from Gustavus Fox, dated April 2. "He is rather disgusted with the flanking expeditions, and predicted their failure from the first," Fox wrote of President Lincoln, "and he always observed that cutting the Rebels in two by our force in the river was of the greater importance. Grant, who I judge by his proceedings has not the brains for great work, has kept our Navy trailing through swamps to protect his soldiers when a force between Vicksburg and Port Hudson, the same length of time, would have been of greater injury to the enemy." [4]

Under the same date Grant, unaware of this official criticism, wrote Porter that the last hope of taking Vicksburg by way of the Yazoo had faded. A reconnaissance made the day before, he reported, convinced him an attack on Haynes' Bluff would result only in terrific slaughter. The offensive must now come from the opposite direction, from New Carthage, either by way of Grand Gulf or Warrenton. Every effort meanwhile, he said, must be made to prevent the Confederates from further fortifying at either place.

Slowly the wheels of a great army turned, and while they were turning the Union Navy scored another success. Involved was the *Queen of the West,* the steamer the Confederates had captured after the youthful Charles R. Ellet was tricked by his pilot back in February. Reports said she had been surrounded and blown up in Grand Lake, a part of the Atchafalaya waterway between the Red River and the Gulf of Mexico.

The *Queen* had steamed innocently to her own destruction. Lieutenant Commander Augustus P. Cooke of the U.S.S. *Estrella,* commanding a squadron of three Union vessels transporting troops across the lake, was largely instrumental in bringing about her end. During the afternoon of April 13 he saw smoke in the distance, apparently in adjoining Lake Chicot, and suspected it was from a Confederate vessel or vessels. Darkness came on, with still no sight of the approaching craft, but preparations were made. Standing by to aid were two other side-wheelers, the *Arizona* and the *Calhoun.*

George W. Baird, third assistant engineer standing the midwatch on the *Calhoun,* wrote in his diary of developments during the postmidnight hours: "About 2:00 o'clock I saw two lights as if on boats, up the lake, and they were moving. Somehow I thought they were on vessels and told the officer of the deck, but he was a phlegmatic old fellow and was not enthused. He noted it and later he reported it. The light came nearer and nearer, but very slowly. At 4:00 I was relieved and I turned in, thinking I had overrated the importance of those lights. At 5:00 the lookout reported the lights as on two steamers. At 5:10 I was awakened by 'All hands to quarters!' for we had no drum, nor fife, nor bugle; it was the call by the boatswain's mate. I was so sleepy I waited a moment to see if there was any excitement; I heard the cable slipped and then a gun fired; then I got out in a hurry." [5]

Baird reached the deck just in time to see a shell from the *Calhoun* strike the roof of the *Queen* and explode, bursting a steampipe. Beside her was another vessel, decks crowded with soldiers, that turned and fled. But the *Queen* was doomed. Her crew leaped into the water to escape death by scalding, and away she floated for three miles before exploding, but not before thirty men had died from hot steam or drowning. Her captain, ironically enough, was Edward W. Fuller of Bayou Teche fame. He had commanded the *J. A. Cotton* and had come in contact often with the *Calhoun*. At sight of her that morning, he was reported to have said: "There is that damned *Calhoun*. I would rather see the devil than that boat." [6]

The night of April 16 was bright with starlight, mellow with the promise of spring, and in Mississippi it was a night more attuned to love-making than to war. Confederates on duty at Vicksburg apparently had no thought that its hours of darkness would witness an attempt by Porter to run past the forts they were manning, defying their markmanship in three ironclads, four Eads gunboats, a ram, and three transports. So confident were they that this particular night would pass in peace that, although on half rations and haggard from the rigors of defense, they turned aside for a bit of levity in the company of all the beauties that could be assembled at a military ball. [7]

It was not this rare resort to social function that caused

Porter to choose the 16th for a run past the forts at Vicksburg. More responsible was a telegram from Gideon Welles telling him that the Navy Department wished him to occupy the river below the city so Farragut could return to his station on the Gulf.[8]

Porter, in the *Benton,* led the little fleet of vessels, each fifty yards apart. The current was running at four miles an hour, and the boats rode with it, turning their wheels only for purposes of direction. Thus they managed to catch the Confederates so off guard that the *Benton* was drifting past the first battery before it was discovered. Tar-barrel fires blazed up suddenly on both sides of the river, and soon several railroad buildings were added to the conflagration. The firing began at 11:16 P.M. and continued for two and a half hours. Both batteries and gunboats were engaged. "The fire from the forts was heavy and rapid," Porter reported, "but was replied to with such spirit that the aim of the enemy was not so good as usual." [9] It was also recorded on the *Benton* that "we passed within forty yards of the town and could hear the rattling of falling walls after our fire." [10]

Again Porter had resorted to gimmicks. Each transport was protected by heavy logs and by bales of wet hay, and each was towing a coal barge loaded with ten thousand bushels of coal.

The gunboats drifted slowly past, pouring in broadside after broadside through smoke so thick the vessels at the rear had to stop firing so their pilots could see. "In that much the Rebels had the advantage over us," it was observed in Federal records, "but in nothing more, for we sent into the town twenty shells where they sent one at the gunboats." [11]

There was an eyewitness to the passing of the fleet—Lorenzo Thomas, Adjutant General of the Union Army. From Young's Point, four miles from Vicksburg, he saw the *Forest Queen,* one of the transports, receive a shot in the hull and steam drum, and he saw another, the *Henry Clay,* to avoid colliding with her, change direction and draw a shot in the stern. It meant this vessel's doom. Soon her captain was taking his men off in boats, leaving only the pilot. A few minutes later she was enveloped in flame, and then the pilot, too, deserted her, floating away on a plank. The boat had on board fifty thousand rations.

"The Rebels burned several houses in Vicksburg and one near the point opposite, which lighted up the whole river," Thomas reported to Washington. "The firing from the Rebels was not near so heavy as I anticipated, and but few shots were given from Warrenton."

Porter, counting his damages after the squadron assembled below at New Carthage, was delighted. Only the *Henry Clay* had been lost, and the damage to the other vessels was surprisingly light. The *Lafayette* had somehow turned around and had headed back upstream until her error was discovered. The *Louisville* collided with the *Carondelet* and then went aground, but she freed herself after cutting loose the coal barge she had in tow. The *Sterling Price* was set afire by shells, but in only a few minutes the blaze was extinguished. And as another cheering development, the casualty list included only fourteen wounded and none killed.

"The passage of the fleet by Vicksburg," Gideon Welles observed, "was a damper to the spirits of all Rebel sympathizers along the Mississippi, for everyone was so impressed with the absurdity of our gunboats getting safely past their batteries without being knocked to pieces that they would not admit to themselves that it would be undertaken until they saw the gunboats moving down the river all safe and sound. Vicksburg was despaired of from that moment." [12]

The appearance of Porter's vessels brought warm cheers at New Carthage where Union troops thought they were facing an emergency. Confederates to the number of a thousand, it was estimated, were in plain sight a mile away, supported by what looked like a huge gun, while the Federals had only two small fieldpieces. But they were making the most of their situation: they had thrown up breastworks of a crude nature and mounted a long stovepipe on a pair of cart wheels as a bluff. Porter immediately sent the gunboats *Lafayette* and *Tuscumbia* down to dislodge the Rebels. This was no problem. The Southerners fled, leaving behind their "big gun," found to be only a log mounted on a pair of timber wheels.[13] Evidently there were poker players on both sides.

A reconnaissance sent across to Grand Gulf, situated on high ground on the east side of the river south of Vicksburg, discovered the Confederates working madly to complete their earthworks atop cliffs eighty feet above the level of the river. Two major forts were in sight, commanded by a deep, covered way that afforded a splendid opportunity for sharpshooters in case of frontal attack, for without being seen they could enter and retire by zigzag paths cut through the hills. Other defenses stretched out along the Big Black River, which emptied into the Mississippi at that point. It was reported that four or five thousand Negroes had been at work on the fortifications since Farragut's passage. Daily, Porter sent gunboats close enough to shell the workmen on duty there, finally forcing them to suspend labor in daylight hours.

While Grant was moving his army down to New Carthage, the Southerners were bringing in men and ammunition by way of the Big Black. Grant arrived on April 24 and called a conference. The immediate problem was the Southern concentration in the area back of Vicksburg, between Jackson, Mississippi, fifty miles to the east, Haynes' Bluff, eleven miles north, and Grand Gulf, fifty miles below. The two enemy armies in this sector, one under John C. Pemberton and the other under Joseph E. Johnston, had an estimated total strength of sixty thousand. Grant at the moment had twenty thousand, but was expecting reinforcements. His first objective would be to capture Grand Gulf for use as a base, after which it would be his aim to defeat the Confederates assembled outside the Vicksburg fortifications.

At this conference it was agreed that Porter would create a

diverson by attacking the Grand Gulf forts with his gunboats while Grant took his troops across the Mississippi. The army would be landed at Bruinsburg, Mississippi, nine miles below, in an area reached by a good road.

Grand Gulf was looked upon as one of the strongest points on the river; some thought it the strongest, because it was favored by natural features and lay near the mouth of the Big Black.[14] The Confederates called it "the Little Gibraltar." But reconnaissance by a couple of Union gunboats revealed that Southern faith had been shaken by the appearance of Porter's fleet and Grant's army. Along the riverbank the Rebels could be seen busily fortifying, while at their backs, heavy clouds of dust along the road leading up the Big Black were stirred up by people running in all directions, herding off Negroes and cattle, and by a string of covered wagons moving off toward Jackson.[15]

The major action came on the 29th. Porter sent seven of his gunboats up the river, three to attack the upper batteries and four the lower, and at the same time ordered eight vessels up the Yazoo to deliver a feint on Haynes' Bluff to prevent reinforcements from coming from that direction. The plan worked. After five hours and thirty-five minutes of bombardment, with Grant witnessing it from a tug, the Confederate batteries were silenced. It was a battle in which shells by the thousands flew in both directions. When Porter's ships withdrew, although they had had almost as much trouble with the current as with the Southerners, they carried plenty of evidence that they had not been welcome visitors. The flagship *Benton* had received forty-seven cannon balls in her hull alone, the *Pittsburg* had been riddled with about fifty, and the *Tuscumbia* had been so cut up—"eighty shot and shell in her hull and over three hundred pieces of shell and grapeshot in her upper works"—that she was marked as "a poor ship in a hot engagement." [16]

"The enemy fought his upper battery with a desperation I have never yet witnessed," Porter wrote Welles, "for though we

engaged him at a distance of fifty yards, we never fairly succeeded in stopping his fire but for a short time. It was remarkable that we did not disable his guns, but though we
knocked the parapets pretty much to pieces, the guns were
apparently uninjured." [17]

A soldier on duty in the forts, a veteran who had seen much
action in General John S. Bowen's Missouri Brigade, wrote a
friend: "The firing beat Oak Hill, Elkhorn, Corinth, Hutchin's
Bridge, or anything I ever heard of." [18]

At 4:30 the morning of May 3, two terrific explosions shook
the hills around Grand Gulf, and the Federals realized the
Southerners had exploded their magazines. When Porter arrived after the Confederates retreated, he found everything so
covered with earth from the bombardment that it was impossible to see what had been there. But he did recognize that
extensive work had gone into the fortifications.

"We had a hard fight for these forts," he jubilantly reported
to Welles, "and it is with great pleasure that I report that the
Navy holds the door to Vicksburg." [19]

His statement was essentially correct. Already, Grant's army,
safely lodged on the eastern bank of the Mississippi, was following the Southerners up the Big Black toward Jackson and
Vicksburg; and now Porter, recognizing the immediate campaign as ended, turned his attention to relieving Farragut at
the Red River. When he took over there, he would have three
fleets under his direction.

Three hours after the capture of the forts, Porter was on his
way down the Mississippi in his flagship. With him went the
Lafayette, Sterling Price, Pittsburg, and *Switzerland.* "The effect of the appearance of the fleet on the people along the
river can better be imagined than described," recorded Secretary Welles. "It shut out the last hope of the Rebels. All the
Rebel world considered Vicksburg as impregnable, and Grand
Gulf as impregnable, and they were now willing to admit that
the former might be taken. The Union people, of whom there
were a few, held up their hands, and as the fleet passed

Natchez the levees were lined with thousands of people to witness the gallant sight, and many there rejoiced at it." [20]

It was only half a day's run from Grand Gulf down to the mouth of the Red River. Porter made it on schedule, arriving just at nightfall, and next morning, with six of his vessels, headed up the Red River. The evening of the following day he arrived at Fort De Russy and found it evacuated, a single gun remaining. Under its protection a heavy raft, constructed at a cost of seventy thousand dollars, was anchored, and this he tore apart. Then he pushed on to Alexandria, Louisiana, taking formal possession of the town without resistance.

"Indeed," he reported to Welles, "there seemed to be great cordiality showed us all along this river. In the town there was great rejoicing among the Union men at our arrival, and no indisposition on the part of anyone to meet us in a friendly spirit." [21]

On the night of the 7th General Banks came into Alexandria from Opelousas, and Porter turned the city over to him. It was a great performance. "Guards were placed, and private property respected," Welles' office noted. "The mayor was told to go on and perform his duties as usual, and everything wore as quiet an aspect as if 'grim-visaged war had smoothed his wrinkled front.'" In such a peaceful setting the Navy prepared to turn back. The dropping level of the Red was hint enough to the fleet captain that he would be unable to go farther up the river.

Porter began the return to Grand Gulf on the 9th. Only the day before, Farragut had departed, heading back to the Gulf. Several vessels, including the *Hartford* and *Albatross,* were left to guard the mouth and valley of the Red.

Along the way back Porter penned a brief report to Grant, giving him advice based on a conversation with Banks: "I don't think you will get any assistance from that quarter, at least for some time. He expects you to cooperate with him." [22] This information was an index to the campaigns ahead. Banks would confine his activities to the territory along the Red River, and Grant would proceed toward the encirclement of Vicksburg, pushing in along the area between that city and Jackson and striking at the separate Confederate armies under Johnston and Pemberton. Grand Gulf as a base would be abandoned, and Grant would daringly launch out with an army living on the countryside until new bases could be established on the Yazoo.

A river unvexed

MAY-JULY 1863

Steady bombardment of Vicksburg began the middle of May. From then until its surrender, shells were rained down upon it daily. Many of its inhabitants literally went underground, digging caves in the hillsides to escape the fury of the shells hurled up from the river by gunboats.

An unidentified Northern woman, caught in the city, wrote that she could not sleep because of the noise. A part of this came from a remarkable gun called "Whistling Dick," a weapon the Confederates took particular delight in firing because it gave off a screeching whistle whenever a shell came from its barrel. "It certainly does sound like a tortured thing," she wrote. Another part of the constant disturbance was the indescribable Rebel yell.

"Whistling Dick," the yell, and everything about the city, even the boldness of the people in continuing with as much of their daily routine as circumstances would permit, combined to make up a massive display of defiance that she could not help but admire. These Southerners who moved and fought and died around her knew that the fall of Vicksburg would be another major defeat for the Confederacy, another indication of approaching collapse. Perhaps that was one reason they seemed resigned to accept the siege and its discomforts as the ordinary penalties of war.

"Clothing cannot be washed, or anything else done," the Northern woman reported. "On the 18th and 22nd when the assaults were made on the lines, I watched the soldiers cooking on the green opposite. The half-spent balls, coming all the way from those lines, were flying so thick that they were obliged to dodge at every turn. At all the caves I could see from my high perch, people were sitting, eating their poor suppers at the cave doors, ready to plunge in again. As the first shell flew, they dived; and not a human being was visible. The sharp crackle of the musketry firing was a strong contrast to the scream of the bombs. I think all the dogs and cats must be killed. . . . Today we heard, while out, that expert swimmers are crossing the Mississippi on logs at night to bring and carry news to Johnston." [1]

As this woman watched, the Southerners fought with their backs to the wall, Pemberton shut up in Vicksburg and Johnston off to the east toward Jackson. Down the river at Port Hudson the fighting, which had been a forerunner of the Vicksburg siege, continued. The bombardment had begun nearly a week before the constant hammering got under way at Vicksburg.

One day the men on the gunboats out in the Mississippi and up the Yazoo, hearing firing in the rear of Vicksburg, knew that Grant's forces were approaching the city. The sound that reached them was the roar of cannon from the battle of Champion's Hill, along the Vicksburg and Jackson Railroad. A day or two later, Grant appeared on Porter's flagship and the two went off in a cutter to survey the situation. Two and a half hours later, when Porter returned, five vessels headed up the Yazoo to establish contact with the Army. Shortly after this was accomplished, one of the vessels, the *De Kalb,* pushed on to

Haynes' Bluff, arriving in time for her crew to see the few remaining Confederates flee upstream, leaving intact their guns, forts, tents, and equipage.

"These works and encampments," Porter wrote Welles, "covered many acres of ground and the fortifications and rifle pits proper of Haynes' Bluff extend for about a mile and a quarter. Such a network of defenses I never saw. The Rebels were a year constructing them, and all were rendered useless in an hour." [2]

Porter wrote with exuberance: "In a very short time a general assault will take place, when I hope to announce that Vicksburg has fallen, after a series of the most brilliant successes that ever attended any army. There never has been a case during the war where the Rebels have been so successfully beaten at all points, and the patience and endurance shown by our Army and Navy for so many months is about to be rewarded. It is a mere question of a few hours, and then, with the exception of Port Hudson (which will follow Vicksburg), the Mississippi will be open its entire length."

After destroying Fort Haynes, the men on the *De Kalb* continued upstream to Yazoo City, their eyes on a towering column of smoke that, while an omen of ruin, seemed to flaunt them with its grandeur. It was rising, they found on arrival, from a fine navy yard, equipped with sawing and planing machines, an extensive machine shop, carpenter and blacksmith shops, and all the necessary appliances for building and repairing ships. Three steamers—rams—were on the stocks. One of these was a 310-foot monster intended to be covered with four-inch iron plates and equipped with six engines, four side wheels and two propellers. All of this, the yard and vessels, was ablaze in a great pyre that blanketed the area in smoke. Out to announce that the place was evacuated came a committee of citizens. They said the work of destruction had been under the direction of Isaac Newton Brown, a perfectionist who again, as with the *Arkansas,* had demonstrated that he believed in doing things well.

Back at Vicksburg, Grant spread his forces in a great circle around the city, under Sherman and McClernand and Mc-Pherson. Along the river, mortars were stationed, each with orders to fire as fast as possible. At night gunboats moved up and dropped shells with five-second fuses in the center of the community. For forty-two days this merciless assault continued.

Down at Port Hudson the same tight siege was in effect, with Banks and Farragut both on hand to direct. On May 28 the General wrote the Admiral: "We made an attack upon the works yesterday, at 2:15 o'clock, advancing up to the breast-works on all sides, and many of our men were upon the parapets; but the enemy was too strong in numbers and the works too formidable to admit our full success, and we hold this position at this time. On the right, the opposing forces are separated only by a few feet, and no man on either side can show himself without being shot." [3]

At both holdout points the Southerners fought desperately. When Porter, at the urgent request of Grant and Sherman, sent the *Cincinnati,* one of the first seven Eads ironclads and Foote's flagship at Fort Henry, to enfilade some rifle pits barring the progress of the left wing of the army around Vicksburg, she was sunk by heavy gunfire and went down in shoal water with flag flying. Twenty-five men were killed and wounded, and fifteen were reported missing, supposedly drowned. This development was particularly distressing to Porter, because the vessel, in line with his belief in gimmicks, had been carefully packed with logs and hay for protection. But the Confederates used a gimmick also, dropping their heavy guns behind the parapets to give the impression they had been moved to the rear of the city, and then suddenly blasting away with deadly accuracy.

More defiance came early in June, this time from Milliken's Bend where a quantity of army stores was guarded by two Negro regiments and a part of the Twenty-ninth Iowa. Somehow Porter was warned that the Confederates were planning to attack, and he hurried the gunboats *Choctaw* and *Lexington* in support. They arrived just in time. An assault, launched by the Southerners before dawn, resulted in wholesale slaughter for the Federals until the two vessels began dropping shells.

Porter himself rushed to the scene in the *Black Hawk* and later wrote Grant that he saw quite an ugly sight. "The dead Negroes lined the ditch inside of the parapet, or levee, and were mostly shot on the top of the head. In front of them, close to the levee, lay an equal number of Rebels, stinking in the sun. Their knapsacks contained four days' provisions. They were miserable looking wretches." [4]

The Confederate attack had been launched by Brigadier General H. E. McCulloch's Brigade. It was well conducted, but doomed to failure. As one General sized up the outcome: "It must be remembered that the enemy behind a Mississippi levee, protected on the flanks by gunboats, is as securely posted as it is possible to be outside a regular fortification." [5]

While the guns barked at Vicksburg and Port Hudson in late June, the Northern part of the nation and many old-navy men fighting with the South were saddened by news of the death of the veteran Foote. He died at the Astor House in New York, while en route to succeed Du Pont as commander of the South Atlantic Blockading Squadron. Welles said of him in a general order: "A gallant and distinguished officer is lost to the country. The Hero of Fort Henry and Fort Donelson, the daring and indomitable spirit that created and led to successive victories the Mississippi Flotilla, the heroic Christian sailor, who in the China Seas and on the coast of Africa, as well as the great interior rivers of our country, sustained with unfaltering fidelity and devotion the honor of our flag and the causes of the Union—Rear Admiral Andrew Hull Foote—is no more."

The fall of Vicksburg was expected at least two weeks before it actually occurred. On June 23, Porter, hearing that the Confederates were about to evacuate, assembled boats at various points to prevent their escape. Three days later he reported to Welles:

"I was in hopes ere this to have announced the fall of Vicksburg, but the Rebels hold out persistently, and will no doubt do so while there is a thing left to eat. In the meantime, they are hoping for relief from General Johnston—a vain hope, for even if he succeeded in getting the better of General Sherman (one of the best soldiers in our Army), his forces would be so cut up that he could take no advantage of any victory that he might gain. General Sherman has only to fall back to our entrenchments at Vicksburg, and he could defy twice his own force."

Deserters, he told the Secretary, reported that the Confederates had six days' provisions and would not surrender until they were all gone. At Port Hudson, he learned, the Southerners were living on parched corn. He expected that point to capitulate within the next few days.[6]

Just about the time Porter was preparing his report to Welles, Pemberton was handed a message dated "In Trenches" and signed "Many Soldiers." It was a direct appeal for food and a warning that the Confederates in the ranks were becoming desperate:

Our rations have been cut down to one biscuit and a small bit of bacon per day, not enough, scarcely, to keep soul and body together, much less to stand the hardships we are called upon to stand. . . . Men don't want to starve, and don't intend to, but they call upon you for justice, if the commissary department can give it; if it can't you must adopt some means to relieve us very soon. The emergency of the case demands prompt and decided action on your part.

If you can't feed us, you had better surrender us, horrible as the idea is, than suffer this noble army to disgrace themselves by desertion. I tell you plainly, men are not going to lie here and perish, if they do love their country dearly. Self-preservation is the first law of nature, and the hunger will compel a man to do almost anything.

You had better heed a warning voice, though it is the voice of the private soldier. This army is now ripe for mutiny, unless it can be fed.[7]

The last Confederate gun to bark at Vicksburg was fired at 5:00 P.M. July 3. The silence threafter denoted that Pemberton had asked armistice to arrange terms of capitulation. Grant sent a telegram to Porter: "I have given the Rebels a few hours to consider the proposition of surrendering; all to be paroled here, the officers to take only side arms. My own feelings are against this, but all my officers think the advantage gained by having our forces and transports for immediate purposes more than counterbalances the effect of sending them North." [8]

At 5:30 next morning, Grant sent Porter another telegram: "The enemy has accepted in the main my terms of capitulation, and will surrender the city, works, and garrison at 10:00 A.M."

So on this historic day in American annals, other things were happening which would set it apart and give it new significance. While Lee's defeated army was falling back from Gettysburg, the Stars and Stripes were run up on the courthouse at Vicksburg, and the *Black Hawk,* bearing Porter and staff, came proudly up to the levee at the city and received on board Grant and many of his officers "with that warmth of feeling and hospitality that delights the heart of a sailor." [9] Bands were playing and Union guns were firing national salutes.

On the 7th, at Port Hudson, the besieged Confederates were startled when the Union forces suddenly fired a salute from the land batteries and then joined in vociferous yelling. Later, some of the Federal soldiers shouted over the trenches that Vicksburg had fallen on the 4th. The Southerners were puzzled but suspected only that the Federals had been given some fictitious news as a spirit-raiser, possibly to stimulate them for a charge the following morning.

But no charge came on the 8th. The cannonading was irregular, never severe, never damaging. On the 9th the Confederate Assistant Adjutant General sent a message to Joe Johnston, off in the direction of Jackson: "Port Hudson surrendered at 9:00 A.M. Our provisions were exhausted, and it was impossible for us to cut our way out on account of the proximity of the enemy's works." [10]

Thus ended the campaign that had brought Farragut his fame and given renown to the lamented Foote. Welles saw in it the finale of the Confederacy: "A slave empire divided by this river into equal parts, with liberty in possession of its banks and freedom upon its waters, can not exist." [11] At Washington there were serenades on the White House lawn, and Lincoln wrote, "The Father of Waters again goes unvexed to the sea."

But it was not yet time for complete celebration. Events in some quarters indicated that a surprising amount of fight was still left in the Confederacy and that a total collapse was not imminent. Up in the harbor of Portland, Maine, for instance, a daring Confederate band had thrown a great scare into Union shipping interests. It was the work of Charles William Read, the 23-year-old Mississippian whom Maffitt back in May had permitted to head to sea as a raider in the captured *Clarence*.

Reports of Read's successes began coming regularly early in June. First victim was the bark *Whistling Wind* of Philadelphia, bound for New Orleans with coal for Farragut. Next the *Alfred H. Partridge* of New York, headed southward with arms and clothing for the citizens of Texas, was captured. This vessel was bonded with the understanding that the bond would end when delivery was made. The *Mary Alvina,* moving from Boston to New Orleans with a cargo of commissary stores, was victim number three.

Read had originally intended to raid in Hampton Roads and, if possible, to cut out a steamer or warship. Before burning his first three prizes, he took from them prisoners and newspapers, but the information he obtained from both convinced him that his plan was not feasible because of the tight guard maintained in that area, and he decided instead to cruise along the coast.

Almost in sight of the Capes of the Chesapeake, he captured two vessels, the bark *Tacony* and the schooner *M. A. Shindler.* The former was a better ship than the *Clarence,* so Read decided to transfer his guns to her. Meanwhile her captain was paroled and allowed to go ashore, and there he spread word of what was happening at sea.

Washington erupted with a batch of orders. In less than three days, thirty-two vessels were searching for Read. While they were in the midst of their hunt, Secretary Welles made an entry in his diary: "None of our vessels have succeeded in capturing the Rebel pirate *Tacony,* which has committed great ravages along the coast, although I have sent out over twenty vessels in search. Had she been promptly taken, I should have been blamed for such a needless and expensive waste of strength; now I shall be censured for not doing more."

Read continued his captures. One by one they came into his net: the brig *Umpire,* the fine packet ship *Isaac Webb,* the clipper ship *Byzantium,* the bark *Goodspeed,* and the fishing schooners *Micawber, Marengo, Florence, Elizabeth Ann, Rufus Choate,* and *Ripple.* Most of these he burned. Late in June, realizing that the enemy had a good description of the *Tacony,* he transferred to a recently taken prize, the schooner *Archer.* Next morning off Portland he picked up two fishermen who mistook him and his crew for pleasure cruisers and innocently steered the *Archer* into the harbor at sunset. Standing by for the night was the revenue cutter *Caleb Cushing.*

At dawn next morning the people of Portland, unaware that the newcomers had been busy during the night, suddenly awakened to the fact that both the *Archer* and the *Caleb Cushing* were missing, the latter now barely visible in the distance. A pursuit was organized by the collector of the port, Jedediah Jewett. The steamers *Forest City* and *Chesapeake* and a small steam tug were rounded up, soldiers from a nearby fort placed on board along with a number of volunteer fighters from the wharf, and off they went at full speed.

The *Cushing,* manned by Read and a crew of nineteen, was overtaken in a few hours. For a time the Southerners resisted desperately, until their ammunition was exhausted, and then they set fire to the vessel and took to the sea in open boats, there to be captured and put in prison in Portland. But this was not the end of Read's career. Exchanged in the fall of '64, he

commanded the C.S.S. *Webb,* one of the last Confederate ships
to surrender. The *Archer* meanwhile was back in Union hands
within a week.

Around midday the *Cushing* exploded. The resulting noise
echoed and re-echoed along the adjacent New England shores,
reminding those within hearing that the war was not over and
that the South was not yet on its knees. This act of defiance
coincided with a disturbing report that had just come up from
North Carolina. Federals on duty there discovered that the
Confederates were busy up the Roanoke River in the construction of another ironclad. It was to be a ram, fashioned much after the original *Merrimack,* covered with five inches of pine,
five inches of oak, and plated with railroad iron. Its name
would be *Albemarle.* Lieutenant Commander C. W. Flusser of
the *Miami,* Union officer nearest the site where this craft was
building, relayed frequent reports concerning her. She was to be
"a formidable affair though of light draft," he warned.[12]

And so the Union Navy advanced into the third year of the
war. Victories it had had along the Mississippi, more so than
along the Atlantic and up the coastal rivers, but its task was far
from ended. The Confederacy, an enemy that had started off
with virtually no naval force at all, was still managing to get
ships in the water. Maffitt and Semmes were still on the high
seas. Mobile, Charleston, and Wilmington were still Rebel
strongholds. There were headaches of all sorts, large and small,
and augmenting all was the intelligence from North Carolina
that the Southerners were building an ironclad in somebody's
cornfield. In Dixie there was still hope.

Notes

[1] Welles reported that Lincoln was so excited he could not deliberate or be satisfied with the opinions of non-professional men. As for himself, he recorded: "Although my Department and the branch of the Government entrusted to me were most interested and most responsible, the President ever after gave me the credit of being, on that occasion, the most calm and self-possessed member of the Government." See *Diary of Gideon Welles* (Boston, Houghton Mifflin Company, 1911), I, 62, referred to hereafter as Welles.

[2] *Ibid.*

[3] *Ibid.*

[4] *Ibid.*, p. 63.

[5] Welles, in describing Stanton's demeanor at this time, said he made "some sneering inquiry" about the *Monitor*. See Welles, p. 63.

[6] *Official Records of the Union and Confederate Navies,* Series 1, IX, 19, referred to hereafter as *O.R.N.*

[7] Fox is wrong in spelling the name of the ironclad without a "k." The *Merrimac* was a side-wheel steamer that was not commissioned until the summer of 1864, while the *Merrimack,* the ship

that fought the *Monitor,* was a frigate. But this error of spelling is one that has existed ever since the *Merrimack* was launched in 1855. At the time this trilogy was started, the author, noting the variation in spelling, addressed an inquiry to Rear Admiral E. M. Eller, Director of Naval History, United States Navy Department. The answer received was that this matter of misspelling first had been the subject of correspondence in the 1930's, and that the Navy Department, then as now, confirmed the correct spelling as *Merrimack.* So do the Official Navy Records. The two ships are separately identified in Series 2, II, 141.

Another fallacy that has carried over from the days of the Civil War has been the reference to the vessel by this name. When the Confederates rebuilt her, they officially recorded her as the CSS *Virginia,* but it was a name that never stuck. Perhaps because of the alliteration, she is generally referred to as the *Merrimack.*

[8] The departmental jealousy between Stanton and Welles existed throughout the war, although the Navy Secretary recorded that never again after this exchange in Lincoln's presence at the White House did the War Secretary address him in such a blustery manner. He reveals that Stanton, from the start, assumed that the Navy was secondary to the Army, something that he himself as naval chief would never admit, claiming they were equal and should be ready at all times to co-operate with each other in demonstrations. Welles claimed Lincoln supported him in his attitude. See Welles, I, 69.

[9] *O.R.N.,* Series 1, VII, 83.

[10] *Ibid.,* p. 84.

[11] Washington, D.C. *Star,* March 11, 1862.

[12] *O.R.N.,* Series 1, I, 129.

[13] *Commodore Vanderbilt,* by Wheaton Joshua Lane (New York, Alfred A. Knopf, Inc., 1942), p. 176.

[14] *Official Records of the Rebellion,* Series 1, IX, 27, referred to hereafter as *O.R.*

[15] *O.R.N.,* Series 1, VII, 98.

[16] *Confidential Correspondence of Gustavus Vasa Fox* (New York, De Vinne Press, 1920), p. 248, referred to hereafter as Fox.

[17] *Ibid.,* p. 30.

[18] *O.R.N.,* Series 1, VII, 134.

[19] This suggestion was advanced by Prince de Joinville. Commented McClellan: "To a landsman it seems a good idea." Fox, p. 439.

[20] *O.R.N.,* Series 1, V, 29.

[21] *O.R.,* Series 1, IX, 64.

[22] *O.R.,* Series 1, IX, 6.

[23] *O.R.,* Series 1, XII, Pt. 1, 223.

[24] *O.R.N.,* Series 1, VII, 764.

[25] *Ibid.,* p. 753.

[26] *The Photographic History of the Civil War* (New York, The Review of Reviews Company, 1911), VI, 182, referred to hereafter as P.H.

[27] *O.R.N.,* Series 1, VII, 756.

[28] Lee's suggestion of moving the *Merrimack* to the York River was strongly endorsed by General Magruder, but he was overruled by Secretary of War G. W. Randolph, who cited that the ironclad near the mouth of the James was still important to the defense of Richmond. See *O.R.,* Series 1, XI, Pt. 3, 494.

[29] *O.R.N.,* Series 1, VII, 764.

[30] This vessel, a twin-propeller, one-hundred-and-ten-foot craft of twenty-foot beam, had one rifle on her deck. She was presented to the Federal Government by E. A. Stevens of New Jersey, her builder, and was sometimes referred to as the Stevens Battery.

[31] These vessels, as well as others of the sailing class, according to Goldsborough, were anchored there against his advice, frequently repeated to authorities on shore. See *O.R.N.,* Series 1, VII, 219.

[32] There seems to be much confusion in the records over which of the Confederate ships made these captures. Professor James Russell Soley of the Naval Academy, writing years later in *Battles and Leaders of the Civil War,* II, 267, referred to hereafter as B. & L., said it was done by the *Jamestown* and *Raleigh;* and in 1894, in an article in the *Confederate Veteran,* II, 86, H. B. Littlepage identified the captors similarly. On the other hand, the log of the British ship *Rinaldo,* standing by, said they were made by the *Patrick Henry.* But Tattnall, who gave the order for the captures, the Baltimore *American* correspondent, Charles Fulton, and the log of the *Minnesota* gave the credit to the *Yorktown.*

[33] See the log of the *Rinaldo* in *O.R.N.,* Series 1, VII, 224.

[34] *O.R.N.,* Series 1, VII, 220.

[35] *Diary of a Southern Refugee,* by Judith White McGuire (New York, E. J. Hale & Son, 1868), p. 106.

[36] *O.R.N.,* Series 1, VII, 249.

[37] *O.R.,* Series 1, XI, Pt. 3, 452.

[38] *O.R.N.,* Series 1, VII, 769.

[39] *Ibid.,* p. 293.

[40] Fox, I, p. 264.

[41] *O.R.,* Series 1, XI, Pt. 3, 488.

[42] *A Pair of Blankets,* by William H. Stewart (New York, Broadway Publishing Company, 1911), p. 55.

[43] *O.R.,* Series 1, XI, Pt. 3, 155.

[44] *O.R.N.,* Series 1, VII, 331. Goldsborough's indication that the Confederate ironclad had refused to fight was emphatically denied by H. B. Littlepage, one of her officers, in an article in the *Confederate Veteran* in 1894, II, 86. "I challenge anyone," he wrote, "to show by any authentic record or statement that the *Merrimack* was ever defeated, that she ever declined an engagement, regardless of the number or strength of her adversaries, or that she ever lost an opportunity to bring on an engagement if possible."

[45] *O.R.N.,* Series 1, VII, 334.

[46] *Ibid.,* p. 335.

[47] *Ibid.,* p. 333.

[48] *Ibid.,* p. 338.

[49] *Ibid.,* p. 336.

[50] New York *Herald,* May 12, 1862.

[51] In his next official report on naval operations, dated August 13, 1862, Secretary Stephen Mallory stated: "The abandonment of Norfolk stripped us not only of a vast amount of valuable property and building material, but deprived us of our only drydock and of tools which are not found and cannot be replaced or made in the Confederacy." See *O.R.N.,* Series 2, II, 243.

Brigadier General John G. Barnard, chief engineer of the U.S. Army, writing in a lengthy report the following January (*O.R.,* Series 1, XI, Pt. 1, 128), said that prominent among the causes of the collapse of McClellan's Peninsular campaign was the inaction on the part of the Union from August, 1861, to April, 1862, and the failure to capture Norfolk that winter. "By its capture," he explained, "the career of the *Merrimack,* which proved so disastrous to our subsequent operations, would have been prevented."

[52] Records indicate that Tattnall placed too much faith in his pilots. Such an experienced naval officer as Franklin Buchanan, who had first commanded the *Merrimack,* said of them: "As to the pilots, I had no confidence in them . . . and less in the master than in either of the others." See his letter to Catesby Jones in *O.R.N.,* Series 1, VII, 788.

[53] Here Tattnall demonstrates one of the hardships of a naval commander of the Civil War era: he was totally dependent on his pilots. This was because in that day there were few reliable charts, and channels had to be navigated by experience.

[54] Tattnall later testified that the part under water was only one inch thick. Higher up the additional plates put in place at the navy yard increased the thickness to three inches.

[55] In January of 1961, the author, while waiting to take part in a Civil War Centennial television program over Station WDBJ at Roanoke, Virginia, received a phone call from Mrs. Annie Hamilton Tucker, who identified herself as the eighty-year-old widow of W. B. Tucker, formerly of Petersburgh in that state. Later, at her apartment, she showed me the remnants of a flag that she said her father, James Wilkey Hamilton, had brought away from the *Merrimack* before it was destroyed. He had been a boilermaker apprentice in the Norfolk Navy Yard prior to the war and had worked on and served on the ironclad.

This flag has since been placed on display in the Confederate Museum at Front Royal, Virginia.

[56] *O.R.*, Series 1, XI, Pt. 3, 163.

[57] New York *Herald,* May 15, 1862.

[58] The *Merrimack* and the *Monitor* had definitely influenced world shipbuilding. On April 11, 1862, Confederate Agent James D. Bulloch wrote Secretary Mallory: "The engagement between the *Virginia* and *Monitor* has changed the entire plan of iron shipbuilding for the British Navy. Several of the largest screw liners have already been selected to be cut down and converted into ironclad vessels . . . and four entirely new ones are to be built at once. . . ." *O.R.N.*, Series 2, II, 184.

[59] This was one of the concluding statements in Tattnall's report on the destruction of the *Merrimack*. See *O.R.N.*, Series 1, VII, 337. At his solicitation, a court of inquiry was convened at Richmond on May 22, 1862. It found that the destruction of the ironclad was "unnecessary at the time and place it was effected." But a court-martial in July cleared the commander of all charges.

CHAPTER TWO

[1] Also referred to as Ward's Bluff. See *O.R.N.*, Series 1, VII, 357, 363.

[2] *O.R.*, Series 1, XI, Pt. 3, 164.

[3] Fox, I, p. 120.

[4] General Lee attributed the shortage of transportation to the demands made in sending troops and provisions to Johnston's army. *O.R.*, Series 1, XI, Pt. 3, 476.

[5] The authority used here for the number of guns in position at Drewry's Bluff at this period is John Taylor Wood. See his article in B. & L., I, 211. Confederate General Joseph E. Johnston, on taking up his new line near Richmond after the fallback from

Manassas, notified General Lee that only three guns were in position. But on May 10, Lee replied: "In addition to the three guns at Drewry's Bluff several guns have been mounted, and every exertion is being made to render the obstructions effective and the battery commanding it as formidable as possible. *O.R.*, Series 1, XI, Pt. 3, 476.

⁶ *R. E. Lee*, by Douglas Southall Freeman (New York, Charles Scribner's Sons, 1935), II, 48.

⁷ *Diary of a Southern Refugee*, by Judith White McGuire, p. 113.

⁸ His feelings concerning the *Galena* were revealed in a private letter he wrote shortly after the visit to Drewry's Bluff: "I was convinced as soon as I came on board that she would be riddled under fire, but the public thought differently, and I resolved to give the matter a fair trial." Rodgers to his wife, one of John Rodgers Papers, Naval Historical Collection, Library of Congress.

⁹ B. & L., II, 268.

¹⁰ *Recollections of a Rebel Reefer*, by James Morris Morgan (Boston, Houghton Mifflin Company, 1917), p. 81.

¹¹ Letter dated July 30, 1959, from Rear Admiral E. M. Eller, Director of Naval History, U.S. Navy Department, to Karl S. Betts, Executive Director of the National Civil War Centennial Commission.

¹² *Sea Dogs of the Sixties*, by Jim Dan Hill (Minneapolis, University of Minnesota Press, 1935), p. 224.

¹³ *Recollections of a Rebel Reefer*, p. 82.

¹⁴ *O.R.N.*, Series 1, VII, 366.

¹⁵ *Ibid.*, p. 370.

¹⁶ *Ibid.*, p. 359.

¹⁷ *Ibid.*, p. 370.

CHAPTER THREE

¹ *Military and Naval Operations During the Civil War*, by Willis C. Humphrey (Detroit, C. H. Smith & Company, 1886), p. 576.

² *Life of Andrew Hull Foote*, by James Mason Hoppin (New York, Harper & Brothers, 1874), p. 331, referred to hereafter as Hoppin.

³ Owing to the frequent changes made by nature in the course of the Mississippi, Island No. 10 has disappeared as a separate body of land today. Some people say it has been washed away by the relentless current of the river, but others claim it has become a part of the neighboring shore.

[4] *O.R.N.,* Series 1, XXII, 664.

[5] *Ibid.,* p. 662.

[6] Rear Admiral Henry Walke tells of this incident in his *Naval Scenes and Reminiscences of the Civil War in the United States* (New York, F. R. Reed and Company, 1877), p. 98, referred to hereafter as Walke. See also *Battles and Leaders,* I, 439.

[7] *Army Life of an Illinois Soldier,* the diary and a compilation of letters of Charles W. Willis to his sister (Washington, D. C., Globe Printing Company, 1906).

[8] *O.R.N.,* Series 1, XXII, 690.

[9] *Ibid.,* p. 753.

[10] New York *Herald,* March 24, 1862.

[11] *O.R.N.,* Series 1, XXII, 752.

[12] *Ibid.,* p. 695.

[13] *Ibid.,* p. 692.

[14] Pope credits the origin of the idea of cutting a canal to General Schuyler Hamilton, one of his division commanders. *O.R.N.,* Series 1, XXII, 724.

[15] Hoppin, p. 278.

[16] *O.R.N.,* Series 1, XXII, 687.

[17] *Ibid.,* p. 697. The "one exception" mentioned by Foote is not identified. Walke, writing afterward in *B. & L.,* I, 441, said "all except myself were opposed to the enterprise, believing with Foote that the attempt to pass the batteries would result in the almost certain destruction of the boat." But Bissell, who had attended the council before setting out up Dry Bayou, wrote in his report on May 14, 1862 (*ibid.,* p. 734): "I strongly urged that one of the gunboats might be allowed to run the batteries, and by her help General Pope would be able to capture the island in a single day. Captain Phelps, at the time commanding the *Benton,* strongly seconded my efforts to induce Commodore Foote to send a boat, and requested to be allowed to command it."

[18] This attitude of commendation for his caution in acting was not borne out by other officers. Colonel J. W. Bissell of the Engineer Regiment charged Island No. 10 could have been taken four weeks earlier if Foote had sent a gunboat down the river. *Ibid.,* p. 734.

[19] *Ibid.,* p. 741.

[20] *Ibid.,* p. 703.

[21] Walke, p. 115.

[22] *O.R.N.,* Series 1, XXII, 704.

[23] *Ibid.,* p. 747.

[24] *The Blue Jackets of '61,* by Willis J. Abbot (New York, Dodd, Mead & Company, 1886), p. 170, referred to hereafter as Abbot.

[25] New York *Herald,* April 15, 1862.

[26] Hoppin, p. 279.

[27] *O.R.N.,* Series 1, XXII, 708.

[28] The New York *Times* correspondent on board the *Carondelet* recorded: "It did not rain in the ordinary meaning of the term, but whole gulfs of water came pouring down in masses. Nor did it thunder and lightning in the usual meaning given to the words, but it roared at us as if all the electric batteries of north, south, east and west had concentrated their forces, and were bellowing at us in unison, while the lightning in each broad flash was so vast and so vivid that it seemed as if the fates of some hell like that of Milton were opened and shut every instant."

[29] *O.R.N.,* Series 1, XXII, 732.

[30] *Ibid.,* p. 766.

[31] Foote, a staunch champion of the Navy, tried repeatedly to obtain the credit he considered due his arm of the service. After the fall of Island No. 10 he wrote Secretary Welles: "I regret to see in the dispatches of Major-General Halleck, from St. Louis, that no reference is made to the capture of forts and continuous shelling of gun and mortar boats, and the Navy's receiving the surrender of No. 10, when, in reality, it should be recorded as an historical fact that both services equally contributed to the victory, the bloodless victory—more creditable to humanity than if thousands had been slain." *Ibid.,* p. 726.

[32] *Ibid.,* p. 724.

[33] New York *Herald,* April 15, 1862.

[34] *The Picket Line and Camp Fire Stories* (New York, Hurst and Company, 1879), p. 89.

CHAPTER FOUR

[1] *The Life of David Glasgow Farragut,* by Loyall Farragut (New York, D. Appleton and Company, 1879), p. 214, referred to hereafter as Farragut.

[2] These words were used by Brigadier General J. G. Barnard, chief engineer of the Army of the Potomac, in a letter to Colonel A. V. Colburn, A.A.G., dated February 7, 1862. See *O.R.,* Series 1, VI, 684.

[3] Frequently during the fall of '61 Governor Moore sent requests to Jefferson Davis for officers, guns, saltpeter, and others items to

aid with the defense of New Orleans. He was looked upon as an alarmist and given half-hearted co-operation. At one time Davis wrote him: "Should your worst apprehensions be realized, which I can not bring myself to believe, when I remember how much has been done for the defense of New Orleans since 1815, both in the construction of works and facilities for transportation, I hope a discriminating public will acquit this Government of having neglected the defenses of your coast and approaches to New Orleans." *O.R.N.,* Series 1, II, 705.

[4] Porter, whose personality and dogmatic attitude robbed him of much of the glory he doubtless deserved, left ample claim for his part in helping with the Mississippi River strategy (see his article, "The Opening of the Lower Mississippi," in B. & L., II, 22). But he is disputed by others. William T. Meredith, secretary to Admiral Farragut, in an article in the same publication (II, 70), was "astonished" at some of Porter's assertions. He maintained that the idea of the advance up the Mississippi was amply fixed by Montgomery Blair and Secretary Welles long before Porter came into the picture. But he left no evidence that Porter did not actually provide the necessary weight and push to further the strategy. In an article in *The Galaxy* magazine, November, 1871, Welles said the plan of offense against New Orleans was under discussion as early as September, 1861. A Dr. Mackie, arriving that month at Nashville after a stay of some months in the North, wrote Governor Moore of Louisiana that "gigantic measures" were being adopted by the Union for a move on his state and that he believed it would be made soon (*O.R.N.,* Series 2, I, 704). But the move apparently did not take shape until November, when Porter came up from the Gulf.

When asked for comment on the matter, Captain W. C. Little, one of the Confederate officers defending New Orleans, replied: "I will leave these matters to the credulity of the American reader not unfamiliar with Admiral Porter's style." Southern Historical Society Papers, XIII, 561, referred to hereafter as S.H.S.P.

But Professor James Russell Soley, one of the most dependable authorities, said: "Commander D. D. Porter undoubtedly had the scheme in mind as early as June, 1861, when he was off the passes in the *Powhatan.*" B. & L., II, 13.

Further support of Porter's claim is provided by Farragut in a message to Welles dated September 13, 1862, transmitting to the Secretary "a proposition" to attack the forts that he identified as coming from Porter. *O.R.N.,* Series 1, XVIII, 195.

[5] Here again there is a difference of opinion, this time in the matter

of who deserved credit for suggesting Farragut. David Porter claimed he first proposed the veteran in a discussion with Gustavus Fox. Writing in his private journal (unpublished and now in the Manuscript Division of the Library of Congress) immediately after the war, Porter recorded that Fox first proposed Captain Frederick Engle and later Commodore Charles H. Bell, both of whom he successfully opposed in favor of Farragut. "It took me some time," he added, "to convince Fox that Farragut was the right man, although to listen to him now anyone would suppose that the idea of selecting Farragut was original with him."

But Farragut's secretary, William Meredith, heartily disagrees with Porter's claim, maintaining his superior was "one of the few officers of sufficient rank to command a squadron who also had the strength and vigor necessary to bear the strain of arduous duty." *B. & L.*, II, 70.

[6] *B. & L.*, II, 26.

[7] *Ibid.*

[8] Farragut's executive officer, George Dewey, hero of a later war, said of him in his autobiography: "Whenever I have been in a difficult situation, or in the midst of such a confusion of details that the simple and right thing to do seemed hazy, I have often asked myself, 'What would Farragut do?' In the course of the preparations for Manila Bay I often asked myself this question, and I confess I was thinking of him the night we entered the bay." *Autobiography of George Dewey* (New York, Charles Scribner's Sons, 1913), p. 50, referred to hereafter as Dewey.

[9] *P.H.*, VI, 184.

[10] *Ibid.*, p. 55.

[11] *Ibid.*, p. 72.

[12] *Ibid.*, p. 186.

[13] *O.R.N.*, Series 1, XVIII, 34.

[14] *Letters of George Hamilton Perkins* (Concord, New Hampshire, The Rumford Press, 1901), p. 68, referred to hereafter as Perkins.

[15] Welles, I, 230.

[16] New York *Herald*, April 29, 1862.

[17] From a letter written by T. Bradley, made available to the author by Rear Admiral E. M. Eller, Director of Naval History.

[18] *Civil War on Western Waters*, by Fletcher Pratt (New York, Henry Holt and Company, 1956), p. 76, referred to hereafter as Pratt.

[19] *O.R.N.*, Series 1, XVIII, 30.

[20] *Ibid.*, p. 59.

[21] *Ibid.*, p. 120.

22 *P.H.,* VI, 188.

23 *O.R.N.,* Series 1, XVIII, 14.

24 *Ibid.,* p. 47.

25 Professor James Russell Soley, in an article in *B. & L.,* I, 628, wrote: "Had one man of force and discretion been in full command and provided with sufficient funds, the defense would at least not have presented a spectacle of complete collapse."

26 New Orleans *Daily True Delta,* January 12, 1862.

27 Porter was not in agreement with Farragut regarding the plan to pass the forts. In a carefully written plan for an attack on New Orleans he had presented to the flag officer, he cited that, by running the forts, they would leave an enemy in their rear, and the mortar vessels would have to be left behind. "Once having possession of the forts," he advised, "New Orleans would be hermetically sealed, and we could repair damages and go up on our own terms, and in our own time." *O.R.N.,* Series 1, XVII, 146.

Opinion would appear to rest on the side of Farragut. When questioned by a court of inquiry, General M. L. Smith, commanding the city's interior line of defenses, gave the opinion: "Had the fall of New Orleans depended upon the enemy's first taking Forts Jackson and St. Philip, I think the city would have been safe against an attack from the Gulf." *O.R.N.,* Series 1, VI, 582.

28 *O.R.N.,* Series 1, XVIII, 253.

29 *Ibid.,* p. 564.

30 General Lovell informed a Confederate court of inquiry that the Mississippi at that time was higher than ever before known. *O.R.,* Series 1, VI, 562.

31 *O.R.N.,* Series 1, XVIII, 731.

32 Perkins, p. 68.

33 *B. & L.,* II, 58.

34 New York *Herald,* April 29, 1862.

35 *O.R.N.,* Series 1, XVIII, 155.

36 This account of ship preparations was gained from an article written by Commander John Russell Bartlett of the U.S.S. *Brooklyn* and published in *B. & L.,* II, 56.

37 *O.R.N.,* Series 1, XVIII, 254.

38 *History of the Confederate States Navy,* by J. Thomas Scharf (New York, Rogers and Sherwood, 1887), p. 266, referred to hereafter as Scharf.

39 In testimony before a Congressional investigating committee, Murray said: "I furnished the plan of the *Merrimack,* though by some jeremy diddling, it is attributed to Lieutenant Brooke." *O.R.N.,* Series 2, I, 757.

[40] E. C. Murray said before the investigating committee of the Confederate Congress that the *Mississippi* was constructed in less time than any vessel of her tonnage and character ever built on the American continent. Scharf, p. 269.

[41] Secretary Mallory was criticized because he did not award the contract for the *Mississippi* to a recognized shipyard, which would have been in position to have started work immediately and would not have had to delay, as the Tift brothers did, until facilities could be provided.

[42] General Lovell testified he first was told by one of the Tift Brothers that the *Mississippi* would be ready by "the January rise of the river." Later, he said, he was advised the ironclad would be completed by April 1. *O.R.*, Series 1, VI, 572, 574.

[43] *O.R.N.*, Series 1, XXII, 671.

[44] *Ibid.*, p. 672.

[45] Farragut, p. 212.

[46] *O.R.N.*, Series 1, XVIII, 254.

[47] New York *Herald*, April 29, 1862.

[48] Rear Admiral E. M. Eller, Director of Naval History, in a talk before the District of Columbia Civil War Round Table, said the current of the river was four knots.

[49] *O.R.N.*, Series 1, XVIII, 423.

[50] While this fleet seemed formidable, at least in numbers, there were those who discounted its offensive strength. Porter said there was not a ship among those sent Farragut that could resist a twelve-pound shot. "Considering the great resources of the Northern states, this supineness of the Government appears inexcusable," he observed. *B. & L.*, II, 29.

[51] Dewey, p. 56.

[52] *O.R.N.*, Series 1, XVIII, 196.

[53] New York *Herald*, May 10, 1862.

[54] The office of fleet captain was somewhat similar to that of chief of staff in the present navy.

[55] Private journal of David D. Porter.

[56] *O.R.N.*, Series 1, XVIII, 131.

[57] See a journal kept by sailors of the U.S.S. *Oneida*, now on file in the University of North Carolina Library.

[58] *O.R.N.*, Series 1, XVIII, 323.

[59] *Ibid.*

[60] "A Historical Sketch of the Confederate Navy," an article by Captain C. H. McBlair published in the military magazine, *The United Service*, copies of which are available in the Bureau of Naval History Library, Washington, D. C.

[61] *O.R.N.*, Series 1, XVIII, 766.

[62] This was the time recorded in the log of the mortar schooner *Norfolk Packet. Ibid.*, p. 399.

[63] *B. & L.*, II, 36.

[64] *O.R.N.*, Series 1, XVIII, 367.

[65] *Ibid.*, p. 162.

[66] *Ibid.*, p. 136.

[67] Professor J. R. Soley later wrote of this assignment: "The vessels of Mitchell's force, if they had been completed and properly officered and manned, would have made a very pretty force for the purpose; but no commander taking hold of them four days before the fight could have made much out of them." *B. & L.*, II, 75.

[68] *O.R.N.*, Series 1, XVIII, 367.

[69] Although John A. Stevenson, whom friends criticized as unable to judge character in others, brought the disfavor of certain Confederates upon his head, he stands out as one of the fathers of the drive for ironclads in the South. When the Hon. C. M. Conrad, chairman of the Committee on Naval Affairs of the Confederate Congress, was asked during an investigation of the fall of New Orleans who first suggested the building of ironclad vessels for the defense of the South's rivers, he replied: "The first suggestion I know of came from Mr. John A. Stevenson, the proprietor of the ram *Manassas*." *O.R.N.*, Series 1, I, 722.

While he later championed the *Merrimack,* Secretary Mallory at the beginning of the war apparently had little faith in iron-plated rams. He so expressed himself in a conversation with Conrad while the capital of the Confederacy was still at Montgomery, Alabama. He was reported as saying at that time that ironclads were not a new invention, that they were as old as the Greeks and Romans, and that the English long ago had tried and abandoned them. Conrad replied that the power of iron-plated rams consisted in the combination of steam power with iron armor, something the Greeks and Romans knew nothing about, and that the English probably had not tried rams with iron plates. The Confederacy soon bought the *Manassas.*

[70] *O.R.N.*, Series 1, XVII, 328.

[71] *Ibid.*, p. 792.

[72] *Ibid.*, p. 442.

[73] *Ibid.*, p. 329.

[74] *Ibid.*, p. 141.

[75] *Ibid.*, p. 768.

[76] *Ibid.*, p. 171.

77 Just how the Confederates first learned that the Union fleet was moving appears to have been lost, although they apparently had lookouts watching the river near the area where the flags had been planted in the afternoon. The general alarm came with the opening fire of the forts about three-thirty, but Beverly Kennon of the C.S.S. *Governor Moore,* in his report (*ibid.,* p. 304), says: "At about three-five A.M. on the morning of the 24th ultimo I was informed that 'The enemy are coming up the river and close aboard of us.' " In writing later in *B. & L.,* II, 79, he states: "At about three-thirty A.M. an unusual noise down the river attracted my attention." Alarmed, he related, he descended the ladder to near the surface of the river and there was able to hear the paddles of a steamer, obviously the *Mississippi.*

78 *O.R.N.,* Series 1, XVII, 282.

79 *Ibid.,* p. 330. Commander Warley (*ibid.,* p. 343), stated in a newspaper article in August, 1862, that "the attack on the enemy of the 24th of April was a complete surprise." In view of Duncan's note, if dated correctly, and the statements of other Confederate officers, he obviously was in error. It would appear, too, from the added precautions the Southerners took after seeing the white flags planted along the bank in the afternoon, that they were expecting the advance.

80 *Ibid.,* p. 510.

81 As late as 1865, the fate of Fairbanks was unknown to some of his fellow Confederates. Commander Warley, in his papers dated in July of that year, states in a footnote (*ibid.,* p. 543) : "Fairbanks proved traitor, drowned his rockets, and made no signal; so the forts were taken by surprise, and it was only the vessels which passed latest that suffered from them. I understand that Fairbanks met his desserts subsequently at the hands of some of the men he betrayed. I can't vouch for the truth of it."

82 *Ibid.,* p. 196.

83 *B. & L.,* II, 65.

84 Humphrey, p. 569.

85 New York *Herald,* April 24, 1862.

86 *O.R.N.,* Series 1, XVIII, 203.

87 *Ibid.,* p. 769.

88 Albert Kautz, lieutenant on the *Hartford,* in a letter to the editors of *B. & L.,* II, 64.

89 *O.R.N.,* Series 1, XVIII, 167.

90 New York *Herald,* May 10, 1862.

91 *O.R.N.,* Series 1, XVIII, 198.

[92] In a report of the battle later written for *B. & L.*, II, 90, Warley gave the number of gunboats as three.

[93] This shell came from the *Iroquois,* the vessel on which Huger was serving when the war started. See *B. & L.*, II, 76. His first service for the Confederacy had been as captain of the *Lady Davis,* the first ship South Carolina had put afloat since the Revolution.

[94] Dewey, p. 75.

[95] *O.R.N.,* Series 1, XVIII, 359.

[96] Kennon, writing in 1885 of his part in the battle (*B. & L.*, II, 82) and obviously confusing details he had so clearly recorded in his report in 1862, said he shot away the light with a musket, "as to have hauled it down would have attracted notice."

[97] The *Stonewall Jackson* alone out of the River Defense Fleet appears to have taken part in the action. Captain J. E. Montgomery, the overall commander who at the moment was fighting Foote higher up the river, said in a later report (*O.R.*, Series 1, LI, I, 40): "The six boats sent by General Lovell to Fort Jackson were not under my control. I learned from one of the captains that on the morning the Federal boats passed the fort our boats were anchored under her guns, in a position where they could not possibly offer any resistance and consequently were destroyed, with the exception of the *Stonewall Jackson,* Captain G. W. Phillips, who succeeded in getting his boat out, ran up the river until he got his boat under good headway, then returned and ran into a large-size Federal vessel and sunk her. He was then overpowered and was compelled to burn his boat."

[98] Writing twenty-three years later, in an article in *B. & L.*, III, 85, Kennon says: "Out of ninety-three all told we lost fifty-seven killed and seventeen wounded, of whom four died in this hospital." This would have given a casualty total of seventy-eight out of ninety-three. Later, in the same account, Kennon places the number of uninjured at eighteen, which would have made the total on board ninety-six instead of ninety-three.

[99] *O.R.N.,* Series 1, XVIII, 308.

[100] *Ibid.,* p. 358.

[101] In the Confederate reports written immediately after the battle, as well as in later years, the river fleet under Stevenson was criticized for not taking a more active part. Beverly Kennon blamed their inactivity on their commander, charging he was still annoyed over the *Manassas. B. & L.*, II, 78.

General Lovell, in his report said: "I will here state that the river defense fleet proved a failure. . . . Unable to govern themselves, and unwilling to be governed by others, their total want of system, vigilance, and discipline rendered them useless and helpless when the enemy finally dashed upon them suddenly in a dark night." *O.R.N.*, Series 1, XVIII, 255.

[102] Absence of light was blamed mainly by General Duncan for the Union success in passing the forts. "I am fully satisfied," he reported, "that the enemy's dash was successful mainly owing to the cover of darkness, as a frigate and several gunboats were forced to retire as day was breaking. Similar results had attended every previous attempt made by the enemy to pass or to reconnoiter when we had sufficient light to fire with accuracy and effect." *Ibid.*, p. 269.

[103] The authority for the number of shots fired at the *Manassas* is Captain M. T. Squires, in command of the stronghold during the battle. *B. & L.*, II, 91.

[104] *O.R.N.*, Series 1, XVIII, 142.

[105] Casualty totals are always an elusive factor. These figures were given by Rear Admiral E. M. Eller, Director of Naval History, in a talk before the District of Columbia Civil War Round Table.

[106] *O.R.N.*, Series 1, XVIII, 143.

[107] *Ibid.*, p. 243.

CHAPTER FIVE

[1] For the membership of this committee see *O.R.N.*, Series 2, I, 726. This group of public-spirited citizens took an active role in the defense of the city. They raised funds, furnished manpower, and supplied technical and professional assistance. After New Orleans had fallen they charged Secretary Mallory with maladministration.

[2] Autobiographical sketch of Thomas L. Bayne, written in 1870 for his children.

[3] Julia LeGrand in *Heroines of Dixie,* by Katherine M. Jones (Indianapolis, The Bobbs-Merrill Company, Inc., 1955), p. 124.

[4] The brothers Tift were among the unsung heroes of the Confederacy. Although dedicated to a cause and working without recompense, circumstances were such that their reputations suffered rather than improved. No doubt the reverse would have been true had their ship ever met the enemy in battle. As it was, they were placed on the defensive, and Nelson, who took credit for originating the idea for the vessel, was forced to tell a court of inquiry: "I know the public mind has been prejudiced against my brother and myself by unfounded rumors and mistaken re-

ports, but I state without fear of contradiction by those who know the facts that our best energies of mind and body were devoted to this work from beginning to end, and that we accomplished all that it was possible for us or any other persons, with the means at our command, to do." When they began work on the *Mississippi* in October, 1861, they estimated they would complete her in four months. *O.R.*, Series 1, VI, 628.

John Ray, a New Orleans constructor, said of the Tifts: "Their ability, not being mechanics, was of the first order . . . In fact, if we had done so well for ourselves as they did, we never would, in my opinion, have lost New Orleans. They worked with all the zeal and energy possible." *O.R.N.*, Series 2, I, 789.

[5] *O.R.N.*, Series 1, XVIII, 353.

[6] *George Hamilton Perkins,* by Carroll Storrs Alden (Boston, Houghton Mifflin Company, 1914), p. 121, referred to hereafter as Alden.

[7] This reply from Mayor Monroe was recorded by the New Orleans *Democrat* reporter after following the two men from the wharf to City Hall.

[8] Alden, p. 121.

[9] *Ibid.,* p. 127.

[10] Morgan, p. 76.

[11] *O.R.N.*, Series 1, XVIII, 229.

[12] *O.R.*, Series 1, VI, 508.

[13] *O.R.N.*, Series 1, XVIII, 361.

[14] *Ibid.,* p. 358.

[15] Baker placed the visit at "about six o'clock" (*B. & L.*, II, 95), but the log of the *Hartford* states: "At seven two gentlemen brought communications on board from the mayor of the city."

[16] *O.R.N.*, Series 1, XVIII, 230.

[17] *Ibid.,* p. 232.

[18] *Ibid.*

[19] *B. & L.*, II, 92.

[20] *O.R.N.*, Series 1, XVIII, 238.

[21] General Lovell, who was of the opinion the Battle of New Orleans was fought and lost at Forts Jackson and St. Philip, wrote (*ibid.,* p. 259): "The extraordinary and remarkable conduct of the garrisons of these forts in breaking out in open mutiny after covering themselves with glory by their heroic defense, is one of those strange anomalies for which I do not pretend to account. The facts are recorded and speak for themselves. The causes will, probably, never be known in full."

[22] *Ibid.,* p. 446.

[23] Colonel Edward Higgins, as recorded in *ibid.*, p. 279.

[24] Over the years Porter seemed to lose track of the exact number of vessels he brought up to the forts on April 28. In 1887, in an article in *B. & L.*, II, 50, he said, ". . . I proceeded with nine gunboats up to Fort Jackson. . . ." But in his official report to Welles, dated May 2, 1862, he speaks of the men on the *Louisiana* "sending her adrift upon the four vessels of ours that were at anchor. . . ."

[25] *O.R.N.*, Series 1, XVIII, 433.

[26] *B. & L.*, II, 51.

[27] The circumstances surrounding the sinking of the *Louisiana* led to harsh treatment of the prisoners captured from her. This was not changed until Lieutenant William C. Whittle of her crew wrote a letter from prison saying he was en route in an open boat to warn Porter when the explosion occurred. *O.R.N.*, Series 1, XVIII, 314.

[28] The exact hour is fixed by Union General John W. Phelps, in command of the occupation, who said at that moment the Rebel flags of the forts were hauled down and the national colors run up, "a part of the ceremony which was greeted by our men with nine hearty cheers." *O.R.*, Series 1, VI, 509.

[29] The exact moment of the *Louisiana*'s explosion is disputed. In his official report of the incident, General Duncan says: "As far as I could learn, the *Louisiana* was fired prior to the time that the enemy's hosts came to an anchor abreast of the forts to negotiate. She was fired in her first and original position, without a change of any kind since her arrival at the forts." This statement, dated April 30, 1862, seems strange in view of the overwhelming evidence that the surrender conference actually was in session at the time of the explosion.

[30] The italics are his. See the journals kept by Philbrick and now on file at National Archives. Philbrick was a zealous and observant diarist, although there were a few factors in the world with which he could never quite catch up. For example, a pile driver was to him invariably a "spile-driver."

[31] *O.R.N.*, Series 1, XVIII, 234.

[32] *Ibid.* Joseph Stinson, local hotelkeeper, reported General Lovell threatened to cut the throat of any man who charged him with running away. Stinson had reasons for remembering this threat, for he was accused of having made just such a remark. See *O.R.*, Series 1, VI, 632.

[33] *O.R.N.*, Series 1, XVIII, 259. General Lovell later explained his reasoning in this instance: "I had deliberately made up my mind

that, although such a step would be entirely indefensible in a military point of view, yet, if the people of New Orleans were desirous of signalizing their patriotism and devotion to the cause by the bombardment and burning of their city, I would return with my troops and not leave as long as one brick remained upon another. The only palliation for such an act would be that it would give unmistakable evidence to the world that our people were in deadly earnest." See his report in *ibid.,* p. 257.

[34] *Ibid.,* p. 235.

[35] This incident was related by James in testimony before a Confederate court of inquiry into the fall of New Orleans. *O.R.,* Series 1, VI, 569.

[36] *O.R.N.,* Series 1, XVIII, 437.

[37] Farragut, p. 261.

[38] Two major factors seem to have led to the fall of New Orleans: (1) failure to complete the ironclads, and (2) the faith placed in the raft. Had the ironclads been ready to fight, they no doubt would have had little trouble overcoming Farragut's wooden fleet, although evidence indicates the *Louisiana* would never have been maneuverable because of the fault in placing the wheels one behind the other and so near the stern that they created an eddy that interfered with the rudder. As for the raft, the Southerners had no way of knowing that the Mississippi River would climb to a height unequaled in the memory of people living at that time.

When asked about the fall of the city, General M. L. Smith, commanding the interior line of defenses, commented: "The forts, in my judgment, were impregnable so long as they were in free and open communication with the city. This communication was not endangered while the obstruction existed. The conclusion, then, is briefly this: while the obstruction existed the city was safe; when it was swept away, as the defenses then existed, it was within the enemy's power. I do not now think it was possible for General Lovell or any other person to have kept the obstruction in place during the continuance of high water and drift, and after it was swept away there was neither time nor materials for building another on a different plan."

[39] Confederate Secretary of War James A. Seddon spoke of the fall of New Orleans as "the darkest hour of the struggle." He said it fell "after resistance so feeble as to arouse not less of shame than indignation." *O.R.,* Series 4, II, 281.

[40] *Ibid.,* VI, 505.

[41] Sarah Morgan in *Heroines of Dixie,* p. 129.

[42] Morgan, p. 54.

[43] *The Naval History of the Civil War,* by Admiral David D. Porter (New York, The Sherman Publishing Company, 1886), p. 237, referred to hereafter as Porter.

CHAPTER SIX

[1] *O.R.,* Series 1, VI, 134.

[2] *The History of the Civil War in America,* by John S. C. Abbott (New York, Henry Bill, 1866), p. 382, referred to hereafter as Abbott.

[3] *Army Life of an Illinois Soldier,* the letters and diary of Charles W. Wills (Washington, Globe Printing Company, 1906), p. 77, referred to hereafter as Wills.

[4] This was the estimate of Henry Walke, commanding the *Carondelet.* See *B. & L.,* I, 447.

[5] This point afterward was called Fort Wright.

[6] New York *Herald,* April 26, 1862.

[7] *Ibid.*

[8] *O.R.N.,* Series 1, XXIII, 8.

[9] New York *Herald,* April 26, 1862.

[10] *O.R.N.,* Series 1, XXIII, 11.

[11] New York *Herald,* May 3, 1862.

[12] Other members of the Board of Detail were Samuel F. du Pont of the Navy, Major General John G. Barnard of the Army, and Alexander D. Bache of the Coast Survey.

[13] Walke, p. 250.

[14] *Life of Charles Henry Davis,* by his son, Charles H. Davis (Boston, Houghton Mifflin Company, 1899), p. 222, referred to hereafter as Davis.

[15] Lieutenant S. L. Phelps, commanding the U.S.S. *Benton,* stated in his report on the 11th: "This I believe is the first purely naval fight of the war." See *O.R.N.,* Series 1, XXIII, 19. His conclusion, of course, ignores the battle between the *Merrimack* and *Monitor* in March, and obviously is based on the number of vessels taking part rather than the engagement's significance in history.

[16] See report of Charles H. Davis, *O.R.N.,* Series 1, XXIII, 13.

[17] *Ibid.,* p. 18.

[18] *Ibid.,* p. 19.

[19] *Ibid.,* p. 56.

[20] *Ibid.,* p. 53.

[21] *Ibid.,* p. 20.

[22] *Ibid.,* p. 24.

[23] *Ibid.*

[24] *O.R.N.,* Series 1, XXII, 681.

[25] *O.R.N.,* Series 1, XXIII, 65.

[26] *Ibid.,* p. 36.

[27] *Ibid.,* p. 38.

[28] *Ibid.,* p. 39.

[29] *Ibid.,* p. 40.

[30] *Ibid.,* p. 43. No explanation of his reluctant attitude at this stage of the campaign was given by Davis. It may have been professional jealousy, the perennial fight to keep one branch of the service from getting ahead of the other, for he wrote in his diary under date of May 29, in the very midst of the exchange with Ellet: "If I could get at them [the enemy's fleet], I should make the attack myself, and my own anxiety is now not to avoid, but to renew the fight clear of the guns of Fort Pillow." *O.R.N.,* Series 1, XXIII, 53.

[31] Davis, p. 236.

[32] *O.R.N.,* Series 1, XXIII, 44.

CHAPTER SEVEN

[1] In testimony during a Confederate Navy Department investigation of the sinking of the *Arkansas,* John T. Shirley said: "I am satisfied that General Polk desired the completion of the vessels, because he recommended the building of them; but for some cause or other, he would not detail the men. I brought, in fact, a letter from him to Mr. Mallory, recommending the plan of the vessels, and expressing a desire for their construction."

[2] Details on the construction of the *Arkansas* are taken largely from the testimony of John T. Shirley, given during the Navy Department investigation of her short-lived career.

[3] *B. & L.,* III, 572.

[4] This commander appears to have been Charles H. McBlair. Midshipman John A. Wilson of the Confederate Navy, who traveled with McBlair from Richmond to the Yazoo, where he said the latter took command of the *Arkansas,* made this entry in a diary he kept during the war: "While at Greenwood Captain McBlair was superseded by Captain I. N. Brown. When we reached Yazoo City Capt. B. insulted Capt. McB., who resented it, and according to orders returned to Richmond and reported Brown for insolence." See *Diary of Midshipman John A. Wilson* at National Archives.

[5] *O.R.N.*, Series 1, XVIII, 647.

[6] *Ibid.*, p. 499.

[7] *Ibid.*, p. 473.

[8] *Ibid.*, p. 491.

[9] *Ibid.*, p. 492.

[10] Defense of Vicksburg was a matter of desperation, of utter stubbornness. Southern military leaders knew it eventually must fall. General Beauregard wrote General Lovell as early as June 10, 1862: "With regard to Vicksburg, as already stated I regard its fate as sealed. You may defend it for a while to hold the enemy at bay, but it must follow ere long the fate of Fort Pillow." *O.R.*, Series 1, XV, 752.

[11] *Ibid.*, Series 1, LII, Pt. II, 324.

[12] Farragut, p. 112.

[13] In his report of the Memphis affair, Montgomery blamed General Lovell for the fuel shortage. He said he had purchased twenty thousand barrels of coal before leaving New Orleans, but that Lovell refused to pay for it, and consequently it was never delivered. *O.R.*, Series 1, LII, Pt. II, 39.

[14] The *Lancaster* sported the figure of an eagle on its prow. This now is on exhibit at the Mariner's Museum at Newport News, Virginia.

[15] Description by Henry Walke.

[16] *O.R.N.*, Series 1, XXIII, 133.

[17] Ellet died as he was approaching Cairo, Illinois, June 21, 1862, en route to New Albany, Indiana, for treatment.

[18] *O.R.N.*, Series 1, XXIII, 133.

[19] *Ibid.*, p. 134.

[20] Fry was an officer who took his soldiering so seriously that it would eventually lead to his death. In 1874, while commanding a filibustering expedition on board the *Virginius*, he was captured by the Spaniards, taken to Santiago de Cuba, and executed.

[21] See the log of the U.S.S. *Lexington*, *O.R.N.*, Series 1, XXIII, 692.

[22] Lieutenant J. W. Dunnington of the Confederate Navy gave this explanation of the shooting of the men in the water: "The vessel was completely deserted, and drifted across the stream into the bank near Captain Fry's battery. He immediately hailed and directed their flag hauled down. They failing to do so, although the order was given by some of their own officers in hearing of our people, our men were directed to shoot those in the water attempting to escape." *Ibid.*, p. 201.

The shooting was blamed on Fry, following his capture, but he stoutly denied any responsibility for it. See *The Life of John*

Ancrum Winslow, by John M. Ellicott (New York, G. P. Putnam's Sons, 1902), p. 82.

Captain A. M. Williams of the Confederate Engineers, commanding a company of sharpshooters, told in his report that the order for the shooting was given by him. *O.R.N.,* Series 1, XXIII, 205.

23 *Ibid.,* p. 166.
24 *Ibid.,* p. 171.
25 *Ibid.,* p. 196.

CHAPTER EIGHT

1 *O.R.N.,* Series 1, XVIII, 584.
2 Farragut, p. 273.
3 Confederate General Earl Van Dorn to Jefferson Davis, *O.R.N.,* Series 1, XVIII, 651.
4 *Ibid.,* p. 588.
5 *Ibid.,* p. 591.
6 *O.R.N.,* Series 1, XXIII, 235.
7 New York *Herald,* July 20, 1862.
8 *O.R.N.,* Series 1, XVIII, 675.
9 *Ibid.*
10 *Ibid.,* p. 594.
11 *O.R.N.,* Series 1, XIX, 19.
12 *Reminiscences of the Confederate States Navy,* by C. W. Read, *S.H.S.P.,* I, 338.
13 *O.R.,* Series 1, LII, Pt. 2, 329.
14 In a note to the editors of *B. & L.,* III, 555, Henry Walke, commander of the *Carondelet,* thus explained this retreat of his vessel: The *Arkansas* "raked the *Carondelet* from stem to stern, striking her forward three times. One shot glanced on the forward plating, one went through it and broke up, one from forward passed through the officers' rooms on the starboard side, and through the captain's cabin. Being a stern-wheel boat, the *Carondelet* required room and time to turn around. To avoid being sunk immediately, she turned and retreated. I was not such a simpleton as to 'take the bull by the horns,' to be fatally rammed, and sacrifice my command through fear of the criticisms of any man, or the vaunting opinion of much less-experienced officers. If I had continued fighting, bows on, in that narrow river, a collision, which the enemy desired, would have been inevitable and would have sunk the *Carondelet* in a few minutes."

[15] *O.R.N.,* Series 1, XIX, 41.

[16] *Ibid.* In his report Walke gives no explanation of this silence on his part, nor does he make mention of it.

[17] *Ibid.,* p. 40.

[18] This phrase was used by the correspondent of the Chicago *Times* in his report of the affair.

[19] *B. & L.,* III, 576.

[20] From the original log on file at National Archives.

[21] Republished in the New York *Times* of August 6, 1862.

[22] *O.R.N.,* Series 1, XIX, 6.

[23] Walke, p. 314.

[24] *O.R.N.,* Series 1, XIX, 137.

[25] *Ibid.,* p. 69.

[26] *Ibid.,* p. 67.

[27] *O.R.,* Series 1, LII, Pt. 2, 329.

[28] *O.R.N.,* Series 1, XIX, 7.

[29] *Ibid.,* p. 8.

[30] *Ibid.,* p. 712.

[31] *Ibid.,* p. 705.

[32] *Ibid.,* p. 748.

[33] H. M. W. Washington.

[34] *O.R.N.,* Series 1, XIX, 712.

[35] *Ibid.,* p. 8.

[36] *O.R.,* Series 1, LII, Pt. 2, 329.

[37] *Diary of Oscar Smith,* Manuscript Division, Library of Congress.

[38] *O.R.N.,* Series 1, XXIII, 237.

[39] *O.R.N.,* Series 1, XIX, 10.

[40] *Ibid.,* p. 4.

[41] *Ibid.,* p. 13.

[42] *Ibid.*

[43] Phelps to Foote, July 29, 1862, as reported in *ibid,* p. 57.

[44] *B. & L.,* III, 577.

[45] *O.R.N.,* Series 1, XIX, 14.

[46] *O.R.N.,* Series 1, XXIII, 238.

[47] *Diary of Oscar Smith.*

[48] *O.R.N.,* Series 1, XIX, 80.

[49] *Ibid.,* p. 44.

[50] Phelps to Foote, July 29, 1862, *ibid.,* p. 57.

[51] In a letter written some weeks after the affair, Farragut charged that Porter wanted all the credit and that he had asked that the remainder of the fleets take no part in the action other than the mortar bombardment.

[52] *O.R.N.,* Series 1, XIX, 61.

[53] These numbers would have totaled half his crew. In a later report he gave his losses as six killed and six badly wounded. *Ibid.,* p. 70.

[54] *B. & L.,* III, 578.

[55] *O.R.N.,* Series 1, XIX, 46. The *Queen of the West* was so badly damaged that it had to be sent north for repairs.

[56] *Ibid.,* p. 17.

[57] *Ibid.,* p. 49.

[58] *Hope Bids Me Onward,* by Harriet Gift Castlen (Savannah, Georgia, Chatham Printing Company, 1945), p. 80.

[59] *O.R.N.,* Series 1, XIX, 74.

[60] *Ibid.,* p. 58.

[61] These were the totals Van Dorn reported to the War Department. *Ibid.,* p. 137.

[62] *Ibid.,* p. 97.

[63] A few days later when Williams' body was transported through the streets of New Orleans, one woman resident was heard to say, "There goes one of the Yankees, and I'd like to see a lot more of them going the same way." Federal soldiers promptly arrested her. Carpenter's Mate William M. C. Philbrick, on board the U.S.S. *Portsmouth,* made note of the incident in his journal and added: "Good [place] for her."

[64] *O.R.N.,* Series 1, XIX, 135.

[65] In his report of the action on August 6, dated September 9, 1862 (*ibid.,* p. 124), W. D. Porter takes full credit for the destruction of the ironclad: "No other vessel was in sight belonging to the fleet off Baton Rouge, fired a gun, or in any way assisted the *Essex* in destroying the *Arkansas.*" A little later, when Ben Butler's General Orders No. 57 appeared in the New Orleans *Picayune,* Porter, having no use for the General, took exception to the clause: "To complete the victory the ironclad steamer *Arkansas,* the last hope of the rebellion, hardly awaited the gallant attack of the *Essex,* but followed the example of her sisters, the *Merrimack,* the *Manassas,* the *Mississippi,* and the *Louisiana,* by her own destruction." He claimed he had exchanged shots with the *Arkansas* at three hundred yards and that a shell from his ship had penetrated her side and set her on fire. Fellow officers, one of them Lieutenant Roe, disputed him, maintaining he never got closer than a mile and three-quarters of the *Rebel* ram, quoting Porter as saying she looked so formidable he "required all the help he could get, and more, too." *Ibid.,* p. 124.

Welles, noticing the discrepancy in the various accounts of the attack on the *Arkansas,* called it to the attention of Farragut, who ordered a court of inquiry. The findings, in the words of the flag officer, proved "there was no justification for the report of Commodore Porter." *Ibid.,* p. 127.

66 *O.R.,* Series 1, XV, 15.

67 *Guns of the Western Waters,* by Harpur Allen Gosnell (Baton Rouge, Louisiana State University Press, 1949), p. 135, referred to hereafter as Gosnell.

68 Farragut, p. 289.

69 *O.R.N.,* Series 1, XIX, 141.

70 Curtis to Halleck, August 7, 1862. *O.R.,* Series 1, XIII, 544.

71 Fox, I, p. 143.

72 *O.R.N.,* Series 2, II, 235.

73 *Ibid.,* Series 1, XIX, 68.

CHAPTER NINE

1 The scenes in this chapter are taken from the book *Hospital Transports,* by Frederick Law Olmsted (Boston, Ticknor and Fields, 1863).

CHAPTER TEN

1 See the journal of Levi Hayden in the Manuscript Division, Library of Congress.

2 Principal prison for Union officers at Richmond, Virginia.

CHAPTER ELEVEN

1 Fox, I, pp. 252, 254.

2 *O.R.N.,* Series 1, VII, 139.

3 *Ibid.,* I, 382.

4 *Ibid.,* VII, 264.

5 These men were quoted as saying the ship was the *William L. Wragg,* obviously an error, for official records show no such vessel. They, of course, meant the *Thomas L. Wragg. Ibid.,* p. 266.

6 *Ibid.,* p. 267.

7 Report of Commander William A. Parker. *Ibid.,* p. 516.

8 *Ibid.,* XIII, 455.

9 Fox, I, p. 318.

10 *Ibid.,* XII, 797.

11 *Ibid.,* XIII, 316.

12 *Ibid.,* V, 752.

13 *Ibid.,* VII, 228.

14 *Ibid.,* p. 304.

15 *History of the Navy During the Rebellion,* by Charles B. Boynton (New York, D. Appleton and Company, 1867), p. 46, referred to hereafter as Boynton.

16 *O.R.N.,* Series 1, I, 413.

17 Fox, I, p. 113.

18 George W. Gift Papers, University of North Carolina Library.

19 *O.R.N.,* Series 1, VII, 583.

20 *Ibid.,* XIII, 4.

21 *Ibid.,* p. 5.

22 Welles, I, 73.

23 John W. Grattan Papers, Manuscript Division, Library of Congress.

24 Scharf, p. 471.

25 *O.R.N.,* Series 1, VIII, 80.

26 *Ibid.,* p. 153.

27 *Ibid.,* p. 155.

28 Scharf, p. 474.

29 *O.R.N.,* Series 2, II, 336.

CHAPTER TWELVE

1 Welles, I, 109.

2 In a report to Farragut dated September 6, 1862, Preble stated: "Had I been officially or unofficially, in any way, informed that a man-of-war steamer was expected or on the ocean I would have known her true character and could have run her down." See *O.R.N.,* Series 1, I, 433. The *Connecticut* arrived with this intelligence on the 6th.

3 *Ibid.,* pp. 433, 435, 438, 439.

4 *Ibid.,* VI, 666.

5 *Ibid.,* VII, 107.

6 *Ibid.,* p. 142.

7 *Ibid.,* Series 2, II, 147.

8 *Ibid.,* Series 1, I, 755.

9 *Ibid.,* VII, 228.

10 See extracts from the journal of John Maffitt, *ibid.,* I, 764.

11 *Ibid.,* p. 397.

12 This quotation is from an editorial that appeared in the Savannah *Republican* and was found in the Maffitt Papers, University of North Carolina Library.

[13] See extracts from the journal of John Maffitt, *O.R.N.* Series 1, I, 764.

[14] Savannah *Republican* editorial in Maffitt Papers, University of North Carolina Library.

[15] The New York *Times* of September 9, 1862, reported that this steamer was standing by to prevent the *Florida* from "going out in pursuit of American vessels."

[16] Savannah *Republican* editorial in Maffitt Papers.

[17] New York *Times,* September 11, 1862.

[18] *O.R.N.,* Series 2, III, 523.

[19] Savannah *Republican* editorial.

[20] *O.R.N.,* Series 1, I, 766. Some confusion seems to have existed over whether or not Maffitt ran up the Confederate flag. Preble and others in the Union ships said that no flag was raised after the English banner was lowered. Apparently Maffitt intended for the flag to be raised and at the time thought it had been done, later discovering differently. At a subsequent court of inquiry he testified: "At this moment I hauled down the English flag, under which I was sailing as a *ruse de guerre,* and gave the order to one of the helmsmen to hoist the Confederate flag. At that moment he was endeavoring to haul up the foot-brail of the spanker, and lost his forefinger with a shrapnel shot, so that my order could not be complied with."

[21] Bulloch, p. 173.

[22] *O.R.N.,* Series 1, I, 767.

[23] "A mile or so of distance, and a few minutes more of daylight, and she must have been ours," Preble estimated in his report. *Ibid.,* p. 434.

[24] Maffitt Papers, University of North Carolina Library.

[25] *Ibid.,* p. 431.

[26] Welles, I, 140.

[27] *O.R.N.,* Series 1, I, 436. Preble did not succeed in getting a court of inquiry until April 20, 1872. The last witness to appear was Maffitt, who did what he could to absolve the Union officer. The report of this inquiry appears in *ibid.,* p. 460.

[28] *Ibid.,* p. 439.

[29] *Ibid.*

CHAPTER THIRTEEN

[1] *O.R.N.,* Series 1, I, 322.

[2] *Ibid.,* p. 685.

[3] See Welles to Francis Winslow, *ibid.,* p. 398.

[4] *Ibid.,* VII, 555.

[5] *Ibid.,* p. 579.

[6] Bulloch, p. 238.

[7] *O.R.N.,* Series 1, I, 773.

[8] *Bulloch,* p. 242.

[9] *The Cruise of the Alabama,* by Philip D. Haywood (Boston, Houghton Mifflin Company, 1886), p. 15, referred to hereafter as Haywood.

[10] *O.R.N.,* Series 1, I, 415.

[11] *Ibid.,* p. 783.

[12] *Ibid.,* p. 784.

[13] *Ibid.,* p. 785.

[14] *Ibid.,* p. 775.

[15] Craven was winding up his career on that side of the Atlantic. Before many weeks he was ordered to the Gulf of Mexico to watch for Confederate cruisers. *Ibid.,* p. 468.

[16] Semmes' journal, *ibid.,* p. 787.

[17] *Ibid.,* p. 805.

[18] New York *Herald,* October 17, 1862.

[19] New York *Times,* December 12, 1862.

[20] Welles, I, 175.

CHAPTER FOURTEEN

[1] *O.R.N.,* Series 1, XIX, 775.

[2] These words were used by David D. Porter in a message to General Sherman dated November 21, 1862. See *O.R.N.,* Series 1, XXIII, 500.

[3] *Ibid.,* XIX, 224.

[4] Report of Commander Charles Steedman of the U.S. gunboat *Paul Jones. O.R.N.,* Series 1, XIII, 358.

[5] *Ibid.,* p. 369.

[6] This conversation was repeated in an article, *How the Mississippi Was Opened,* by W. A. C. Michael, read before the Nebraska Commandery, Military Order of the Loyal Legion, at Omaha in 1887.

[7] *O.R.N.,* Series 1, XXIII, 512.

[8] J. Thomas Scharf, in his volume, *The Confederate States Navy,* p. 752, gives credit for the construction of the mines in the Yazoo to Acting Masters Zedekiah McDaniel and Francis M. Ewing, but the *Confederate Veteran,* XXIII, 167, attributes their origin to the

engineer Thomas Weldon, who had helped build the *Arkansas*. He was aided, according to this source, by H. Clay Sharkey, residing at the time of publication at Jackson, Mississippi.

9 *O.R.N.*, Series 1, XXIII, 689.

10 *Ibid.*, VII, 98.

11 *Ibid.*, XXIII, 547.

12 *Ibid.*, p. 548.

13 The time required for the *Cairo* to sink has been variously estimated. The Official Records of the Navy, Series 2, I, 49, places it as "within less than five minutes." It was reported by eyewitnesses, including Selfridge, as twelve minutes. The following entry concerning the sinking appears in the log of the *Marmora:* "This occurred at eleven-fifty-five, and at twelve-three the *Cairo* was no more." O.R.N., Series 1, XXIII, 689.

14 The site where the *Cairo* sank was lost for ninety-four years. In 1956, Edwin Bearss, professional historian at the Vicksburg National Military Park, Warren Grabau, professional geologist, and Don Jacks, National Military Park employee, found it by means of a compass and a long iron bar used as a prober beneath the water. In 1960, the pilothouse and one of its cannon were brought to the surface. The carriage of the gun, thickly coated with mud, was well preserved. A drive now is under way to raise the entire vessel by the centennial of its sinking, December 12, 1962.

15 Statement of Lieutenant George W. Brown of the tinclad *Forest Rose*. See *Personal Recollections of the War of the Rebellion* (New York, printed by the Military Order of the Loyal Legion, 1891), p. 302.

16 See the Selfridge Papers, now on file in the Manuscript Division, Library of Congress.

17 *O.R.N.*, Series 1, XXIII, 544.

18 *Ibid.*, p. 580.

19 *Ibid.*

20 Selfridge Papers.

21 *O.R.N.*, Series 1, XXIII, 545.

22 *Ibid.*, p. 567.

23 *Ibid.*, p. 569

24 *Ibid.*, p. 579.

25 *Ibid.*, p. 580.

26 *Ibid.*, p. 577.

27 *Ibid.*, p. 598.

28 *Ibid.*, p. 574.

29 Estimate of David D. Porter, made in a report dated January 3, 1863. See *ibid.*, p. 602.

[30] *Ibid.*, p. 607.
[31] *Ibid.*, p. 587.
[32] *Ibid.*, p. 597.
[33] *Ibid.*, p. 607.

CHAPTER FIFTEEN

[1] *O.R.N.,* Series 1, XIII, 513.
[2] *Ibid.*, VII, 170.
[3] *Ibid.*, VIII, 14.
[4] Fox, I, p. 273.
[5] *O.R.N.,* Series 1, VIII, 203.
[6] *Ibid.*, p. 338.
[7] *Reminiscences of the Old Navy,* by Edgar Stanton Maclay (New York, G. P. Putnam's Sons, 1898), p. 212.
[8] Francis B. Butts, in an article published by the Rhode Island Soldiers and Sailors Historical Association at Providence in 1890, Fourth Series, No. 6, referred to hereafter as Butts.
[9] *O.R.N.,* Series 1, VIII, 351.
[10] This was a statement by Francis B. Butts.
[11] Butts.
[12] *Ibid.*
[13] Just where the *Monitor* lies today has never been definitely established, although the general location is known. At 1:00 P.M. on December 30, 1862, official reports indicate, she was fourteen miles from Cape Hatteras light, which bore W.S.W. At sunset of that day she was seventeen miles distant, with the light bearing N.W. The last report of her location placed her twenty miles S.S.W. of the light at eleven o'clock that night. *O.R.N.,* Series 1, VIII, 344.
[14] The last survivor of this group was Thomas L. Taylor, who was buried at Putnam, Connecticut. For many years his grave went unnoticed. Then in January, 1960, the Sons of Union Veterans, realizing the distinction due his memory, erected a suitable headstone to mark his grave.
[15] The missing were identified as Norman Atwater, acting ensign; George Frederickson, acting ensign; R. W. Hands, third assistant engineer; Samuel A. Lewis, third assistant engineer; John Stocking, boatswain's mate; James Fenwick, quarter gunner; William Bryan, yeoman; Daniel Moore, officers' steward; Robert Howard, officers' cook; William Allen, landsman; William Eagan, landsman; Jacob Nickles, ordinary seaman; Robert Cook, first-class

boy; Thomas Joice, first-class fireman; Robert Williams, first-class fireman, and George Littlefield, coal heaver. *O.R.N.*, Series 1, VIII, 340.

[16] Welles, I, 213.

[17] *Ibid.*, p. 216.

[18] *O.R.N.*, Series 1, VIII, 354.

CHAPTER SIXTEEN

[1] See Magruder's report, *O.R.N.*, Series 1, XIX, 470.

[2] *Ibid.*, p. 468.

[3] *Ibid.*, p. 439.

[4] *Ibid.*, p. 468.

[5] *Ibid.*, pp. 468, 735.

[6] *Ibid.*, p. 441.

[7] *Ibid.*, p. 447.

[8] *Ibid.*, p. 470.

[9] *Ibid.*, p. 475.

[10] *Ibid.*, p. 479.

[11] *Ibid.*

[12] *Ibid.*, p. 464. In subsequent correspondence Commodore H. H. Bell, who re-established the blockade at Galveston, maintained that the truce was violated by the ring of cannon and small arms by the Confederates on shore, "as he had been informed." But this Magruder denied. "Not a gun or small arm was discharged during the stipulated period or until the enemy's vessels were discovered to be creeping off out of the harbor," he claimed. See *ibid.*

[13] *Ibid.*, p. 440.

[14] *Ibid.*, p. 481.

[15] Welles, I, 220.

[16] Fox, I, p. 178.

[17] *Ibid.*, p. 735.

[18] *Ibid.*, p. 738.

[19] *Ibid.*, p. 507.

[20] Witnesses vary in their estimate of the period that the firing lasted. Bell judged it to be twenty minutes, as reported in *ibid.*, p. 737. Acting Master Partridge of the *Hatteras* was reported in *ibid* as placing it at fifteen minutes. But Semmes, in his report to Secretary Mallory (*ibid.*, II, 683), fixes it at thirteen minutes.

[21] *Ibid.*, p. 18.

[22] There seems to be some confusion over this reply. The name of the steamer mentioned is given as the *Petrel* by some of the par-

ticipants and as the *Spitfire* by others. See *ibid.,* XIX, 737, and II, 721.

²³ Semmes says in his journal that the name of the *Hatteras* could not be heard distinctly enough to be understood.

²⁴ This exchange has been resurrected from accounts given by Commodore Bell in his private diary, *ibid.,* XIX, 737, and by Commander Semmes in his report to Secretary Mallory, *ibid.,* II, 683.

²⁵ *Ibid.,* p. 721.

²⁶ *Ibid.,* p. 722.

²⁷ *Ibid.*

²⁸ Farragut, p. 307.

²⁹ *Ibid.,* p. 309.

CHAPTER SEVENTEEN

¹ These words were used by Grant in a telegram sent Halleck on January 11, at the very time that McClernand's forces were drawing near for the attack on the fort. *O.R.N.,* Series 1, XXIV, 130.

² *Ibid.,* p. 130.

³ *Ibid.,* p. 174.

⁴ *Ibid.,* p. 124. Despite this claim by McClernand, the Navy Secretary's office records state: "General Sherman then proposed to Admiral Porter to make a combined attack on Arkansas Post, which was at that time being heavily fortified." See *ibid.,* XXIII, 398.

⁵ *Ibid.,* XXIV, 100.

⁶ *Ibid.*

⁷ *O.R.,* Series 1, III, 58.

⁸ *O.R.N.,* Series 1, XXIV, 129.

⁹ *Ibid.*

¹⁰ *Ibid.,* p. 129.

¹¹ *Ibid.,* p. 130.

¹² *Ibid.,* XXIII, 401.

¹³ *Ibid.,* XXIV, 114.

¹⁴ *Ibid.,* p. 127.

¹⁵ *Ibid.,* p. 116.

¹⁶ *Ibid.,* p. 174.

CHAPTER EIGHTEEN

¹ *O.R.N.,* Series 1, XIX, 344.

² *Ibid.,* I, 768.

3 *Ibid.*, II, 17.

4 *The Life and Services of John Newland Maffitt,* by Emma Martin Maffitt (New York, The Neale Publishing Company, 1906), p. 266, referred to hereafter as Maffitt.

5 Diary of A. L. Drayton, Manuscript Division, Library of Congress.

6 *O.R.N.,* Series 1, I, 769.

7 Maffitt, p. 267.

8 This attempt is reported both by Maffitt and by A. L. Drayton, who shipped on board the *Florida* at Mobile October 24, 1862. See his dairy in the Manuscript Division, Library of Congress.

9 The period of time that elapsed before the *Cuyler* got under way in chase is not made clear by the record. Emmons said in his report: "I had just retired . . . but was on deck, partly dressed, in a few minutes, and in a few more, [the officer of the deck says four, in his remarks in the log book] say five or six, we were turning to pursue." *O.R.N.,* Series 1, II, 30. But James Russell Soley records in his *The Navy in the Civil War,* I, 139: "It is stated by an officer of the *Cuyler,* in a letter quoted by Maffitt that half an hour was lost in getting under way, owing to a regulation of the ship by which the officer of the watch was required to report and wait for the captain to come on deck before slipping the cable."

10 *Ibid.*, p. 639.

11 *Ibid.*, p. 33.

12 *Ibid.*, p. 30.

13 *Ibid.*, XIX, 529.

14 *Ibid.*, p. 528.

15 The original log book of the *Florida* was thrown overboard, but this information on her whereabouts was taken from a certified abstract made by Acting Master G. D. Bryan, one of her officers. *Ibid.*, II, 673.

16 Maffitt, p. 271.

17 *Ibid.*

18 *O.R.N.,* Series 1, II, 639.

19 New York *Herald,* January 23, 1863.

20 *O.R.N.,* Series 1, II, 639.

21 *Ibid.*, p. 642.

22 Diary of A. L. Drayton.

23 Maffitt, p. 274.

24 *Ibid.*, p. 276.

25 *O.R.N.,* Series 1, II, 668.

26 *Ibid.*

[27] *Ibid.,* I, 768.
[28] *Ibid.*

CHAPTER NINETEEN

[1] *O.R.N.,* Series 1, XX, 25.
[2] Fox, I, p. 122.
[3] *Ibid.,* p. 156.
[4] *Ibid.*
[5] Bankhead, son of a soldier father, had been born in Castle Pinckney in Charleston Harbor and had been popular in local social circles before the war. See *Military Essays and Recollections* (Chicago, A. C. McClurg and Company, 1891), I, 193.
[6] Du Pont in *O.R.N.,* Series 1, XIII, 292.
[7] For this exchange of correspondence, see *ibid.,* pp. 353, 377, 389, and 416.
[8] *Ibid.,* p. 563.
[9] George Bacon's report in *ibid.,* p. 558.
[10] *Ibid.,* p. 622.
[11] Stellwagen's report in *ibid.,* p. 579.
[12] When Abbot wrote his report he was unable to give the name of the senior Confederate officer with whom he had conferred. See *ibid.,* p. 580.
[13] *Ibid.*
[14] *Ibid.,* p. 598.
[15] *Ibid.,* p. 622.
[16] *Ibid.,* p. 586.
[17] Scharf, p. 677.
[18] Report of Commander John R. Tucker in *O.R.N.,* Series 1, XIII, 619.
[19] *Ibid.,* p. 593.
[20] *Ibid.,* p. 620.
[21] The Confederacy charged that the *Mercedita,* her officers, and her crew were surrendered by Abbot at the time of his oral pledge. The Union, after a court of inquiry, maintained that the officers and crew, but not the vessel, were included in the surrender. In its reply, the Federal Government overlooked, if it featured in the inquiry at all, the report of Abbot dated January 31, 1863, in which he stated that he told the captain of the Confederate ram that "I have come in the name of Captain Stellwagen to give up the U.S.S. *Mercedita,* she being then in a sinking and perfectly defenseless condition." See *ibid.,* p. 580.

Commenting on the action in his definitive volume, *The Navy in the Civil War,* Professor James Russell Soley says: "It can only be excused on the supposition that the enemy [Confederates] were unable to take possession owing to the presence of a superior force."

[22] Commander Le Roy, captain of the *Keystone State,* explained his action thus: "Being unable to communicate with the senior officer present personally or by signal, I deemed it my duty to make the best of my way to Port Royal." *O.R.N.,* Series 1, XIII, 582.

[23] *Ibid.,* p. 616.

[24] The Savannah *Republican,* February 2, 1863.

[25] *O.R.N.,* Series 1, XIII, 617.

[26] *Ibid.,* p. 600.

[27] *Ibid.,* XVIII, 623.

[28] *Ibid.,* XIX, 519.

[29] This vessel was on its final expedition. The following month it struck a snag and sank. *Ibid.,* p. 624.

[30] *Ibid.,* p. 523.

[31] *Deeds of Valor—How America's Heroes Won the Medal of Honor* (Detroit, Michigan, The Perrien-Keydel Company, 1905), p. 130.

CHAPTER TWENTY

[1] Fox, I, p. 138.

[2] Narrative by Paymaster Samuel T. Browne, *Rhode Island Soldiers and Sailors Historical Society Papers* (Providence, Rhode Island, N. Bang Williams Company, 1880), Number 1, Second Series, p. 36.

[3] Du Pont was aware that Osbon was on board the *Montauk,* but he blocked the reporter's long and detailed account of the operations mainly because of a decision that no announcement should be made of them until after an attack on Charleston had been attempted. See *O.R.N.,* Series 1, XIII, 549.

[4] *A Sailor of Fortune,* by Captain B. S. Osbon (New York, McClure, Phillips and Company, 1906), p. 233, referred to hereafter as Osbon.

[5] *Ibid.*

[6] *O.R.N.,* Series 1, XIII, 637.

[7] The exact time of the *Nashville*'s discovery was recorded by Second Assistant Engineer Thomas A. Stephens of the *Montauk. Ibid.,* p. 700.

8 Osbon, p. 240.

9 *Ibid.,* p. 242.

10 In this report Worden was not completely accurate. A part of the *Nashville* remained, for a century later journalists were writing in the Atlanta *Journal* and *Constitution:* "You can see her bare bones thrusting above the water." An effort has been launched by the Georgia Historical Commission to preserve what is left of her.

11 Words used in the report of Captain Anderson, commanding Fort McAllister. See *O.R.N.,* Series 1, XIII, 709.

12 *Ibid.,* p. 700.

13 *Ibid.,* p. 705.

14 I. E. Vail in *Three Years on the Blockade* (New York, The Abbey Press, 1902), p. 103.

CHAPTER TWENTY-ONE

1 Both of these vessels had been built by the Union at Cincinnati, Ohio, and completed during the preceding fall.

2 *Bohemian Brigade,* by Louis M. Starr (New York, Alfred A. Knopf, Inc., 1954), p. 193.

3 *O.R.N.,* Series 1, XXIV, 385.

4 *Ibid.,* p. 376.

5 *Ibid.,* p. 375.

6 *Ibid.,* p. 403.

7 See the report of H. M. Mixer, acting assistant surgeon on the *Indianola,* in *ibid.,* p. 392.

8 *Ibid.,* p. 379.

9 *Ibid.,* p. 392.

10 *Ibid.,* p. 404.

11 *Ibid.,* p. 210.

12 *Ibid.,* p. 297.

CHAPTER TWENTY-TWO

1 *O.R.N.,* Series 1, XX, 783.

2 Banks' report to Grant, *ibid.,* p. 5.

3 Banks' part in the operations was to be strictly a diversion. He wrote Grant on the 13th: "The best information we have of the enemy's force places it at twenty-five thousand or thirty thousand. This and his position precludes the idea of an assault upon our part. . . ." *Ibid.*

[4] The Spanish-American War hero, George Dewey, serving at the battle of Port Hudson as executive officer of the *Mississippi,* is said to have considered Bacon's account of the fight the best in existence. See Gosnell, p. 205.

[5] *O.R.N.,* Series 1, XIX, 666.

[6] R. W. Campbell of Rogillioville, Louisiana, in the *Confederate Veteran,* July, 1918, p. 288.

[7] *O.R.N.,* Series 1, XIX, 769.

[8] Dewey, p. 101.

[9] *O.R.N.,* Series 1, XX, 5.

[10] *Ibid.,* p. 11.

[11] From the Navy Secretary's Office Records, *ibid.,* XXIII, 404.

[12] *B. & L.,* I, 625.

[13] *O.R.N.,* Series 1, XXIV, 474.

[14] *Ibid.,* p. 475.

[15] *Ibid.*

[16] *Ibid.*

[17] *Ibid.,* p. 492.

[18] *Ibid.,* p. 479.

CHAPTER TWENTY-THREE

[1] *O.R.N.,* Series 1, XX, 24.

[2] *Ibid.,* XXIII, 407.

[3] When Welles questioned the attempt of the two rams to run the blockade, Porter replied with a letter in which he sharply denounced Ellet and concluded: "The Department can imagine my embarrassment when associated with persons who are thinking more of their own personal aggrandizement than they do of this Union." *Ibid.,* XXIV, 522.

In a memorandum (*ibid.,* XX, 52) Ellet recorded: "Porter wrote me a very sharp letter denying my right to give orders to my subordinate officers without receiving them from him, and informed me that he had ordered the arrest of Lieutenant Colonel Ellet and would try him by court-martial for disrespect, which he has not done."

[4] Fox, I, p. 331.

[5] *O.R.N.,* Series 1, XX, 137.

[6] *Ibid.,* p. 138.

[7] Farragut wrote at this period: "I have been holding the enemy very uneasy by the stomach." *Ibid.,* p. 62.

[8] *Ibid.,* XXIV, 552.

[9] *Ibid.*
[10] *Ibid.,* p. 556.
[11] *Ibid.,* XXIII, 409.
[12] *Ibid.,* p. 410.
[13] *Ibid.*
[14] Porter wrote Welles after he had captured the stronghold: "Grand Gulf is the strongest place on the Mississippi. Had the enemy succeeded in finishing the fortifications no fleet could have taken them." *Ibid.,* XXIV, 627.
[15] *Ibid.,* p. 600.
[16] Porter's description in *ibid.,* p. 611.
[17] *Ibid.*
[18] Alfred Mitchell to Ainsworth, April 30, 1862. *Ibid.,* p. 628.
[19] *Ibid.,* p. 627.
[20] *Ibid.,* XXIII, 415.
[21] *Ibid.,* XXIV, 645.
[22] *Ibid.,* p. 650.

CHAPTER TWENTY-FOUR

[1] Abbot, p. 274.
[2] *O.R.N.,* Series 1, XXV, 5.
[3] *Ibid.,* XX, 213.
[4] *Ibid.,* XXV, 164.
[5] Major General J. G. Walker, *ibid.,* p. 166.
[6] *Ibid.,* p. 96.
[7] *Ibid.,* p. 118.
[8] *Ibid.,* p. 102.
[9] P.H., VI, 37.
[10] *O.R.N.,* Series 1, XX, 272.
[11] *Ibid.,* XXV, 109.
[12] Scharf, p. 403.

Bibliography

GENERAL HISTORICAL WORKS

Abbot, Willis J., *The Blue Jackets of '61* (New York, Dodd, Mead and Company, 1886).

Abbott, John S. C., *The History of the Civil War in America* (New York, Henry Bill, 1866).

Albion, Robert G., and Pope, Jennie Barres, *Sea Lanes in Wartime* (New York, W. W. Norton and Company, Inc., 1942).

Alden, Carroll Stors, and Earle, Ralph, *Makers of Naval Tradition* (Boston, Ginn and Company, 1925).

Ammen, Daniel, *The Old Navy and the New* (Philadelphia, J. B. Lippincott Company, 1891).

Battles and Leaders of the Civil War (New York, The Century Company, 1887).

Bigelow, John, *France and the Confederate Navy* (New York, Harper and Brothers, 1888).

Boynton, Dr. Charles B., *The History of the Navy During the Rebellion* (New York, D. Appleton and Company, 1867).

Bradlee, Francis B. C., *Blockade Running During the Civil War* (Salem, Massachusetts, The Essex Institute, 1925).

Brockett, Dr. Linus Pierpont, *The Camp, the Battlefield, and the*

Hospital (Philadelphia, The National Publishing Company, 1866).

Bulloch, James D., *The Secret Service of the Confederate States in Europe* (New York, G. P. Putnam's Sons, 1884).

Carse, Robert, *Blockade* (New York, Rinehart & Company, Inc., 1958).

Church, W. C., *The Life of John Ericcson* (New York, Charles Scribner's Sons, 1891).

Coffin, Charles Carleton, *Four Years of Fighting* (Boston, Ticknor and Fields, 1866).

Confederate Blockade Running Through Bermuda 1861-1865, edited by Frank E. Vandiver (Austin, University of Texas Press, 1947).

Confidential Correspondence of Gustavus Vasa Fox, edited by Robert Means Thompson (New York, De Vinne Press, 1920).

Cranwell, John Phillips, *Spoilers of the Sea* (New York, W. W. Norton & Company, Inc., 1941).

Daly, Robert Walter, *How the Merrimac Won* (New York, Thomas Y. Crowell Company, 1957).

Dudley, Dean, *Officers of the Union Army and Navy* (Boston, L. Prang and Company, 1862).

Du Pont, H. A., *Rear Admiral Samuel Francis du Pont* (New York, National Americana Society, 1926).

Frothingham, Jessie Peabody, *Seafighters from Drake to Farragut* (New York, Charles Scribner's Sons, 1902).

Fullam, George Townley, *The Cruise of the Alabama* (Liverpool, Lee and Nightingale, 1863).

Gosnell, Harpur Allen, *Guns of the Western Waters* (Baton Rouge, Louisiana State University Press, 1949).

Hackett, Frank Warren, *Deck and Field* (Washington, W. H. Lowdermilk and Company, 1909).

Hanks, Charles C., *Blockaders off the American Coast*, U.S. Naval Institute Proceedings (Menasha, Wisconsin, 1941).

Haywood, Philip D., *The Cruise of the Alabama* (Boston, Houghton Mifflin Company, 1886).

Headley, Joel Tyler, *Farragut and Our Naval Commanders* (New York, E. B. Treat and Company, 1867).

———— *Heroes and Battles of the War, 1861-1865* (New York, E. B. Treat and Company, 1891).

Hero Tales of the American Soldier and Sailor (Philadelphia, Century Manufacturing Company, 1899).

Hill, Frederic Stanhope, *Twenty Historic Ships* (New York, The Knickerbocker Press, 1902).

Hill, Jim Dan, *Sea Dogs of the Sixties* (Minneapolis, The University of Minnesota Press, 1935).

History of the Ram Fleet and the Mississippi Marine Brigade in the War for the Union on the Mississippi and Its Tributaries (St. Louis, Society of Survivors, 1907).

Hubbell, Raynor, *Confederate Stamps, Old Letters, and History* (published at Griffin, Georgia).

Humphrey, Willis C., *Military and Naval Operations During the Civil War* (Detroit, C. H. Smith and Company, 1886).

Jones, Katherine M., *Heroines of Dixie* (Indianapolis, The Bobbs-Merrill Company, Inc., 1955).

Lewis, Charles L., *David Glasgow Farragut, Our First Admiral* (Annapolis, U. S. Naval Institute, 1943).

Lonn, Ella, *Foreigners in the Confederacy* (Chapel Hill, University of North Carolina Press, 1940).

MacNeill, Ben Dixon, *The Hatterasman* (Winston-Salem, North Carolina, John F. Blair, 1958).

Mahan, Alfred T., *The Navy in the Civil War* (New York, Charles Scribner's Sons, 1895).

Matthews, Franklin, *Our Navy in Time of War* (New York, D. Appleton and Company, 1899).

Merrill, James M., *The Rebel Shore* (Boston, Little, Brown & Company, 1957).

Murphy, D. F., *Full Report of the Trial of William Smith for Piracy* (Philadelphia, King and Baird, 1861).

Ninety Years of Marine Insurance (New York, Triggs Color Printing Corporation, 1932).

Olmstead, Frederic Law, *Hospital Transports* (Boston, Ticknor and Fields, 1863).

Parker, Foxhall A., *The Battle of Mobile Bay and the Capture of Forts Powell, Gaines, and Morgan* (Boston, A. Williams and Company, 1878).

Parrott, Enoch G., *Description and Cruise of the U.S.S. Augusta* (New York, Francis McCarten, 1876).

The Photographic History of the Civil War (New York, The Review of Reviews Company, 1911).

Trial of the Officers and Crew of the Privateer Savannah, as reported by A. F. Warburton (New York, Baker and Godwin, 1862).

Porter, David D., *The Naval History of the Civil War* (New York, The Sherman Publishing Company, 1886).

Porter, John W. H., *A Record of Events in Norfolk County, Virginia* (Portsmouth, Virginia, W. A. Fisher, 1892).

Pratt, Fletcher, *Civil War on Western Waters* (New York, Henry Holt and Company, 1956).

Quad, M., *Field, Fort, and Fleet* (Detroit, Detroit Free Press Publishing Company, 1885).

Robinson, William Morrison, *The Confederate Privateers* (New Haven, Yale University Press, 1928).

Ross, Fitzgerald, *Cities and Camps of the United States* (Urbana, University of Illinois Press, 1958).

Sands, Benjamin Franklin, *From Reefer to Rear Admiral* (New York, Frederick A. Stokes Company, 1899).

Scharf, J. Thomas, *History of the Confederate States Navy* (New York, Rogers and Sherwood, 1887).

Semmes, Raphael, *Service Afloat* (New York, P. J. Kenedy, 1903).

———— *The Cruise of the Alabama and Sumter* (London, Saunders, Otley and Company, 1864).

Sinclair, Arthur, *Two Years on the Alabama* (Boston, Lee and Shepard, 1895).

Soley, James Russell, *The Blockade and the Cruisers* (New York, Charles Scribner's Sons, 1890).

Sprunt, James, *Derelicts* (Wilmington, North Carolina, 1920).

———— *Chronicles of the Cape Fear River* (Raleigh, North Carolina, Edwards and Broughton Company, 1914).

Starr, Louis M., *Bohemian Brigade* (New York, Alfred A. Knopf, Inc., 1954).

Stern, Philip Van Doren, *Secret Missions of the Civil War* (Chicago, Rand, McNally & Company, 1959).

Vail, I. E., *Three Years on the Blockade* (New York, The Abbey Press, 1902).

West, R. S., Jr., *Gideon Welles: Lincoln's Navy Department* (Indianapolis, The Bobbs-Merrill Company, Inc., 1943).

———— *Mr. Lincoln's Navy* (New York, Longmans, Green & Co., Inc., 1957).

———— *The Second Admiral: A Life of David Dixon Porter* (New York, Coward-McCann, Inc., 1937).

White, E. V., *The First Iron-clad Engagement in the World* (New York, J. S. Ogilvie Publishing Company, 1906).

White, William Chapman and Ruth, *Tin Can on a Shingle* (New York, E. P. Dutton & Company, Inc., 1957).

LETTERS, MANUSCRIPTS, AND PAMPHLETS

Abstract of U.S.S. *Tioga*'s log, on file at National Archives.

Address by Joseph Adams Smith on the Alabama and Kearsarge, delivered before the Union League of Philadelphia in 1906.

Anonymous journal kept on the U.S.S. *Carondelet,* Manuscript Division, Library of Congress.

Augustus C. Evans Papers, Manuscript Division, University of North Carolina Library.

Buchanan-Screven Papers, Manuscript Division, University of North Carolina Library.

Cout-martial of Commodore Charles Wilkes, House of Representatives Executive Document No. 102, Thirty-eighth Congress, First Session.

David D. Porter's Private Journal, Manuscript Division, Library of Congress.

Diary of A. L. Drayton, Manuscript Division, Library of Congress.

Diary of Current Events, by I. T. Gordon, National Archives.

Diary of Edwin F. Ludwig, Manuscript Division, Library of Congress.

Diary of Isaac DeGraff, National Archives.

Diary of J. C. Gregg, National Archives.

Diary of Midshipman John A. Wilson, National Archives.

Diary of Thomas F. Galway, in possession of family.

Diary of William B. Cushing, National Archives.

Edmund Rose Calhoun Papers, Manuscript Division, Library of Congress.

E. N. Kellogg Letters, Manuscript Division, Library of Congress.

F. A. Roe Papers, Manuscript Division, Library of Congress.

Frederick Milnes Edge letter on destruction of United States carrying trade, National Archives.

Hayes, Rear Admiral John B., "Lee Against the Sea," paper read before the District of Columbia Civil War Round Table.

Insurgent Privateers in Foreign Ports, House of Representatives Executive Document No. 103, Thirty-seventh Congress, Second Session.

"Ironclads of the Sixties," paper prepared by Thomas W. Green and read before the Confederate Research Club, London, England, in 1959.

James B. Jones letter, Manuscript Division, University of North Carolina Library.

James Rider Randall Papers, Manuscript Division, University of North Carolina Library.

John Mercer Brooke Papers, Manuscript Division, University of North Carolina Library.

John Rapier Letters, copied from originals in possession of Mrs. Ted Trigg, Mobile, Alabama.

Journal of George F. Emmons, National Archives.

Journal of the *Oneida,* Manuscript Division, University of North Carolina Library.

Journals of Carpenter's Mate William M. C. Philbrick, National Archives.

Journals of Levi Hayden, Manuscript Division, Library of Congress.

Katherine McCook Knox Papers, Manuscript Division, Library of Congress.

Letter of S. D. Greene, National Historical Foundation.

Letter of G. J. Van Brunt, furnished the author through the kindness of W. Norman FitzGerald, Jr., Milwaukee, Wisconsin.

Letters of Asa Beetham, Manuscript Division, Library of Congress.

Letters of George Hamilton Perkins (Concord, New Hampshire, The Rumford Press, 1901).

Letters of George W. Gift, Manuscript Division, University of North Carolina Library.

Letters of Henry L. Graves, Manuscript Division, University of North Carolina Library.

Letters of S. P. Gillett, Manuscript Division, University of North Carolina Library.

Lloyd Phoenix Biography, Manuscript Division, Library of Congress.

Log of the U.S. ram *Lancaster,* National Archives.

Log of the U.S.S. *Santee,* National Archives.

Maffitt Papers, Manuscript Division, University of North Carolina Library.

Mark de Wolf Stevenson Papers, Manuscript Division, University of North Carolina Library.

Messages and Papers of the Confederacy (Nashville, United States Publishing Company, 1905).

Military Historical Society of Massachusetts Papers.

Military Order of the Loyal Legion Papers.

Napoleon Smith Papers, Manuscript Division, University of North Carolina Library.

"Naval Lieutenant Matthew Fontaine Maury," by Catherine Cate Coblentz, Manuscript Division, Library of Congress.

Official Records of the Union and Confederate Navies in the War of the Rebellion (Washington, Government Printing Office, 1894).

Papers of Joseph Bloomfield Osborn, Manuscript Division, Library of Congress.

Peter Evans Smith Papers, Manuscript Division, University of North Carolina Library.

"President Lincoln's Campaign Against the Merrimac," pamphlet prepared by Dr. Chester D. Bradley.

Radford Papers, abstract from log book of *Battery Brooke,* National Archives.

Rhode Island Soldiers and Sailors Historical Society Papers.

Ruffin Thompson Papers, Manuscript Division, University of North Carolina Library.

Rupert C. Jarvis, "The Alabama and the Law," paper read before the Confederate Research Club, London, England, in 1959.

"The Merrimack," a manuscript by Colonel George M. Brooke, Jr., grandson of John Mercer Brooke.

"The Virginia or Merrimac; Her Real Projector," by John Mercer Brooke.

T. O. Selfridge Papers, Manuscript Division, Library of Congress.

Violet G. Alexander Papers, Manuscript Division, University of North Carolina Library.

War Papers (Portland, Maine, The Thurston Print, 1898).

William Calder Papers, Manuscript Division, Library of Congress.

BIOGRAPHIES, DIARIES, MEMOIRS, ETC.

Alden, Carroll Storrs, *George Hamilton Perkins* (Boston, Houghton Mifflin Company, 1914).

Autobiography of George Dewey (New York, Charles Scribner's Sons, 1913).

Barr, James W., *Diaries, Letters, and Recollections of the War Between the States,* Vol. 3 of the Winchester-Frederick County Historical Society Papers, privately published by the Society, Winchester, Virginia, 1955.

Batten, Dr. John M., *Reminiscences of Two Years in the United States Navy* (Lancaster, Pennsylvania, Inquirer Printing and Publishing Company, 1881).

Butts, Frank B., *The First Cruise at Sea and the Loss of the Ironclad Monitor* (Providence, Rhode Island, Sidney S. Rider, 1878).

Castlen, Harriet Gift, *Hope Bids Me Onward* (Savannah, Georgia, Chatham Printing Company, 1945).

Davis, C. H., *Life of Henry Davis* (Boston, Houghton Mifflin Company, 1899).

Diary of Gideon Welles (Boston, Houghton Mifflin Company, 1911).

Diary of Henry Kloeppel, Manuscript Division, Library of Congress.

Diary of John A. Wilson, National Archives.

Diary of Oscar Smith, Manuscript Division, Library of Congress.

Ellicott, John M., *The Life of John Ancrum Winslow* (New York, G. P. Putnam's Sons, 1902).

Evans, Robley D., *A Sailor's Log* (New York, D. Appleton Company, 1901).

Farenholt, Oscar Walter, *The Monitor Catskill, a Year's Reminiscences, 1863-1864* (San Francisco, Shannon-Conney Printing Company, 1912).

Farragut, Loyall, *The Life of David Glasgow Farragut* (New York, D. Appleton and Company, 1879).

Franklin, S. R., *Memories of a Rear Admiral* (New York, Harper and Brothers, 1898).

Gordon, I. T., *Diary of Current Events,* National Archives.

Hill, Frederick Stanhope, *Twenty Years at Sea* (Boston, Houghton Mifflin and Company, 1891).

Hoppin, James Mason, *Life of Andrew Hull Foote* (New York, Harper and Brothers, 1874).

John Taylor Wood Diary, Manuscript Division, University of North Carolina Library.

Jones, John Beauchamp, *A Rebel War Clerk's Diary* (New York, Old Hickory Bookshop, 1935).

Journal of Midshipman Clarence Cary, National Archives.

Kell, John McIntosh, *Recollections of a Naval Life* (Washington, The Neale Company, 1900).

Letterbook of Commander J. N. Barney, National Archives.

Life of Charles Henry Davis, by Charles H. Davis (Boston, Houghton Mifflin Company, 1899).

Maffitt, Emma Martin, *The Life and Services of John Newland Maffitt* (New York, The Neale Publishing Company, 1906).

McGuire, Judith White, *Diary of a Southern Refugee* (New York, E. J. Hale and Son, 1868).

Meade, Rebecca Paulding, *Life of Hiram Paulding* (New York, The Baker and Taylor Company, 1910).

Memoir and Correspondence of Charles Steedman (Cambridge, Massachusetts, privately printed at The Riverside Press, 1912).

Memoirs of James H. Tomb, Manuscript Division, University of North Carolina Library.

Memoirs of Thomas O. Selfridge, Jr. (New York, The Knicker-bocker Press, 1924).

Morgan, James Morris, *Recollections of a Rebel Reefer* (Boston, Houghton Mifflin Company, 1917).

Paine, Albert Bigelow, *A Sailor of Fortune,* memoirs of B. S. Osbon, Manuscript Division, Library of Congress.

Pasha, Hobart, *Sketches from My Life* (New York, D. Appleton and Company, 1887).

Reminiscences of George C. Remey, Manuscript Division, Library of Congress.

Reminiscences of the Old Navy, by Edgar Stanton Maclay (New York, G. P. Putnam's Sons, 1898).

Rochelle, Captain James Henry, *Life of Rear Admiral John Randolph Tucker* (Washington, The Neale Publishing Company, 1903).

Scales, Cordelia Lewis, *Dear Darling Loulie* (Boulder, Colorado, Ben Gray Lumpkin, 1955).

Smith, H. D., and others, *Under Both Flags* (Philadelphia, Peoples' Publishing Company, 1896).

Stewart, William H., *A Pair of Blankets* (New York, Broadway Publishing Company, 1911).

The Story of American Heroism (New York, The Werner Company, 1896).

Walke, Rear Admiral Henry, *Naval Scenes and Reminiscences of the Civil War in the United States* (New York, F. R. Reed and Company, 1877).

Watson, William, *The Adventures of a Blockade Runner* (New York, The Macmillan Company, 1892).

Wilkinson, John, *The Narrative of a Blockade Runner* (New York, Sheldon and Company, 1877).

Wells, Charles W., *Army Life of an Illinois Soldier* (Washington, Globe Printing Company, 1906).

Worden, J. L., and others, *The Monitor and the Merrimac* (New York, Harper and Brothers, 1912).

Wyeth, John Allen, *Life of Lieutenant General Nathan Bedford Forrest* (New York, Harper and Brothers, 1899).

NEWSPAPERS AND PERIODICAL PUBLICATIONS

All Hands, Bureau of Personnel Information Bulletin, U. S. Navy.
Atlanta *Constitution.*
Baltimore *Sun.*

The Bellman.
Century magazine.
Civil War Times.
The Confederacy magazine.
Confederate Veteran.
Confederate War Journal (New York, War Journal Publishing Company, 1893).
Galaxy magazine.
Harper's magazine.
The Independent magazine.
The Journal of American History.
Maryland Historical Society magazine.
McClure's magazine.
Montgomery (Alabama) *Weekly Mail.*
Munsey magazine.
New Orleans *Daily Picayune.*
New Orleans *Daily True Delta.*
New York *Evening Post.*
New York *Herald.*
New York *Times.*
New York *Tribune.*
Putnam's Monthly.
Richmond *Dispatch.*
Savannah *Republican.*
Scribner's magazine.
Southern Historical Society Papers.
The State magazine.
The United Service magazine.
Washington *Evening Star.*
Washington *Intelligencer.*

Index